Praise for
Assessment Essentials

"Banta and Palomba's new edition of *Assessment Essentials* covers a wide range of current topics that are crucial for faculty, staff, and administrators to follow as they strive to sustain effective assessments. I highly recommend this comprehensive resource for academic leaders and others in higher education who want to maintain the quality of their assessment efforts.

I regularly teach graduate courses and used the original Banta and Palomba book as required reading that helped students learn critical knowledge and skills in implementing and sustaining assessments. I plan to use the comprehensive new edition of this book for my upcoming graduate courses and highly recommend this valuable resource to other faculty members."

—Elizabeth A. Jones, Ph.D., professor of education and director,
Doctoral Program, Holy Family University

◆ ◆ ◆

"It's hard to improve on a classic, but Banta and Palomba have done so with this updated edition of *Assessment Essentials*, which is replete with examples of what effective assessment work looks like in different types of institutions."

—George D. Kuh, adjunct professor and director,
National Institute for Learning Outcomes Assessment,
University of Illinois and Indiana University

◆ ◆ ◆

"A sweeping update that brilliantly reflects the evolution of the field. Institutions should use it to build the assessment infrastructure they will need in the brave new world of prior learning assessment and competency-based education."

—Barbara D. Wright, vice president,
WASC Senior College and University Commission,
Alameda, California

Assessment Essentials

Planning, Implementing, and Improving Assessment in Higher Education

SECOND EDITION

Trudy W. Banta, Catherine A. Palomba

Foreword by Jillian Kinzie

JOSSEY-BASS™
A Wiley Brand

Cover Design: Lauryn Tom
Cover Image: © iStockphoto/VikaSuh

Published by Jossey-Bass
A Wiley Brand
One Montgomery Street, Suite 1200, San Francisco, CA 94104-4594
www.josseybass.com/highereducation

Jossey-Bass books and products are available through most bookstores. To contact Jossey-Bass directly call our Customer Care Department within the U.S. at 800-956-7739, outside the U.S. at 317-572-3986, or fax 317-572-4002.

Wiley publishes in a variety of print and electronic formats and by print-on-demand. Some material included with standard print versions of this book may not be included in e-books or in print-on-demand. If this book refers to media such as a CD or DVD that is not included in the version you purchased, you may download this material at http://booksupport.wiley.com. For more information about Wiley products, visit www.wiley.com.

Library of Congress Cataloging-in-Publication Data has been applied for and is on file with the Library of Congress.

ISBN 9781118903322 (cloth); ISBN 9781118903766 (ebk.); ISBN 9781118903650 (ebk.)

Printed in the United States of America
FIRST EDITION
HB Printing 10 9 8 7 6 5 4 3 2 1

THE JOSSEY-BASS HIGHER AND ADULT
EDUCATION SERIES

CONTENTS

12. Summing Up   263

LIST OF EXHIBITS AND FIGURES

FOREWORD

The pressures for colleges and universities to demonstrate educational effectiveness and use empirical evidence to make improvements have only intensified since 1999, when *Assessment Essentials* debuted as a comprehensive resource for those responsible for assessment in higher education. Now, with the prospect of the tenth reauthorization of the Higher Education Act, lawmakers are pushing to enact new ways to hold colleges and universities accountable for their costs and outcomes. How are colleges and universities navigating this period of heightened demands for accountability?

Results from the 2009 and 2013 National Institute for Learning Outcomes Assessment (NILOA) survey of provosts suggest that most institutions are engaged in considerable assessment activity and are using multiple approaches to gather evidence in response to a variety of drivers, most notably accreditation. In 2009, the vast majority (92 percent) of all colleges and universities participating in the survey used at least one assessment approach at the institution level, and the average was three. In 2013, that average increased to five. Institutional use of assessment evidence for every category—including accreditation, external accountability, strategic planning, and institutional improvement—was also higher in 2013 than in 2009.

Indeed, much has changed in the world of assessment since the first edition of *Assessment Essentials* was published, and results demonstrating the amount of assessment activity going on at most institutions suggest significant progress on the assessment agenda. Yet strong interest in learning more about how to effectively implement, organize, support, and sustain assessment activities continues to grow. In this second edition, Trudy Banta and Catherine Palomba make a substantial and timely contribution to enriching the knowledge base regarding how assessment is carried out and the best ways to organize and structure effective assessment work.

This updated edition of *Assessment Essentials* serves as a good checkup of the robustness of assessment practice. The practical examples it presents are a source of reassurance that assessment in colleges and universities is healthy and that institutions are not ignoring important assessment behaviors—while also serving as an alarm system, raising questions about current conditions of assessment before they become chronic. The Contents list alone could function as an annual checklist for healthy assessment practice in colleges and universities. These respected general practitioners of assessment have done a thorough examination of the overall health of assessment.

Banta and Palomba are exactly right to place considerable emphasis throughout this book on increasing the involvement of faculty in assessment. They make the case that effective assessment of student learning cannot occur without the participation of faculty in every step of the assessment process. Quite simply, faculty involvement is key to meaningful assessment, and the meaning of assessment is only as good as the scope and quality of faculty involvement. Notably, the authors also acknowledge the importance of assessing student learning and program effectiveness in student affairs and have added a new chapter to address this expansion in assessment work. In particular, the chapters dedicated to engaging faculty and students in assessment and evidence of focused efforts to assess learning in student affairs make a significant contribution to documenting effective work and discussing current needs in the field.

It is heartening to see that ensuring the use of assessment results is a consistent theme across all chapters in *Assessment Essentials*. For almost a dozen years, I have had the good fortune to work with the National Survey of Student Engagement (NSSE) to further the assessment of student engagement in educationally effective practice and provide colleges and universities with diagnostic, actionable information to inform efforts to improve the quality of undergraduate education. While it is rewarding to see campuses adopt NSSE as an important component of their assessment programs that provides them concise summaries of the strengths and shortcomings of their students' experience, it is disappointing when campuses fail to share results with faculty, draw clear lessons from their assessment data, or formulate concrete improvement priorities. Motivated by the understanding that campuses are much better at gathering data than using assessment to improve, Banta and Palomba dedicate much-needed attention to outlining approaches that campuses can use to encourage faculty and staff to take action on assessment information, and in several chapters they highlight examples of closing the assessment loop, or taking action and then determining the results of these actions. Quite simply, assessment has little to no value if results are not shared and used in meaningful ways. This book aims to make assessment results meaningful and used.

Assessment has taken on greater importance across all areas and units of colleges and universities. The widespread use of national surveys, rubrics, and portfolios to assess learning; the emergence of assessment technologies, including an array of data management systems; and the increase in assessment specialists are all signals of serious investment in assessment. While "assessment cynics" do still exist, the shallow compliance approach to assessment—simply to satisfy the expectations of accreditation—is clearly untenable and no longer holds sway. Although previously common, the compliance approach to assessment has been supplanted by an approach favoring assessment for learning and improvement. Now, assessment more often than not is viewed as vital to improving educational quality and effectiveness. The first edition of *Assessment Essentials* helped guide this shift, and this new edition updates and extends the guidance. More important, Banta and Palomba demonstrate how faculty and staff have made meaning of assessment results to demonstrate educational effectiveness and inform institutional improvement.

Improving quality in undergraduate education to foster learning and success for all students is imperative for US higher education. The challenge that this presents to institutional leaders, faculty, and staff demands meaningful assessment and concerted action to enhance educational effectiveness. The stock-taking activities undertaken by NILOA indicate that assessment has become a permanent fixture in the structure of colleges and universities, yet there is clearly more to do for assessment at these institutions to advance and mature. Moreover, assessment in higher education has grown increasingly more complicated as demands for evidence and expectations for ensuring student learning and institutional improvement have intensified. Faculty and staff with assessment responsibilities and students of assessment need practical resources and achievable assessment examples to advance their assessment skills and repertoire. *Assessment Essentials* is precisely the resource to guide the field in these demanding times.

Jillian Kinzie
associate director, Indiana University
Center for Postsecondary Research,
and NILOA senior scholar
Bloomington, Indiana

PREFACE

When we were considering the possibility of undertaking the task of revising the 1999 version of *Assessment Essentials*, our Jossey-Bass editor, David Brightman, offered to ask three experienced assessment professionals to review the original and give us advice about approaching a revision. We are indebted to this anonymous trio because they gave us a perspective that opened our eyes to the distinctive character of the first edition and to the possibilities for continuing to make a unique contribution to the literature with a revision.

Our reviewers told us that we had offered a practical guide to assessment practice, with principles, examples, and advice about decisions that must be made in the course of implementing an outcomes assessment initiative. In addition to the guidance for practice, we had provided history and context with perspective and vision. The reviewers asked us for a similar approach in our revision, and we have tried to fulfill that request.

When we wrote the 1999 edition, there were few such resources to guide faculty and staff who needed a basic introduction to outcomes assessment, with connections to current references that would help even experienced assessment leaders acquire fresh examples and extended understanding. Now there are many books, several journals, numerous conferences, new organizations, and a panoply of examples of good practice available on institutions' websites. This has made it extremely difficult to produce, as we were instructed by our publisher, a work of as few pages as the first edition!

In addition to the principles, examples, and perspectives offered in the first edition, our three reviewers asked us to add information about these topics:

- The use of technology in assessment, including electronic student portfolios
- Capstone courses as assessment vehicles
- Assessment in student affairs
- The link between outcomes assessment and such valued institutional processes as strategic planning, curriculum revision, and comprehensive program review

So much has changed since 1999 that we have replaced virtually all of our original examples, and of course this required new surrounding text. So while we have retained much of our original organization, most of the words are new. We have expanded our original focus on assessment of student learning to include institutional effectiveness. Accordingly, there are new chapters on assessment in student affairs and assessing institutional effectiveness.

Audience

The three reviewers of our first edition identified our audience as *learners*: faculty and staff engaged in leading outcomes assessment on their campuses, faculty and staff new to assessment and seeking a comprehensive overview, faculty and staff teaching master's and doctoral students in higher education and student affairs. We have attempted to provide some history, context, perspective, and vision for these populations.

The Contents

In Chapter 1 we introduce our broad definition of *outcomes assessment,* encompassing all institutional programs and services. We also include some history and perspective on assessment's progress. Chapter 2 presents our assessment essentials envisioned in three phases: planning, implementing, and improving/sustaining assessment. The essential step of engaging faculty and students in outcomes assessment is the subject of Chapter 3.

Chapters 4, 5, and 6 prepare readers to develop outcomes statements and make decisions about appropriate outcomes. Curriculum mapping, instrument validity and reliability, rubrics, and examples of direct and indirect measures are introduced.

Chapters 7, 8, and 9 contain illustrations of the ways measures can be applied in assessing student learning in the major, general education, and student affairs, respectively. Chapter 10 addresses the essential processes of analyzing, reporting, and using assessment findings.

Chapter 11 offers examples of comprehensive institution-wide assessment programs. In Chapter 12 we characterize the current assessment scene as one fraught with uncertainties, making it difficult to predict a clear way forward. Yet much has been achieved in the four-decade history of outcomes assessment in higher education, and we conclude with some of those achievements, as well as some continuing challenges.

Acknowledgments

We are indebted to the thousands of assessment professionals who have moved this field forward over the past four decades and have unselfishly shared their successes, failures, and continuing challenges in books, journals, and conference presentations, as well as on websites. They have provided the hundreds of examples we cite in illustrating our *Assessment Essentials*.

Cindy Ahonen Cogswell, a doctoral candidate in Indiana University's higher education program, has contributed her considerable research skills and editing expertise on our behalf. We could not have produced this book without the amazing clerical assistance of Shirley Yorger. And finally we appreciate the review of the final manuscript by Kenneth Gilliam, a master's-level student in the student affairs program at Indiana University.

Trudy W. Banta
Indianapolis, Indiana
Catherine A. Palomba
Durham, North Carolina

To Our Essentials:

Ruth and Ky
Logan, Holly, and T.J.

Mady and Max
Neil, Mary Frances, and Nick

ABOUT THE AUTHORS

Trudy W. Banta is professor of higher education and senior advisor to the chancellor for academic planning and evaluation at Indiana University-Purdue University Indianapolis (IUPUI). Considered a pioneer in outcomes assessment in higher education, Banta has received ten national awards for her work in this field. Before moving to IUPUI in 1992, she was the founding director of the Center for Assessment Research and Development at the University of Tennessee, Knoxville.

Banta has developed and coordinated twenty-seven national conferences and fifteen international conferences on the topic of assessing quality in higher education. She has written or edited eighteen books on assessment, contributed thirty chapters to other published works, and written more than three hundred articles and reports. She is the founding editor of *Assessment Update*, a bimonthly periodical published since 1989 by Jossey-Bass.

◆ ◆ ◆

Catherine A. Palomba is director emeritus of assessment and institutional research at Ball State University. Prior to leading a nationally recognized assessment program on that campus, she taught economics at West Virginia

University and Iowa State University. She also was a research analyst at the Center for Naval Analyses in Virginia. She earned her PhD in economics from Iowa State University and her master's degree in economics from the University of Minnesota. Her assessment work includes two books, as well as several articles and presentations.

ASSESSMENT ESSENTIALS

CHAPTER 1

DEFINING ASSESSMENT

The concept of assessment resides in the eye of the beholder. It many definitions, so it is essential that anyone who writes or speaks about assessment defines it at the outset.

Some Definitions

In common parlance, *assessment* as applied in education describes the measurement of what an *individual* knows and can do. Over the past three decades, the term *outcomes assessment* in higher education has come to imply aggregating individual measures for the purpose of discovering *group* strengths and weaknesses that can guide improvement actions.

Some higher education scholars have focused their attention on the assessment of student learning. Linda Suskie, for instance, in the second edition of her book *Assessing Student Learning: A Common Sense Guide* (2009) tells us that for her, the term *assessment* "refers to the assessment of student learning." In the first edition of this book, we also adopted the focus on student learning:

> Assessment is the systematic collection, review, and use of information about educational programs undertaken for the purpose

of improving student learning and development. (Palomba and Banta, 1999, p. 4)

The term *assessment* in higher education has also come to encompass the entire process of evaluating institutional effectiveness. Reflecting her career in applying her background in educational psychology in program evaluation, the first author of this book uses this definition:

Assessment is the process of providing credible evidence of

- resources
- implementation actions, and
- outcomes

undertaken for the purpose of improving the effectiveness of

- instruction,
- programs, and
- services

in higher education.

In this book, the term *assessment* will certainly apply to student learning. But we also use it to describe the evaluation of academic programs, student support services such as advising, and even administrative services as we look at overall institutional effectiveness.

We will describe the assessment of student learning as well as of instructional and curricular effectiveness in general education and major fields of study. We will consider methods for assessing student learning and program effectiveness in student services areas. We also will present approaches to assessing student learning and program and process effectiveness at the institutional level. In fact, the most meaningful assessment is related to institutional mission.

Disciplinary accreditation is a form of assessing program effectiveness in a major field. Regional accreditation is a form of assessing institutional effectiveness. Both are powerful influences in motivating and guiding campus approaches to assessment. Federal, state, and trustee mandates for measures that demonstrate accountability may determine levels of performance funding and also shape campus assessment responses. We will discuss the many external factors that impel college faculty and administrators to undertake assessment activities.

Our guiding principle in this book, however, will be to present approaches to assessment that are designed to help faculty and staff improve instruction, programs, and services, and thus student learning, continuously. Assessment for improvement can also be used to demonstrate accountability. Unfortunately, assessment undertaken primarily to comply with accountability mandates often does not result in campus improvements.

Pioneering in Assessment

In his book *The Self-Regarding Institution* (1984), Peter Ewell portrays the first work in outcomes assessment of three institutions. In the early 1970s, Sister Joel Reed, president of Alverno College, and Charles McClain, president of Northeast Missouri State University, determined that the assessment of student learning outcomes could be a powerful force in improving the effectiveness of their respective institutions. Alverno faculty surveyed their alumnae to find out what their graduates valued most in terms of their learning at Alverno (Loacker and Mentkowski, 1993). Survey findings shaped faculty development of eight abilities, including communication, analysis, and aesthetic responsiveness, that would become the foundation for curriculum and instruction at Alverno. In addition to work in their own discipline, Alverno faculty were asked to join cross-disciplinary faculty specializing in one of the eight core abilities. Alverno's (2011) "assessment as learning" approach has transformed that college, increasing its reputation among students and parents, its enrollment, and its visibility in the United States and abroad as a leader in conducting conscientious and mission-centric assessment.

At Northeast Missouri State University, President McClain and his chief academic officer, Darrell Krueger, became early advocates of value-added assessment, giving tests of generic skills to their freshmen and seniors and tracking the gain scores. In addition, department faculty were strongly encouraged to give their seniors an appropriate nationally normed test in their major field if one existed. McClain famously asked his department chairs one persistent question: "Are we making a difference?" meaning, "How are our students doing on those tests we're giving?" (Krueger, 1993). The early emphasis on test scores had the effect of raising the ability profile of Northeast Missouri's entering students. Subsequently the faculty and administration decided to pursue and gain approval from the state as Missouri's public liberal arts institution, with the new name of Truman State University.

The third pioneering institution profiled in Ewell's book was the University of Tennessee, Knoxville (UTK). Whereas Alverno's and Northeast Missouri's assessment initiatives were internal in their origins and aimed at improving institutional effectiveness in accordance with institutional mission, UTK was confronted with the need to address an external mandate—a performance funding program instituted in 1979 by the Tennessee Higher Education Commission and the Tennessee state legislature. Initially UTK's chancellor, Jack Reese, called the requirements to test freshmen and seniors in general education and seniors in their major field, conduct annual surveys of graduates, and accredit all accreditable programs "an abridgement of academic freedom." His administrative intern at the time, Trudy Banta, thought the performance funding components looked like elements of her chosen field, program evaluation. She took advantage of a timely opportunity to write a proposal for a grant that the Kellogg Foundation would subsequently fund: "Increasing the Use of Student Information in Decision-Making." For the first three years of addressing the external accountability mandate, faculty and administrators charted their own course on the performance funding measures on the basis of their Kellogg Project. While the amount of the Kellogg funding was tiny—just ten thousand dollars—for research-oriented faculty, the "Kellogg grant" gave them the opportunity to begin testing of students and questioning of graduates in their own way. Within five years, UTK was recognized by the National Council for Measurement in Education for outstanding practice in "using measurement technology" (Banta, 1984).

By 1985 three additional states joined Tennessee in establishing performance funding programs for their public colleges and universities. Colorado, New Jersey, and Virginia issued far less prescriptive guidelines than Tennessee, however. The state higher education organizations and legislatures in the three new entries provided examples, but left it to their public institutions to select or design tests and other measures to demonstrate their accountability.

In his 2009 paper for the newly formed National Institute for Learning Outcomes Assessment (NILOA), Ewell notes that "two decades ago, the principal actors external to colleges and universities requiring attention to assessment were state governments." However, by the 1990s, mandates in several states were no longer being enforced because of budget constraints, and so attention turned to other goals, such as higher degree completion rates. Tennessee remained an exception in continuing to employ several learning outcomes measures in its long-established performance funding program.

In 1988, Secretary of Education William Bennett issued an executive order requiring all federally approved accreditation organizations to include in their criteria for accreditation evidence of institutional outcomes (US Department of Education, 1988). During the next several years, the primary external stimulus for assessment moved from states to regional associations as they began to issue specific outcomes assessment directives for institutional accreditation, and discipline-specific bodies created such guidelines for program accreditation. The 1992 Amendments to the federal Higher Education Act (HEA) codified assessment obligations for accrediting agencies, and subsequent renewals of the HEA have continued to require accreditors to include standards specifying that student achievement and program outcomes be assessed. It has taken some accreditors longer than others to comply, however. Accreditors of health professions were in the vanguard, followed by social science professions like education, social work, and business. Engineering accreditors initiated "ABET 2000" standards in 1997 (ABET, 2013). The first trial balloon for standards related to student learning outcomes in law was launched in 2013, for approval within three years (American Bar Association, 2013).

By the time NILOA's first survey of chief academic officers was undertaken in 2009, accreditation—either disciplinary or regional, or both—was being cited as the most important reason for undertaking assessment. According to Ewell (2009), the shift in stimulus from state governments to regional accreditors had the important effect of increasing the emphasis on assessment to guide improvement in addition to demonstrating accountability. Advocating congruence of assessment and campus mission is another hallmark of the influence of accrediting agencies on outcomes assessment. A July 19, 2013, statement of Principles of Effective Assessment of Student Achievement endorsed by leaders of the six regional accrediting commissions and six national higher education associations begins, "[This] statement is intended to emphasize the need to assess effectively student achievement, and the importance of conducting such assessments in ways that are congruent with the institution's mission" (American Association of Community Colleges et al., 2013).

The pendulum is swinging once again with respect to state interest in assessment. In spring 2010, the National Center for Higher Education Management Systems surveyed state higher education executive offices concerning policies, mandates, and requirements regarding student outcomes assessment (Zis, Boeke, and Ewell, 2010). According to study results, eight states, including Minnesota, Georgia, Tennessee, and West Virginia, were unusually active in assessment, some requiring common testing. Some states have systemwide requirements rather than state requirements. For many years, students at the campuses of the City University of New York were required to obtain a minimum score on a locally developed standardized examination in order to earn their degrees.

More recently, declining global rankings, rising tuition and student debt, and poor prospects for employment of college graduates have alarmed state and federal decision makers (Miller, 2013). This has prompted an emphasis on productivity and efficiency in higher education, which is now seen as an engine of the economy and of the nation's competitiveness (Hazelkorn, 2013). Many state reporting systems are focusing more on graduation rates, job placement, and debt-to-earnings ratios than on measures of student learning. The Voluntary Framework of Accountability for community colleges contains measures not only of how many students obtain degrees, but of how many pass remedial courses, earn academic credit, transfer to another institution, and get a job (American Association of Community Colleges, 2013). President Barack Obama's administration has proposed a College Scorecard (White House, 2013). The emphasis on producing numbers of degrees and job-ready employees has alarmed educators. They fear that educational quality will suffer if too much weight in funding regimes is placed on simply graduating more students or turning out majors who are prepared for today's jobs rather than with the abilities to adapt to ever-changing workplace demands. As Margaret Miller puts it, "The completion goal is downright pernicious if it entails the minting of an increasingly worthless currency" (2013, p. 4). In addition, emphasizing college completion in a shorter time frame could encourage institutions to raise their entrance requirements to be sure they enroll students who are best prepared for college work, which could make a college education unattainable for those who need it most.

As a result of all these external influences, as well as internal interests in obtaining guidance for continuous improvement of student learning and institutional effectiveness, increasing numbers of faculty have been called on to participate in assessment. Some assume leadership roles, serving on campuswide committees charged with planning the institution's overall approach to assessment or designing a program to assess general education. A greater number are involved at the department level, helping to design and carry out assessment of programs or courses for majors. Attendance at national, regional, state, and discipline-specific assessment conferences attests to continued interest in sharing assessment information. In fact, for more than a decade, the number of participants at the annual Assessment Institute in Indianapolis, the oldest and largest assessment conference in the United States, has approached or exceeded one thousand. This book is designed to fill some of the continuing need for information about assessment.

Quality Assurance: An International Perspective

Interest in obtaining evidence of accountability from postsecondary institutions emerged as a worldwide phenomenon in the mid-1980s. In Europe, China, Australia, South Africa, and other countries, as in the United States, stakeholders in higher education have become increasingly concerned about the value received for resources invested, accommodating increasing numbers and diversity of students, covering cost increases with resources spread over an ever-growing array of services, developing a workforce with skills competitive in a global marketplace, and producing graduates with credentials that are transferable across cultural and national boundaries. Since postsecondary education is managed by the central government in most other countries, initial accountability-related actions were national in scope and focused on a process commonly referred to as quality assurance (QA). Self-study and external peer review, including site visits, were encouraged. Given the commanding role of central education ministries, voluntary associations of institutions like the regional accrediting agencies in the United States were virtually unknown in Europe and elsewhere prior to 1985. In that year, thirteen universities in the Netherlands formed the Association of Cooperating Universities and began a six-year cycle designed to conduct peer reviews in the same year of all universities offering degrees in a particular discipline (Vroeijenstijn, 1994). Few other countries have followed the Netherlands in developing associations of institutions to carry out QA procedures.

Prior to 1990, higher education in most other countries had been a privilege for the economically and intellectually elite: only 10 to 15 percent of the college-going age population was enrolled. In the next three decades, this percentage increased to 50 percent and higher in Europe and beyond. When only the privileged and gifted, who were generally motivated to succeed and able to navigate postsecondary education with minimal guidance, constituted the population of university students and their tuition was paid by governments, student services beyond an admissions office and a student housing staff were not needed. But with "massification," students with diverse needs necessitated the creation of a full range of student services and the institutional research function to support this infrastructure (Banta, 2013).

Although an emphasis on student success has come only recently to Europe and elsewhere, European students are much more influential in steering QA initiatives than US students are in shaping outcomes assessment. At the University of Freiburg in Germany, undergraduates in psychology made their own list of learning outcomes and presented it to the psychology faculty (Banta, 2009). In the United Kingdom, the National Student Survey is administered at all universities. The results, reported publicly, have become an important factor in judging the quality of institutions. There is now a European Students' Union (ESU, 2014) that voices its concerns about quality assessment on occasion. The ESU is an umbrella organization for forty-seven national unions of students and has headquarters in Brussels, from whence its officers can lobby the European Union.

Policies of the European Union have created transparent borders and a common currency that combine to encourage workers to migrate from one country to another. By 1999, it was clear that some standardization was needed in order to make sense of university degrees produced by programs differing in content, length, and curricular structure. In that year education ministers representing twenty-nine European countries met in Italy and drew up the Bologna Declaration, which called for comparable degrees based on a common framework of degree levels, a credit-based system that would facilitate international transfer, and a cooperative system of quality assurance (Ewell, 2004). In 2000 the European Network for Quality Assurance in Higher Education (ENQA) was established to promote European cooperation in ensuring quality. Australia, New Zealand, and Hong Kong are among the many other countries that also have national QA organizations that conduct institutional audits and disseminate information about good practice.

In 2000 ENQA initiated a process designed to develop field-specific reference points, including learning outcomes, that could guide students to a credential in a field of study. The process is called "tuning" to reflect its "attempt to steer a course between identical cross-national standards and institutional autonomy with respect to degree standards" (Ewell, 2004, p. 12). Tuning in Europe has inspired similar efforts in Latin America and Russia, as well as the Lumina Foundation's Tuning USA project involving several disciplines in Indiana, Kentucky, Minnesota, Texas, and Utah (Adelman et al., 2014, p. 38).

Faculty development has been a hallmark of QA initiatives, particularly in Britain. But that has not kept British academics from voicing their resentment toward QA because it is imposed by external authorities (Banta, 2009). In addition, the tension between assessment for improvement and assessment to address accountability demands is as palpable in Europe and elsewhere as it is in the United States (Harvey and Williams, 2010).

Prior to 2000, most of the scholarship in postsecondary outcomes assessment in other countries emphasized national and state (e.g., *landers* in Germany) quality assurance initiatives, while in the United States, this emphasis was on classroom assessment and assessment in general education and academic disciplines (Banta, 2000). Since 2000, assessment scholarship in all countries has also included a focus on institutional effectiveness: electronic institutional portfolios, quality management (e.g., Total Quality Management and ISO 9000), academic audits (external peer review), performance indicators (e.g., key performance indicators), league tables or rankings (e.g., *U.S. News & World Report* rankings and U-Multirank in Europe), and surveys for students (e.g., the National Survey of Student Engagement, the Australian Survey of Student Engagement), faculty, graduates, and employers.

Assessment Purposes

Assessment is more than the collection of data. To make assessment work, educators must be purposeful about what they collect. As a basis for data gathering, they must clarify their goals and objectives for student learning and be aware of where these goals and objectives are addressed in the curriculum. After data are gathered, educators must examine and use assessment results to improve educational programs.

Alexander Astin (1985, 1991) helped refocus thinking about the quality of higher education from resources such as library holdings and student SAT scores toward educational outputs such as knowledge, skills, and values. He also argued that the results of education must be understood in relationship to both inputs and environment. Knowing where students wind up is only part of the story; information about where they start and what they encounter along the way is also necessary. Without this context, it is difficult to use outcome results for improvement. Questions about student experiences need to be considered in planning assessment programs. What kinds of courses do students take? What opportunities are available for out-of-class learning and development?

The overriding purpose of outcomes assessment is to understand how educational programs are working and to determine whether they are contributing to student growth and development. Hence, the ultimate emphasis of outcomes assessment is on programs rather than individual students. At its most useful, assessment provides information about students as a group—information that can be aggregated across sections of a single course and is meaningful across courses. Assessment indicates what the experiences of students add up to and what these experiences imply about educational programs. It enables educators to examine whether the curriculum makes sense in its entirety and whether students, as a result of all their experiences, have the knowledge, skills, and values that graduates should possess. Program assessment helps determine whether students can integrate learning from individual courses into a coherent whole. Interest is focused on the cumulative effects of the educational process. Assessment helps us look at programs in a holistic way.

Assessment participants on most campuses recognize that assessment contributes to improved teaching and learning and that it also satisfies reporting requirements, but it serves other purposes as well. For some institutions, assessment's greatest benefit is fostering academic introspection—making the institution more self-conscious about what its programs are accomplishing. In 2004, Calvin College faculty redesigned their assessment program after receiving a negative review from an accreditation team. A first step was to articulate a philosophy of assessment that was compatible with institutional culture. Assessment is strongly affirmed and framed within the concept of reflection. Everyone is encouraged to be reflective, not just as an individual but as a member of a department and the community as a whole (Bradley, 2009).

St. John's University (2014) leaders conceptualize assessment as a three-way conversation among students, faculty, and administration. It is a continuing dialogue in which all participants learn from each other. At Carnegie Mellon University (n.d.a), assessment information is intended to help instructors "refine their teaching practices and grow as educators."

Other recognized benefits of assessment include attracting prospective students, improving institutional image, and developing funding opportunities. Montgomery College (n.d.) leaders see assessment as providing a way for faculty and administrators to tell their story to others, including politicians, employers, and potential donors. And at the Massachusetts College of Liberal Arts (2013), faculty find that they can use assessment information to inform planning, document needs, assist with grant writing, and improve each academic program and its standing in its discipline.

The purposes a particular university or college chooses for assessment may be captured in an assessment definition. Occasionally campuses use an existing definition, such as the ones we offered at the start of this chapter. More often, they develop their own unique definitions. Baruch College faculty (2014) describe assessment as an important way to make informed decisions and a means to pursue excellence in teaching and learning.

Values and Guiding Principles

In addition to a definition of assessment, many campuses develop statements of values or guidelines for carrying out assessment, as well as lists of best practices. Examining such documents reveals a great deal about the particular campus approach to assessment.

Some statements emphasize collaboration and inclusion in developing assessment initiatives, and many affirm that faculty are the individuals best suited to carry out assessment in their disciplines. Many also specify that assessment results will be used to evaluate academic programs, activities, and student services but not individual faculty or staff.

Issues of timing and methods also are addressed. Montgomery College (n.d.) educators value an assessment approach that is "as simple and manageable as possible. The process cannot become so onerous that it hampers or interferes with the delivery of the educational experience that it attempts to assess and improve." College leaders also expect faculty and staff to use assessment results. If assessment is primarily a reporting tool, "then this effort will have been deemed a failure."

St. Ambrose University (2014) faculty value assessment efforts that are timely, efficient, and feasible; use existing data and instruments if possible; and are informed by scholarship and good practice. Hartwick College (2014a) educators value assessing "smarter not harder" by using methods and strategies that are simple, sustainable, and iterative and inform efforts to improve teaching and learning.

Along with, or in place of, a statement of values, some educators find it helpful to develop a set of operating principles or guidelines that clarify the purposes and intended uses of assessment information. Guiding principles at North Carolina State University (2006) call for curiosity and intellectual dialogue, involvement that is recognized and rewarded, and relevant evidence that is used in many ways, including highlighting excellence and informing planning and resource management. At Cabrillo College (n.d.),

faculty and staff view assessment as a way to identify issues that can benefit from campuswide discussion.

Rather than guiding principles that often set specific expectations for a particular campus, lists of good practices may present ideals to which campuses can aspire. For example, the "Characteristics of an Effective Assessment Program" statement shared on the James Madison University (n.d.) website calls for evidence that resources are moved or reallocated in response to assessment results and that traditional and technological delivery modes are compared with respect to student learning and development.

Practitioners on many campuses find it useful to prepare a set of frequently asked questions for faculty, staff, and students. In addition to answering questions about the who, what, and why of assessment, FAQs can deal directly with issues that are problematic. Most lists answer the question of how faculty grades and assessment information differ from each other. As we elaborate in Chapter 3, grades reflect participation, effort, and attendance, as well as learning. And grades alone generally fail to capture enough information about mastery of learning objectives to provide direction for improvement.

Other frequently asked questions may reflect specific campus interests. For example, the set of FAQs available on Stanford University's (2014) website asks: "What is the difference between assessment and research?" The answer explains that assessment is a type of action research with the primary goal of improving practice rather than generating theoretical knowledge. Experimental control and random assignment are often not possible in instructional settings. Nyack College (2014) FAQs address the practical question of whether all faculty teaching the same course will be required to use the same textbook as the result of participating in program assessment. The answer is, "Not necessarily." It is the skills and knowledge to be assessed that are common, not the textbook.

On some campuses, the greatest challenge in implementing department-based, faculty-involved assessment is to develop a common language about the meaning of and uses for student assessment. Faculty are used to thinking about assessment of individual student learning and dealing with curriculum issues; they are much less familiar with using assessment for the purpose of improving programs. Thus, on a number of campuses, sets of definitions or glossaries for faculty and staff have been developed. The Internet Resources for Higher Education Outcomes Assessment site maintained at North Carolina State University provides links to nearly fifty campus glossaries. The web page for California State University Long Beach (n.d.b) contains some two dozen assessment definitions.

All of these materials should reflect the values and interests of the many stakeholders in assessment, not just of a few decision makers. Formal and informal discussions about the aims of assessment need to be inclusive if the campus is to embrace assessment as a way to provide evidence to guide improvement.

As we have illustrated, outcomes assessment is a many-faceted concept. When one uses the term, a definition must follow to ensure that the ensuing conversation will take place in the appropriate context. Statements of values and guiding principles are important to the clarity of this conversation.

CHAPTER 2

THE ESSENTIALS OF ASSESSMENT

In the first edition of this book (Palomba and Banta, 1999), we offered six strategies that we deemed essential for effective conduct of outcomes assessment:

1. Agree on goals and objectives for learning.
2. Design and implement a thoughtful approach to assessment planning.
3. Involve individuals from on and off campus.
4. Select or design and implement data collection approaches.
5. Examine, share, and act on assessment findings.
6. Regularly reexamine the assessment process.

This list provides direction that is as relevant to good practice today as it was in 1999. Nevertheless, our deeper experience now suggests a fuller list incorporating more nuance. The approach described in this chapter follows an outline first published in *Designing Effective Assessment: Principles and Profiles of Good Practice* (Banta, Jones, and Black, 2008). Here we view assessment as a continuum comprising three phases: planning, implementing, and improving and sustaining the process. In the *planning* phase, stakeholders are engaged and purposes identified. A written plan, with milestones established over multiple years, will guide a successful process.

In the *implementation* phase, leadership for assessment is provided, with champions at the classroom, department, and college levels and coordination at the institution level. After data collection strategies are conceived, resources must be made available for development or purchase of appropriate measurement instruments. Faculty and staff require orientation and education to assume their roles in outcomes assessment because most have not been prepared to develop or use reliable and valid measures. As suggested in our comprehensive definition of assessment in Chapter 1, it is essential to consider resources and processes, as well as outcomes, in the design of effective assessment. When assessment information has been collected, it must be organized and analyzed. Then findings are summarized and communicated in ways that encourage action.

In the third phase of outcomes assessment, processes are *improved* and *sustained.* Assessment evidence must be credible for stakeholders; if it isn't, improvements in collection methods may be in order. Assessment leaders should ensure that assessment findings are examined, shared, and acted on when action is warranted. Provision of resources for making improvements is essential. The assessment plan and processes should be reexamined periodically, and appropriate changes enacted.

Planning Effective Assessment

Planning Effective Assessment

- Engaging stakeholders
- Establishing purpose
- Designing a thoughtful approach to assessment planning
- Creating a written plan
- Timing assessment

Engaging Stakeholders

An initial step in planning is to identify and involve relevant stakeholders. Faculty, academic administrators, and student affairs professionals need to play leading roles in charting the course for assessment. Students can contribute ideas, as can their parents, employers, advisory board members, and other community representatives. Trustees of an institution may play important roles. Both regional accreditors and the Association of Governing Boards have set expectations that trustees will

be cognizant of assessment information and processes and will participate in the conversation about institutional effectiveness (Hinton and
MacDowell, 2012).

Faculty must establish broad learning outcomes for general education and more specific objectives for academic majors. Trustees, alumni,
employers, and other community representatives can review draft statements of these outcomes and suggest revisions based on their perspectives
on community needs. Student affairs professionals can contribute to the
development of academic outcomes and devise their own complemen-
tary outcomes based on their plans to extend learning into campus environments beyond the classroom. For instance, West Virginia University's
(2014) office of student affairs has developed student learning goals organized around five Cs: commitment to excellence, competence, compas-
sion, citizenship, and communication.

Students can translate the language of the academy into terms their
peers will comprehend. Students may also assist in designing data-gathering
strategies and instruments. At the College of Saint Benedict and Saint
John's University, assessment workshop participants have included several
student scholars, as well as faculty, academic affairs staff, and student development staff (Kramer, Knuesel, and Jones, 2012).

Regional accrediting associations and national disciplinary and professional organizations provide resources for the planning phase of assessment. They may set standards and expectations for assessing student
learning, furnish written materials, and offer workshops at their periodic
meetings. Although the six regional accreditors have similar expectations
for assessment, they are experimenting with different assessment strategies,
including innovative approaches to providing assessment resources such as
the Leadership Academy offered by the Western Association of Schools and
Colleges (Provezis, 2010; Wright, 2013).

Establishing Purpose

Reaching agreement about goals and objectives for educational programs
and having an understanding of where and how they are addressed is
essential to effective planning. This foundation guides the selection of
assessment instruments and facilitates the use of assessment results. It also
provides explicit information to students and the public about the aims of
higher education.

As a starting point for assessment, faculty must consider the institution's values, goals, and vision. Some campuses are strongly committed

to experiential education, some value knowledge and understanding of arts and humanities, and others focus on service-learning. In 2008, Hartwick College (2014b) faculty adopted their organizing principles and strategic framework with the goal of being the best at "melding a liberal arts education with experiential learning." St. Olaf College leaders seek to develop the whole person in mind, body, and spirit and to enhance the global perspective of their students (Jankowski, 2012). Inspired by their institution's namesake, Justice Louis Brandeis, faculty at Brandeis University (n.d.b) expect their graduates to endeavor to advance justice in the world. Regional accreditors require their members to make their educational goals clear, public, and appropriate to higher education. Thus, mission statements should capture the special qualities that graduates are expected to possess. Assessment itself can be a strong factor in pushing institutions to become more focused and specific in their mission statements and in the ways they convey their missions to the public.

Developing goals and objectives for general education necessarily involves a group of campus representatives who describe the knowledge, skills, and values graduates should possess regardless of their discipline. Agreement about the role of general education on campus will guide this discussion. The Provost's Advisory Committee on Assessment of Student Learning at Brandeis (n.d.b) worked for more than a year to create a draft of learning goals for its graduates. Committee members, consisting of faculty, academic staff, and student life staff, researched goals at other universities as part of the development process. Before finalizing their statement, they submitted the draft for review to many campus groups, including a subcommittee of the board of trustees.

Faculty who are developing goals and objectives for a major field will be most concerned with the standards of the field, but will likely consider learning outcomes traditionally associated with general education programs such as valuing lifelong learning or working cooperatively. At Bismarck State College (2014), for example, program outcomes align with the overall goals and mission of the College.

Designing a Thoughtful Approach to Assessment Planning

At either the institution or department level, members of the committee or task force charged with developing an approach to assessment need to begin with a discussion about its purposes. Several authors distinguish between activities aimed at improvement and those aimed at demonstrating accountability. Ewell (2009) refers to a "simmering tension" between these competing forces. The two categories often are referred to as *formative* and *summative* evaluations. The first is meant to "form" the program or performance, the second to make judgments about it. *Formative assessment* is conducted during the life of a program (or performance) with the purpose of providing feedback that can be used to modify, shape, and improve the program (or performance). *Summative assessment* is conducted after a program has been in operation for a while, or at its conclusion, to make judgments about its quality or worth compared to previously defined standards for performance. If activities are to continue or be repeated, the results of summative assessment can be used to help form the program (or performance) for the future.

Although the overall focus of the assessment movement has centered on improvement of educational programs, elements of summative assessment are in practice on college campuses, not only in responding to external accreditors and state governments but also in internal processes. For example, general education assessment programs that are course based may include an evaluation of whether courses should remain in the program. These reviews usually contain strong elements of formative as well as summative assessment.

The terms *formative* and *summative assessment* are applied to activities focused on individual students as well as those focused on overall programs. Summative assessment activities aimed at students include such things as junior-level writing competence exams and comprehensive exams in the major that must be passed for advancement or certification. Since 1984, Ball State University (2014c) graduates have completed a writing competence requirement. Students must register for and pass a proctored and timed writing examination that carries no credit hours. A writing proficiency course is available for those who do not pass the exam after two attempts or who have test anxiety. Formative assessment measures include performance reviews accompanied by feedback, perhaps provided by a panel of experts (who may also certify the work). The strongly held view that students should learn from assessment has increased the use of formative assessment approaches focused on individual students. In their argument for integrated learning, Hersh and Keeling (2013) write that assessment must be systematic, cumulative, formative, and summative in order to signal and reinforce learning expectations and standards. They believe standards should be in place so that students can demonstrate mastery of a subject before they move on to the next level of learning.

Creating a Written Plan

One of the major tasks facing assessment planners is the development of a planning document. An assessment plan captures agreement about what matters, gives direction for actions, and provides a means to determine if progress is being made. Many institutions adopt a model for assessment that becomes the basis of their plan. At Marquette University (2014), the assessment cycle is viewed as a continuum with four steps: define, measure, reflect, and improve. Edmonds Community College (n.d.) faculty have named their planning document the SIMPLE (Strategic, Informed, Measurable Process Leading to Improvement) plan. The plan provides for ongoing assessment of processes to make sure each area of the college is meeting students' needs.

Creating a plan helps the institution or program see the big picture of assessment, including the who, what, when, and why. The plan need not be elaborate. It may be a simple time line or a matrix of activities, but there needs to be agreement at the institution and within departments about the overall objectives of an assessment program and how it will be carried out. Faculty at Del Mar College (n.d.), a two-year institution in Texas, use an annual assessment time line. The cycle begins each August when department chairs review assessment plans from the previous year. In September student learning outcomes are reviewed and measures to be implemented during the current year are selected. Action plans based on findings are completed by mid-July.

Although regional accrediting bodies now ask their members to have written assessment plans at the institution level, emphasis in the plans should be on the process and discussion that produce and implement the plan rather than on the document itself. Individuals involved in assessment planning can adopt strategic planning methods such as brainstorming, seeking input, and revising. These strategies work for department planners as well. At a panel discussion for new assessment coordinators at California State University Fresno (2007), veteran assessment coordinators urged their colleagues to view their assessment plans as "something you're constantly rewriting and changing . . . Revise it all the time." No plan is unchangeable.

Institutions may have assessment plans or designs at several levels, including campus, program, course, and classroom. Assessment at each level can provide information for the others and may reflect a variety of purposes. For example, a department assessment plan aimed at improvement may reflect institutional reporting requirements and those of one or more disciplinary accrediting bodies. Lancaster Bible College and Graduate School has a plan in place requiring assessment at five levels (Mort, 2012): course, program, division, core knowledge and skills, and institution. All academic and support units must create comprehensive plans that include purposes, intended outcomes, means of assessment, data summary, and use of results. Based on assessment findings, units indicate whether an action plan or strategic initiative is needed. Action plans are follow-up activities that can be undertaken with the unit's own resources. Strategic initiatives require additional resources from outside the unit.

An important consideration when planning an assessment program is to link the results of assessment to other educational processes such as curriculum review, planning, and budgeting. Some campus leaders require that proposals for curriculum change be accompanied by relevant assessment information. Insisting that assessment information be provided in support of budgeting requests is another approach for linking assessment to decision making. In the Division of Continuing Education at Brigham Young University, an existing planning and budgeting template was modified to include assessment reporting (Hoyt, 2009). Directors are required to report on and consider assessment results in establishing annual budgeting priorities, making assessment part of a meaningful established process.

Timing Assessment

Ideally assessment is a component of strategic planning for an institution or department and is part of any new program from the outset. Adding assessment to an ongoing program or event will require time to convince the developers of the value of assessment for improving and sustaining their efforts. Since assessment requires multiple methods, it is not usually necessary to implement every method immediately or even every year. A comprehensive assessment plan should have a schedule for implementing each data-gathering method at least once over a period of three to five years. Assessment leaders at St. Olaf (n.d.) maintain a detailed time schedule of planned activities at the institution, program, and general education levels through 2018. National surveys will be conducted intermittently, and assessment of individual general education courses is planned for 2015–2016.

Institutional requirements generally set the time table for program-level assessment, often with some flexibility. Emory University (2014a) leaders expect faculty to collect evidence over time and analyze data longitudinally.

Assessment reports are completed annually, and program faculty are to evaluate all outcomes within three- to five-year cycles. Administrators at Long Island University (2013) recently announced a revised assessment cycle for their Post campus. In the new three-year cycle, program faculty are required to report assessment results for two learning objectives each year rather than four.

Implementing Effective Assessment

> ## Implementing Effective Assessment
>
> - Providing leadership
> - Selecting or designing data collection approaches
> - Providing resources
> - Educating faculty and staff
> - Assessing resources and process as well as outcomes
> - Sharing findings

Providing Leadership

Successful assessment requires effective leadership at all levels: presidents, provosts, deans, department chairs, and student affairs professionals. Through their public and private statements and actions, these leaders can convey the message that they value the assessment process and will sustain it. They can foster innovation by offering valued incentives for participants. Some universities provide written messages from respected administrators to set the tone for assessment. The provost at American University (2014) includes a written welcome for visitors on web pages for learning outcomes and assessment. He tells readers that American University is dedicated to "articulating expectations for student learning, and assessing the degree to which these expectations are met." He also commits to making every effort to support faculty as they engage in assessment and curricular enhancement.

Selecting or Designing Data Collection Approaches

To select among assessment instruments, faculty must discuss and establish their selection criteria and become familiar with various assessment methods. The most important criterion is whether the method will provide

useful information—information that indicates whether students are learning and developing in ways faculty have agreed are important. Assessment
methods must be linked to goals and objectives for learning and to the
instructional activities that support these goals. For example, future teachers should be observed interacting with students, not simply examined with
a multiple-choice test. Although the information comes from an online
survey of assessment professionals rather than from faculty, Eubanks and
Royal (2011) provide information about what constitutes quality assessment methodology. Assessment practitioners place high value on evidence-
based results. They place less importance on the randomness of data,
whether results are original, or if they can be replicated. Because results
are considered through dialogue and politics rather than in a scientific way,
the authors conclude that professionals likely look for practical assessment
strategies and less formal methods that work. Assessment coordinators at
California State University Fresno (2007) identify some realistic issues in
choosing methods. For example, alumni surveys did not work for one program because faculty could not locate their former students. Most graduates were women and their surnames had changed when they married.

Assessment methods (also called techniques or instruments) include
both direct and indirect approaches. *Direct measures* of learning require
students to display their knowledge and skills as they respond to the
instrument itself. Direct assessment techniques include both objective
tests, in which students select a response from among those provided,
and performance measures, for which students generate their own
responses. Performance measures include essays, presentations, and
projects, as well as comprehensive portfolios containing material accu-
mulated over time. These measures allow students to demonstrate skills
as well as knowledge.

Indirect methods such as questionnaires and interviews ask students to
reflect on their learning rather than to demonstrate it. Many assessment
programs include exit surveys or interviews of graduating seniors, alumni
surveys of recent or long-term graduates, or both. These allow faculty to
hear from their students about how their programs are working or what
could be improved. They also yield details about instructional or curricular
strengths that direct measures alone cannot provide. Nevertheless, when
specific assessment techniques are being selected, activities that directly
assess learning must be included if the assessment program is to have credibility. Several institutions have standards for academic departments or
programs that address required methods. Faculty at American University
(2014) are asked to use a variety of methods, including one direct measure

for each program outcome. Long Island University (2013) faculty must use two direct measures for each outcome assessed in a given year.

A further distinction that may be made is between *quantitative* methods, which rely on numerical scores or ratings, and *qualitative* methods, which rely on descriptions rather than numbers. The latter include use of logs, journals, participant observations, focus groups, and interviews. Faculty who ask seniors to write about important learning experiences and then prepare an overall summary of prevalent themes are using a qualitative approach. To gather feedback from their students, faculty in the Physical Education-Teacher Education program at Southern Illinois University-Edwardsville asked students to write daily in electronic journals. Seniors from the Department of Kinesiology and Health Education who were engaged in full-time student teaching activities responded to the same questions every day, including: "What were your duties/responsibilities today?" and "What happened that you did/did not feel prepared to deal with?" A careful review of the journal entries yielded several themes that guided improvement. For example, faculty added a dedicated class in behavior modification strategies to the first semester and also infused this topic into other classes (Cluphf and Lox, 2009).

Performance measures and qualitative approaches provide rich information and therefore are increasingly recommended. Because learning is enhanced by doing, it makes sense to design assessment strategies that actively engage students. Such methods should also allow students the chance to receive feedback and respond to it. Assessment practitioners should ask focused questions about each assessment strategy—for example, "Will it, by itself, enhance student learning?" "Will it provide students with opportunities for self-evaluation?"

In addition to the methods decision, faculty must decide when information will be collected: From students at entry, midpoint, or exit? From alumni one, two, or five years after graduation? If students are the source, faculty must decide how the information will affect student progress. Will it be required or graded? The site of data collection also must be determined. One possibility is to create (or take advantage of) data collection opportunities outside the classroom. Educators can administer an entry-level test during orientation, and students can be required to attend a special session to complete a writing competence exam. South Mountain Community College (2011) established the fifth week of each semester as its "Academic Assessment Week." During this week instructors administer several assessment instruments, including a humanities survey. In addition, student focus group sessions are conducted and videotaped.

Faculty collect assessment information within the classroom not simply for convenience but because of the opportunity this provides to use already-in-place assignments and course work for assessment purposes. The latter approach, called *course-embedded assessment,* involves taking a second look at materials generated in the classroom; in addition to providing a basis for grading students, these materials allow faculty to evaluate their approaches to instruction and course design. Course-embedded assessment is cost-efficient and is least likely to have problems related to student motivation. A variant involves designing exam questions or other assignments that are inserted into classroom work for the purpose of providing group-level information. During the NILOA focus groups, several campus leaders pointed to what faculty are doing in the classroom as "the natural place to begin to advance assessment" (Kinzie, 2010, p. 15; also see Chapter 5, this volume).

Providing Resources

Campus leaders must budget for staff time and relevant materials, but also for giving faculty and staff opportunities to hone their assessment skills. Rewards should be available for those who engage in assessment, whether through promotion and tenure and staff advancement or through other means, such as *assessment grants* or awards. Lane Crothers describes a retreat held for faculty in the Department of Politics and Government at Illinois State University (2013) that was funded by an assessment initiative award from University Assessment Services. The off-campus retreat allowed faculty to discuss and eventually revise their learning outcomes. At Bluefield State College, faculty were awarded stipends to attend summer assessment workshops designed to help them develop assessment plans (Anderson, 2013).

Particularly at research universities, faculty and staff can contribute to the resource base by competing for external grants or awards. External grants are useful in launching an assessment program, but continuation with soft money can be a temporary expedient only. Campus leaders at the College of Saint Benedict and Saint John's University created a series of four year-long on-campus "Assessment 101" workshops for faculty, staff, and students using a forty-eight-month grant from the Teagle Foundation (Kramer et al., 2012). Participants were introduced to assessment literature, explored assessment issues, and applied what they learned to their own programs. The provost has made a commitment to provide the funds necessary to continue the assessment workshops indefinitely, although likely in a shorter and more cost-conscious way.

Educating Faculty and Staff

Most faculty members have not been prepared as teachers, and certainly not as assessors. Thus it is imperative that special programming be offered to help faculty and staff understand the potential range of effective assessment practices and how to implement them. This special programming may be offered through an assessment office, a center for teaching and learning, or a faculty-staff development unit. The Eberly Center for Teaching Excellence and Educational Innovation at Carnegie Mellon University (n.d.a) offers support for faculty engaged in assessment, including one-on-one consultations. When they invigorated their assessment program, administrators at Zayed University in the United Arab Emirates also reestablished the Center for Teaching and Learning. They recognized a need to help faculty as they implement actions based on assessment findings (Schoepp, 2012).

While attention to professional development is usually focused on academic personnel, similar programming should be offered for student affairs leaders and staff. John Carroll University's (n.d.) web pages for Student Affairs Assessment include a link for Building Assessment Capacity: Staff Development Resources. The page provides access to material from several workshops. In 2006, the American College Personnel Association's Commission Directorate for Assessment and Evaluation released a set of Assessment Skills and Knowledge (ASK) Standards for student affairs professionals with assessment-related responsibilities. The standards, illustrated in practice in a companion guidebook (Timm, Barham, McKinney, and Knerr, 2013), supply an excellent foundation for staff development.

In both academic affairs and student affairs, sustaining program effectiveness represents a significant challenge to leaders of professional development initiatives that involve planning and implementing assessment processes. Elizabeth Jones (2009) cites research that single-session workshops have little effect on behavior and then provides several examples of ongoing professional development initiatives. At Northern Iowa University, a three-phase faculty development plan began with workshops on curriculum mapping. A second set of workshops focused on how to assess student learning in the classroom, and the third addressed how to use results to create action plans. West Virginia University officials offered a set of six development seminars to staff and leaders in student affairs to help them develop assessment plans for their units.

Faculty learning communities represent a more sustained initiative that may have a greater impact. In learning communities, instructors work together for a semester or more on a focused topic. Campus leaders at Blinn College have developed a faculty learning community focused on understanding and sharing assessment information. In addition to meetings, it includes readings, videos, and online chats (Reynolds-Sundet and Adam, 2014).

Without knowing the types of help faculty need to assess student outcomes, creating development opportunities is difficult. A needs assessment survey of faculty may help leaders identify the most useful assessment topics to address and suggest how to offer educational opportunities. In spring 2010, faculty at the Community College of Baltimore County were invited to complete an online general education survey designed to elicit information for improving faculty support. The results indicated that faculty wanted help designing assessable assignments and using assessment results (Mince, Mason, and Bogage, 2011). An online survey of faculty at Saint Xavier University found similar needs (McCullough and Robinson, 2014).

Faculty development opportunities are essential during the entire assessment cycle—from the outset as plans are developed, through the implementation phase, to interpretation of results, and use of results to make improvements. The three-phase program at Northern Iowa University described earlier contains these opportunities. Many assessment web pages provide resources for each stage of the assessment process.

Faculty can attend workshops to assist them with developing clear and measurable learning outcomes, an essential early step in the assessment process. Linkages between program-level learning outcomes and individual course-level outcomes can then be illustrated in curriculum maps that identify gaps and redundancies in the program and improve the articulation of outcomes across all program segments. Faculty also can participate in workshops to assist in designing and using rubrics and consistently applying the criteria to increase interrater reliability. In addition, faculty may create portfolios to document their assignments and rubrics. The rubrics make faculty intentions explicit and public so that students gain a better understanding of key expectations for individual courses.

The need for faculty development continues as new full-time and adjunct faculty come to campus. Senior faculty can help these individuals understand how to teach courses and measure student learning in alignment with program learning outcomes. At the Community College of Baltimore County, new faculty attend a year-long New Faculty Learning Community that addresses assessment. Adjunct faculty, who contribute to assessment of multisection courses, must participate in an Assessment Essentials for Adjunct Faculty workshop (Mince et al., 2011). Long Beach City College (2012) leaders have prepared a white paper on the participation of adjunct faculty in outcomes assessment. They urge full-time faculty to maintain a dialogue with adjunct faculty about assessment, explaining the implementation protocols for course and program assessment and stressing the important role assessment plays in improving curriculum effectiveness.

Assessing Resources and Processes as Well as Outcomes

Processes that lead to the outcomes of student learning must be examined in order to improve those outcomes. Simply measuring an outcome will do little to improve it without inspecting the processes that led to the outcome. What students and faculty do does make a difference. Thus, student engagement is a key to student success. Student engagement is commonly assessed using instruments such as the National Survey of Student Engagement, as well as locally developed approaches. In 2000, faculty at the University of North Dakota began an interview project involving more than one hundred students (Hawthorne and Kelsch, 2012). These students were interviewed by team members once each semester for the duration of their time at the university. Questions focused on how students learn and how they think about their own learning.

Reviews of thousands of studies on the influence of college on students that Pascarella and Terenzini conducted in 1991 (twenty-six hundred studies) and again in 2005 (twenty-five hundred studies) reveal the important influence that teacher behavior has on student learning (Pascarella and Terenzini, 1991, 2005). Specifically, faculty organization and preparation have positive effects. These studies confirm the notion that process, or how we arrive at an outcome, is essential to good results.

Although classroom processes are critical to student learning, equally important is the assessment process itself. Assessing and reporting results may coincide with improved student learning but can coincide equally with no improvement if the process itself is not sound. Continuously reviewing and exploring new ways to assess student learning is critical. At Lehman College (n.d.), staff from the Office of Assessment and Planning are committed to keeping abreast of best practices in outcomes assessment, and at the Rochester Institute of Technology (n.d.), office staff implement new technologies to encourage meaningful and sustainable outcomes assessment practices.

Sharing Findings

Assessment should foster conditions in which meaningful questions are raised and addressed and in which assessment evidence is valued and used. Well-chosen assessment methods will produce information that can lead to improvement. However, the information must be analyzed and shared before it can provide a basis for action. One of the tenets of good research has always been that results should be communicated and vetted so that the research can benefit others as they pursue similar studies. Those assessing student learning should be held to the same standards and provided opportunities to learn from colleagues engaged in the process. Although disseminating assessment findings is a step that often is considered last and may even be ignored, faculty can benefit from the willingness of their colleagues to describe their work in *Assessment Update, Assessment and Evaluation in Higher Education,* the online *Research and Practice in Assessment,* and other journals.

Assessment practitioners and researchers ask faculty and staff to make assessment an ongoing process that communicates about learning outcomes and educational processes and how well these work to improve student learning and development. Assessment results must be compiled and disseminated at the campus level in ways that help to improve teaching and programming at the unit level.

Various assessment audiences and their needs must be considered. Often separate reports are required to serve distinct audiences. Regional and disciplinary accrediting associations and state governments all have distinct reporting requirements that affect the content and timing of assessment programs. Provezis (2010) indicates that regional accreditors have raised their expectations for institutional assessment of student learning outcomes. Renewed interest in assessment in some states, as well as a resurgence of performance funding schemes based on indicators such as graduation rates, indicates that states also will continue to seek information (Zis, Boeke, and Ewell, 2010).

Current and future students, as well as their parents, are interested in the performance of academic institutions. Potential students may seek information on job placement of graduating students as they select their campus or major. Employers, community leaders, and donors may value assessment information as well. Detailed project reports probably will not suit the needs of these audiences, but highlights of assessment findings may be well received. Providing information on assessment web pages is an important means of sharing this information.

The National Institute for Learning Outcomes Assessment (n.d.) has developed a *transparency framework* that an institution can use to evaluate how well it is doing in making evidence of student accomplishments readily accessible and useful to various audiences. The framework has six components that may be shared on a transparent website. These include not only plans and resources, but also evidence of student learning. While Provezis (2010) includes transparency as one area in which regional accreditors could accomplish more, she also notes the challenge of sharing assessment information without compromising the accreditation process. Jankowski and Makela (2010) have found that most assessment information is located on internally focused web pages rather than on home or admissions pages, making the information less accessible to students and the public. During our examination of many institutional websites, we found that web pages specifically directed at students and their assessment needs are the exception rather than the rule.

Internal audiences, including committees and task forces, may have specific requests for reports. Assessment program leaders at many institutions provide reporting templates for unit reports that often are mirror images of planning templates. And as with planning templates, an annual assessment report may be in the form of a grid, a time line, or a series of questions that must be answered by the unit. The Academic Program Assessment Template for Malone University (n.d.) contains four categories: program-level intended learning outcomes, means of program assessment and criteria of success, summary of data collected, and use of results. Each category contains directions and definitions. On the final section of the assessment report, faculty must show that they used results to "close the loop" by making improvements in curriculum, academic processes, and assessment planning.

Where possible, assessment programs should produce information that can be shared with several audiences for a variety of purposes. For example, results from a writing competence exam can provide information to students about their progress, help assess the overall effectiveness of the general education program, and provide disaggregated data to individual academic programs about the progress of their majors. The best assessment programs share timely information in varied ways, including project reports, theme reports, and feedback to students.

Improving and Sustaining Assessment

Improving and Sustaining Assessment

- Obtaining credible evidence
- Ensuring the use of assessment findings
- Reexamining the assessment process

Obtaining Credible Evidence

Many faculty and staff members collect relevant and meaningful assessment information pertaining to their students, often using multiple assessments over time to determine how well their students have mastered their intended learning outcomes. Although some assessment leaders may be tempted to rely mainly or solely on indirect methods to capture students' perceptions of their learning and the campus environment, this approach does not generate enough meaningful information. Effective assessment plans incorporate a combination of indirect and direct assessments, increasing credibility for the process by allowing faculty to compare results from multiple approaches. Faculty at Florida A&M University reviewed several years of evidence from direct and indirect measures to see if results were consistent and to evaluate general lessons learned. Although direct results from a nationally normed standardized test showed only small gains of 3 to 6 percent in reading, critical thinking, writing, and mathematics, more than 90 percent of survey respondents indicated they were satisfied with their educational outcomes. To improve student learning and satisfaction with student services and to reduce discrepancies between direct and indirect findings, the assessment committee developed a new process to collect data from the same subjects during the freshman and senior years, and the Florida A&M board of trustees approved a policy requiring students to participate in institutional tests and surveys. Additional initiatives, including faculty development efforts, were introduced to improve student learning of critical thinking skills (Ohia and Diallo, 2012).

Providing evidence of student learning that is credible and meaningful to a variety of stakeholders, particularly for professional and regional accreditors with explicit standards related to assessment, is a challenge. Teacher education is an example of a field that must respond to professional accreditation and state-level requirements, as well as to institutional expectations. Most professional accrediting organizations expect faculty in accredited academic programs to demonstrate accountability regarding student performance on a continuous basis. Accreditors want evidence that faculty and staff "identify the knowledge and skills required of all students receiving a degree and determine in advance the level of student performance that will be acceptable" (Diamond, 2008, p. 19).

Although regional accreditors require assessment in all disciplines, liberal arts faculty traditionally have not had disciplinary associations that require or encourage assessment. Ford (2010) reports that more disciplinary associations are supporting assessment in the liberal arts. These associations are articulating positions on assessment, suggesting learning outcomes, producing guides and other written materials, and hosting assessment sessions at their conferences.

As faculty and staff review the potential range of instruments and assessments to measure student learning, there are numerous factors to consider. First, *validity* should be examined to determine "the degree to which evidence supports the interpretation of test scores" (Millett et al., 2008, p. 5). A valid method provides a direct and accurate assessment of the learning described in program- or course-level outcomes statements. *Reliability* should also be examined to answer "questions about the consistency and stability of [student] scores" (Millett et al., 2008, p. 8). As faculty members increasingly rely on applying rubrics to student work, interrater reliability becomes another matter to address. Although multiple raters may use the same rubric, assessment leaders should carefully determine how consistently individual assessors are judging student work. The goal is to have a high level of consistency among different raters. Validity and reliability are very important to address in a formal manner and on a regular basis in order to provide the most credible evidence of student learning.

Other factors that may affect major decisions about the best assessment methods include the amount of time required for students to complete the assessment, the degree of motivation that students will have to produce their best work, and the cost of purchasing commercial instruments or the amount of time needed to develop assessments.

Although many of these factors will have been considered before methods are selected and implemented, they need to be revisited periodically to determine if the chosen methods are producing results that will lead to improvement. How well rubrics are working, for example, can be determined only through actual practice. Martins (2010) reports on efforts to develop and improve a writing rubric to be used at the Rochester Institute of Technology. Workshops for faculty allowed them to revise a draft and pilot the rubric, and eventually Martins was able to turn the scoring guide into an online survey that readers can complete as they evaluate portfolios in the writing lab.

One of the features of a credible assessment project is the willingness of investigators to verify initial findings with additional research before implementing changes to a program. Results from the University of North Dakota student interviews mentioned earlier showed that seniors assigned little value to distribution-based general education courses in contributing to their learning of cross-disciplinary general education goals, crediting their major, employment, and extracurricular activities instead. To explore this finding, department chairs helped map goals to courses, and transcript analysis enabled faculty to see course-taking patterns. Then courses in the distribution program were revalidated to ensure that general education goals were being addressed. In addition, small groups of seniors participated in focus groups. Only when all of the analysis was complete did the university redesign its general education program (Hawthorne and Kelsch, 2012).

Developing credible evidence is an area in which faculty could use more assistance. During interviews with faculty who are experienced with assessment, Ebersole (2009) asked how assessment could be changed to improve student learning. Experienced faculty asked for more training in instrument design. Training in how to develop valid interventions suggested by assessment findings was also suggested.

Ensuring the Use of Assessment Findings

Using the results from assessment should not be a burden, especially for faculty members who typically adapt and regularly modify their courses with the intention of improving student learning. Some individuals may be inclined to make decisions based on intuition, but the critical value of assessment is that faculty have data or concrete information that can be used to make informed, strategic decisions. Administrators and staff also should continuously collect information about student performance in relation to established program outcomes and use that information to improve their programs.

Faculty frequently use results from their assessments to change their undergraduate programs. Assessment results may provide faculty and administrators with vital information to guide key decisions about the allocation of resources. When financial support is provided to make informed, targeted changes based on assessment results, it becomes evident that an institutional culture is embracing assessment and making enhancements that serve students.

Hawthorne and Kelsch (2012) suggest five principles that help make assessment "actionable." First, as just suggested here, assessment needs scholarly credibility in method and conception. It needs authenticity, the feeling of truthfulness. It needs to be local, that is, grounded in the context of a specific campus, and it needs to be faculty owned. Finally, to be actionable, assessment needs to be driven by genuine inquiry about real questions. The authors point to their student interview project at the University of North Dakota as an "actionable" study. The study had institutional review board approval, included quotes from student interviews, and was designed locally. It was faculty owned and revolved around a key question about what was happening in the general education program. As the examples in this book illustrate, faculty at many institutions have been able to act on their assessment findings and improve student learning.

Reexamining the Assessment Process

Assessment is about learning. Much of what is learned is about the assessment process itself. Attention to the way assessment is carried out invariably points to opportunities for improvement. Although a regular meeting each year should be reserved for discussing the way the program is functioning, introspection about assessment should occur throughout the process, not just intermittently.

The strategies highlighted in this chapter provide direction for assessing assessment. For example, faculty can examine the program to see if important constituents are involved, if clear statements of learning outcomes are available, if methods are meaningfully aligned with these outcomes, and if results are being integrated into curriculum and budget decisions.

One of the important developments in assessment in the past several years has been the creation of meta-rubrics that can be used to assess the plans and reports of individual departments and programs. Ory (1992) uses the term *meta-assessment* to describe the evaluation of assessment. Rather than asking whether program faculty participate in assessment, meta-assessment asks how well they conduct assessment. A "small but growing number of universities" have developed meta-assessment rubrics (MARs) to evaluate assessment reports (Fulcher, Swain, and Orem, 2012, p. 1). These rubrics specify characteristics of a good assessment report and provide behavioral descriptions for each level of performance associated with the criteria. Rubrics are shared with program faculty before they submit their assessment reports and are used as the basis for ratings. Results can be used for feedback to units and can be aggregated to see how well a college or university is doing. At James Madison University, Fulcher and his coauthors gathered information on fifty-one MARs used elsewhere. More than 90 percent of these include objectives/outcomes and methods as criteria and about 75 percent also include results and use of results as criteria. More than 50 percent examine whether faculty are using multiple measures, including those that are direct and indirect. In many cases, communication with stakeholders must occur when using results. Fewer than 10 percent of the rubrics include participation of students in the assessment process or good psychometrics as criteria (Fulcher et al., 2012).

Penn (2012) provides some general suggestions for improving unit assessment processes, plans, and reports. These include providing faculty development on the ability to self-assess, using assessment mentors who help throughout the assessment process rather than providing a critique at the end, and creating online communities and disciplinary collaborations across institutions.

The Joint Committee on Standards for Educational Evaluation (2011) has established several standards for program evaluation that a committee charged with evaluating an assessment program can apply or adapt. An initial set of standards for program evaluation was developed by the Joint Committee in 1981. *The Program Evaluation Standards*, published in 1994 and revised in 2011, guide evaluation practice for education and training programs and for materials. Because of the wall created between personnel evaluation and assessment in the 1980s, the standards have not been used to help design assessment programs. Axelson and Flick (2009) believe that applying these standards could enrich campus discussion about sustainable assessment systems. The current program standards are organized around five dimensions: utility, feasibility, propriety, accuracy (valid and reliable information), and evaluation accountability.

An important consideration in evaluating an assessment program is whether it provides for both continuity and flexibility. Assessment information is most helpful to the decision-making process if it is provided in a consistent format over a period of time. If the same test or survey is administered over a series of semesters, educators can see trends in the results and can more confidently identify issues or make necessary changes. Collecting the same information before and after an academic program has been modified allows decision makers to judge more readily if the modification had an impact.

Although continuity is important, so is flexibility. Viewing the assessment process itself as dynamic rather than fixed encourages experimentation and helps overcome the fear that a measure will become a permanent fixture regardless of its value. This is one reason that multiple measures are recommended. With multiple measures, a nonproductive method can be dropped without having to start data collection from scratch. In addition, finding similar results with more than one assessment measure increases confidence in making a decision to change an academic program. For example, faculty may be more willing to require additional library work if both senior surveys and research papers demonstrate a need.

Additional Thoughts

Provezis (2010) notes that deficiencies in student learning outcomes assessment are the most common shortcoming in regional accreditors' evaluations of institutions. Accreditors are asking increasing numbers of institutions for follow-up actions or reports focused on these issues. Staff from the New England Association of Schools and Colleges indicate that 80 percent of institutions in their region have been asked for follow-up actions related to assessment. In 2010, 70 percent of community colleges in the southern region were out of compliance with the Southern Association of Colleges and Schools standard related to institutional effectiveness (Nunley, Bers, and Manning, 2011). As expectations of accreditors increase, the number of institutions receiving approval for less than the traditional ten years is also increasing.

Aware of their influence on assessment, representatives of accreditors agree that "it would be far better for institutions themselves, as part of their cultures, to drive student learning outcomes assessment" (Provezis, 2010, p. 18). Ewell (2009) believes that accreditors can foster a focus on improvement and notes the attempts of several accreditors to separate "compliance" activities from "deep engagement" activities. In spite of this emphasis on improvement, Ewell still believes that "the need to report measures of student achievement that can be benchmarked or compared" will increase (p. 20).

We believe that institutions can and should make concerted efforts to develop assessment approaches that work and have found that many institutions already are doing this. In subsequent chapters, we address several of the issues involved in establishing successful assessment programs and provide many examples of the creative assessment initiatives that are already in place on university and college campuses.

While similarities exist in approaches to assessment, many campuses have something unique to recommend. For example, faculty at California

Lutheran University (2014a) conceptualize assessment as a three-step process of decision making and planning, gathering evidence and analysis, and communication and reflection. The emphasis of assessment is on supporting educational effectiveness with evidence. Leaders at Northern Arizona University (2014a) also distinguish three stages for assessment reporting. The first phase provides the program's mission, learning outcomes, and curriculum map, as well as the assessment questions and design. The second phase focuses entirely on collecting quality data. The third phase includes interpretation of findings, recommendations, and dissemination of findings. Providing three phases recognizes that programs demonstrate a wide variety of assessment experience and allows program faculty to complete reporting requirements without feeling overwhelmed.

At the beginning of this chapter, we offered an assessment approach based on the three-phase process of planning, implementing, and improving and sustaining assessment. We believe this is a useful approach for conceptualizing the assessment process. In the remainder of this book, we return to many of the ideas presented in this chapter.

CHAPTER 3

ENGAGING FACULTY AND STUDENTS IN ASSESSMENT

E ffective assessment of student learning cannot occur without involving *faculty* in setting goals and objectives for learning, selecting or developing assessment methods, collecting evidence of student learning, determining the meaning of the findings, and taking warranted improvement actions. While a single faculty member may engage in all of these activities in her classroom, effective assessment of program and institutional effectiveness requires collaboration among faculty. Collaboration may not come naturally to academics, whose graduate work has encouraged them to develop unique knowledge of a narrow area of their field and to value their autonomy and academic freedom to develop their own teaching style and methods in their classrooms. Moreover, many graduate programs do not prepare their graduates particularly well as teachers, and most provide no training or experience in outcomes assessment. Thus, faculty need support from each other and from administrators to become engaged in assessment.

The support of *administrators*—presidents, provosts, deans, and directors—is essential in planning and carrying out program reviews for academic and administrative units and self studies for disciplinary and regional accreditation. They can:

- Provide important support for faculty involvement in outcomes assessment.
- Bring faculty and student affairs professionals together to enhance student learning in and outside the classroom. (We say more about engaging student affairs professionals in assessment in Chapter 9.)
- Appoint committees focused on curriculum development and improvement, general education, teaching excellence, or assessment that bring faculty and student affairs personnel together to devise ways to strengthen student learning and development.
- Bring assessment experts to campus to provide workshops and small group consultation.
- Send faculty and staff to assessment conferences, including meetings of disciplinary associations that have tracks or individual sessions on outcomes assessment in the discipline.
- Invest in professional development experts who can offer specialized and sustained training and support to enable faculty and staff to develop assessment expertise.
- Provide funds for purchase of questionnaires and tests, software programs for data storage and analysis, report preparation, and certainly for the purpose of making improvements that are warranted on the basis of assessment findings.

Effective assessment of student learning cannot take place without the conscientious participation of *students*. Students must be informed of the role of outcomes assessment in gauging and improving their learning. Then they must carry out their assignments, complete projects and internships, and take exams—always doing their best work—in order to demonstrate honestly what they have learned.

Employers are important contributors to, and consumers of, outcomes assessment. (We say more about their involvement in Chapter 7.) They can convey a vital external perspective on the workplace as those responsible for institutions and for individual academic and administrative programs set goals, select and administer data-gathering tools, ponder the meaning of findings, and implement improvements. Program *graduates* and students' *parents* can play similar roles on program or institutional advisory boards or stakeholder focus groups. Examples of the involvement of these external groups are found throughout this book.

In this chapter, we concentrate on strategies for engaging faculty and students. We describe their assessment-related responsibilities, the resources they need to carry out these responsibilities, and the rewards that encourage deeper involvement. Attending to these three Rs—responsibilities, resources, and rewards—will help to overcome another R of assessment: resistance.

Involving Faculty in Assessment

Because of the pivotal role of faculty, we begin by discussing the three Rs of faculty involvement.

Faculty Responsibility

To ensure that assessment is a faculty-driven activity, faculty must have responsibility for carrying out all steps of the process, from articulating the purposes of assessment for the campus or unit to acting on assessment findings. Carrying out these responsibilities takes several forms and differs from individual to individual. Some faculty serve as assessment coordinators in their departments. Some serve on department, division, or campuswide committees that provide direction for assessment. Serving on assessment committees puts faculty in leadership roles with respect to assessment and often is a major responsibility for them. Committee members generally are knowledgeable about assessment matters and involved in making decisions about assessment. Although the number of faculty members serving on assessment committees may be small, faculty participate in assessment in many other ways: by attending meetings, administering assessment instruments in their classes, providing comments, and responding to requests about assessment. Some faculty have responsibility for analyzing data or writing reports. Hutchings advises "matching tasks to talents" and "needs to interests" (2010, p. 17). For example, those who enjoy working with data can help analyze and interpret results.

Certain approaches to assessment lead to more involvement than others. On some campuses, faculty who teach general studies courses are asked to demonstrate that these courses are meeting the learning goals of the program. Thus, course instructors must work together as they develop and carry out a plan for assessing a course. In this approach, the responsibility for assessment is placed directly on individual classroom teachers, usually with a campuswide committee that acts as a review body for the reports it receives from faculty.

An explicit list showing expectations for each individual or group helps clarify roles and delineates responsibilities. A bulleted list created at Del Mar College (2012) shows four overall responsibilities for faculty: participate fully in the development and implementation of the program assessment plan, integrate student learning outcomes into the curriculum, identify and implement effective action plans based on assessment results, and participate in professional development. The list defines responsibilities for several other participants in the assessment process as well. For example, the president is expected to advocate for assessment as an institutional priority and provide the resources necessary to maintain a culture of assessment. Such lists vary among colleges and universities, reflecting the unique approaches campuses take to assessment of student learning. To be effective, the list needs to be endorsed by campus leaders, key assessment committees, and faculty.

Job responsibility lists also can be helpful for specific projects. When an updated assessment management system was launched at Milliken University's School of Education, a handout describing involvement, protocol, and instructions was created for each group of stakeholders (Magoulias, 2011).

Assessment Resources for Faculty

The resources provided for faculty need to mirror faculty responsibilities. Information about the reasons for undertaking assessment, strategies for formulating learning outcomes, and approaches for writing plans, selecting methods, and using results are all important topics.

Written Materials   Leaders at many institutions have developed assessment materials for internal use. Examples include handbooks, workbooks, and assessment newsletters that keep faculty up to date on what is happening locally, as well as in the overall field of assessment. Several campuses have created lending libraries that contain assessment-related books and materials.

One of the major developments of the past several years has been the increase of assessment materials available on university and college websites. On many campuses, these websites are an important source of faculty support and development. Staff from the Office of Institutional Assessment at the University of Florida (2014) maintain online modules and newsletters to assist faculty with assessment responsibilities.

Many websites include a definition of *assessment*, often framing it as an opportunity for conversation. The Baruch College (2014) website contains the following answer to the question: "Why Assessment?": "Outcomes assessment helps to define what happens and what matters . . . Through data collection and analysis, outcomes assessment provides a forum for discussion that leads to understanding and informed decision-making." Websites often include one or more of the following helpful materials: an assessment philosophy, a statement of assessment values, a list of effective practices, definitions of terms, and a list of frequently asked questions (FAQs). Some assessment web pages contain a resource link to websites of other institutions and/or to national sites.

General descriptive materials about the assessment process are helpful in building a foundation for assessment. In addition, at specific points in the assessment process, faculty can benefit from resource materials that facilitate their tasks. Many web pages provide downloadable grids for faculty to use as they create assessment plans or reports. Long Island University (2013) provides annotated exemplars of assessment plans on its website. Other helpful materials include a list of characteristics of good assessment plans or a list of criteria that will be used to critique plans after they are submitted. On several campuses, criteria for evaluating reports about assessment activities have been developed and shared with faculty (Fulcher, Swain, and Orem, 2012).

Websites of national groups such as the Association of American Colleges and Universities and the National Institute for Learning Outcomes Assessment (NILOA) provide additional resources for faculty. Websites of disciplinary associations in chemistry, communication studies, and psychology, among others, have web pages devoted to assessment. In her *Assessment Update* article, Ford (2010) describes resources available for assessment in the liberal arts, including several books focused on particular disciplines.

National, Regional, and State Conferences   The annual Assessment Institute in Indianapolis is now in its third decade, providing preconference workshops, plenary panels of assessment experts, and concurrent sessions by experienced practitioners. The thirty-five-year-old Alverno College Institute for Educational Outreach (2013) offers three-day and week-long summer workshops on assessment, introducing educators to Alverno's ability-based curriculum design and its assessment-as-learning approach to education. The Virginia Assessment Group convenes assessment practitioners from within the state's boundaries and beyond for annual conferences. Several other states have their own assessment conferences. Regional associations, including the Middle States Commission on Higher Education and the North Central Association's Higher Learning Commission, also hold annual conferences, and several discipline-specific conferences such as business and physical education highlight assessment issues. In fact, the Association to Advance Collegiate Schools of Business is one of several national associations that sponsors an annual conference focused specifically on assessment.

Campus Gatherings   In addition to attending national or regional conferences, faculty have opportunities to learn about assessment on their own campuses. Many departments regularly offer lectures or symposia for faculty. External assessment experts are invited to share general or specific information at these gatherings, and campus websites often contain slides from these presentations. Campus experts also share their knowledge with others, providing an accessible source of expertise. For example, faculty in teachers' colleges who have experience with portfolios often share their knowledge with faculty in other units. Workshops serve similar purposes but usually are designed to give participants a chance to work with the information they are receiving. The director of institutional research and assessment at Lancaster Bible College and Graduate School conducted a full-day workshop in which course-embedded assessment was emphasized. Faculty were asked to develop one course-embedded assignment focused on information literacy. To overcome resistance from faculty and staff, workshop leaders began the day with an overview of assessment highlighting faculty responsibilities in assessing student learning for the benefit of students (Mort, 2012).

Rather than responding to a particular situation, some campuses have regularly scheduled assessment activities. Retreats held once each semester are the most important professional development activity at Zayed University (Schoepp, 2012). Based on recommendations of faculty members who attended a national conference, Gonzaga University introduced Student Learning Outcomes Day (SLOD), an annual half-day event. Soon renamed Learning Assessment Day (LeAD), the day provides an opportunity for national and local faculty experts to share their knowledge about assessment, framing it as an effort to improve teaching. During the day, department faculty work on creating assessment reports as well as data-gathering instruments and rubrics. The event includes a session in which faculty report on their work (Bubb, Herzog, Terry, and Geithner, 2010).

Because workshops tend to last no longer than a day or two, an alternate strategy is to create a working group, which tends to meet over a period of several weeks, generally with the goal of completing some task.

This strategy has been used with classroom assessment where faculty meet once a week for two or three weeks to learn techniques and then meet several additional times to report on their experiences. Discussion groups are a similar strategy but tend to be more open-ended and less focused on completing a particular task. To engage more participants in the assessment process, David Martins (2010), associate professor and writing program director at the Rochester Institute of Technology, invited all of the writing faculty to participate in a reading group focused on academic writing. In addition, the university's teaching and learning center helped create a faculty learning community focused on engaging students in writing and revision activities. Faculty used some of their time to help develop a scoring rubric. Other ways to gather faculty together to learn about assessment include brown bag lunches, roundtables, and town hall–style meetings. The web can be used for virtual gatherings and additional interaction using listservs, blogs, and other means. In addition to learning about assessment, formal and informal campus gatherings provide opportunities for the continuing conversations that assessment needs to thrive.

Institutional Support   Appropriate institutional and administrative support for assessment greatly contributes to faculty efforts. A director of assessment (or similar office) often plays a strong role in working with faculty at both the institutional and unit levels. Leaders in the Department of Industrial Design at Metropolitan State College of Denver, where faculty had no real data collection instruments and no system to take action based on assessment results, sought to strengthen their existing assessment processes. The position of director of student learning assessment had just been created, and the newly hired director "became a source of guidance for the development of the new ID assessment program" (Phillips and Thompson, 2011). At James Madison University (n.d.), staff from the Center for Assessment and Research Studies support assessment activities. Consultants in the program assessment support service also are available to facilitate assessment projects.

Other professional staff and administrators can be helpful as well. When some individuals at Bluefield State College remained reluctant to participate in assessment, a faculty member in social sciences was appointed associate dean for assessment in arts and sciences and met individually with faculty who were having difficulty (Anderson, 2013). To make the assessment process most useful on their campus, American University (2014) leaders advise faculty to work with the learning outcomes and assessment team and the Center for Teaching and Learning.

Faculty Rewards

Faculty who participate in assessment should receive recognition for their efforts. Some rewards are intrinsic. A well-designed assessment program will result in interaction with other faculty that may have been lacking in the past. It will lead to improved clarity with respect to goals and objectives for learning and ultimately to improved learning (Ebersole, 2009). Faculty may also see a supportive link between assessment and other important processes such as internal program review, planning, and budgeting. Faculty in units that are accredited by professional organizations often show strong support for assessment, reflecting the increased interest of accreditors.

What about more explicit rewards? In some units, faculty receive release time to serve as assessment coordinators or undertake projects. This may provide time for individuals to study assessment, attend campus workshops and national conferences, and prepare to lead colleagues in their own assessment activities. At Albany State University in Georgia, faculty assessment experts were created using a two-year rotating appointment with course release. After serving as assessment director for two years, faculty return to their departments with assessment experience to share with their colleagues (Kinzie, 2010).

In a 2010 NILOA survey of program heads from randomly selected programs, additional release time for faculty to engage in assessment was selected as the most important factor in advancing assessment. This item was followed by additional stipends and more faculty involvement. Of note, nearly 70 percent of respondents indicated they had a person devoted to assessment either full time (15 percent) or part time (54 percent). The authors urge caution in evaluating specific results due to the 30 percent response rate, which was lower than desired (Ewell, Paulson, and Kinzie, 2011).

Promotion and tenure processes should recognize assessment efforts. In some units, faculty are encouraged to report assessment activities on their annual reports under the heading of teaching and teaching-related activities. Assessment also may be recognized as service to the department, division, or campus. Faculty at the Community College of Baltimore County who score course-embedded assessment activities can be paid a stipend or count their work as service for their faculty evaluations (Mince, Mason, and Bogage, 2011).

Recognition   At many institutions, participation in assessment leads to recognition through activities such as presenting posters or giving on-campus presentations. Faculty have opportunities to publish articles about their assessment activities in disciplinary journals, including those in accounting, mathematics, and economics. The bimonthly newsletter from John Wiley & Sons, *Assessment Update*, publishes accounts of assessment work of faculty, as do *Assessment and Evaluation in Higher Education, Research and Practice in Assessment*, and other journals. The web page for the Center for Teaching and Learning at the University of Minnesota (2012) lists several journals that publish assessment work. And the assessment scholarship web page at Northern Illinois University (2012) lists relevant papers and presentations by faculty and staff.

To recognize faculty efforts, college and university websites contain information about notable assessment efforts. Loyola Marymount University's (2014) web pages list "Assessment Success Stories" and ask readers to join in "celebrating" these successes. The site includes several examples of programs that used assessment to make improvements. For example, the dance program incorporated scaffolded writing lessons in its capstone writing assignment after reviewing information from rubrics and surveys.

Grant Programs   At several universities, faculty may receive grants to undertake assessment projects. One approach to awarding grants is to ask for proposals that are then reviewed by a committee of peers. Guidelines for grants generally ask for a description of the project, a statement of how the project fits into department assessment plans, and an explanation of how results will be used.

At the Rochester Institute of Technology (n.d.), faculty can apply for grants through the Student Learning Outcomes Assessment Office. Small grants are offered for projects that address assessment plans, methods, or "closing-the-loop" activities. The Office of Assessment and Evaluation at Virginia Polytechnic and State University (2014b) offers several types of grants to help develop assessment skills and abilities; encourage best practice in assessment; and foster the scholarship of teaching, learning, and assessment. High-impact-practice grants support assessment of educational practices such as undergraduate research, internships, service-learning, and capstone experiences.

Another approach is to award grants for work that can be accomplished during the summer. Summer grants give faculty the opportunity to focus their energies on specific projects in a concentrated time frame. At James Madison University (n.d.) an assessment fellowship program encourages faculty and staff to work on assessment projects. Faculty must agree to be in residence at the Center for Assessment and Research Studies for a specified period during the summer to work with center staff to learn about assessment practice.

Faculty may need guidance in applying for assessment grants because they are not quite sure what a credible assessment project involves. At Shepherd University (2014), staff from the Center for Teaching and Learning suggest topics for faculty interested in applying for mini-grants. To ensure that proposals focus on important tasks needed to move a department's overall assessment program forward, faculty should be encouraged to consult with chairs or assessment committee members about what might be included in a proposal. A letter of support from a program's head may be required.

Travel Funds   Because several conferences focus on assessment, faculty have opportunities to learn about assessment or give presentations about their assessment activities. The Office of Assessment and Evaluation at Virginia Polytechnic and State University (2014b) offers two types of travel grants. *Assessment education grants* support faculty who are just beginning in assessment to engage in professional development opportunities. Teams of faculty are encouraged to apply. *Assessment dissemination grants* support faculty to present their assessment findings to either discipline-specific or broader-themed audiences. These grants require applicants to verify institutional review board (IRB) approval prior to funding.

Maximizing the Role of Faculty and Faculty Acceptance

The 2010 NILOA survey of program heads suggests substantial faculty engagement in assessment. About 60 percent of respondents indicated that most (23 percent) or all (38 percent) of their faculty are involved. Yet 44 percent of all respondents indicated they would like greater faculty involvement, as would 70 percent of liberal arts respondents (Ewell et al., 2011).

At most institutions there is a desire to maximize the role of faculty in assessment—to involve as many individuals as possible and engage them in meaningful ways. In this section, we share some strategies to maximize the role of faculty in assessment, and because faculty can play a role in assessment without necessarily valuing it, we also address the issue of faculty acceptance.

Share Tasks Wisely   Involvement in assessment is maximized if each faculty member is given at least some role in the process. That role may be something easy to accomplish, such as reviewing a plan developed by a committee or ranking the importance of program goals. It may be much more extensive, such as developing an assessment plan to reflect the contributions of individual courses to an overall academic program. The important point is that faculty cannot be involved in assessment if they have no responsibility for its undertaking.

A related strategy is to put in place a plan or project that divides the assessment process into a series of specific assignments. It is easier to involve faculty if they know the task at hand and can approach assessment as a series of steps rather than an overwhelming burden. When Martins (2010) began planning an assessment project at the Rochester Institute of Technology, he and a few other writing specialists planned a three-year project but started with assessment of one learning objective. Although they were thinking "big picture," they decided to use an approach rooted in psychology to "shrink the change" (p. 4): they started with specific activities for faculty, allowing them to engage in and practice assessment skills.

Next, make sure that faculty are involved in all steps of the process. Too often faculty are asked to articulate learning objectives for their courses, but the department chair writes the assessment plan. A faculty committee should be responsible for actually creating the assessment plan, not for providing comments on approaches proposed by administrators. Both Hatfield (n.d.) and Hutchings (2010) warn against pitfalls associated with centralizing assessment activities within a specific office or with a single individual. The danger is in marginalizing regular faculty.

A similar pitfall occurs when a small committee takes so much control of the process that the typical faculty member has little role. Thus broadly representative committees, rotating memberships, and shared tasks are preferred. At Southern Illinois University Edwardsville, Min Liu (2011) engaged five other untenured faculty in conversations about assessment. Although several were involved at the program level, none was engaged in assessment at the college or university level. These faculty felt they were not adequately prepared for assessment of student learning. While some attended campus workshops about specific aspects of assessment, one specifically commented, "What's lacking for me is the big picture" (p. 6). In one department, a faculty member felt the chair took the burden for assessment and shielded untenured faculty from doing it. Another felt assessment was a privilege of the few. Junior faculty did feel that excellent teaching, and therefore assessment, were important to tenure.

Encourage Teamwork and Team Building   Educators understand the value of teamwork for students and frequently give group assignments in the classroom. Similarly, assessment flourishes when faculty, staff, and students work together rather than alone. Not only the assessment committee, but additional faculty members, should have opportunities to work in teams. For instance, several faculty can be invited to design a performance task. Ewell (2010) believes that younger faculty are more team oriented and therefore more positive about assessment. He believes that less "isolation in the classroom" will be good for assessment (p. 5).

Team-building activities for groups that will be working together on planning or other projects can be valuable. Strategies include brainstorming—getting all the ideas out on the table for careful attention—and consensus taking to see if there is substantial agreement on essential points. Ground rules for group conversations might include providing evidence for assertions, taking periodic breaks to allow those who have not spoken to do so, and limiting the time any one person can speak. For the activity to be meaningful, each group must set up its own ground rules and, of course, follow them. Occasionally inviting an outsider to help facilitate meetings is a good idea. An assessment specialist may be able to help faculty make progress.

Use Local Instruments   The role of faculty is maximized if local rather than nationally available instruments are used. Assessment programs that are built around regular faculty classroom work necessarily lead to increased faculty involvement and provide the most promise to answer faculty questions about student learning. Hutchings (2010) favors approaches that "bring the purposes of assessment and the regular work of faculty closer together" (p. 6), resulting in both greater faculty involvement and more useful assessment.

Foster Acceptance of Assessment   Maximizing the role of faculty may contribute to faculty acceptance, but it is only one of several ingredients. At the most basic level, it helps to concentrate on important questions (Wehlburg, 2013). Start with what matters most; then concentrate on three or four major learning outcomes rather than trying to assess every possible program goal. Faculty often have concerns about the methods and instruments used to collect assessment data. They are not likely to accept results generated with instruments that are not of high quality, and they will not support decisions based on information they consider inadequate. Issues of reliability and validity need to be addressed, and campus experts on instrument design should review data collection instruments and procedures. Penn (2011) warns that overlooking issues of data quality is a mistake. A better approach is to provide support from a graduate student or staff member and to encourage triangulation of results through the use of multiple measures. In fact, 50 percent of program leaders, particularly in business disciplines (68 percent), believe better tests or measures would further their assessment efforts. And more than 50 percent agree that improved faculty expertise in methodology would be beneficial (Ewell et al., 2011).

Faculty acceptance of assessment also is enhanced if assessment information is used in appropriate ways. If information is collected but not acted on, faculty soon lose interest in continued participation. Ewell (2009) urges leaders to create opportunities for "thoughtful collective reflection about evidence" (p. 16), encouraging faculty and staff to work together as they consider assessment information.

Helpful Administrative Actions　Key administrators have an important role in the assessment process because the actions they take can hinder assessment or foster it. If administrators view assessment as an unpleasant burden, many faculty will as well. Administrators need to express a sincere commitment to assessment; allow adequate time for faculty to understand, accept, and carry out assessment; and encourage and support the use of assessment information. At St. John's University (2014) administrators are expected to nurture the culture of assessment, for example, by providing faculty with necessary tools and direction.

As assessment has matured, a number of practitioners have developed expertise that they can share with others to help assessment succeed. Penn (2011) warns against "best intentions" that can impede assessment. First is the tendency to oversell what can be accomplished through assessment. If great promises are made but results are modest, initial claims can appear outlandish. Penn recommends that a realistic perspective be presented, framing assessment as a tool to help gather information about student learning and provide information for decision making. He also warns against using accreditation as an enforcer. Assessment needs to be part of the daily life of the institution, not just a periodic activity.

Watch Your Language　Hatfield (n.d.) recommends that "one of the first and foremost important steps an institution can take when it comes to starting an assessment initiative is clarifying the terminology" (p. 2). In the absence of universal standards, Goldman and Zackel also believe that "individual institutions must agree on terms and ensure that their own terminology is widely available and utilized" (2009, p. 9). Bubb and his coauthors from Gonzaga University (2010) recommend caution about language. In their view, *outcomes assessment* is a phrase that has negative associations for faculty. *Student learning outcomes* is a more comfortable term because it implies successful teaching experiences. Acronyms matter too. The name of the university's Student Learning Outcomes Day (SLOD) was changed to Learning Assessment Day (LeAD) to improve the acronym. Many websites include a list of definitions among their materials. Nevertheless, Penn (2011) warns against too many acronyms and too much jargon.

View Faculty Development as a Continuing Process   Just as the student body changes from year to year, so do at least some members of the faculty. Thus, faculty development related to assessment must be seen as a continuing process. On many campuses, new faculty receive an introduction to outcomes assessment during the annual orientation for newcomers. At Lancaster Bible College and Graduate School (Mort, 2012), new faculty and staff receive widely read assessment books, such as *Classroom Assessment Techniques* by Angelo and Cross (1993).

Some Stumbling Blocks in Understanding Assessment

Some points of confusion create stumbling blocks in the way faculty view assessment, and these are areas in which clarification is particularly important. Cochise College (2009) faculty describe what student outcomes assessment is not. Their list includes grading, faculty evaluation, course evaluation, and program review.

Entry-Level Placement   Faculty in many programs collect and use information about potential students to determine their qualifications for majoring in the program or to select the appropriate level for them to begin their studies. This information often provides a good starting point for assessing academic programs. Reviewing initial papers, performances, and portfolios provides valuable information about where students begin. Program assessment also requires faculty to know where students end up, as well as something about what happens along the way.

To gather information about general education outcomes, leaders in the Association of American Colleges and Universities (2008) urge institutions to develop a comprehensive assessment framework that begins with orientation and includes both milestone and capstone experiences. They believe that progress in achieving liberal outcomes needs to be assessed from entry to the final year in both general education programs and the major.

Course Grades   Confusion often arises about the role of course grades in assessment. In fact, faculty understanding of the difference between grading and assessing learning outcomes was the biggest hurdle that leaders at Texas Christian University faced when they introduced a new learning management system (King, 2011).

Why aren't course grades enough? The assignment of a grade to an individual student provides a summary measure about the student's performance in the class and perhaps tells something about the teacher's standards. But it does not usually convey direct information about which of the course's goals and objectives for learning have been met or how well they have been met by the student. Likewise, the grade distribution for the class as a whole tells something about the relative performance of the group of students but not about what or how much they have learned. Course grades alone do not necessarily help students improve.

Tests and activities on which grades are based can be meaningful for assessment. As staff from Carnegie Mellon's (n.d.a) Eberly Center for Teaching Excellence explain, if grades are to be used as the basis of learning outcomes, they need to be decomposed into indicators that reflect learning and those that reflect other behaviors, such as class attendance and participation. Grades must be based on consistently applied criteria, and separate grades or subscores should be assigned to major components of knowledge and skills so that specific strengths and weaknesses can be identified. Then subscores can be aggregated across students and assignments to assess the performance of the group in specific areas.

Early in the history of assessment, assessment practices were "consciously separated from what went on in the classroom" (Ewell, 2009, p. 19), often causing practitioners to overlook the role that classroom activities and assignments could play in assessment. The work of Walvoord and others (Walvoord and Anderson, 1998) helped practitioners understand the great value of close-to-the-classroom approaches.

Faculty Evaluation   Many faculty fear the relationship between assessment and faculty evaluation, often thinking the two processes are the same. Thus, it is important to make a clear distinction between them. Information collected through assessment strategies is used to evaluate programs, not faculty members. Yet many times assessment activities generate results that may reflect on individuals. In situations where only one or two individuals are responsible for a program, for example, experienced assessment practitioners from California State University Fresno (2007) urge extreme care. Assessment findings can be made available to instructors to guide improvement, but should not be included in their personnel folders or as summative evidence in making tenure, promotion, or salary decisions. A clear distinction must be made between rewarding assessment activities and using assessment findings in judging individuals.

The Nature of Resistance

Although we saved a description of the last R, faculty resistance, until the end of our discussion about faculty involvement, it is important to be aware of its nature. Ewell (2009) notes that "the majority of academics now realize that engaging in assessment has become a condition of doing business" (p. 6). Nevertheless, some faculty, as well as administrators, continue to resist assessment for a number of reasons. Some believe that assessment is primarily for external audiences and fail to see its potential to improve programs. Some resent the cost of assessment in terms of time and resources. Others question the quality of the data collected. Some fear their efforts will be for naught if the information is not used; others worry that the information will be used in some way that is harmful to their interests.

Many faculty consider teaching to be a private activity, and they do not want to open themselves to judgment on the results of this endeavor. Assessment requires a sharing of information and a commonality of goals that can cause individuals to be uncomfortable at times.

Because of these issues, some faculty question the value of assessment. Fortunately, many who initially resist assessment come to accept it over time. If faculty have responsibility, resources, and rewards for participating in assessment, the chance they will come to appreciate its value greatly increases.

Involving Students in Assessment

Assessment is an activity in which students must be active partners. Here we discuss several ways to engage them. As with our discussion of involving faculty, we refer to three areas of importance: responsibility, resources, and rewards. Students need to know what is expected of them, have appropriate support and information to live up to these expectations, and have some incentive or reward for their participation. If educators are thoughtful about how they include students in the assessment process, they can help overcome motivation problems that can hinder assessment. Hutchings (2010) believes that "bringing students more actively into the processes of assessment may well be the most powerful route to greater faculty engagement" (p.16).

Student Responsibility

Assessment information that directly demonstrates the learning of students originates with students themselves. Thus, the most basic responsibility of students is to participate in direct assessment activities such as tests and performance measures, as well as indirect activities such as interviews and focus groups. Specifics vary by campus. For example, students at Southeastern Oklahoma State University (n.d.) are selected to participate in university-wide midlevel testing either on scheduled assessment days or in targeted courses each semester. Their enrollment for the following semester is delayed if the requirement is not completed. In addition to participating in assessment activities, students on many campuses play other roles in the assessment process.

Serving on Committees   On several campuses, students serve on institution-wide or unit assessment committees conceptualizing, designing, and consequently learning about the program. Students also may serve on task forces that are concerned with specific assessment instruments, helping to plan measures such as portfolios or performance projects. Some colleges or departments have student advisory boards that contribute advice on a variety of topics including assessment. At Grand Valley State University, students are represented on the University Assessment Committee as well as on unit assessment committees (Schuurman, Berlin, Langlois, and Guevara, 2012). Faculty at Macalester College (2012) include students on their Student Learning Committee.

Providing Feedback about Assessment   Whether or not they are serving in an official advisory capacity, students should be encouraged to provide comments about the assessment activities in which they participate. This can happen in both formal and informal ways. Students who are completing portfolios often are asked to reflect on the value of their experiences and activities. They also can be asked to participate in focus groups that are concerned with various aspects of the assessment process, perhaps providing insight about test or survey results that are surprising. As Ewell (2010) points out, students are closer than faculty and administrators to the data and often can offer better interpretations. Even without a specific request for comments, students can be quite vocal about an assessment activity that they do not feel is worthwhile. Educators should consider these opinions very carefully and may need to make some modifications in their approach. For example, faculty at one university revised the writing competence examination for juniors after receiving a steady stream of negative comments. The exam was changed so that students receive topics specifically related to their majors.

Students made a valuable contribution to an assessment project at Saint Mary's College, which participated in a grant from the Lumina Foundation to the Higher Learning Commission (HLC) to gather information about the Degree Qualifications Profile (DQP). The DQP defines the learning that each degree should reflect regardless of major. Saint Mary's students were asked to reflect on the Specialized Knowledge outcomes contained in the profile. On a survey, students in the nursing, biology, psychology, and modern languages departments used their own words to explain the meaning of the DQP outcomes in relationship to their majors. Although interpretations varied by discipline, students generally understood the meanings of the outcomes (Ickes and Flowers, 2013).

Providing Feedback about Instruction   In promoting wider use of classroom assessment techniques, faculty may collect midcourse information from students about how their classes are proceeding. Brigham Young University (2014) faculty use a midcourse evaluation tool that allows them to create simple surveys to gather student feedback on learning experiences in their courses. Faculty in the Fiek School of Pharmacy at the University of the Incarnate Word in San Antonio use student focus groups to obtain student feedback about their teaching practices during, rather than after, the course. The LEAD (Learning, Education, Assessment, and Development) team is made up of representatives from mentoring teams formed in each class. The team meets with a facilitator midway through the semester to discuss the courses in progress. The facilitator, a faculty member from outside the program, leads the discussion and later meets with the program's steering committee to share program-related comments about issues such as scheduling, content, or resources. Students feel the LEAD focus groups provide a nonthreatening way of communicating with faculty. Resulting changes in classes include peer tutoring and dissemination of videotaped lectures (Martin and Martinez, 2010).

Conducting and Facilitating Assessment   At some institutions, students play yet another role with respect to assessment: acting as assessors themselves. During group work projects, they often evaluate the functioning of the group and the contributions of other students, as well as themselves, to the group. Students also critique class projects or presentations of other students. At the Grand Valley State University School of Social Work, the capstone course includes peer assessment as a central component. Student groups meet for an hour of each class session to share and critique cover pages for their required electronic portfolios. The student who is seeking feedback documents responses on a peer assessment form. As a guide to their responses, the students providing feedback use the same rubric as course instructors do to grade final portfolios (Schuurman et al., 2012). At Aristotle University in Greece, a voluntary portfolio project includes six assignments. As part of the project, students work in teams and evaluate the work of other teams (Papadimitriou, 2009). Students also can help the assessment process by acting as mentors for other students. To facilitate use of e-portfolios at LaGuardia Community College (2014), students hold peer mentorships called Student Technology Mentors.

Student members of the Ad Club at Fontbonne University were asked to help institutional research and assessment (IRA) staff with administration of the National Survey of Student Engagement (NSSE), which captures student involvement during the first and senior years. For results to be useful, Fontbonne, a small university, needed a response rate closer to 50 percent rather than the 27 percent it was experiencing. The club was given a budget of one thousand dollars and an incentive plan based on response rate. The student team identified promotional strategies and met with their client, the director of IRA. Most of the budget was spent on printed banners and T-shirts to be given to those who completed the survey. Laptops were placed around campus to facilitate immediate survey completion. The final response rate was 54 percent (Feldmann and Jackson, 2011).

In some cases, graduate students work with professional staff to conduct assessment activities. When site visits were conducted as part of a self-study for George Washington University's Student Affairs Division, each team included one graduate fellow who had attended GW as an undergraduate (Konwerski, Sonn, and Hamluk, 2010). At James Madison University, graduate students worked with faculty on two-member teams on a special project designed to evaluate the assessment office (Fulcher and Bashkov, 2012).

Resources for Students

Faculty and staff must provide information for students to help them fulfill their assessment responsibilities. These materials help students understand what assessment is about, why they are asked to participate, what is expected of them, and how they will be evaluated.

Statements of Goals and Objectives for Learning   It is of great importance for students to be aware of the goals and objectives for learning that drive programs. If they understand what faculty want them to know, do and value, they have a much better likelihood of achieving these objectives. Ewell (2009) believes that "learning objectives must be inescapable" (p. 16) and appear in catalogues, syllabi, and grading criteria. At Montgomery College (2011), faculty share learning outcomes with students early in the course either as part of a syllabus or in other printed material. If a rubric is to be used, students receive this prior to participating in assessment.

Leaders at Brigham Young University (2014) maintain a web page that allows readers to see the learning outcomes for each college, department, and program by selecting the unit of interest from a dropdown menu. Students are urged to review program outcomes to see "the big picture" of the knowledge and skills they will attain upon finishing a program.

Written Materials about Assessment   Catalogue statements about assessment can be helpful to students and are particularly important if assessment is a required rather than an expected activity. James Madison University's (2013b) catalogue contains several paragraphs describing the assessment process. As explained, the university requires students to take a three-stage series of student outcomes assessments: as entering students, at the midpoint in undergraduate studies, and as graduating seniors in their academic major. Testing at the first two stages occurs on scheduled assessment days in the fall and spring semesters. Testing of seniors in their major occurs on the spring assessment day or is embedded in academic courses. Students are required to participate. Those who miss the scheduled assessments are unable to register for the next semester until the assessments are completed. Staff from the Center for Assessment and Research Studies provide a web page describing Assessment Day at James Madison University (n.d.). Students are advised that thinking of test items as a challenge will encourage them to try harder, have more fun, and ultimately perform better.

Several college leaders provide flyers or brochures for entering students. To help students become more aware of assessment at LaGuardia Community College, staff distribute brochures during orientation (Provezis, 2012). Parents may also receive materials at that time. This information is particularly helpful if students are being asked to participate in entry-level testing. Flyers can be used to describe the purposes of testing, how it will affect grades and placement in courses, how much time it will take, and who will see results.

If students are required to achieve a satisfactory level of performance on an assessment activity such as a writing competence exam, they should be made aware of this as well. Expectations about assessment activities in particular majors, including requirements to complete standardized exams, also should be in the catalogue and other materials.

In addition to establishing assessment requirements, some institutions' web pages familiarize students with the purposes of assessment. Leaders at Long Beach City College (n.d.) provide a Student Guide to Learning Outcomes among their web pages. The page includes FAQs about learning outcomes and explains their importance in helping students choose classes and programs. Faculty are told that they can refer students to the page or use it as a teaching tool.

Project Instructions   Students need to have specific directions for all the assessment activities in which they participate. Instructions are particularly important for comprehensive projects such as portfolios, where students are asked to accumulate materials for an extended time. As they begin their portfolios, students must have enough information to understand the overall dimensions of the project. They should know what is currently expected, as well as what they will be asked to provide in subsequent classes. They also need to be aware of the specific criteria that will be used to judge their portfolios. On some campuses, faculty provide written guidelines; on others, they ask students to attend orientation sessions. It is important to indicate how information will be used and to assure students that their results will be treated confidentially. Leaders at Truman State University (2014) provide a web page for students describing a required portfolio project. In addition to instructions and suggestions, the page gives a rationale for portfolios, explaining that faculty use portfolio assessment to gain a deeper understanding of student learning than is provided by standardized exams. Because the Portfolio Project is an evolving system with prompts rotating in and out each year, students are asked to store their work online for later use in their senior portfolios.

Examples   Another helpful approach for providing assessment information is to let students examine a range of previously completed work. Reviewing examples of average as well as excellent work can be very useful. Versions of tests that are no longer in use also can be made available. Leaders at Casper

College (n.d.a) recommend that students receive models or samples of successful performance.

Student Rewards

Just as some faculty rewards from assessment are intrinsic and others extrinsic, the same is true for student rewards. Students should benefit from assessment in a variety of ways.

Improved Programs   Assessment frequently leads to changes in academic programs. Although some improvements may be introduced after current students have left campus, many faculty have been able to introduce changes rather quickly so that current students benefit as well. Improvements such as clearer syllabi, more fully articulated goals and objectives for learning, and more explicit evaluation standards are often introduced soon after assessment programs are initiated. In addition, improvements to instruction based on classroom assessment activities may occur immediately. Nevertheless, some change is slower in coming. Fortunately, current students often welcome the opportunity to provide feedback about their experiences even if it is future students, not themselves, who may benefit.

Feedback   Direct feedback to students about their own performances is a benefit of many assessment projects. Although some tests provide only group results, many assessment instruments provide results at the individual level. In these cases, it is recommended that students be given their scores. James Madison University (n.d.) faculty provide a student feedback web page to help students understand their test scores. Students can compare their scientific reasoning and quantitative reasoning scores to faculty standards or to other students' scores. Students also may receive feedback from survey projects. Both the Engage survey from ACT and MAP-Works from Educational Benchmarking Inc. provide individualized student reports.

One of the primary advantages of performance assessment is the opportunity for faculty to give direct and immediate feedback to students. In some cases, feedback will be provided by professionals in the field as well as by department faculty. Peer review also is included in many assessment projects. Yavapai College (2008) faculty encourage peer and instructor dialogue using podcasts, discussion boards, and online chats. Baepler (2011) describes the use of screencasts to provide audio and video feedback on student essays. Faculty can record and save comments before sending the URL of the screencast to their students. Developers of the Catalyst for Learning (2014) website share research on e-portfolios indicating that learning is deeper when students receive feedback from meaningful audiences in addition to their instructors. Many projects are being structured to provide these opportunities (Bass, 2014; Eynon, Gambino, and Torok, 2014a).

Faculty in the Department of Sociology and Anthropology at Winthrop University assess how well their majors' self-perceptions match the impressions they give to others (Marx, Crew Solomon, and Tripp, 2011). In the required senior seminar, a group of students directs their classmates in a discussion of reading material. The classroom is equipped with remote control recording equipment, and taping is of audience members rather than group leaders. The students consent to be taped but do not know when the taping will occur. Class members are asked to evaluate the presentations. The form includes a self-rating of the student's own reaction to the presentation along a five-point continuum ranging from Very Engaged to Bored. Then edited videos are placed on a protected website and class members watch and rate each student's involvement, including their own. Students are surprised to see the impressions they make on others.

Opportunities for Reflection and Self-Assessment   Although students often need time to develop self-assessment skills, among the greatest benefits from many assessment projects is the opportunity they provide students to reflect on their own learning and development. In most portfolio projects, students are asked to justify their choice of artifacts and to reflect on their growth through written statements or essays in their portfolios. Integrative e-portfolio strategies allowing students to connect learning in one course to learning in other courses, to cocurricular activities, and to life experiences appear particularly effective in helping students to reflect and learn (Eynon, Gambino, and Torok, 2014b). Other direct assessment methods can be used for self-reflection, including journal entries and essays.

Indirect assessment methods provide additional opportunities for self-assessment. Many surveys include blocks of questions asking students to reflect on their learning and development. Students often comment on surveys that they appreciate the chance to think about what they have experienced and to provide their reactions. Focus groups too provide an opportunity for students to consider and react to various aspects of their education.

The Office of Academic Assessment web pages at Brandeis University (n.d.a) provide a link to a series of student reflective guides—one for each student class level. The first-year reflective guide urges students to become familiar with the university's learning goals and to reflect on them as they choose a class schedule.

Tangible Rewards Some incentives for students to participate in assessment projects may be appropriate. Rewards such as passes to movies, coupons for free food, or small payments of money are sometimes used to increase participation in projects. Coupons can be included in mailings inviting eligible students to participate, or respondents can be sent coupons after they have returned their assessment instruments. Students who participate in focus groups may be treated to pizza and soft drinks. To evaluate a campus outreach facility, student affairs staff at Queen's University in Kingston, Ontario, conducted focus groups with students. A buffet dinner and twenty-dollar gift cards were provided to participants (Massey and Gouthro, 2011). At California State University, San Bernardino (2014), seniors who take the Collegiate Learning Assessment (CLA) in the spring have their commencement fee paid (a fifty-dollar value) and also are entered into a raffle for extra commencement tickets. While rewards may encourage students to participate in outcomes assessment, only intrinsic motivation will elicit their best work.

Maximizing Student Acceptance of Assessment

The most important element in eliciting student acceptance of assessment is the commitment to it that faculty demonstrate. The messages faculty give about assessment are powerful motivators. If faculty care about assessment, students are much more likely to care too. Alternatively, if students perceive from the way faculty introduce an assessment project that they are not interested, students will lack interest as well. Even the most enthusiastic faculty need to share information with students about the purposes of assessment and the way the information will be used. Tying assessment to classroom activities is helpful. If assessment is seen as a natural part of the teaching and learning process, students are motivated to do well. Practical concerns also are important. In cases where students are required to attend testing sessions, provisions should be made for their convenience. Offering alternate test days may be necessary.

As with faculty, assessment practitioners should recognize that students need time to develop assessment skills. Students who participated in course-related focus groups at the Fiek School of Pharmacy at the University of the Incarnate Word initially focused on criticisms and what they did not like. With guidance from the facilitator, their feedback became more recommendation specific. Now they identify issues and make suggestions for the benefit of the group (Martin and Martinez, 2010).

Acting with Integrity

Assessment programs should incorporate strategies designed to protect participants from unintended consequences. For example, a principle for assessment at Buffalo State University (n.d.) is that the results of assessment activities will be used only at the campus level to improve institutional effectiveness. Assessment results will never be used to punish or embarrass students, faculty, courses, programs, or departments either individually or collectively. Confidentiality of assessment data will be maintained.

Faculty and staff should clarify the effect of assessment on grades. Although some assessment activities, such as large-scale testing, may not affect grades, assessment information that comes from the natural process of classroom activities ordinarily will be graded. It is important that the purposes and consequences of assessment be explained to students, as well as the specifics of when and where assessment will occur. Any commitments for follow-up information or prizes to be awarded for performance or participation must be kept.

Purdue University (2012) faculty and staff have developed a policy on the use of student survey data collected for internal management, planning, and policy research issues. Surveys are coordinated under the auspices of the Purdue Assessment Coordinators Team, which approves appropriate use of survey data. Student survey data must be kept confidential. Shared data must not include student identifiers such as social security number or name, and reports (paper, electronic, or verbal) using the data must not identify individual students. Summary data with small sample sizes (generally four or fewer) must not be reported if the information could potentially reveal findings about an individual student. Student survey data for scholarly research (defined as potentially publishable research) also must be approved by Purdue's institutional review board (IRB).

Institutional review board policies vary by campus, but in general, group data collected for internal evaluation are exempt from IRB approval, while data collection for use in publications requires IRB review. At Casper College (n.d.b), activities used to collect routine data about class or program effectiveness do not need to be reviewed by the IRB. These activities include student course evaluations, student surveys assessing perceptions of an academic program or sequence, and student exit interviews that address only curriculum and program concerns. However, assessment activities that address students' personal lives (e.g., dating behaviors, drug use, social life) go beyond routine data collection and may involve some element of risk to subjects or investigators, or both. Therefore, these types of assessments require IRB review and probably written consent from students.

Staff from the Office of Assessment and Evaluation at Virginia Polytechnic and State University (2014b) remind faculty that students own the copyright to their own work, so they should be informed if any part of it will be disseminated beyond the department. They recommend that reporting of results should be done in the aggregate and focus on process, including purpose and methods.

As these examples illustrate, faculty and staff carefully develop guidelines and procedures to protect their students and to act with integrity.

CHAPTER 4

SETTING EXPECTATIONS AND PREPARING TO SELECT MEASURES

Planning an effective assessment initiative begins with setting expectations for success. What are the goals and objectives—the outcomes—for student learning that guide our curriculum design and our teaching, and therefore suggest our assessment methods? What are the goals and objectives for community engagement activities and other programs and services that support student development in college, and therefore become guides for segments of our assessment of institutional effectiveness? We outline the process of developing goals, objectives, and outcomes in the first part of this chapter. Then we demonstrate the connections between stated outcomes and assessment methods and note some general principles that should be taken into account when selecting assessment measures.

Intentions for Learning: Goals, Objectives, Outcomes

As Don Noel Smith (2009) points out, "Assessment necessarily begins before, not after, the learning experience" (p. 7). Statements about the intended results of educational activities are the starting point for assessment, providing faculty and staff with direction for their other choices. In addition, these statements enhance communication about expectations for graduates, not only among faculty and staff themselves but also with their current and future students. Writing clear statements about what students should know, value, and be able to do is easier when agreement exists about language.

Defining Terms

Historically educators have drawn a distinction between learning goals and learning objectives. Both can be used to describe the intended results of educational activities. The difference between the two is their level of precision. *Goals* are used to express intended results in general terms and consist of broad learning concepts such as clear communication, problem solving, and ethical awareness. Often included in the institution's mission statement, general education goals are typically developed through consensus of a cross-section of the campus community. In contrast, *learning objectives* for specific academic or cocurricular programs are developed by faculty and staff who provide those programs. Objectives describe expected learning and behavior in precise terms, providing guidance for what needs to be assessed. For example, graduates in speech communication should be able to interpret nonverbal behavior and support arguments with credible evidence.

As assessment websites and glossaries reveal, most assessment practitioners have embraced the term *student learning outcomes* (SLOs). Faculty and staff at the University of Hawaii at Manoa (2013) use the terms *outcomes* and *objectives* interchangeably. Both are clear, concise statements describing how students can demonstrate their mastery of program goals. Although practitioners on some campuses still use the term *goals* to refer to institution-level expectations for learning, on other campuses faculty and staff refer to *institutional outcomes*. For example, Zayed University faculty in the United Arab Emirates are committed to six institution-wide learning outcomes known as the Zayed University Learning Outcomes (ZULOs; Schoepp, 2012).

As long as campuswide consensus exists, the exact language that faculty use is not important. What is important is that faculty reach agreement about expectations for their graduates and express these intended results with enough precision to guide accurately the selection of suitable assessment instruments.

Learning Taxonomies

Educators distinguish between cognitive, affective, and psychomotor learning outcomes—what students know, value, and can do. Faculty who are asked to write cognitive outcomes often refer to Bloom's taxonomy (Bloom, 1956). The original taxonomy focuses on cognitive learning objectives arranged in six levels of increasing complexity: knowledge, comprehension, application, analysis, synthesis, and evaluation. Each level is associated with related behaviors; those for evaluation include concluding and recommending. Because levels above comprehension require students to use information in various ways, they are sometimes called higher-order thinking skills. Several assessment websites contain this taxonomy, along with lists of verbs (behaviors) suggested by each of its six levels.

A revision of Bloom's taxonomy (Anderson and Krathwohl, 2001) describes six levels of thinking using verbs rather than nouns and adds a top level—creating—that encompasses the original level of synthesis. The first two levels are remembering (recalling, recognizing) and understanding (explaining, interpreting). Higher levels are applying (executing, implementing), analyzing (differentiating, organizing), and evaluating (checking, judging). The top level, creating, includes designing and producing.

In addition to the six levels of thinking, the revised taxonomy identifies four levels of knowledge:

- Factual knowledge—essential terms and details
- Conceptual knowledge—classifications, models, and theories
- Procedural knowledge—techniques and methods that help students do something
- Metacognitive knowledge—awareness of one's own thinking in relation to various subjects

Having two dimensions in the new taxonomy allows educators to be more specific about the level of cognitive complexity appropriate for their students (Munzenmaier and Rubin, 2013). In writing outcomes statements, faculty can choose a verb associated with a cognitive process such as *evaluate* and then select a type of knowledge such as *procedural*. For example, expecting students to be able to judge the effectiveness of a pottery technique is an outcome that involves *evaluating procedural knowledge*. An interactive graph prepared by Rex Heer (2012) at the Center for Excellence in Teaching and Learning at Iowa State University can help faculty compare the four classifications of knowledge to the various levels of cognitive processes as they create statements about expected learning.

Whereas *cognitive objectives* refer to thinking skills, *affective objectives* refer to attitudes and values. Attitudes capture feelings toward people, ideas, situations, and institutions. Values are enduring beliefs about what is good and what is not in terms of life goals and ways of living. No affective taxonomy is in wide use, but the ideas captured by Krathwohl, Bloom, and Masia (1956) are helpful. The authors distinguish among five levels of commitment to an idea or object, beginning with an initial level of awareness, followed by responding to and then valuing the idea or object. The final stages of the taxonomy include integrating the new value with other values and acting consistently with respect to the new value. Pennsylvania State University's (n.d.a) Learning Design Community Hub contains a summary of this taxonomy. Examples of intended outcomes for affective dimensions include being sensitive to the values of others, practicing ethical behavior, and developing an appreciation for lifelong learning. Faculty at Weber State University (2014a) have developed a set of affective outcomes for students in the College of Health Professions. Students are expected to demonstrate honesty by maintaining strict patient confidentiality and to exhibit appropriate professional behavior by interacting with coworkers in a positive manner. Affective outcomes can be examined by observing behaviors that occur, for example, in group work or simulations, monitoring participation rates in activities related to the attitude, and asking students to report on their own behavior or attitudes.

A third major category of intended learning outcomes is the area of *psychomotor skills.* Penn State's Hub (n.d.a) contains a psychomotor taxonomy, as do other sites. Generally these taxonomies recognize different levels of skill development, ranging from performing a physical activity based on observation or instruction to performing the activity independently, and eventually to performing with high levels of proficiency. A skilled individual is one who has developed expertise based on training and practice. Areas such as the performing arts, health professions, and physical education emphasize psychomotor skills that should be assessed using performance measures that include direct observation.

Thinking skills, affective skills, and psychomotor skills are often interrelated. Communication skills, for example, include both cognitive and psychomotor elements. The curriculum at Alverno College (2011) is based on integrated developmental abilities that are assessed through individual performances. Among others, these abilities include communication, social interaction, effective citizenship, and aesthetic response—abilities that combine cognitive, affective, and psychomotor dimensions.

Educators also may be concerned with the success of their students in areas such as retention, persistence, time to degree, satisfaction, and workplace readiness. While development of workplace skills may be captured in the outcomes described above, statements reflecting expectations about program completion, satisfaction, and success also must be developed.

Developing Statements of Expectations

Developing statements of expected learning outcomes is a challenging and time-consuming aspect of assessment and necessarily requires consensus. The six learning outcomes at Zayed University were prepared during a two-year period and now provide the basis for the assessment program (Schoepp, 2012). At Portland State University (2014b), initial development of campuswide learning outcomes occurred between 2007 and 2009 with follow-up during 2010 and 2011. The Institutional Assessment Council met with senate committees and held work sessions, committee meetings, and focus groups with students. The process to create specific learning criteria for each of several broad outcomes involved additional discussion with stakeholders. For example, members of the Internationalization Committee helped establish criteria for that outcome.

Developing statements of expected student learning outcomes (SLOs) at the program level also is challenging. Many campuses provide excellent advice through committees, offices, and websites. Staff from the Office of Institutional Assessment at George Mason University (2014) advise faculty to prepare concise written statements of knowledge, skills, and values students will achieve on completing a course or degree program. Statements about SLOs require action verbs that are not open to interpretation. Words like *identify*, *solve*, and *construct* are better than vague words such as *understand* and *appreciate*. In addition to an action verb, the statement needs an object, as in, "Students will create an *abstract painting*." The statement may include additional details as well, such as "in the Cubist style." Although too much precision should be avoided, faculty need to make sure their goals can be assessed. It does not make sense to claim that a program develops the whole person if there is no way to demonstrate this. In asking departments to revisit their outcomes to ensure they are high quality, assessment leaders at St. Ambrose University (2014) recommend that the outcomes be stated clearly rather than in the language of experts, focused on students rather than on what the course instructor intends to do, and appropriate for the level of the program rather than too simple or overly complex. Indicating that "students will be able to explain categories of the labor force" is an appropriate learning outcome for an introductory economics class. Indicating that "the instructor will develop a regression model to explain unemployment" is not.

Practitioners at the University of Connecticut (n.d.) advise that an outcome statement should be single, not bundled, and should be worded so that more than one method can be used for assessment. Viewed overall, the outcomes should reflect all key elements of a program or service. Outcomes that are aggregated across courses or majors should be written at a similar level of precision. At Cornell University (n.d.b) the Center for Teaching Excellence provides an eight-item outcome review checklist encouraging faculty and staff to consider whether the statements they have written include measurable, student-centered outcomes that contain effective action verbs and appropriate conditions for performance.

Statement Content

When creating or revising outcome statements, how do faculty decide what to include? The University of Connecticut's (n.d.) document "How to Write Program Objectives/Outcomes" provides helpful advice. Faculty can examine existing materials describing the program, including catalogue copy, online statements, and current reports for program review or other purposes. Classroom-specific materials such as syllabi, assignments, and instructional materials can be examined to help faculty clarify how program content fits together.

Practitioners at Anoka Ramsey Community College (2014) advise their faculty not to overlook information that is external to the program, such as statements from employers about their expectations for graduates. The standards and guidelines for learning developed by professional associations or accrediting bodies often are important sources. Faculty in the Department of Industrial Design at Metropolitan State College of Denver considered the requirements of the National Association of Schools of Art and Design as they developed their outcome statements (Phillips and Thompson, 2011). In the Grand Valley State University School of Social Work, the new standards introduced by the Council on Social Work Education were helpful to faculty (Schuurman, Berlin, Langlois, and Guevara, 2012). Statements of the expected outcomes of similar programs on other campuses also can be valuable and may be available online. When the Department of Political Science faculty at Fort Hays University

EXHIBIT 4.1 CONTENT-BY-PROCESS MATRIX

	Beginning	Intermediate	Advanced
Writing			
Math			
History			

reenergized their assessment efforts, they chose three programs at other universities for comparison purposes (Mills, Bennett, Crawford, and Gould, 2009). Drawing on the advice of current and former students and involving them in developing statements also is recommended. Portland State University (2014b) faculty included a team of graduate students to provide assistance when they were developing their university-wide outcomes.

At St. Ambrose (2014) faculty review the Lumina Foundation's Degree Qualifications Profile (DQP) to help determine if their own outcomes statements are appropriate to the level of the program. The profile provides a set of reference points describing what students should know and be able to do in order to earn associate, bachelor's, and master's degrees regardless of their field of specialization.

Based on the materials they examine, faculty can consider characteristics of an "ideal" graduate, expectations of alumni five years after graduation, and characteristics necessary for graduates to succeed in the workplace or in advanced programs of study. Creating a content-by-process matrix (see exhibit 4.1) with subject matter as row headings and thinking levels as column headings can be useful. Discussing these materials should lead faulty to develop or revise their outcomes in ways that will guide improvement. At Bluefield State College, the process each program faculty worked through and the number and level of outcomes varied greatly, but the results were ultimately successful (Anderson, 2013). Faculty and staff at Rice University (n.d.) use a two-step process to strengthen their programs. Stage 1 involves developing course and program outcomes as well as a curriculum map. Stage 2 involves taking a closer look at philosophy and methodology to ensure that program mission and values are reflected in the curriculum.

Curriculum Maps

For students to learn what is expected of them, the relevant subject matter must be addressed and reinforced in the curriculum. As Smith (2009) points

EXHIBIT 4.2 CURRICULUM MAP

Course	Expected Outcome 1	Expected Outcome 2	Expected Outcome 3
Course 101			
Course 205			
Course 310			
Course 420			

out, programs need to be delivered in coherently related and appropriately sequenced learning experiences. An increasing number of campuses, including Long Island University (2013), require faculty to submit curriculum maps as part of the program's assessment plan. A *curriculum map* is a grid that shows all of the program's courses as row headings and expected outcomes as column headings (see exhibit 4.2). Filling in the grid or matrix allows faculty to see the outcomes covered in each course. If a particular outcome is getting too much coverage or too little, the curriculum map will reveal the imbalance. Faculty at George Mason University (2014) are encouraged to discuss these results, particularly for courses that do not cover any of the objectives shown in the matrix. In their curriculum maps, faculty at California Polytechnic State University San Luis Obispo (2014a) are asked to show for each course and outcome whether the material is introduced, practiced, or reinforced. Rather than a simple check mark, the cells of the matrix are marked with an I, P, or R to capture the expected level of coverage. In addition to a curriculum map, faculty at Chaffey College (2013) complete a worksheet showing the correspondence between program learning goals and the college's core competences.

Using Matrices and Other Tools

Many faculty find *matrices*, such as curriculum grids, very helpful in facilitating their assessment work. For their assessment planning, the political science faculty at Fort Hays University used affinity diagrams that map connections between learning outcomes, curriculum, and assessment methods (Mills et al., 2009) and Southeastern Oklahoma State University's (2010) assessment plan features a similar matrix that includes methods and benchmarks. Exhibit 4.3 provides a useful guide for linking goals and objectives, teaching strategies, and assessment methods. It associates broad outcomes with more specific outcomes and asks faculty to think through all of the in-class and out-of-class experiences that address these expected outcomes.

EXHIBIT 4.3 PLANNING FOR LEARNING AND ASSESSMENT

1. What general learning outcome are you seeking?	2. How would you know it (the outcome) if you saw it? (What will the student know or be able to do?)	3. How will you help students learn it (in class or out of class)?	4. How could you measure each of the desired behaviors listed in #2?	5. What are the assessment findings?	6. What improvements might be made based on assessment findings?

Furthermore, it asks faculty to think about how they will measure the outcome, and to anticipate assessment findings and their use.

Selecting Methods and Approaches

As faculty develop or revise their assessment plans, they must decide how they will gather the information they need. An extensive array of possible assessment techniques exists, and some strategies are available to help choose among them. Faculty can consult inventories to determine the methods that are being used elsewhere on campus. They also can establish selection criteria to help them identify the best methods to answer their assessment questions. Selection criteria include validity and reliability, the hallmarks of technical quality. They also include timeliness, cost-benefit comparison, and student motivation. Once faculty review possible assessment techniques, they can compare them with their selection criteria to make final choices. The steps we suggest may occur simultaneously rather than sequentially. Faculty may develop their criteria for good assessment methods as they examine various instruments. This section of the chapter summarizes assessment methods and concludes with some suggestions about developing local instruments.

Inventories of Existing Activities

A campuswide inventory of assessment methods currently being used in departments and programs can be helpful to faculty who are considering a technique that may have been tried elsewhere. In its traditional form, an assessment inventory is presented as a matrix showing the department or program names as the headings for the rows and the various assessment techniques, such as capstone projects or exit interviews, as the headings for the columns. A quick glance at the matrix provides an overview of how much activity is taking place and which activities are used most frequently.

The Eastern Connecticut State University (n.d.) website includes an inventory of assessment activities grouped in five broad categories: comprehensive exams (national and local), skill tests (labs, performances, and fieldwork), writing, surveys, and graduate/alumni data. Faculty who are interested in trying a new approach are encouraged to contact departments that are already using the method.

Practitioners at the University of Iowa (2013b), have created the Assessment Exchange, an online database that faculty and staff can use to find out what other departments are doing. The database is searchable by department or type of assessment method.

The transparency framework that staff developed at the National Institute for Learning Outcomes Assessment (n.d.) includes "current assessment activities" as one of its components. Transparent activities are clearly stated in understandable language describing how the method is used in relationship to the institution's mission. The work reported by several campuses, including St. Olaf College, Slippery Rock University, Spelman College, and University of Cincinnati, is highlighted.

Developing Criteria for Choosing Methods

A useful strategy for selecting among assessment techniques is to ask faculty to identify and create a list of the qualities they consider most important with respect to data collection methods. Here we examine several characteristics to consider.

Assessment Questions   To select assessment instruments that will provide useful results, faculty must consider their assessment questions. Patton (2008) recommends that stakeholders begin by thinking about what they would like to know that would make a difference in what they do. Wiggins and McTighe (2005) advocate a "backward design" when thinking about educational programs: starting from a set of desired results, faculty ask what evidence would demonstrate these results and then plan instruction and activities designed to lead to the outcome. This approach asks faculty to think about assessment before they think about teaching and is used at Capella University (Jankowski, 2011b).

In program assessment, statements of expectations about student learning provide the natural starting point for selecting methods. But even in this case, faculty can frame specific questions that are of most concern. For example, they might want to know if communication skills are enhanced by self-assessment. When creating assessment plans, staff from the Office of Institutional Effectiveness at Rice University (n.d.) advise faculty to ask questions that are of genuine importance to them and relevant to their needs.

Hatfield (n.d.) recommends that the link between learning outcomes and assessment methods be logical and appropriate. Many methods have the potential to answer several assessment questions but are stronger for some purposes than others. Objective tests are quite useful in measuring knowledge and recall but less useful in determining skills, particularly as compared to performance measures. Questionnaires and focus groups are very helpful for determining student satisfaction and success but can only infer cognitive gains. The relative advantages of various methods need to be examined in light of specific assessment questions and the way the information will be used.

Reliability   Reliable measures are those that can be counted on to produce consistent responses over time. Technically it is the scores or data derived from using an instrument that are considered reliable rather than the instrument itself. An instrument yields reliable data to the extent that the variance in scores is attributable to actual differences in what is being measured, such as knowledge, performance, or attitudes. Data are unreliable to the extent that score variance is due to measurement error. Sources of measurement error include the individuals responding to the instrument, the administration and scoring of the instrument, and the instrument itself. The instrument must be well constructed: items must be worded clearly, words must be unambiguous, and possible responses to test or survey items must be developed appropriately. The length of the instrument must be consistent with the time available to administer it. If raters are used, they must agree on the meaning of items in a well-designed scale.

Information about the *internal consistency* of items is important. That is, all of the items on a scale designed to measure test anxiety, for example, should actually measure that. Techniques to determine internal consistency—how well items are related to each other—are available for both tests and surveys. Using split-half reliability or inter-item reliability, instruments can be examined to see if responses to questions designed to measure the same construct, such as critical thinking, actually do appear to measure that construct. With respect to instrument administration, the instructions given and the time allowed for completion must be consistent across administrations.

The use of well-developed standards to train those who will be rating or scoring student responses is an additional concern. Various measures of *interrater reliability* for instruments that have rating scales are commonly used to compare ratings assigned by two or more raters. Coefficients of 0.80 or higher are recommended, with 1.0 being perfect reliability and 0.0 representing total unreliability. During a presentation at the Assessment Institute in Indianapolis, Penn, Ray, and Kominsky (2010) reviewed some considerations with respect to measuring interrater reliability. As they point out, if interrater reliability is low, the specific rater who grades a student's performance may matter more than the quality of the performance. Low interrater reliability may occur because of problems with the scoring scale, the student artifacts, or the particular raters. Interrater reliability can be significantly improved by careful training of evaluators, and reliability and validity also are enhanced by the development of clear, articulate scoring rubrics.

An additional issue related to performance-based assessment deals with the trade-off between reliability and validity. As the performance task increases in complexity and authenticity, which serves to increase validity, the lack of standardization serves to decrease reliability. The challenge becomes to design or select assessment methods and instruments that achieve the most effective balance between these two concerns.

Validity   Once faculty have determined that an instrument is reliable, that is, that it will provide similar information time after time, they need to determine if it is appropriate for the use to which it will be put. Validity is thought of as accuracy, honesty, or truthfulness. It asks, "Does an instrument measure what we intend it to measure?" As with reliability, validity is not a property of the instrument itself, although the term is commonly used in this way. Validity requires evidence to support the interpretation and use of test or survey data for a particular purpose. Clarity about purposes, intended interpretations, and likely uses are the starting point when evaluating validity.

Validity has many aspects; the most common are construct, criterion, and content. *Construct-related validity* refers to the congruence between the meaning of the underlying construct and the items on the test or survey. To support a claim of congruence, faculty need to consider if results correlate with those obtained with other instruments examining the same construct and whether results differ for groups of individuals expected to show differences. Results also should change in expected ways based on factors that are expected to affect the construct. For example, scores on an instrument measuring anxiety should increase prior to taking high-stakes examinations.

Criterion-related validity includes predictive validity: How dependable is the relationship between the scores or answers on an instrument and a particular future outcome? It also includes concurrent validity: How well do scores estimate students' current standing on the characteristic of interest? *Content-related validity* refers to the overall match between the content of the instrument and the content of the curriculum or other domain of interest. Questions include: Does the instrument cover a representative sample of the curriculum? Is it thorough in its coverage?

For program assessment, validity issues also include the following: Does the instrument address desired levels of cognitive complexity? To what extent can results be generalized? Are tasks credible to those who will use the results? Are tasks valuable to students? Will results provide useful information for improving programs? The most important consideration is whether the instrument contains items related to the curriculum being assessed.

Faculty at St. Ambrose University (2014) are expected to examine the validity of both nationally available and locally developed assessment instruments. For commercial instruments, information from test or survey developers is to be referenced. To demonstrate validity of locally developed methods, faculty are advised to examine the alignment of the instrument with student learning outcomes, use common rubrics, and involve multiple faculty in evaluating work. Staff from the Institutional Research and Evaluation Office at St. Olaf College (2014) provide research design and evaluation advice, including a helpful description of reliability and validity.

Timeliness and Cost   About two-thirds of program heads responding to a survey about assessment practices indicated that more release time for faculty would be helpful in advancing assessment (Ewell, Paulson, and Kinzie, 2011). This reflects the great concern of faculty that working on assessment projects will take time away from other important tasks. Thus, the likely time demands of developing, administering, and evaluating various assessment instruments should be examined. Even if exact estimates are unavailable, rough comparisons can be made. For example, commercial instruments require time for selection but not for development. Portfolio projects require a great deal of time for both development and implementation (Andrade, 2013). Developing rubrics can be time-consuming as well (Martins, 2010).

Cost is also important and is related to time. That is, using faculty time on assessment rather than other activities has an opportunity cost. An assessment model developed by decision makers in Virginia recognizes three levels of faculty effort in carrying out assessment projects. Assigned time for faculty is lowest for consulting and advising when a commercially available instrument is used, more for developing an internal instrument, and most for evaluating true-to-life performances, portfolios, or other labor-intensive methods (Harper, 2010). Tangible costs of various methods need to be considered. Costing procedures for commercial instruments differ by company and instrument. For example, campuses that administer the ETS Major Field Tests can purchase various types of data analysis packages.

Swing and Coogan (2010) urge consideration of both benefits and costs when choosing among assessment measures. For example, a multiple-choice test to evaluate writing may be less costly than a performance-based test, but if faculty do not have confidence in its results, the multiple-choice test is in fact the weaker selection. The authors argue that "what ultimately matters most is not the amount spent on assessment but the amount gained compared to the amount spent" (p. 18).

Motivation   It is important to choose instruments that will be valuable for students and will elicit their cooperation. Case studies, simulations, role-playing, and problem-solving exercises require students to apply what they have learned and can be used effectively for assessment. These techniques also provide opportunities for people who learn in different ways to demonstrate their accomplishments. Yavapai College (2008) educators believe that a connection is necessary between the way students learn and the way they are assessed. Hutchings (2010) recommends that students be given more opportunities for self-assessment. She cites both e-portfolios and rubrics that students can use to evaluate their own work as serving this purpose. Working with information from the multi-institutional national Wabash Study, Blaich and Wise (2011) find four dimensions of good practice as particularly beneficial for students: good teaching and high-quality interactions with faculty; academic challenge and high expectations; diversity experiences; and higher-order, integrative, and reflective learning.

These dimensions can be captured by effective assessment practices, perhaps through interviews with faculty or challenging senior projects.

Other Considerations   Additional questions can be raised about potential assessment instruments. Will results be easy to interpret? Will fluctuations in results reflect changes in academic programs rather than poorly constructed instruments? Will instruments provide information valuable for program assessment as well as for documenting the achievement of individual students? Will the information be manageable? The consequences of using various methods also need to be anticipated. Some critics of standardized tests believe that they narrow the curriculum and reinforce the use of instructional techniques inconsistent with active learning. RiCharde (2009) fears that rubrics also may have unintended consequences, locking faculty into an overly simplified view of the concept they are measuring.

Fairness to individuals is an additional consideration. An assessment instrument should not be biased in favor of particular groups. Results should not reflect characteristics such as culture, gender, or socioeconomic background. Leaders at North Carolina State University (2006) call for assessment practices that are sensitive to diversity and consider a broad spectrum of perspectives.

An Overview of Methods

After (or while) faculty develop criteria for selecting methods, they need to review the methods that are available, consider how they might adapt these methods to their own use, and contemplate methods that may be completely new. One important distinction is between techniques that directly determine whether students have mastered the content of their academic programs and those that ask students to reflect on their learning. Regional accreditors, although careful not to require specific methods, call for multiple measures using both direct and indirect approaches (Provezis, 2010).

Among *direct* assessment methods, most familiar are exams of all kinds, including multiple-choice and true-false tests where students select a response, as well as essays and problems where students produce an answer. Oral exams provide an alternative to pencil-and-paper tests and allow for extensive probing of student learning.

Direct measures include performance assessments that require students to demonstrate their competence in one or more skills. Many kinds of performance measures are in use, including projects, oral presentations, demonstrations, case studies, design competitions, and simulations. Simulations are used when it is not feasible to demonstrate a skill in a real-world setting. Medical schools, including Johns Hopkins University School of Medicine (n.d.), use "standardized patients" to assess their students' capabilities. These "patients" are actors who have been trained to describe particular illnesses to medical students, who are then evaluated on their diagnostic skills.

Portfolios constitute an important kind of performance assessment in which student work is collected over time. Their appeal is their ability to provide longitudinal information and opportunities for student reflection. Portfolios are powerful tools for guiding as well as assessing student learning, encouraging students to take responsibility for their own learning, and giving students a voice in assessment (Yancey, 2009). Additional direct measures are juried activities with outside panels that rate student work, evaluations of performance in internships or other fieldwork, and scores on national licensure or professional exams. Many times direct measures of learning are embedded in a capstone course or referred to as a capstone experience. However, a capstone course must be more than just the course most students take in the last semester to be used effectively for assessment (Hatfield, n.d.).

Indirect methods ask students to reflect on what they have learned and experienced rather than to demonstrate their knowledge and skills, providing proxy information about student learning. Methods such as questionnaires, interviews, and focus groups fall in this category. Each of these methods allows faculty to listen to their students' voices concerning what they have learned and experienced in academic programs.

Part of the appeal of indirect methods is the wide variety of information that can be collected. Students can be asked about their attitudes, opinions, experiences, expectations, perceptions, and needs and provide reactions and reflections. Surveys are frequently used to address issues of student satisfaction and success. Self-ratings of learning obtained from surveys can be compared to direct measures of learning to see if results are consistent. Faculty at Florida A&M University found this kind of comparison helpful in their assessment of student learning (Ohia and Diallo, 2012).

Besides allowing for a wide range of subject matter, surveys and focus groups have the advantage of reaching many different target groups. Thus, as part of their assessment plan, department faculty could design and administer surveys to such groups as entering students, current students, graduating seniors, alumni, faculty, or employers, with each group responding to some of the same questions. These methods are the most common approaches for collecting information from alumni.

During the past several years, practitioners have shown increasing interest in qualitative approaches to assessment that provide descriptions of learning rather than assign numbers to tests or performances. Qualitative methods can yield direct as well as indirect evidence of learning. For example, faculty can examine materials in students' portfolios for evidence of critical or creative thinking and then provide a narrative summary of how students have grown in college. This contrasts with the use of rubrics to evaluate products and performances. As Flick (2009) points out, using rubrics is a way of turning qualitative data into quantitative data. Qualitative methods are helpful in evaluating student services as well as learning (see Chapter 6.)

Down and In: Assessment Practices at the Program Level (Ewell et al., 2011), a NILOA report, provides an overview of activities currently in place nationwide within broad disciplinary groupings. Capstone courses are endorsed most frequently, followed by rubrics, performance assessment, and culminating projects. At the program level, local surveys and tests are used more than standardized versions. And a great deal of variation exists across disciplines.

Use of Existing Information

Practitioners involved with the Wabash Study, a longitudinal research and assessment project designed to provide participating institutions with extensive evidence about student learning, quickly came to realize that campuses have lots of actionable information but little experience with how to use it. They recommend that institutions conduct an institutional data audit listing all the data they produce from surveys, tests, and other projects (Blaich and Wise, 2011).

In addition to consulting an inventory of departmental activities, program faculty can benefit from being aware of the institutional assessment plan and the campuswide activities that are in place. At several institutions, survey extracts are made available to departments to enable faculty to see how their own graduates compare to campuswide averages. Institutional research offices often have data that can help a unit interpret the results of their assessment projects. Data about the characteristics of students in the program and how these characteristics have changed over time can be important when looking at assessment results. Information about course-taking patterns can be valuable as well. When seniors who were interviewed at the University of North Dakota attributed little value to distribution-based general education courses, faculty followed up with transcript analysis to examine students' course-taking patterns (Hawthorne and Kelsch, 2012).

Locally Developed versus Commercial Measures

An important choice that must be made when selecting assessment methods is whether to purchase and use nationally available standardized instruments or to use locally developed instruments. Standardized measures are those for which questions, scoring procedures, and interpretation of results are consistent across administrations, allowing group comparisons to be made. Some commercial examinations cover a broad range of general education outcomes; others address specific learning skills such as writing or critical thinking. Some instruments examine learning in specific disciplines and are appropriate for graduating seniors. The Mental Measurements Yearbook series, published by the Buros Center for Testing at the University of Nebraska, contains reviews of hundreds of commercially available instruments. The most recent volume was published in 2014. In addition to commercially available tests, a number of survey instruments can be purchased. These address assessment issues such as involvement, preparation, and success and may be targeted to various audiences, from freshmen to alumni.

One important advantage of nationally available instruments is that reliability and validity will have been addressed by the instrument developers, and their efforts should be described in supporting documents. Gary Pike discusses the technical quality of specific instruments as well as general topics about testing and survey usage in his regular *Assessment Update* column, "Assessment Measures."

Another advantage of commercially available instruments is that they are *norm referenced*. That is, summary results will be available, allowing faculty to examine how their own students are performing or responding on the instrument compared to a norm group of similar students elsewhere. Results for the ETS Major Field Tests are available online for all test takers from the current year; cumulative results for all seniors who have taken the current version of a test are also available. Developers of the National Survey of Student Engagement (NSSE) prepare an annual written report that describes lessons learned from the previous year's administration, with results shown by institutional type and class level. Also of interest, the NSSE website contains the Public Report Builder, which researchers can use to focus on questions of interest. In contrast, locally developed instruments can provide results only for local test or survey takers over time or for subgroups of local students.

Generally, comparative results are obtained from institutions that have previously purchased and used the commercial instrument. Although they may provide results for a large body of users, the information generally does not come from a representative national sample of possible test or survey takers. For this reason, it is important to be aware of the types of institutions that have used the instrument and to determine whether results for these institutions are meaningful locally.

Although it does take time to become familiar with commercial instruments, including their content and properties, these instruments have the advantage of being readily available. In contrast, locally developed instruments can take a great deal of time to construct and may provide results that are difficult to interpret. Quite often local tests are *criterion-referenced examinations.* In these tests, faculty determine absolute levels of mastery or proficiency that denote competence in the subject matter, providing a yardstick for helping them judge whether students are reaching the level of competence established as appropriate. Although such absolute standards are very helpful, they leave faculty unable to answer questions about how local students compare to students elsewhere.

The significant advantages of locally developed instruments are the opportunities they provide for involving faculty in the assessment process and the likely result that the instruments they develop will closely match the local curriculum as well as local issues and concerns. If the purpose of using the instrument is to assess the extent to which students are mastering the content of the institution's curricula, well-designed locally developed methods should yield the most valid inferences about student learning. Unlike commercial instruments, locally developed tests and surveys can be modified to reflect changes in the curriculum and can be analyzed according to local needs.

Opinions on the value of standardized tests continue to be divided. Ewell (2012) points to three reasons that many in higher education do not like standardized exams: first, faculty do not control the content; second, faculty do not like giving money to testing organizations; and third, faculty equate standardized tests with accountability. Furthermore, because they are developed externally, the subject matter of these exams may not match the curriculum and foster improvement in learning. Banta and Pike (2012) point out that test administration for commercial examinations may not be as standardized as it appears given that motivation among students differs greatly. Some students take the test for extra credit; others take it because it satisfies a course or graduation requirement; some have no motivation to do well other than the chance to win a prize if they attain a high score.

Benjamin (2012) argues that external comparisons, however flawed, are necessary to gauge how well an institution is doing and to learn from others who are doing well. He thinks the right direction is to continue to improve the tests that are available rather than to abandon external comparisons and points to promising developments in test construction, including the use of authentic performance tasks. Although Benjamin is against it, others feel that allowing test and survey organizations to make individual institutions' results public would encourage curricular improvement.

In addition to nationally available or locally developed instruments, faculty can contact their peers at other institutions to see what they are doing. Faculty elsewhere often are willing to share their assessment instruments and may welcome the opportunity to compare results across campuses. Many interesting collaborations exist. For example, Gonzaga faculty worked with colleagues at Seattle University on a Teagle Foundation Assessment Grant to evaluate social justice, a value common to both institutions (Bubb, Herzog, Terry, and Geithner, 2010).

In the final analysis, many campuses adopt assessment plans that include a combination of nationally and locally developed instruments. For example, George Mason University (2014) faculty and staff use both locally developed and commercial surveys. And campuses that use commercially available examinations often use course-based assessment as well to evaluate general education programs.

Comparing Potential Methods to Criteria

Once faculty have had the opportunity to discuss the criteria they want to apply and decide on the relative importance of these characteristics, they can consider how well various assessment techniques match the criteria. One possibility is to complete a matrix comparing possible methods to selection criteria. In this matrix (see exhibit 4.4 for an example), the potential methods are used to create the column headings, and the row headings contain the selection criteria. Exhibit 4.4 includes the following characteristics (row headings) for consideration: curriculum match, technical quality, preparation time, value to students, and program information. Clearly the row headings for this type of matrix should be based on the criteria that are important to the unit doing the assessment. It does not always matter if the matrix is completely filled out; what matters is that it provides a basis for focused discussion. Another type of useful matrix is shown in exhibit 4.5. The column headings are, again, the possible techniques being considered, and the row headings are the learning objectives for the program. This type of matrix is particularly useful in determining whether the methods that are selected match the curriculum goals of the program.

EXHIBIT 4.4 SELECTION CRITERIA MATRIX

	Measures				
Criteria	Objective Tests	Performances	Portfolios	Classroom Assignments	Surveys
Match to curriculum					
Technical quality					
Preparation time					
Value to students					
Program information					

EXHIBIT 4.5. OBJECTIVE-BY-MEASURES MATRIX

	Measures		
Objectives	Term Paper	Questionnaire	Speech
Write at a scholarly level			
Adapt verbal messages to a specific audience			
Value lifelong learning			

Designing Instruments

In this section we share a few suggestions about designing assessment instruments locally, including recognizing the uniqueness of the task, drawing on campus experts, and taking steps to enhance the reliability and validity of instruments.

Recognizing the Uniqueness of Designing Instruments for Assessment

Assessment methods and techniques such as tests and writing assignments are approaches faculty routinely develop and use. So why does outcomes assessment seem so different? The principal difference is the group effort that is necessary to undertake assessment activities. Faculty who have traditionally worked independently to design and administer assessment instruments for their own classes now find that these decisions need to be made in concert with others. A second difference is the way results are gathered and summarized. Assessment focuses on group rather than individual performance. For program assessment, faculty must accumulate results across students and across courses and ask what the results imply about the program as a whole. Blaich and Wise (2011) point out that in contrast to the often solitary research endeavors that faculty typically pursue, assessment involves an "entirely public process" with individuals of different levels of experience and intellectual backgrounds working together toward a common end. They believe the unfamiliar group approach needed for assessment explains why, in some cases, assessment data are collected and then not used. They urge faculty to work together to "try to change something and see what happens" (p. 13).

Enlisting Help from Campus Experts

Several studies indicate that faculty would like help with instrument design (Mince, Mason, and Bogage, 2011; Ebersole, 2009). Measurement specialists in administrative units or other departments or divisions can provide valuable advice in designing and using tests and assignments for assessment purposes and can also help with questionnaire construction. Survey questions and response options need to be designed with care in order to obtain valid and reliable results. Because survey design is not a routine part of the job for most faculty, seeking help from campus experts in social sciences, institutional research, or elsewhere is a good strategy. On many campuses, faculty and staff find SurveyMonkey, Qualtrics, and other online programs helpful when creating short surveys. At North Carolina State University (2006), best practice calls for every program or unit to have an assigned assessment professional to help with assessment, including with the choice of appropriate tools and activities.

Enhancing Instrument Reliability and Validity

Drawing on the advice of campus experts is one way to enhance reliability and validity of measures, as is asking peers on and off campus to review instruments. Combining data from several years is helpful for programs that have small numbers of students. Using item analysis for objective tests and surveys is valuable. Computer programs that analyze test items will indicate item difficulty (the proportion of students answering the item correctly), as well as item discrimination. Discrimination scores show how well the item distinguishes between students with good performances and those with poor performances. If those with low overall scores perform better on an item than those with high overall scores, the item will have a negative discrimination score and should be rewritten or dropped. Staff from Vanderbilt University's Center for Teaching (n.d.) offer an excellent document about writing good multiple choice test items.

As noted in Chapter 3, listening to student comments is also important. If students frequently complain about an exam or if their performances do not compare to what would be expected based on their other work, faculty may have evidence that the instrument they are using needs to be modified. Pilot-testing items before they are used on a large scale is also important. Rubrics designed for assessment projects should always be tried on a small number of students and then revised if necessary (Martins, 2010).

Because consensus in the design of instruments is so important in assessment, a *test blueprint* can help faculty reach agreement as a group about appropriate test content. A test blueprint is a matrix in which the subjects covered by the test appear as row headings. Column headings represent skill levels, such as comprehension and application, which are to be addressed by the items. The cells of the matrix include the number of items or the percentage of the test that addresses the content-skill combination. Blueprints help ensure that test items cover the content of the curriculum at sufficiently challenging levels—a key issue with respect to the test's validity. Practitioners from the Office of Assessment and Institutional Research (AIR) at the New York City College of Technology (2008) provide information for faculty about how to construct a test blueprint. At the college, faculty work together to assess critical courses. If a test is going to be developed as a direct assessment measure, AIR office staff recommend that multiple faculty members be included in the process so that the assessment activity will be valued as a department initiative. An outline, similar to a blueprint, can also help in creating surveys.

Determining Approaches for Implementation

Several planning questions need to be addressed when deciding on methods to use and ways to implement them. Faculty must decide on a research strategy, identify participants, and consider whether to use a sample.

Research Strategies

Assessment researchers use a variety of designs. In practice, as Upcraft and Schuh (2002) point out, limits of time, cost, and the organizational context may force compromises. But they also point out that a study with limitations is better than no study at all. Some assessment studies are purely descriptive, collecting information about a group of students at a particular point in time to answer a relatively narrow question. For example, focus groups can be used to gather descriptive data on current issues or as a prelude to designing a questionnaire. Many teachers use classroom assessment techniques to find out about learning as it occurs.

Assessment studies often involve more complex designs. Some researchers use a *cross-sectional approach*, comparing different groups of students at a common point in time. For example, entering students and junior students may be asked to complete writing competence examinations, and their respective performances can be compared. However, it is difficult to attribute any differences in ratings to academic experiences if the characteristics of students differ greatly. Thus, it is very important to describe any characteristics of the two groups of students that are likely to affect their performances, such as high school class rank or test scores on other entry-level assessment instruments.

Many assessment leaders are interested in tracking and comparing successive cohorts of students. If characteristics of the student body stay relatively constant over time, this approach can help faculty understand how programs are working. For example, they can use results from successive senior surveys to see if attitude and satisfaction ratings improve after various program changes are introduced.

Longitudinal designs involve collecting information from the same set of students over a period of time. General education assessment often includes the use of pre- and post-results. Students are asked to take the same test, survey, or performance assessment when they enter the university and again two, three, or four years later. Because the same students participate in both assessments, it is possible to calculate changes in their scores or ratings between the two time periods. Faculty at Florida A&M University have adopted this approach (Ohia and Diallo, 2012).

When using longitudinal designs, researchers need to be cautious about attributing changes in scores, ratings, or opinions strictly to academic programs. Over time students mature and change in many ways, for many reasons. In addition, comparisons made between beginning and end points provide little information about why changes have occurred and thus little evidence about what is working or not with respect to academic programs. One of the great values of portfolios is the opportunity they provide to collect comprehensive longitudinal information. Rather than looking only at the beginning and end points in terms of students' programs, portfolios can provide rich details about what happens along the way.

On a practical note, longitudinal approaches can be difficult to implement in terms of tracking students. Because some students drop out over a period of years, researchers need to be aware of how this affects results. When reporting conclusions, they must describe how characteristics of students who have remained in the study compare to those who have left. A good strategy when using sampling techniques is to begin a study with more students than will be needed for making reliable generalizations in order to allow for expected attrition. Faculty who conduct course-level assessment often develop pre-post measures for in-class use. Because these are usually focused on course content and application and are administered within a relatively short time frame, they suffer less from the limitations just mentioned.

Occasionally as new programs are introduced, educators have a chance to design a true experiment. In these studies, students are randomly assigned to experimental and control groups. Thus, improvements in student learning can be more confidently attributed to the treatment that is introduced. Unfortunately, it is usually difficult to introduce random assignment of students to treatment and nontreatment groups because it is not ethical to withhold treatment from students who are eligible for programs (Pike, 2009).

When random assignment is not possible, statistical analysis may be used to control for differences in important characteristics that exist between students who are in a treatment group and those who are not. Regression and analysis of variance can be quite helpful in this regard. However, researchers always need to be aware of selection bias. If students have volunteered to be in the treatment group, they may differ greatly from another group of students in motivation and interest, even if matched on demographic characteristics. In practice, it is extremely difficult to control for differences in motivation and therefore difficult to determine program effects (Pike, 2009).

The specific research design that faculty use is often limited by circumstances. The most important consideration is that it provides faculty with useful information for making decisions. Although few opportunities for true experiments exist, possibilities to engage in interesting and valuable assessment projects are plentiful.

Identifying Eligible Participants

Practitioners must develop clear criteria to identify individuals who will be required or invited to participate in assessment projects. For example, participation may be open to all entering freshmen or restricted to degree-seeking students only. At the upper-division level, general education assessment may include only those from a particular entering cohort or all those who have achieved a certain classification level, such as sophomore or junior. Most often, all graduating seniors will be eligible for assessment that occurs at the completion of the major. Even here there may be conditions for eligibility, such as a minimum number of courses taken on campus. At George Mason University (2014), leaders remind faculty that program-level assessment in various courses should include majors only. Although nonmajors may participate in assessment activities, their results should be excluded from data analysis. In general, the selection of participants depends on the population to which educators wish to generalize after data are collected and analyzed.

Sampling and Sample Size

After determining who is eligible, faculty need to decide whether they will assess every student or only a sample. Assessing a sample is less costly and is feasible if results for each individual student are not needed. However, to ensure student motivation, the same data may be collected from every student and assessed to give individual feedback; then a sample of student work can be selected for program assessment. This strategy is often used with course-embedded assessment.

Several sampling approaches are in use. In a *random sample*, every individual has the same chance of being selected. *Stratified sampling* is used when researchers want to make sure they have adequate numbers of individuals in some subgroups. The overall group of interest is divided into subgroups or strata based on a categorical variable such as class standing or declared major. Individuals are then randomly selected within the subgroups. Some groups are over- or undersampled based on particular characteristics in order to have each subgroup large enough to detect differences in an outcome variable. Conclusions about the population are based on weights that represent the proportion of each subgroup in the population.

Many times information is collected from a *convenience sample*. This essentially means that researchers cannot comply with the rules for appropriate sampling and have simply done the best they can in locating individuals to participate in the assessment. For example, tests given during class periods include only those attending on the day the exam is administered. The characteristics of these students may not be representative of the group as a whole. Reports of results should include a comparison of characteristics of those in the actual study group with those who were eligible.

If sampling is appropriate in terms of time, cost, or other issues, an important decision regards the number of cases to study. Project results based on samples are usually reported with a sampling error—the possible difference between project findings and true results. For example, faculty may report that 80 percent of students are satisfied with their majors, with a sampling error of plus or minus 3 percent. Sampling error primarily depends on the desired confidence level (typically 95 percent), the error in the overall population, and the sample size. The larger the sample size is, the smaller the sampling error, and therefore the more accurate are project results. Statistical textbooks often include tables to help estimate sample size, and Raosoft's online program contains an easy-to-use sample size calculator (http://raosoft.com/samplesize.html).

An additional factor in determining final sample size is the likely response rate of those invited to participate in the project. If a 50 percent response rate is expected, researchers need to double the number of people invited to achieve a desired number of completed cases. Sample size also has to be large enough to disaggregate results if data will be reported for subgroups of the population. Thirty cases per subgroup is considered a minimum number. However, if results are going to be studied using multivariate analysis, it is desirable to have a few hundred cases overall. Staff from St. Olaf's (2014) Institutional Research and Evaluation Office provide a helpful discussion of sample size.

Putting Everything Together

Once faculty determine criteria for instrument selection, think through implementation strategies, and evaluate possible instruments, they are ready to make choices about what to do. At this point, it is a good idea to look at choices as a whole to make sure that assessment activities have the characteristics that are important to a successful assessment program. Activities must make sense overall, reveal details about student experiences along the way, and provide information that can direct actions. Although various instruments differ in their strengths and weaknesses, the totality of selections must provide the needed information. This is, of course, part of the argument for using multiple methods.

CHAPTER 5

USING DIRECT MEASURES

W hen assessment began to filter into institutions of higher education, it was often through the large-scale use of commercially available objective tests. Although this type of information gathering is still in
place, assessment programs now include many other techniques, such
as performance measures, e-portfolios, surveys, and focus groups. At the
institution level, surveys of current students are the most frequently used
assessment method. Among direct measures, provosts report that rubrics
and classroom-based performance assessments are used most frequently;
fewer than 50 percent use commercial tests (Kuh, Jankowski, Ikenberry,
and Kinzie, 2014). In this chapter, we take a closer look at several of the
direct assessment methods that help faculty investigate how well students
are learning and developing.

Using Classroom Assignments for Outcomes Assessment

Nearly twenty years ago, Walvoord and Anderson (1995, 1998) were
among the few practitioners advocating the use of graded materials as
the basis for outcomes assessment. They noted at the time that grading
is a process that "has nearly universal faculty participation, enjoys superb

student participation, is never accused of violating academic freedom" (1995, p. 8; 1998, p. xvii). It is closely linked to objectives for learning and to the planning of classroom teachers. Walvoord and Anderson, although quite aware of the criticisms of using course grades for outcomes assessment, argued for use of "the process by which a teacher assesses student learning through classroom tests and assignments, the context in which good teachers establish that process, and the dialogue that surrounds grades and defines their meaning to various audiences" (1998, p. 1). They encouraged faculty to use the information gathered from evaluating individual students to assess the effectiveness of programs, departments, and institutions.

Now faculty routinely use course-embedded assessment information to evaluate outcomes in general education programs and the major. Generally these assessment projects are collaborative in nature, with faculty discussing and reaching agreement about the process they will use for gathering materials and reviewing results. For example, Benner and Kapcsos (2010) describe an assessment project that led to changes in teaching and to improved student learning at Northampton Community College. Faculty examined six student learning outcomes from elementary algebra. They collected information from a developmental math course using a set of four embedded math questions and a shared rubric. In addition to scoring work of their own students, faculty submitted a selection of work across a range of performances to create a blind sample that was distributed and scored. Faculty created aggregated tables showing both sets of scores so they could consider results. Through discussion about how they were using the rubric, they found that they were sometimes giving credit because they inferred student understanding rather than scoring what was actually in the work, especially when grading their own students. Faculty also discussed the meaning of grades and the need to reach consensus when evaluating student work. To improve learning, faculty added emphasis on word problems to the course.

Embedded assessment can be used for online courses as well. At Pennsylvania State University, two course instructors collaborated with instructional consultants from the Schreyer Institute for Teaching Excellence to try out embedded assessment in their online courses. Test questions and assignments were matched with previously developed course learning objectives. Instructors forwarded results to the institute's consultants, who calculated the percentages of students who answered the associated questions correctly and presented these as data points. The instructors used the aggregated information to make changes in their instruction and in test questions. The assessment approach worked because faculty were able to see data "from the point of view of the learning objective rather than the student" (Weinstein, Ching, Shapiro, and Martin, 2010, p. 6).

As these examples illustrate, course-embedded assessment can be applied to objective tests, as well as to problem sets. In most cases, course-embedded assessment involves evaluating performance assessment tasks using a rubric developed for that purpose. Here we describe performance assessment and provide some examples. Then we turn to issues such as how to design assignments that effectively reflect student learning outcomes, how to develop and use rubrics appropriately, and how to aggregate results in ways that are efficient and meaningful.

Performance Assessment

Performance assessment is the process of using student activities or products, as opposed to tests or surveys, to evaluate students' knowledge, skills, and development. As part of this process, the performances generated by students are rated or scored by faculty or other qualified observers, who also provide feedback to students. Using the broadest definition, performance assessment includes any technique that requires students to construct their own responses rather than to select among responses that have been provided for them. By this definition, all direct assessment methods, with the exception of multiple-choice and other objective examinations, fall under the heading of performance assessment. Among others, these methods include essays, oral presentations, exhibitions, and demonstrations. To be called *authentic assessment,* tasks should meet a higher standard: they should demonstrate learning directly related to the nature of the discipline in which students are engaged and reflect the outcome being assessed. Boughton (2013) points out that asking students to answer questions about color scales is not an authentic assessment if the intent is to see if students can draw a house. Wiggins has taken an even more restrictive view, reserving the label of authentic assessment for tasks that "closely simulate or actually replicate challenges faced by adults or professionals" (1998, p. 141). Mueller (2012) defines authentic assessment as "that in which students are asked to perform real-world tasks that demonstrate meaningful application of essential knowledge and skills." In Boughton's example, asking fine arts students to create imaginative drawings of a house would come closer to meeting the standard.

Advantages of performance assessment include increased opportunities for instructors to provide feedback as they draw on the comprehensive evidence captured through performance assessment, increased possibilities for students to engage in self-assessment based on the feedback they receive and their own observations of the performances of others, and increased student engagement and motivation as they respond to tasks that are directly related to their programs. Although faculty may choose the topic and format, authentic assessment allows students to make choices about the way they present evidence of their learning. In the arts, Boughton argues for assessment practices that allow evidence of risk taking and sustained independent investigation in order to encourage creativity.

As with all other good assessment methods, performance assessment requires clear statements about desired learning outcomes. Because performance-based assessments are expected to be indistinguishable from the goals of instruction, teaching to these assessments is considered not only acceptable but exemplary. To that end, students need to see models of performance at various levels, as well as the rubrics that will be used to score their performances.

Attention to validity requires faculty to ask questions such as: Does the particular assessment cover the appropriate content? Is it assessing the appropriate level of cognitive complexity? Are tasks meaningful for students? Faculty also should ask if tasks are fair in terms of reflecting cultural diversity and differences in instructional experiences. Leaders of the Conference on College Composition and Communication (2009) assert that standardized tests of writing may disadvantage students whose dialect is not the dominant one because these tests often rely on identifying grammatical errors rather than on evaluating authentic rhetorical choices. In contrast, assessing authentic acts of writing provides multiple avenues to success.

Types of Performance Assessment

Many types of performance assessment are applicable across a wide range of subjects, including essays, research papers, problem sets, and oral examinations. Orals involve one or more examiners who use both planned and unplanned questions to gather evidence from students about their understanding of and ability to apply what they have learned. Faculty in the Stillman School of Business at Seton Hall University (2014) use a variant of this approach to assess their students. In sophomore and senior assessment panels, students analyze a current business situation and are evaluated by outside business practitioners. In addition, students write short essays and prepare self- and peer evaluations of team performances.

Many well-known examples of performance assessment are specific to the major, asking students to create and exhibit products or present demonstrations that are representative of work done by professionals in the discipline. Journalism, art, music, and architecture have long traditions of examining products and performances of this type. At Carnegie Mellon University, faculty are encouraged to use methods customized to the disciplines as well as reflective of local culture (Kinzie, 2012).

In some cases, assessment of student performances is conducted in a naturalistic setting. Observing a student teacher managing a classroom is a well-known example. In other cases, performances are simulated. Simulations allow faculty to assess the ability of students to perform in lifelike situations. At LaGuardia Community College, students in the physical therapy assistant program role-play clinicians with patients. Their conversations are recorded and analyzed using a communication rubric (Provezis, 2012). Online software also can be used for simulations such as designing buildings or planning landscapes. At Fox Valley Technical College, the new Health Simulation and Technology Center features a virtual hospital, a virtual training lab, and simulation sites, providing students with preparation for real-world situations (Wisconsin Technical College News, 2013).

Using Performance Measures for Outcomes Assessment

To gather information to assess their programs, faculty must decide how they will collect evidence about the performances of their students. Perhaps, as at the Stillman School of Business, student presentations will be rated by professionals from the field. More likely, evidence will come from tasks that individual students complete in their classrooms and classroom instructors grade. In assessing general education outcomes, faculty at the University of North Carolina Wilmington use a curriculum map to identify appropriate courses and then select a stratified random sample of sections from which artifacts are drawn (Siefert, 2013).

After evidence is gathered, a standing or ad hoc assessment committee or a working group of faculty can take another look at the evidence to see if it demonstrates that students are achieving the expected learning outcomes addressed by the program. Perhaps a departmental committee will use a rubric to reevaluate a sample of work from individual classes. Once results are obtained, focused discussion needs to occur. Looking collectively at assessment results allows faculty to examine how well their programs are working, identify areas where students seem to be weak, and compare the performances of current students to those of previous students. A regularly scheduled department or college meeting can be used for this purpose.

In the College of Business at Lewis University, members of a faculty team thought carefully about how they would present results from a recent assessment project to the entire faculty at a college-wide meeting. The team's analysis of writing samples from several business courses had identified some shortcomings in student writing. Team members recommended to college faculty that they provide better prompts and directions for students, and the rubric used for the project was revised (Cherry and Klemic, 2013).

To encourage group discussion, faculty who have been involved in an assessment project can complete reflection sheets sharing their reactions and conclusions about the student performances they have observed. Then a summary of narrative responses can be used to guide faculty discussion. This approach has been used at St. Olaf College in what is called mission-driven, meaningful, and manageable assessment. Rather than creating additional rubrics or instruments, faculty who are teaching courses that meet general education requirements are asked to describe and reflect on the work of their students using a General Education Student Learning Report. These reports are aggregated for each outcome to create a composite picture for consideration (Jankowski, 2012).

At Globe University and Minnesota School of Business, faculty offer several programs that share curriculum, course objectives, and assessment techniques such as rubrics and exams. Faculty across several campuses submit assessment scores with their final grades. Information is aggregated across programs and campuses for systemwide curriculum planning. Outcomes that are uniformly weak are the subject of focused discussions. Those that are high on a particular campus can be identified, with that campus serving as a model for good practice (Peterson and Gustafson, 2013).

Although the approaches differ in specifics, performance assessment is used on many campuses to improve student learning. To be done well, it requires attention to all aspects of the process: identifying skills to be examined, designing appropriate tasks to demonstrate the skills, articulating a reliable process for rating performances, and appropriately using results. We turn now to a very important aspect of the process, designing effective assignments.

Designing Effective Assignments

In course-embedded assessment, course assignments provide the primary means of determining student competence. Several campuses use the concept of a *signature assignment.* At California Lutheran University (2014b), this is the assignment or examination that most effectively displays that the outcomes of a course have been achieved.

In order for performance assessment to generate useful information, the tasks or assignments that are the basis for evaluation must be effectively designed. Schneider and Rhodes (2011) point out that assignments should "invite students to produce their best work in response to significant questions and information" (p. vi). Of most importance, students must be able to demonstrate the competence of interest. Many faculty use effective approaches. For example, at Carnegie Mellon University, an arts instructor developed course "project briefs" as concise guides for her students, specifying assignment objectives, including expected behaviors and reflection tasks as well (Kinzie, 2012).

Ewell (2013) believes, however, that too few faculty create assignments or open-ended examination questions that provide students with enough information to respond appropriately. To provide guidance to students, faculty need to identify the properties of an appropriate response and then design the assignment so that students understand what is expected of them. To assist faculty in designing assignments, Ewell offers an assignment template containing three basic elements: the central task that must be completed and the competence it is addressing, a description of how the task should be achieved and its results communicated, and an indication of how much evidence is expected in the response. For example, to demonstrate quantitative literacy, students can be asked to contrast and compare the results of several research studies and construct tables of data for three items that differ in study results. Using a specific approach such as this makes it more likely that students will be able to demonstrate their knowledge and skills fully. Staff from the Eberly Center at Carnegie Mellon University (n.d.a) offer similar advice with respect to open-ended examination questions, urging faculty to provide explicit directions. For example, if an open-ended question needs to be answered in a paragraph format rather than bulleted points, students should be told. If steps in a solution need to be shown, students need to know this as well. In addition to the task, successful performance assessment requires effective rubrics.

Rubrics

One of the biggest challenges of performance assessment is developing a useful approach for evaluating the activities or products generated by students. In most cases, faculty will want to examine several aspects of a performance or product and evaluate these behaviors or attributes at several different levels. If so, a scoring rubric will be necessary.

In some cases, faculty use *holistic scoring*, giving a performance or product a single overall score. Each possible score is accompanied by a statement that describes performance at that level. Although the description will refer to several characteristics of interest, these characteristics are not scored separately. Holistic scoring is based on an overall impression of the work and is most useful if only a few characteristics are of interest. Holistic scores do not give feedback about what scorers consider strengths and weaknesses. High scores mean students have performed well or satisfied all, or nearly all, aspects of the assignment. For example, students who receive the highest possible score on a critical thinking assignment may be expected to interpret evidence, identify and evaluate arguments, and draw appropriate conclusions. Low scores mean that few, if any, important aspects of the performance were met satisfactorily.

In most cases, faculty use an *analytic rubric* to rate separately the various important characteristics of a performance or product. A teacher grading a research project may look at aspects of the performance such as "includes statement of hypothesis," "analyzes information," and "develops appropriate conclusions." For each characteristic, a three- to five-point scoring scale is developed with an explicit statement describing performance at each level. For example, "includes statement of hypothesis" may be given a score of 3 if the hypothesis is clearly stated, of 2 if it is present but unclear, or of 1 if it is incomplete or missing.

In practice, each possible score will ordinarily be described by several aspects of performance. A score of 5 on a "develops appropriate conclusions" section of a research paper may require an overview of issues, a restatement of major positions, and the student's own judgment about the position that is superior. Lower grades will be assigned to students whose "conclusions" section is incomplete on one or more aspects of the performance necessary to receive a grade of 5. Well-designed rubrics contain specific descriptive language about what the presence or absence of a quality looks like. Rubrics should be tried out in practice and revised if necessary. Faculty in the College of Business at Lewis University revised their analytic writing rubric when they found it was overweighting certain factors due to redundancy. The rubric had to be adjusted because some papers were receiving a passing score even though they were judged incoherent (Cherry and Klemic, 2013).

The characteristics of interest in the rubric may be expressed using nouns or verbs. The number of possible scores and how they are labeled also varies. For example, each aspect of a performance can be rated from unsatisfactory to outstanding. Alternatively, a scale may include the categories "standard met," "standard partially met," and "standard not met." Some rating scales ask for a narrative explanation justifying extreme scores. Online resources such as RubiStar are available to help faculty develop rubrics (http://rubistar.4teachers.org/).

If rating scales are to be used to generate programmatic information, faculty should discuss and agree on the aspects of a product or performance to measure and how these characteristics will be described. The most important reference in developing the list of characteristics is the student learning outcomes for the course and program. The process of developing rubrics can be lengthy. Faculty at Winston-Salem State University report spending a year developing their rubrics (Berry, 2013). Both well-developed rating scales and careful training of raters contribute to inter-rater reliability. At the University of North Carolina Wilmington, scorers begin by working together, perhaps scoring a few papers. Then they create guidelines to help them apply rubrics in a similar manner. After a scoring session is completed, feedback is solicited from both scorers and instructors of those classes from which artifacts were chosen in order to determine any issues with the process (Siefert, 2013).

VALUE Rubrics

The Association of American Colleges and Universities' (AAC&U, 2014d) sixteen Valid Assessment of Learning in Undergraduate Education (VALUE) rubrics are an important resource. The rubrics were developed to help link the assessment work done by faculty in individual classrooms to the assessment work that is often done separately by faculty and evaluators at the program or institution level. The rubrics help create a set of shared expectations about student performance on stated learning outcomes. They allow faculty to communicate expectations for performance to students and others and students to assess their own performances. The VALUE rubrics went through several rounds of drafting and redrafting and involved more than one hundred faculty from campuses across the country. Existing rubrics were referenced as the project proceeded, but additions were made where necessary to allow forms of presentation such as visual, graphical, digital, or artistic. These criterion-referenced rubrics exhibit content validity because they have been developed by faculty and academic professionals in each of the areas of learning represented (Rhodes, 2011).

AAC&U staff expected faculty to modify the VALUE rubrics to fit their own needs, and many have done so. At Carroll Community College, the rubrics were used as a starting point, but faculty soon moved to a three-point scale rather than use the four-point scale contained in the VALUE rubrics (Davis and Ohlemacher, 2013). Because the VALUE rubrics do not address scientific inquiry, faculty at Winston-Salem began by considering two other VALUE rubrics—problem solving and inquiry and analysis. Ultimately they were able to use criteria from the National Science Education Standards of the National Academy of Sciences to construct an appropriate rubric (Berry, 2013). Faculty at the University of North Carolina Wilmington also considered multiple VALUE rubrics as they worked to create a rubric to assess student reflections (Siefert, 2013).

Developing good rubrics takes effort from many participants. Griffin (2009) cautions that a scoring rubric may appear as a precise, technical, scientific-looking document, but a "rubric is more like a cake than a rock" (p. 4). Rather than a mirror of some absolute reality, a rubric is a record of negotiated compromises—a product of many minds and therefore more thoughtful than any one person could conceive alone.

The ability to use well-developed rubrics has changed the way many campuses undertake assessment. Yet some faculty approach rubrics with caution.

Some Rubric Issues

RiCharde (2009) believes that both interrater reliability statistics and rubrics themselves suffer because they convert concepts that are abstract and nonlinear into concrete numbers. Although interrater reliability statistics appear to quantify the level of agreement among scorers, RiCharde questions what partial agreement actually means. RiCharde believes that rubrics often are adopted without sufficient local input and that they tie faculty to overly simplified views of the constructs they are assessing. In particular, he finds that critical thinking rubrics are not up to the task of assessing critical thinking. RiCharde (2008) also argues that these methods are at odds with the nonlinear dialectical pedagogy favored by faculty in the humanities. In contrast, Flick (2009) believes that, used judiciously, rubrics are as valuable in the humanities as they are elsewhere and argues that higher-order thinking involves debate and disagreement in all disciplines, not just in the humanities. Problems arise only when members of a discipline disagree on the kind of thinking or performance that is valued. Although RiCharde argues that assessment leads to standardization of instruction, in Flick's view nothing about interrater reliability, rubrics, or defined outcomes leads to standardization. Outcomes can be written with fluidity, and faculty can add unique outcomes to their own courses. Flick believes faculty can and should reach consensus on a few core outcomes and seek to measure them reliably.

The use of electronic portfolios (discussed below) presents additional issues with respect to rubric use. Portfolio scores are based on evaluation of student work produced over time and are most often obtained using rubrics. Secolsky and Wentland (2010) examine the effect that differences in product topics have on the validity of portfolio assessment. Rubrics typically use criteria such as organization, relevance, and creativity. But because topics themselves can vary on these dimensions, the nature of the topic may influence judgment of the quality of work. If topic selection is not taken into account, conclusions about program effects on learning outcomes may be incorrect. How can faculty determine if creativity, for example, has shown growth over time unless the topics and tasks are the same? One approach would be to rate individual assignments on their sensitivity to each criterion included in the portfolio assessment rating and take these different sensitivities into account when evaluating student products. Another approach would be to collect and examine the topics, task descriptions, and rubrics associated with the original assignments and use these to create an overall rubric. The authors note that topics used as essay prompts share similar problems. To compensate, writing tasks on the SAT and ACT exams are very narrow in the range of topics covered. Testing companies regularly undertake comparability studies to determine if score differences exist across prompts. Faculty should be aware of these rubric issues as they develop performance assessments and portfolios.

Here we turn to another developing area of programmatic assessment: the ability to efficiently aggregate results across students and courses. These approaches use faculty grading to provide program-level information without requiring a second scoring of artifacts.

Aggregating Assessment Results in and across Courses

As campuses increasingly integrate student learning outcomes at the university, program, and course levels, the connections among classroom assignments, expected outcomes, and grades assigned to tasks by instructors become more explicit. As a result, the possibility of using already graded materials as the direct source of evidence for program assessment becomes both feasible and efficient.

Greville (2009) argues not that grades alone constitute outcomes assessment, but that assessment and grading do not have to be mutually exclusive. She proposes reassembling a syllabus to connect each piece of graded work to a specific learning outcome. If faculty can articulate outcomes and the degree to which students master the outcomes, an A or an "exceeds expectations" or a 95 percent all signify that learning has occurred. What is needed is clarity about what is being assessed and about the basis for judgment. Faculty must consistently assign scores for each element of each assignment. Then scores can be totaled across assignments to obtain an individual student's course grade. Scores also can be totaled by learning outcome for the entire class, yielding outcomes assessment information.

Similar to the approach Greville suggested, faculty at Prince George's Community College (2013) have developed a system to integrate assessment of course, program, and general education outcomes and to connect outcomes assessment with classroom grading (Ariovich and Richman, 2013). Called All-in-One, the advantage of the system is that faculty do not need to allocate time for additional reading of papers or separate processes for general education or program assessment. At the course level, interconnections begin with a key or culminating assignment that demonstrates all of the course outcomes. Faculty who teach the course collaborate to design the assignment and the rubric. Rubrics are created using the template in the database software. A set of assignment-specific domains is entered as row headings and five performance levels appear as column headings. In addition to the number of points (which can represent a range of possibilities), each cell contains a description of expected performance at that level. The rubric is completed online for each student by selecting the points he or she has received in each domain. Then total points and percentage scores are calculated for each student. After the semester is over, scores are cumulated by performance level for each domain. And because each domain is linked by number to a course learning outcome, and these in turn are linked to program and general education outcomes, results can be aggregated to these levels as well.

The approach requires faculty to maintain connections carefully across course, program, and general education learning outcomes. The authors acknowledge that the system, developed using Tk20 software, takes a lot of work, but the focus of the work is on curriculum design rather than assessment. Each department has a three-member faculty team to shepherd the assessment process. And each academic division has two members who serve on an institution-wide committee. Strong administrative support is necessary to make sure all divisions and departments are contributing. The faculty invested a great deal of time working to connect course outcomes to program outcomes and integrate skills from the general education program into the curriculum. One result has been the development of a preferred sequence of courses within both the general education program and the major. Following the preferred sequence allows students to build skills coherently, eventually culminating in the expected general education and program outcomes.

Faculty at Texas Christian University have undertaken a similar approach at the program level to assess online graduate programs in nursing and liberal arts. Using Learning Outcome Manager, the assessment and reporting application of Pearson LearningStudio, faculty tie learning outcomes to assignments. They write outcomes statements, map these to courses, and create and store rubrics. At first faculty thought the new system was just a form of grading, but they soon found it was different. Faculty training assisted the process. With Learning Outcome Manager, a student's performance is rated on learning outcomes, and a dashboard summarizing that performance is created. Results also can be aggregated to the program or institution level. The process has helped faculty identify redundant assignments (King, 2011).

The use of course-embedded assessment has caused faculty on several campuses to rethink the way this information can be aggregated and used. The availability of new technology has hastened change in this regard and is likely to cause more change in the future.

Using Objective Tests for Outcomes Assessment

Objective tests are a normal and expected part of the classroom experience and are a type of direct measure included in many assessment programs. Objective tests allow students to demonstrate the knowledge they have acquired and their ability to process and use that knowledge. Students select a correct answer from a set of responses that have been provided for them. Multiple-choice, true-false, and matching items fit this description.

Several commercial instruments are available to assess general education outcomes. Overall, these instruments examine analytical skills as well as recall, include performance tasks and writing samples as well as multiple-choice items, and in some versions provide group rather than individual scores.

Standardized objective tests also are used for assessment in several disciplines. Seniors in programs such as education and nursing take licensure exams. The Educational Testing Service provides major field tests in a dozen areas, including biology, computer science, mathematics, political science, and psychology. Tests are also available for associate, bachelor's, and master's levels in business. Faculty can add up to fifty locally developed questions to these tests. The Area Concentration Achievement Tests (ACAT) available through PACAT, Inc., provide an additional approach to testing content knowledge acquired in the major. ACAT areas include art, criminal justice, geology, history, social work, and others. Program faculty using ACAT can select from specific components so that the test most closely matches the local curriculum. To identify additional possibilities, faculty can consult the Measuring Quality Inventory, a searchable online database developed by Borden and Kernel (2012).

Results from a study of program heads that Ewell et al. (2011) conducted indicate that many faculty develop their own content examinations for assessment purposes. These may include short answers and essays, as well as objective questions. The percentage of program heads reporting that they use this assessment method is above 50 percent for trade programs, health sciences, computer science, business, and engineering.

On a given campus, department faculty vary in their approaches to using examinations, with some using locally developed tests and others using purchased instruments. At St. Olaf College, biology faculty use the ETS Major Field Exam, an exam from the American Chemical Society is used in chemistry, nursing faculty use the California Critical Thinking Skills Test, and ACAT is the choice for psychology. Chemistry faculty also use a locally developed safety quiz for all lab students, statistics faculty employ a collectively written final exam essay question, and physics faculty use common test items in introductory and advanced seminar courses (Beld, 2013).

Some tests cover all or most of the subjects addressed in general education or the major. In fact, assessment has renewed the interest of faculty in senior comprehensive examinations, with about 30 percent of programs using them (Ewell et al., 2011). In the School of Journalism at the University of Arizona (2013), all students take a pretest during their beginning premajor course and a posttest as they complete their capstone course. The test covers nine of the program's eleven learning outcomes.

Many times a test addressing a program-related issue is administered within a particular course or class. For example, Harrell (n.d.), who was teaching introduction to philosophy at Carnegie Mellon University (n.d.a), designed a pre- and post-strategy to see if the use of argument mapping software contributed to learning. Some sections of the course served as a control group that did not learn argument mapping but still participated in the pre- and post-testing. Harrell found that students who learned argument mapping showed greater gains in analytic skill than those who did not learn it.

Advantages and Disadvantages of Objective Tests

Using objective tests allows faculty to examine a wide range of content knowledge in a single instrument—one that is comparatively easy to administer, score, and summarize. Faculty can ask several questions about each content area, contributing to precision in measurement and to the test's reliability. In fact, objective tests can be subjected readily to well-established measures of reliability and validity. Although it may take considerable effort to develop (or select) an objective test, the biggest time investment usually occurs at the initial stages of development and implementation. Once they are developed, the time needed to administer and score objective tests is minimal compared with other measures. An appropriately developed test often can be used for several administrations, allowing faculty to create a longitudinal data set.

The extensive time required to create good local examinations is a deterrent to many potential users, as is the difficulty of writing items that examine higher-order thinking skills. Many critics believe that objective test items rarely operate beyond levels of simple recall or recognition. Even experienced item writers have difficulty producing items that test above this level. In addition, some tests are focused at such a general level of information that they do not yield detailed results useful for improvement of teaching and learning.

Developing Good Tests and Writing Good Items

Information about reliability and validity must be examined during the development of objective tests. In Chapter 4, we provided some advice about developing good assessment measures, including creating test blue-prints, piloting items, and using item analysis to determine the difficulty and discrimination of individual items.

A standardized test is one for which conditions of administration and scoring are constant. Tests that are developed locally for program assessment typically reflect a group effort. Because these tests often are used by several faculty, documentation about content, scoring procedures, and administration needs to be available and understood by all users. Procedures for administering the test should include introductory comments and directions. Time allocated for administration must be constant from one test administration to the next, which is sometimes difficult to achieve when test conditions vary. For example, the time available in orientation for entry-level testing may differ from that allowed for upper-division testing in classrooms or online.

On several campuses, assessment or teaching and learning specialists provide guidelines for faculty to use as they develop tests. The web pages of the Eberly Center for Teaching Excellence at Carnegie Mellon University (n.d.a) contain advice for faculty, such as considering their cognitive objectives for learning as they select the types of items they will use. Multiple-choice items, for example, may be useful in asking students to recognize or distinguish among alternatives, but they do not allow students to articulate anything. Items should be checked against the test blueprint to see if there is correspondence between the content and level of thought addressed by the items and that which was planned. Faculty should be explicit on the exam about the learning objectives that are to be addressed. This helps students understand how course objectives fit together and prompts them to think about what they have learned. Point values assigned to questions should reflect the difficulty of the questions, the time students will likely need to complete them, and the importance of the skills being addressed. To ensure the test can be completed in the time allowed, faculty should take the test themselves. Students typically need three times the amount of time it takes the instructor to complete the exam.

Eberly Center staff also provide some general rules to help in writing objective test questions. A typical test item consists of a question (the stem) and a set of possible responses. The most important strategy for writing good test items is to use clear, easily understood language for all parts of the item and to include as much of the item in the stem as possible to avoid repetition. Objective test questions should have only one best answer, and overlapping alternatives should be avoided. Wrong answers (distractors) should be plausible choices. The position of the correct answer should vary randomly from item to item. Response items should be similar in length and complexity. Using "All of the above" and "None of the above" in responses should be avoided. Students need to eliminate only one response to eliminate "all of the above" as an answer. Using "none of the above" as the correct response tests students' ability to detect incorrect answers, but not whether they know the correct answer.

Pike (2013a) has reviewed a software system that increases the usefulness of traditional examinations for assessment purposes. The ExamSoft examination management system is a tool to create, score, and report assessment results. Faculty design the exams and the system administers the tests, scores performances, and reports results. To work for assessment, each exam question is linked to one or more student outcomes by the instructor who is designing the test. Simple reports can then show the proportion of items answered correctly by outcome, and this information can be made available to students. Results can be aggregated across exams as well. The study of online courses at Pennsylvania State University described earlier in this chapter represents a local attempt to link objective test results to learning objectives (Weinstein et al., 2010).

Implications for Students

Because objective tests provide an opportunity to examine large numbers of students simultaneously, faculty must think carefully about the way students will be affected. If interest is in the performance of the group rather than in individual performance, students may be asked to participate in assessment testing that does not affect their grades. At some institutions, participation is required as a condition for graduation. In these cases, notations may be entered on students' records when they have met test requirements. If individual scores are generated, they should be shared with students to help increase their motivation to perform well.

With locally developed assessment instruments, faculty are often more comfortable with test content and its relationship to the curriculum, and are more likely to include results in the course grade. In fact, faculty may choose part or all of a test they already use for grading as an outcomes assessment measure. Because of the many possible approaches, students must be informed of the effect, if any, that their performance or participation will have on their grades. They need to know the overall purpose of testing and how the information will be used. Faculty and staff at St. Olaf College provide materials to students that stress the value of assessment results to the campus (Jankowski, 2012).

Consideration also must be given to when and where a test will be given to students. At St. Olaf, large-scale testing of entering students is completed during orientation week on that campus (Jankowski, 2012). Testing of upper-division students may be scheduled in campus testing facilities on designated days or may be administered during selected class periods. Rather than occurring in a fixed time frame, some tests are designed for online administration at students' convenience. Tests that contain well-written items covering the appropriate subject matter and level of thinking can reveal much about student learning. Because of their increasing use and great potential, we now turn to a discussion of e-portfolios.

Electronic Portfolios

Electronic portfolios are digital collections of student work including multimedia artifacts, reflective commentary, and evidence linked to institutional outcomes, personal outcomes, or both. E-portfolios allow students to integrate information across courses, disciplines, and experiences and to become "authors who study their own learning" (Clark and Eynon, 2009, p. 18). Clark and Eynon attribute the increased use of e-portfolios to their elasticity—their large number of potential uses. Possibilities include learning portfolios, assessment (documentation) portfolios, and showcase (career) portfolios, but objectives often are combined (Matthews-DeNatale, 2014).

Many companies offer e-portfolio systems. In addition, several universities have developed platforms for their own use and for licensing to others. Integrating e-portfolios with existing learning management systems (LMSs) can prove difficult. Faculty at Utah Valley University found that e-portfolios supported by their LMS did not allow data to be easily retrieved across courses without additional programming (Andrade, 2013). At St. John's University (2014), faculty use WEAVE as their database for assessment plans and results and Digication to support e-portfolios.

Evidence is accumulating that e-portfolios contribute to student success as measured by pass rates, retention rates, and grade point averages (Eynon, Gambino, and Torok, 2014a). In addition, e-portfolios that encourage students to reflect on and connect their experiences appear to contribute to higher-order thinking and integrative learning. Great possibilities exist for using e-portfolios to aid student learning. The related question is whether that potential also can enhance outcomes assessment efforts without jeopardizing student engagement and ownership.

Using E-Portfolios for Outcomes Assessment

Using e-portfolios for outcomes assessment requires carefully reviewing collections of student work and reflections for evidence of learning and development with respect to agreed-on student learning outcomes. Because e-portfolios contain systematically collected artifacts that students add to their portfolios as they progress through their academic programs, portfolios can be evaluated for degree of improvement as well as for overall quality. Both the selection of items for portfolios and the evaluation of portfolios are based on criteria that are established by faculty and should be available to and understood by students.

In practice, portfolios have been implemented for a variety of purposes: to assess learning in general education and in the major, examine freshman learning communities and other cocurricular programs, and evaluate various aspects of learning such as integration of concepts across subject areas. At Clemson University, required e-portfolios are used for assessment of general education competences. Students begin their portfolios in the first semester and add evidence in the following semesters. They tag their artifacts to indicate the specific competence they are meant to satisfy. For program assessment, faculty evaluate the portfolios during summer workshops. After viewing initial results, the number of competences was reduced and criteria addressing communication skills were included in all the competences (Rhodes, 2011).

Within disciplines, traditional portfolios have been used for many years in the arts, as well as in architecture, English, and engineering. Now program heads in education report more use of portfolios than in any other program (Ewell et al., 2011). At Virginia Polytechnic and State University (2014a), faculty in several education programs participate in the campus's ePortfolio Initiative. While portfolios can be linked to a single course or group of courses, in many cases they are used to demonstrate that students can integrate what they have learned across their curricular and cocurricular experiences. Florida State University (2011) students, for example, place artifacts in multiple cells reflecting both the type of learning skill demonstrated (communication, critical thinking, leadership, and others) and the type of experience involved (courses, internships, service-learning, and life experiences).

Choices for E-Portfolios

To use portfolios effectively for assessment of student learning, faculty and other stakeholders must consider what they want to achieve, as well as what they want their students to achieve. Answering questions about purposes provides the conceptual framework for e-portfolios and guides the many other decisions that are necessary.

Faculty at Salt Lake Community College (2014) have multiple purposes for student e-portfolios, including providing opportunities for students to reflect on their work and make connections across their learning. Also of importance, portfolios promote coherence of their general education program. The college has a cafeteria-style program that can make it difficult for students to see how general education courses provide a foundation for career success or continued educational advancement. The e-portfolio serves as a pseudo-capstone for the program, allowing students to see how their courses reinforce each other. In their portfolios, students create a page for each course where they store assignments from the course. Then they connect these assignments to the page that displays student learning outcomes for the general education program.

Faculty must agree on the type and quantity of materials that will be collected, the timetable for submissions, and the way materials will be evaluated. Faculty agreements about the way portfolios will be organized—the format—need to reflect the portfolios' conceptual framework or purposes. Most often students select artifacts that demonstrate their learning and development. If portfolios also are intended to help students as they enter the job market, the types of items they include will reflect this as well. Students at St. John's University (2014) use their e-portfolios to present themselves both academically and professionally.

The specific items contained in portfolios vary widely and may include, for example, essays, computer programs, photographs, and videos. Clemson University (2014) students may select from classroom assignments; materials from internship, co-op, or study-abroad experiences; and evidence from cocurricular activities. Case studies, research reports, and projects are other possibilities. In some cases, students are required to submit specific types of items in their portfolios. At Florida State University (2014), students in the Teacher Education Unit complete special assignments, referred to as critical tasks, which are designed to demonstrate that students have met the standards of the Florida Department of Education and the National Association of Colleges of Teacher Education. Once tasks are completed, students upload them to assessment portfolios created through Chalk and Wire, and the system notifies the instructor when assignments are ready to be graded using a rubric.

As at Clemson, faculty most often provide general directions and allow students to select the specific materials. Students may need help in seeing the connections among learning goals and objectives, appropriate evidence that they have met these objectives, and items to include in their portfolios. Because each artifact will be judged as acceptable or unacceptable, Clemson University (2014) educators provide specific advice organized according to each of the learning outcomes addressed in their program. For example, materials that demonstrate critical thinking must be selected from upper-division courses rather than from earlier work.

Most portfolios contain what students judge to be their best work. However, particularly in e-portfolios that are focused on enhancing learning, student artifacts may demonstrate a range of work. They may show student progress or how their thinking has changed about a subject. Artifacts may include a draft of a paper as well as the finished product. The way students use evidence in portfolios is the subject of ongoing research. In well-constructed portfolios, student reflection appropriately frames the evidence that has been submitted (Yancey, 2009).

Student Reflection

In most e-portfolios, students write reflective statements connecting their evidence to outcomes and justifying their choice of artifacts. Faculty may provide structured reflection prompts to guide these statements. In the Graduate Childhood Education program at Lehman College, students are asked to describe each artifact, analyze its relationship to a professional standard, indicate how it demonstrates personal growth, and explain how they intend to use what they have learned to improve their teaching (Ross, 2013). Reflection about portfolio items requires students to view possible choices from various perspectives and consider how others will view their choices. It also may include making connections across items and perhaps describing future interests and commitments. Reflection provides an essential way for students to demonstrate critical thinking, analytic reasoning, and integrative learning (Yancey, 2009; Rhodes, 2011).

Students must be given specific directions about all possibilities and requirements for reflective statements. Truman State University (2011, 2014) faculty ask students to include a cover letter providing overall reflections about their portfolios, including the process and time used in creating them and their attitudes toward the activity. In their portfolios, students write about their most satisfying experience at the university. This information is analyzed for type of experience and reasons for selection, such as challenge, growth, and professional focus.

Students may not come to a class or portfolio project with the ability to reflect on their learning and may need practice to develop this skill (Penny Light, Chen, and Ittelson, 2012). Practitioners at Salt Lake Community College (SLCC, n.d.a) advise students to think of reflections as conversations they are having with themselves. The faculty developed a rubric to evaluate reflective writing that addresses the depth of reflection (how well the student connects the assignment to learning) and the context and references for reflection (recognizing audiences other than the instructor and referring to the work itself) (SLCC, n.d.b).

Scoring

As faculty consider what kind and how much evidence will be collected, they also must decide how e-portfolios will be evaluated. They may begin by using a simple checklist to indicate that a portfolio contains all of the required items and meets other explicit criteria. Then the portfolio can be examined more closely for its appropriateness and quality.

In some cases, an e-portfolio is scored holistically. The overall collection of work it contains is examined and given one score based on how well it demonstrates that the student has mastered program outcomes. More likely, the overall portfolio will be evaluated using an analytic rubric that provides separate scores on multiple traits or criteria such as organization, creative thinking, and integration of ideas.

For an e-portfolio to function effectively as a means for program assessment, faculty should examine the individual items contained in the portfolio for evidence that the outcomes of the program have been met. Scores can be assigned to all or a sample of the items based on separate criteria for each of the outcomes they address. At Truman State University (2011), students provide an artifact that is scored for both critical thinking and writing. Critical thinking is evaluated using a holistic rubric, and writing is scored with an analytic rubric. A Salt Lake Community College team used rubrics to examine a sample of portfolio items for evidence of quantitative literacy, including the abilities to explain information presented as equations, graphs, diagrams, words, or tables; convert information from one of these forms to another; and express quantitative evidence in support of the work (Hubert and Lewis, 2013).

Samples of previous work, expectations about various levels of performance, and scoring guides developed elsewhere can be used to identify appropriate criteria for assessing various items. The VALUE rubrics have the advantage of being developed by panels of experts and provide an excellent place to start.

Portfolios are generally viewed as valid in terms of being fundamentally related to the curriculum content of academic programs. But as with all other assessment methods, issues of reliability and validity need to be addressed. To achieve reliability, procedures need to be in place that will lead to accurate and consistent results when scoring portfolios. Seyferth (2012) reports on a study she conducted using information from e-portfolios developed with software from Chalk and Wire Learning Assessment. Her interest was in validity issues of competence-based portfolio assessment. Seyferth suggests that establishing validity requires examining the entire system as well as individual instruments and learning tasks. Using thematic content analysis, she uncovered several validity issues in the portfolios she examined—for example, the use of too few scores to discern distinctions in quality, a failure to agree on and use key words and phrases, and a tendency to set the target level of performance as the highest level so that exceptional students are not identified. Seyferth found cases too where feedback to students was unavailable or too late to allow students to revise their work before final evaluation. Seyferth recommends that faculty examine validity issues so they will be able to support conclusions that come from e-portfolios.

Rhodes (2011) identifies the ability of faculty and staff to meaningfully communicate e-portfolio results to internal and external audiences as a great remaining challenge. He describes Washington State University's use of spider diagrams to present rubric scores for learning outcomes as an interesting possibility. To address potential criticism that faculty are examining the work of their own students, faculty from other programs or other campuses can serve as evaluators. Washington State faculty ask employers to participate in evaluating portfolios.

Resources and Training

The effective use of e-portfolios requires thorough training of all participants, particularly when e-portfolios are being developed and introduced. The Salt Lake Community College (2014) site contains online tutorials to help faculty create signature assignments, and suggested rubrics are available as well. Students and faculty also can benefit from an online library of previous e-portfolios with examples of various levels of performances. Assessment leaders from the multicampus Connect to Learning project led by the Making Connections National Resource Center at LaGuardia Community College have developed an e-portfolio website, Catalyst for Learning: ePortfolio Resources and Research, which contains many ideas about implementing e-portfolios (http://c2l.mcnrc.org/).

Andrade (2013) describes the implementation process used at Utah Valley University to introduce e-portfolios for assessment of learning outcomes in the general education program. Two faculty members, one an expert in e-portfolios and the other in technology, were given release time to work with a general education subcommittee to develop models for training and recruitment. Committee members also organized a learning circle focused on the 2004 book by Zubizarreta, *The Learning Portfolio.* Faculty who were recruited to be part of the pilot attended a week of training, and each was paid a stipend of five hundred dollars.

Feedback

Evidence suggests that the e-portfolio experience for students is heightened when they know instructors are viewing their portfolios. In fact, feedback from peers as well as instructors is beneficial (Eynon et al., 2014a). New technologies can support this effort. For example, Baepler (2011) describes an application that can be used to embed written feedback in multimedia text. Instructors use three windows as they review videos contained in portfolios: one for the video, one for a time line, and the third for comments. The time line is marked when the reviewer makes a comment and rubric scores can be stored along with comments.

At Clemson (2014), peer reviewers and faculty facilitators provide formative feedback to students online. Using an iterative process, students are expected to make changes until they receive a passing score. E-portfolios are scored by a creative team specific to a competence. The team uses a four-point scale, with 1 indicating the student has failed to demonstrate competence. Students are alerted if the artifact might work for a different competence or if more information is needed.

Regular opportunities for feedback and review should be identified as part of the portfolio process. Reviews should be completed according to an established time line and should be frequent enough to help students make necessary adjustments as they proceed with their portfolios. Technology allows for frequent online review, but students still need to have a reasonable expectation of when feedback is likely to occur. In many cases, more than one person will be looking at portfolios. A team may include one or more faculty, an advisor, and perhaps student peers, as well as community representatives.

Impact on Students

The ability of students to use e-portfolios to exercise their voices in presenting and representing their learning has been found to be a significant motivator for students to do their best work (Cambridge, Cambridge, and Yancey, 2009). Because portfolios are often useful when seeking work after graduation, students have another incentive to do their best. At Florida State University (2014), students in the Teacher Education Unit use Chalk and Wire to create a program assessment portfolio and also can use it to make separate e-portfolios for career or other purposes.

On some campuses, students have great control over the appearance of their portfolios, using either customized templates or starting from scratch. Clark and Eynon (2009) point out that e-portfolio platforms often develop an increasingly standardized appearance and format as they become easier to use and manage. They believe e-portfolios should allow for more than just the translation of text, videos, and photos to screen. The best e-portfolios allow students to personalize the organization and appearance of their portfolios and to tell their "reflective personal digital stories" (Penny Light et al., 2012, p. 98).

To increase student enthusiasm and engagement, some campuses are linking e-portfolios to social networking and other new technologies. At Bowling Green State University (2013), campus leaders have adopted a new system that uses Web 2.0 tools and social media platforms like Google Docs and Facebook. The new system provides a place, public or private, where students can display and discuss their submissions and experiences.

Before portfolios are introduced, faculty must decide how they will affect the progress of students through the program. At both Clemson University (2014) and Truman State University (2014), faculty require students to submit portfolios as a condition of graduation. In addition, at Clemson, each required artifact has to be judged acceptable in order for students to complete their portfolio requirements. If portfolios are an additional requirement for graduation, students need to be informed, and they need to know the standards that will be used for decision making.

The ownership and confidentiality of portfolio materials is an additional consideration. At Truman State University (2014, n.d.), faculty retain portfolios for ten years to conduct longitudinal research about the university and its effectiveness. They routinely include anonymous quotes from student materials in project reports, and student artifacts are used for faculty training. Before they graduate, students are asked to complete and return a "permission for use" document agreeing to other potential uses of their portfolios, such as serving as models for other students.

Using Results

To be useful for guiding improvement, faculty must reach agreement about how portfolios will be viewed collectively, including the process for making decisions. Generating scores is only one step in the process of outcomes assessment. A collective look at results is necessary to reach agreement on how findings can be used for improvement.

Faculty at LaGuardia Community College examine student artifacts contained in e-portfolios during the program review cycle. Students submit a major assignment to the e-portfolio assessment area for selected courses in each program. During program review, a team of faculty, including some individuals from outside the program, uses a scoring rubric to examine the artifacts and assess core and program competences. Based on results, the team prepares recommendations for the program that are then addressed in the program's action plan. To concentrate more specifically on general education outcomes in 2011–2012, LaGuardia faculty conducted a benchmark assessment reading. A campuswide group used rubrics to score blind samples drawn from beginning and advanced students. Faculty worked in teams based on the core competences to take a comprehensive look at student learning (Provezis, 2012).

Developing E-Portfolios

Users of e-portfolios often point to the effort required to implement them successfully. Based on reviewing many e-portfolio projects in the United Kingdom, Joyes, Gray, and Hartnell-Young (2010) relate the idea of "threshold concepts" to e-portfolios. Threshold concepts are ideas that must be understood to move forward in thinking about a subject. With respect to e-portfolios, practitioners must understand the importance of aligning purposes with context; helping stakeholders comprehend the process, including the need for reflection and feedback; and providing learning activities to support faculty and students.

An additional threshold concept is the understanding that introducing portfolios is a disruptive process. Accounts from many campuses about the time, resources, and energy required in developing e-portfolio projects confirms this conclusion. Faculty and administrators at Utah Valley University took two years to gather materials and understand what would be involved in introducing e-portfolios. Then they spent many additional months designing and piloting an approach (Andrade, 2013). Members of a task force at Bowling Green State University (2013) spent several months reviewing possibilities for a new portfolio system before selecting Canvas by Instructure. Faculty teaching courses in different colleges and at different levels with different pedagogies were included in the study group. Multiple surveys of student and faculty opinions were conducted as well.

Appeal of Portfolios and Some Cautions

E-portfolios appeal for many reasons. As compared to traditional portfolios, they facilitate management and archiving of information. They permit students to efficiently use multimedia in providing evidence and reflections, and they allow faculty to use creative means to provide feedback to students. Innovative technologies are making it easier for e-portfolios to serve multiple purposes simultaneously, such as enhancing student learning and facilitating program assessment. As with all other portfolios, e-portfolios provide a great deal of information about what students are experiencing, and therefore more information about what they might need to improve. Sternberg, Penn, and Hawkins (2011) point out that portfolios encourage students to display creative, analytical, and practical thinking. Kahn (2014) believes that e-portfolios help students prepare for purposeful lifelong learning. Portfolios lead faculty toward collaboration, reflection, and discussion both within and across campuses (Eynon et al., 2014a).

Criticisms exist, however. Because students prepare their portfolios independently, it is not always possible to tell if they did all of the work themselves. Allowing students to draft and revise items may be criticized as allowing too much support. Issues of reliability and validity are raised. As noted earlier, the greater inclusiveness of portfolios increases scoring difficulties (Secolsky and Wentland, 2010). Clearly portfolios represent an assessment technique that requires a substantial amount of time from both students and faculty. Exhibit 5.1 captures planning issues that must be addressed when designing a portfolio process. In spite of some concerns, many faculty have enthusiastically embraced e-portfolios. By allowing faculty to link learning goals with rich evidence about learning, e-portfolios have much potential to strengthen academic programs.

EXHIBIT 5.1 PLANNING SHEET FOR E-PORTFOLIOS

- Establish purpose of e-portfolios.
  Emphasis on: assessment, learning, career?

- Decide the impact on students.
  How will students be affected? Required? Graded?
  What should students demonstrate? Learn?

- Determine content of portfolios.
  Types of items?
  Selection criteria for items?
  Opportunities for reflection?

- Determine feedback opportunities.
  What process will be used for review?
  When will feedback occur?

- Establish scoring approach.
  What criteria will be used?
  Will rubrics be developed, or will they be adopted or adapted?
  What process will be used for scoring?
  How will raters be trained?

- Establish procedures for program assessment.
  Will all portfolios be reviewed or a sample?
  How will results be summarized?
  What process will be used for discussing results and making recommendations?

- Practical considerations
  What is the time line for activities and review?
  What software will be used?
  How will e-portfolios integrate with other assessment systems?

CHAPTER 6

USING INDIRECT ASSESSMENT METHODS

In contrast to direct assessment methods that ask students to demonstrate their learning explicitly, indirect methods ask students to reflect on their learning. Through questionnaires, interviews, focus groups, and other listening and observing approaches, educators can be receptive to the voices of their students. Because indirect methods address a wide range of topics and a variety of target groups, these methods often provide information that cannot be collected easily in any other way. Indirect approaches are frequently used in student affairs divisions and units, as well as in academic departments. At the institution level, student surveys are the most common means of assessment (Kuh, Jankowski, Ikenberry, and Kinzie 2014).

Using Surveys in Assessment

Surveying is the process of administering a set of predetermined questions— a questionnaire—to collect information from individuals in a target group about their characteristics, behaviors, attitudes, perceptions, and needs. Surveys most often make use of paper- or web-based questionnaires, but phone interviews, such as those conducted for marketing research, also can be used to administer the questions. To begin a survey project, researchers must decide on the purposes for the study; possibilities include gathering descriptive information on specific issues, comparing subgroups of respondents, tracking information over time, and examining relationships among variables (Woosley and Miller, n.d.).

Topics for Assessment Surveys

Faculty and staff should refer to their assessment plans for guidance in selecting among possible survey topics, asking themselves precisely what questions need to be answered. Surveys often are used to examine the values and attitudes of students, including the importance they place on college goals such as gaining a broad education. Carnegie Mellon University (n.d.a) students in an art history class were surveyed to gauge their confidence, motivation, and goals for writing. The results helped the professor frame his discussions of a writing assignment. Reynolds (n.d.), who assisted with the study, notes that affective traits like motivation and expectations for achievement can greatly influence a student's writing.

Survey questions may ask students to indicate their level of satisfaction with specific aspects of their experiences. Faculty at Grinnell College (n.d.) developed the Survey of Undergraduate Research Experiences (SURE) to collect data from undergraduates who completed a summer research experience. A later survey, the SURE-III, collected quantitative data on the benefits of undergraduate research projects completed during the academic year. It also addressed peer and mentor roles of undergraduate researchers. Many surveys ask students to report on their actual experiences, including their class attendance patterns and their out-of-class activities. Students also can indicate their future plans, including those for continuing education after college.

Some surveys gather information about student needs for various support services. At Ball State University (2014a) the MAP-Works system from Educational Benchmarking allows administrators such as residence hall staff and advisors to identify at-risk students. This questionnaire is administered to incoming first-year and second-year students during the early part of fall semester. Students are asked about their adjustment to college life such as their degree of homesickness and their intention to stay at the institution. After completing the questionnaire, all students receive a customized report that helps them understand their strengths and weaknesses in areas that are important to persistence and retention.

To determine relative areas of strength and weakness with respect to specific learning outcomes, students may be asked to reflect on their preparation by completing various rating scales or responding to open-ended questions. For example, principals at the Higher Education Data Sharing Consortium (HEDS) administer a survey that assesses the literacy skills and research experiences of current students. To assist with analysis, surveys may include demographic and background questions asking for such data as age, gender, class level, and major. To help interpret answers about specific courses or programs, filtering questions such as attendance or participation are helpful (Cooper, 2009).

Selecting and Using Various Target Groups

A great strength of surveys is that they can reach a wide variety of specific audiences, including current and future students, nonreturning students, graduates, faculty, employers, and parents. Often interest is in comparing groups of individuals, so more than one target is chosen. Separate surveys for the selected groups can contain a common core of questions.

Some survey projects include a broad range of students. In 2013, the Student Experience in the Research University (SERU) questionnaire was administered for the first time at the University of Iowa (2014), and all degree-seeking undergraduates were invited to participate. Tell Us, the name the university uses for this survey, is an initiative of the Center for Studies in Higher Education at the University of California-Berkeley and is used at a consortium of fifteen universities. It provides an overview of student experiences with a focus on the major. All students receive the same set of core questions and one randomly assigned module that addresses areas such as global experiences or student life and development.

More often, a specific group of students is targeted. Staff from Ball State University's Office of Institutional Effectiveness (2014a) conduct an orientation survey of incoming first-year students during the second day of freshman orientation. The questionnaire gathers data in eleven categories, including students' high school background and experiences, decision to attend Ball State, choice of major and career, and competence with various technologies.

Surveys often are used to obtain information from alumni. In addition to employment information, the alumni questionnaire available through HEDS assesses the long-term impact of various teaching practices on learning outcomes. Office of Assessment Services staff at Northern Illinois University (2014) administer an annual alumni survey to all graduates from the past calendar year. To satisfy requirements of the Illinois Board of Higher Education, office personnel also regularly conduct a baccalaureate survey for graduates five and nine years out.

To determine employment outcomes for students who participated in career technical education programs at community colleges in California, the Research and Planning Group for California Community Colleges (n.d.) collaborated with the Bay Area Community College Consortium and practitioners from around the state to develop a universally available survey methodology. Students who were enrolled in 2010–2011 but not in 2011–2012 (including completers) were surveyed. Questions asked whether students became employed within their field of study, if their course work had a positive effect on their earning potential, and why dropouts did not return. The questionnaire was administered to forty-seven thousand students in early 2013, first by e-mail, then by US mail, and then by telephone. The respective response rates were 8 percent, 7 percent, and 10 percent.

Employers too can be surveyed to find out in general about their expectations for the skills of college graduates they hire or about the preparation of graduates from specific institutions. Since 1993, a locally developed employer questionnaire has been administered by staff at Missouri State University (2013) to determine how well the institution is responding to educational needs related to employment. The survey also assesses the quality of the career planning and placement office and the office of cooperative education.

Faculty comprise another group that may be asked to participate in surveys. The Higher Education Research Institute at UCLA, for example, maintains a faculty survey that has been used at more than one thousand institutions since 1989 to examine faculty practices, values, and priorities. Staff at the University of North Dakota (2011) recently administered the Faculty Survey of Student Engagement, a companion to the National Survey of Student Engagement; a summary of results is available on the university's website.

Response Types and Scales

Some survey questions are open-ended, allowing participants to use their own words as they respond. Alumni, for example, are frequently asked to provide suggestions for improvements to programs and services. Most survey questions are closed-ended, with a list of possible options provided for respondents to select.

Several response options are available for closed-ended questions and must be carefully chosen to fit the topic of interest and the anticipated analysis. Because assessment surveys are often concerned with student attitudes and opinions, response categories based on a Likert scale are commonly used. Students choose among the categories: Strongly Agree, Agree, Neither Agree nor Disagree, Disagree, and Strongly Disagree. Variations in the number of categories and the exact wording of options are common. To force a choice between agreeing and disagreeing, the middle option may be eliminated. Usually "I am satisfied with . . ." is included as a stem and followed by a series of items. Alternatively, students can be asked to agree or disagree with a series of free-standing statements such as, "My advisor was very helpful." If the latter approach is used, some items should be stated in a negative way to make sure respondents answer carefully.

The term *Likert-like scale* may be used to refer to various ordered response categories that are symmetrical, with an equal number of positive and negative possible answers. *Importance* and *preparation ratings* scales of this type often are used together. Porter (2011) criticizes the use of scales that gather self-reported information about preparation because he believes the results may be biased in a way that puts respondents in a good light. The tendency to answer questions in socially desirable ways can be a source of bias for some survey questions.

Questions asking for self-reports about gains in learning also have been criticized (Bowman, 2013). To answer correctly, students need to estimate their current and previous levels of skills and calculate the difference. Although they are reasonably accurate in assessing their current skill levels, they tend to overestimate growth in skills. Furthermore, the tendency to estimate skill gains incorrectly is related to factors such as class level (seniors are more accurate), the particular skill (gains for well-defined skills are more accurately reported), and survey length (accuracy declines as students complete a long questionnaire). Response categories that address these questions must allow students to indicate negative as well as positive growth. Bowman suggests that questions about self-reported gains be abandoned, at least with respect to cognitive items.

Assessment surveys that contain questions about student participation in various activities can include a response scale with categories such as Not at All, A Few Times, and Once a Month. Saunders and Cooper (2009) criticize a scale of Never, Rarely, Occasionally, and Frequently as too vague. Another approach is to provide a series of categories containing intervals of numbers or hours as a response scale, but the categories must be chosen realistically. The selection among these approaches is important because it affects the type of analysis that can be conducted. Porter (2011) believes that college students, like the rest of us, have trouble accurately reporting on activities and behaviors. He encourages researchers to pay more attention to the time frame for questions about the frequency of activities. For example, the time frame for a question about the frequency of coming to class without reading the assignment should be no longer than a week. Some questions should refer to the previous twenty-four hours.

Response categories that contain ordered choices do not fit all questions. For example, if students are asked why they entered a particular program, faculty need to provide a set of responses from which to choose, such as academic reputation, location, and size. All possibilities that have a high likelihood of being chosen by respondents should be included. In some cases, respondents will be able to choose more than one response, or they may be asked to rank-order their responses. Instructions must be clear.

Writing Survey Questions

Some general guidelines are helpful when designing questionnaires. Items should be worded as clearly as possible and should ask for information that respondents will be able to provide. For example, alumni should not be asked about programs or services using new names or titles. To reduce bias, questions should avoid leading respondents into providing particular answers. Asking students about their "level of agreement" with a series of statements is preferable to simply asking them how much they agree. Each question should be able to stand alone. Inquiring whether students received helpful career information from faculty or career counselors is actually asking two separate questions. Response categories provided for questions about continuous variables such as grade point average should cover all possibilities and not overlap. Complex concepts such as leadership should be addressed by several items (Bowman, 2013). Cornell University's (n.d.c) Office of Institutional Research and Planning website provides a helpful overview of survey design, including item construction.

In general, the layout of questions should be logical, with related questions appearing together. Skip patterns that allow respondents to bypass some questions on surveys should be clearly marked. Web delivery is creating new survey opportunities. Qualtrics, for example, allows for customized design, skip patterns, and randomization of questions and response choices. Ehrmann and Peterson (2010) describe matrix surveys. In a matrix survey, the questions that participants see and the wording of response alternatives are determined in advance based on the personal characteristics of the respondents. Using this approach, numerous stakeholders can contribute their own questions for a subset of respondents.

Questionnaire Administration

The possibilities for survey administration have expanded greatly in the past several years. Several companies provide survey software containing user-friendly analysis tools (counts, percentages, graphs, and cross-tabs), and the speed with which results are available is very attractive. The division of student affairs at the University of Utah (2012b) provides a protocol for survey administration methods based on Campus Labs technology. The application can be used to load surveys to several iPod Touches. Then the iPod Touches can be used to collect data from respondents while they are at an event, with survey results immediately available for viewing. Staff from the Student Affairs Research Evaluation and Planning Office at Oregon State University (2012) use thirty iPod Touches to collect data from rubrics and checklists, as well as from surveys at workshops and events on their campus.

Cover Letter and Invitation Surveys generally include a cover letter or e-mail invitation that provides a clear explanation of the reasons for the survey and how the information will be used. Typically the invitation comes from the most important person in the unit or division. College or university presidents often sign cover letters for alumni questionnaires. Gansemer-Topf and Wohlgemuth (2009) suggest that for some surveys, such as those in a residence hall, a cover letter from a student staff member may be more effective than one from a top administrator. At the University of Utah (2012b), staff can send e-mail invitations in their own name using the Campus Labs mailing information form. Each individual receiving the invitation is sent a unique link so that reminders can be sent to nonrespondents. Questionnaires can also be administered using a link posted directly to a website rather than using an e-mail list.

Anonymous versus Confidential Questionnaires Practitioners must decide whether questionnaire respondents will be anonymous or identified. If current or former students are identified, the institution's student records can be used to gather background information for analysis. Identification of respondents also facilitates awarding prizes and sending follow-up mailings. However, surveys that focus on personal behaviors may be answered more accurately by students who are given the opportunity to respond anonymously. In cases where students are identified, it is important to remind them that information will be treated confidentially. Similar to paper surveys, those conducted online can be *confidential* or *anonymous*. Washington State University's (2014) Skylight Survey System automatically provides anonymity by separating log-in information containing the respondent's identity from the individual's responses.

Encouraging Responses   Good choices about topics, wording, instructions, layout, and length can increase a survey's appeal—and therefore the response rate. Anything that takes more than ten minutes to complete is considered long. Reminder e-mails or follow-up mailings must be used to boost the overall response rate. In some cases, a notice is sent before the actual mailing to alert study subjects that a survey will be coming (Nulty, 2008). Incentives such as prizes or coupons can be offered to respondents. Some research suggests that a small, certain incentive, such as a coin or a dollar bill, provided with the survey request is more effective than a chance for something bigger at a later date (Gansemer-Topf and Wohlgemuth, 2009). The Residence Satisfaction Survey available through EBI is administered online at the University of Maryland Baltimore County (2014). Students are entered to win one of several prizes, including a tablet, funds for food, or priority for a single room in the residence hall. In addition, residence halls that achieve a 75 percent response rate receive three hundred dollars to spend on community needs.

An increase in the number of online surveys has led to a decline in response rates. Oregon State University (2012) experienced a drop in response to the National Survey of Student Engagement (NSSE) and asked faculty and staff to refrain from surveying first-year and senior students in the winter term when NSSE is administered. Faculty also were asked to encourage eligible students to respond to the questionnaire. To combat survey fatigue on some campuses, students are being contacted on their cell phones (Gansemer-Topf and Wohlgemuth, 2009). Phone interviews may be preferable when practitioners think respondents (such as nonreturning students) will have little interest in completing an online survey or returning a mailed questionnaire. To increase response rates, Gansemer-Topf and Wohlgemuth (2009) recommend that units consider sampling, coordinate efforts with other units, use a variety of delivery methods, and provide feedback. Concerned that the proliferation of surveys is becoming annoying, Cornell University's (n.d.c) IRP staff help to coordinate the timing of various surveys.

Other Considerations   Regardless of response rate, it is important to demonstrate how well those who completed a survey represent the overall group of potential respondents. Those who respond may not be representative of the entire group.

Staff from the Indiana University (IU) Center for Postsecondary Research have investigated whether conducting their annual survey of arts graduates strictly online has led to biased results. Researchers conducted a shadow study to solicit respondents using a variety of delivery modes, including paper, web, and phone. They found no meaningful difference in results between the shadow group and other respondents (Lindemann and Tipper, n.d.). The Strategic National Arts Alumni Project (SNAAP) is conducted in cooperation with degree-granting institutions that provide e-mail information for alumni (Indiana University, 2013).

Designing a good questionnaire is challenging. Surveys are very useful when quantitative information on a variety of topics is needed in a timely way. However, surveys may suffer from low response rates, and if response options are not chosen well, researchers may not be able to determine the answers to their assessment questions. Sometimes results are difficult to interpret and can be affected by the placement and wording of items. Except for open-ended questions, surveys offer few opportunities to probe areas of interest that are not predetermined. In addition, survey information is self-reported. Evidence about learning is indirect, and even factual information such as grade point average may not be provided accurately. Surveys nevertheless remain an extremely popular assessment technique.

Practitioners have a choice of paper, web-based, and telephone surveys, although relatively few campuses use telephone surveys for assessment (Cooper, 2009). Studies of response rates for the various approaches produce mixed results. Sending a paper questionnaire in the mail with the opportunity to also fill it out online may solicit the best response, but negates some of the cost advantages of using the web. The first consideration in deciding among the various survey methods should be the assessment questions and the approach that will lead to the most accurate and useful results. As Knerr (2013) points out, practitioners must select questions of interest first, then methodology.

Seeking Help   Pike and Ouimet (2009) advise drawing on theory and expert opinion when constructing surveys. They applied a theory of socialization in graduate education when they developed a questionnaire for graduate and professional students. Pretesting questionnaires and having them reviewed by survey experts before they are distributed also is beneficial. They strongly recommend using a variety of methods and resources to "clarify unclear instructions or items, fix generation-gap items, and otherwise fine-tune" questionnaires (p. 9). Asking individual students to engage in cognitive interviews—reading a question and then voicing their understanding of it—can be particularly helpful in this regard. Many assessment websites, including those in student affairs divisions, share valuable information on creating and using surveys. Administrators at Oregon State University (2012) used their *Perspective* newsletter to deliver advice on designing a local survey.

Much of the information needed for outcomes assessment is already available on campus. Comprehensive surveys of current students or alumni gather information for divisions and departments about their own majors. If respondents are identified through mailing labels or other means, campus records can be used to determine their majors and other demographic information. Separate reports can then be created for each unit. In cases where students are not identified, they can be asked to self-report their major, and this information can be used to disaggregate results. At Northern Illinois University (2014), raw data and program-level reports for departments are made available using a secure Blackboard website. Raw data are available in Excel format so that program-level reports on data from alumni surveys can be created easily. On many campuses, academic and administrative units are invited to prepare supplemental questions for institution-wide surveys, an approach that allows faculty and staff to ask questions that are of most concern to them.

National Surveys for Assessment

Many campuses use commercially available standardized surveys in their assessment programs, particularly if they are interested in obtaining comparable data. Some widely used questionnaires are the ACT Engage survey, surveys from the Cooperative Institutional Research Program (CIRP), and the National Survey of Student Engagement (NSSE).

The ACT Engage survey, designed for use with college freshmen prior to the start of college, measures student behaviors and psychosocial skills that research holds are related to success in college. Questions focus on three domains—student motivation and skills, social engagement, and self-regulation—and results are reported for ten scales within these domains. The survey yields reports for students, advisors, and campus administrators. Students receive a score report that shows how they compare to similar students, identifies strengths, and shares opportunities for improvement. The advisors' reports contain similar information along with success indices predicting retention and grade point averages. Approximately 24 percent of those who do drop out are identified through this survey (Pike, 2012b). In addition to identifying at-risk students, survey results are used for assessment and evaluation studies of intervention programs focused on student success. Researchers can control for differences in student characteristics as they examine the effects of various programs. The EBI survey MAP-Works uses a similar framework but is administered after students begin their programs.

The CIRP survey for freshmen has been available for nearly fifty years and is currently administered by the Higher Education Research Institute (HERI) at UCLA. The Freshman Survey is administered before students begin their college work and gathers background information on student characteristics, as well as student perceptions about their academic preparation for college, information about reasons for attending college, and expectations for their academic success. Participating institutions receive a report, including summary data by gender and full- and part-time status, as well as comparison data from other institutions. The CIRP program also includes a questionnaire to be used at the end of the first year (Your First College Year) and one for seniors (College Senior Survey). An online Diverse Learning Environments (DLE) questionnaire can be administered at the end of the second and third years. It measures campus climate and educational outcomes related to areas such as diversity and civic engagement.

NSSE leadership recently revised their questionnaire to reflect feedback and research and to update terminology. Approximately 27 percent of NSSE items have been substantially rewritten, and an additional 23 percent are new. The new questionnaire provides ten engagement indicators organized into four themes: academic challenge, learning with peers, campus environments, and experiences with faculty. The revised instrument provides information on student involvement in high-impact educational practices and includes questions about what instructors do in their classes. Participants also can include optional modules on topics such as writing and learning with technology. Pike (2013b) notes that the ability to compare results from the two versions of the questionnaire is limited. Even with respect to items that have stayed the same, format and order effects may influence responses. In fall 2013, NSSE staff released results from the first administration of the revised instrument based on responses for about 335,000 students from nearly six hundred colleges. The report, *A Fresh Look at Student Engagement,* includes several findings. For example, as a group, freshmen who participate in high-impact practices achieve greater self-reported gains in knowledge, skills, and personal development.

Pike (2012a) used an "Assessment Measures" column in *Assessment Update* to discuss the validity of survey instruments. Before selecting an instrument, assessment professionals must develop a clear idea of its purpose. For example, the NSSE benchmarks were developed to support institutional and group-level decisions, not to make decisions about individuals. CIRP's Your First College Year survey also is designed to provide aggregated data for decisions such as whether to continue offering freshman learning communities. As Pike notes, finding that these surveys do not predict student grades or persistence is not a valid criticism because they were not designed for this purpose. Pike concludes that the CIRP and NSSE surveys have been useful to institutions in many ways and thus pass the test of consequential validity. Ewell (2009) points out that surveys addressing campus climate and behavior may be more amenable to action than assessment methods such as standardized tests that produce general conclusions that are difficult to interpret.

NSSE administrators (2012) have published a second volume of examples, *Moving from Data to Action*, demonstrating the actions universities and colleges have taken based on NSSE findings. Among many others, these actions include using results to improve retention at Allegheny College, improving writing across the curriculum at Auburn University, and improving the first-year experience at Franklin Pierce University.

Using Focus Groups in Assessment

Focus groups provide an excellent opportunity to listen to the voices of students, explore issues in depth, and obtain insights that might not occur without the discussion they provide. Focus groups are carefully planned discussions designed to generate in-depth consideration of a narrowly defined topic. A small number of questions is developed in advance of the meeting and serves as the basis for discussion. Typically the goal is to examine perceptions, feelings, attitudes, and ideas rather than to reach consensus or solve problems. Focus group participants are given adequate time to discuss topics at length, and group interaction is encouraged. Participants generally include a trained moderator, an assistant moderator, and a small number of carefully selected interview subjects. Focus group projects should begin with a specific plan that identifies how information will be used. Goals may include determining key ideas, describing participants' language, examining consensus on a topic, and finding direction for further analysis. Assistance with planning and conducting focus groups is available on many campuses. For example, the Office of Assessment Evaluation and Research in the division of student affairs at the University of Utah

(2012a) conducts focus groups for clients in order to gather qualitative information on various issues.

Topics, Target Groups, and Participants

Focus groups can be used for many purposes. They are often conducted before surveys are designed as a means of gathering preliminary evidence on an issue. Alternatively, they may be conducted after survey results have been gathered to help interpret findings. Pike and Ouimet (2009) used focus groups to help develop response categories for a survey of graduate and professional students. The focus groups revealed that experiences in graduate school such as research and teaching assistantships and practica are dependent on the particular program in which students are enrolled. To reflect these differences, the researchers designed a web-based survey with multiple branches.

In addition to their use in conjunction with questionnaires, focus groups can be used to examine other topics, such as student satisfaction with various aspects of their academic programs. In the College of Education at James Madison University, faculty used focus groups to examine student opinions about the best way to administer course evaluations (Thelk, 2014). Often a specific group of students is of interest. To find out more about the curricular and cocurricular experiences of students who transfer to their institution, educators at Augustana College held a series of on-campus focus groups. Campus leaders were hopeful that they could use the information gained to improve the experiences of these students. The focus groups revealed that transfer students not only varied in age, but also in their economic and educational backgrounds, suggesting the need for a variety of services (Salisbury, 2013).

Recent or longer-term graduates, employers of graduates, and local business leaders are often willing to share their opinions. As part of a study of student services, researchers at the University of Alabama Birmingham conducted several focus groups with frontline staff members. The focus groups helped participants identify strategies and resources to do their jobs more effectively and had beneficial results in terms of improved communication among staff (Perkins and Fifolt, 2013).

Focus group participants should be well matched on characteristics of interest so that results can be associated with these characteristics. Matching also avoids a situation where the thinking of one group dominates that of another. Focus groups at St. Louis Community College were conducted to study issues related to transfer enrollment. Transfer Education Assessment

Committee members were particularly interested in whether the college's students were well prepared to succeed at the most popular transfer university. The committee developed research questions for three groups of students who already had transferred: recent, established, and graduating transfers. Although findings differed for the three groups, the focus group process revealed overall that students did not seek advice as much as college administrators preferred. One outcome of the study was to bring students who had transferred back to the campus to speak with current students (Cosgrove and McDoniel, 2009).

To identify specific participants, campus records can be used to generate a list of students' names from which a random sample can be drawn. Convenience sampling involves inviting students who are readily available. To find willing participants for assessment related to specific courses, teachers may give small incentives such as extra points toward students' grades. Occasionally a snowball technique is used in which selected participants are asked to suggest other individuals who have characteristics similar to their own, perhaps to participate in a later group. It is not necessary for all participants to be strangers, but too much familiarity can inhibit discussion. Some practitioners encourage students to participate in focus groups by providing sodas and pizza or offering a prize or a small stipend (Gansemer-Topf and Wohlgemuth, 2009).

The Moderator's Role

The success of a focus group is largely dependent on the preparation of the moderator, who must be an impartial participant with good listening skills. Although they need not be experts on the topic being considered, moderators need enough familiarity with the subject matter to be able to lead the discussion effectively. Moderators must create a comfortable environment where all participants feel free to express their thoughts and opinions. To start, moderators should say why the group has been brought together and what will occur. Ground rules for appropriate behavior, such as speaking one at a time, also can be presented. Participants should be told that they need not reach consensus in their thinking and that, in fact, a variety of viewpoints is encouraged.

At North Carolina A&T State University (NCA&T), students have the opportunity to lead focus groups (Baker, 2012a). Faculty and administrators on that campus have created a unique project, the Wabash-Provost Scholars Program (WPSP), through which undergraduate students participate in the campuses' culture of inquiry, collecting evidence that is used to improve the university. The scholars are trained to conduct student focus groups, implement surveys, and use institutional review board (IRB) protocols. NCA&T educators initially created the WPSP to examine how students felt about faculty interest in their growth. The question was generated after reviewing evidence from the university's participation in the Wabash National Study of Liberal Arts Education. In subsequent years, topics have focused on NCA&T's intellectual climate, including issues such as admissions policies. With faculty guidance, scholars analyze and summarize data, develop written reports, and present their results on and off campus. Scholars enroll in a one-credit-hour course that may be repeated.

Developing Questions and Summarizing Results

Focus groups require a precise set of clear questions. Ordinarily the first question will be one that all participants can answer so that each participant has the chance to speak. This is followed by four or five questions about the topic of interest, usually starting with questions that are general and following with those that are more specific and of greatest interest. Frequently the last question is used to identify participants' conclusions, preferences, or recommendations.

Student affairs professionals at the University of Alabama Birmingham developed a detailed protocol of this kind for a series of focus groups and interviews conducted on their campus (Fifolt, 2013). With respect to types of questions, asking participants to "think back" about their experiences is preferred to asking them to project forward. Asking "why" should be avoided because this can be difficult to answer and may be threatening (Saunders and Cooper, 2009). If the project involves several types of groups, the questions should be coordinated but need not be exactly the same for each group. Questions for subsequent sessions may be modified on the basis of findings from initial sessions. The object is to find useful information, not to follow a protocol rigidly.

An assistant moderator take notes capturing important themes, various points of view, and quotes that seem representative. Tone of voice and group dynamics should be noted if they are important. Even if focus groups are being taped, assistant moderators need to take notes as a backup. Notes taken by assistant moderators should be summarized by either question or topic. To analyze the information, investigators code and sort responses into a number of broad categories After three audiotaped focus groups were completed with students who had been resident assistants at

Pennsylvania State University, co-investigators coded transcript material for emerging themes (Knerr, 2013). Then they met to review their findings and develop a final theme structure. A fourth reviewer synthesized and checked the information for completeness and consistency. In some cases, focus groups are videotaped, and researchers analyze the tapes looking for particular responses or behaviors.

Other Considerations

Neutral meeting rooms with appropriate seating where everyone is visible are essential. To be confident in their conclusions, researchers should replicate focus groups. Generally six to nine people per group and three to four replications for each type of group are recommended. However, researchers should be guided by their needs, working until they are no longer gathering new information (Knerr, 2013). Some find the value of individual opinions to be the most compelling aspect of focus groups, but a drawback is the restricted ability to generalize from results. Participants are usually not selected at random and may not reflect accurately the opinions of a larger group. Focus groups do not yield results suitable for statistical testing and may not work with sensitive issues. Moderators need to be adept at eliciting accurate rather than socially desirable responses. Training is helpful. As Knerr (2013) points out, interview and focus group methods are "not as easy as they first appear" (p. 38).

With respect to their strengths, focus groups allow in-depth discussion of a topic. Because of their flexible format, they also allow consideration of ideas and insights that may be entirely new to those who are conducting the focus group. Writing about his insights after conducting focus groups with students who had transferred to Augustana's campus, Salisbury (2013) stated, "I was certainly one who had not thought through the implications of this diversity among our transfer students before holding these focus groups and hearing what these students had to say." Focus groups must contain appropriate participants, a good protocol for questions, and an effective moderator. If these aspects are well planned, focus groups should provide useful information (Woosley, 2009).

Additional Indirect Methods

In addition to surveys and focus groups, indirect assessment methods include techniques such as interviews, analysis of written materials, and examination of various documents and records. We provide some discussion and examples here.

Interviews

Although structured *interviews* contain preset sequential questions and strict guidelines for interviewers, other interviews permit dialogue to proceed in various directions, thus allowing researchers to get an in-depth look at the subject's perspective. Open-ended or unstructured interviews contain a topic or theme but no predetermined questions. In contrast, semi-structured interviews usually have a set of questions that can be answered in any order and for which wording can vary. In either case, additional questions can be added to pursue promising directions.

Staff from the division of student affairs at the University of Alabama Birmingham conducted hundreds of interviews with students, alumni, faculty, staff, and others (Fifolt, 2013). Using a process called *appreciative inquiry*, internal and external stakeholders shared experiences and stories in considering the organization's future. All conversations followed a general protocol using an interview summary sheet. Midlevel student affairs staff served as facilitators and later hand-coded the interview results. Verification techniques included triangulation (looking at the division through multiple perspectives and different observers), allowing stakeholders to view drafts of results on the website and through town hall meetings, and providing an audit of all agendas and minutes.

Faculty interviews of students provide an excellent opportunity for student reflection. In the Physics and Astronomy Department at the University of Iowa (2013a), the department chair conducts an exit interview with each graduating senior. Students also can be interviewed for more specific reasons, such as to gather information before or after questionnaires are administered. Pike and Ouimet (2009) used one-on-one interviews with students to complete the design of a survey about civic engagement. Students were interviewed as they completed an online version of the proposed questionnaire to find out if they were interpreting the questions correctly and to see how they worked through survey instructions.

As with focus groups, the value of interviews reflects the skill of the interviewer, who should guide rather than influence the subject's responses. The interviewer must be able to paraphrase and summarize the direction of the conversation so that the purposes of the study are accomplished. The Vanderbilt University (n.d.) website contains helpful advice, including a recommendation to let subjects know the questions in advance.

Written Materials

Reflective statements, journal writing, and open-ended comments on surveys can be used to gather indirect assessment evidence. Portfolios provide important opportunities for students to reflect on their learning—to share their understanding of what they have learned and their reactions to that learning (Sternberg, Penn, and Hawkins, 2011). Rubrics provide a way to quantify results from portfolios. However, to summarize the indirect evidence contained in reflective statements, faculty and/or staff can read a sample of student reflections and use content analysis to group findings in various meaningful categories. At Truman State University (2011) this approach is used to categorize student descriptions of their most important learning experience.

Talisman and Westcott (2012) from Juniata College have examined student reflections as they study the effects on student outcomes of attendance at cultural events. First-year students enrolled in a writing seminar submitted reflection papers for each event they attended, describing their expectations for the event as well as summarizing and critiquing it. Approximately seven hundred reflection papers were coded across several dimensions to gauge how attendance at these campus events influences student development, particularly thinking or behavior. Students were involved in the data analysis.

Staff at Sullivan University analyzed *student writing* to address concerns about the quality of student services provided on campus. Several students were asked to write about what they mean when they say they get the runaround, define the term *runaround*, and describe what happened the last time they experienced it. To interpret these stories, researchers used techniques from computational linguistics, including the identification of important entities, events, and themes. Researchers discovered that the Financial Planning Office was most often the source of a runaround, but was also frequently mentioned as providing good service if problems were solved. A year later, after training of financial aid staff, focus groups and interviews showed students were no longer experiencing the runaround from Financial Planning. The researchers conclude that linguistic approaches provide an effective way to analyze qualitative data (Houlette, 2012).

Journal writing provides another approach that students can use to share their reactions and explore their experiences. Moon (2010) suggests learning journals, logs, and reflective diaries as methods to personalize and deepen learning. Journals allow students to use their own language as well as personal concepts and definitions as they write about their experiences.

Journals may involve freewriting or have some structure. Double-entry journals can be used to encourage students to revisit their original reflections. Reflective comments can be examined for indirect evidence of learning, including thoughts about experiences and perceptions of learning.

At Carnegie Mellon University (n.d.a), a faculty member used student journals to monitor thinking in his statistics course (DiPietro, n.d.). To initiate dialogue with students and support their thinking, students were required to write in their journals weekly in response to a prompt. The teacher examined the journals to provide written feedback, such as suggesting a website or asking a follow-up question. If the entries collectively revealed a misunderstanding, the topic was addressed in class.

Analysis of open-ended comments from surveys is a frequently used approach to indirect assessment. At the University of Iowa, a locally developed senior survey is administered at the time students apply to graduate and enjoys a 90 percent response rate, with two-thirds of respondents completing open-ended questions (Jacobson, 2012). A group of faculty and staff was asked to examine a set of open-ended responses and to tally the number falling into each of several categories based on the stem: "Student response suggests the effect of . . ." Possible response categories were "institution, "particular faculty or staff," "external events," "student's own actions," "other students' actions," or "nothing to report." Themes or comments that stood out also were recorded.

At the University of Alabama Birmingham, representatives from several student affairs offices came together to explore the possibility of a one-stop model of student services (Perkins and Fifolt, 2013). As at Sullivan University, staff looked at several sources of information to determine what students mean when they say they get the "runaround." The group looked at open-ended questions from previous surveys. Negative comments were organized into three groups: people, process, or information. Researchers found that the runaround was both physical and metaphorical and that it applied to the website too in the form of a virtual runaround.

Documents and Records

Documents and records provide another opportunity to examine the environment for learning on a given campus (Knerr, 2013). Documents may be preexisting, such as newsletters, minutes, or syllabi, or they may be generated as part of an assessment project, such as records of activities or time logs. Saunders and Cooper (2009) note the importance of developing a protocol before engaging in *document review*. The protocol should address the type and source of the documents to be reviewed, the questions to be asked about the documents, and an acceptable time frame for selecting the documents.

At Northern Illinois University, members of the Student Advisory Council on Learning Outcomes (SACLO) engaged in a review of *syllabi* (Niemi and Douglass, 2013). SALCO includes faculty, staff, and administrators, as well as students. The group addresses concerns that students are not well informed about learning objectives. One of its first projects was to examine how effectively learning objectives are communicated. SALCO members individually reviewed and evaluated syllabi from sixty general education courses. Results showed that only 35 percent of syllabi identified the courses as general education courses, and fewer stated general education or even course learning objectives. Members of SALCO made several recommendations for improving syllabi, including one that assignments be explicitly connected to learning objectives.

Student activities transcripts provide another set of records that can be useful for assessment. While they do not yield actual observations of student behavior, activities transcripts provide a record of student involvement. Students use their transcripts to record participation in athletics, student clubs, leadership experiences, employment, internships, and community service. They also may record honors received and programs attended. At the State University of New York at New Paltz (2013), students can enter more than two hundred possible experiences using an online form. On the form, they choose from some twenty possibilities the five skills or learning outcomes they believe they have gained from the experience. Completing the form generates e-mail to an appropriate campus employee who can verify the experience before it appears on the transcript. When linked to goals for learning and development, cocurricular transcripts have the potential to help student affairs professionals answer important questions about how well their students are achieving expected learning outcomes. The transcripts permit tracking student participation in activities and programs, and they provide information for units to use to strengthen their programs. Transcripts help students to prepare résumés and graduate school applications, as well as to make better choices about using their time outside class. Several companies provide transcripts, including CollegiateLink.

Often several indirect methods are used together. An assessment project at Queen's University in Ontario, Canada, implemented multiple techniques to study a problem in the residence halls. Two service units were merged to form Housing and Hospitality Services. Custodial staff were not familiar with new processes, and students were experiencing delays in service responses. Surveys were administered to employees and students and external reviewers interviewed supervisors and staff and shadowed employees. Documentation of the current system processes also was reviewed. The study found that an online maintenance request order process was not working and that many staff wanted more authority for decision making. The director of Housing and Hospitality Services personally delivered the results of the study to staff. Several changes have been made, and processes continue to be documented and improved (Massey, Griffiths, and Corrigan, 2011).

Qualitative versus Quantitative Approaches

In this chapter, we have described several techniques that provide indirect evidence of learning. In addition to distinguishing between direct and indirect assessment methods, researchers distinguish between qualitative and quantitative approaches. Qualitative methods such as in-depth, open-ended interviews; observations of activities, behaviors, and interactions; and analysis of written documents yield direct quotations, descriptions, and excerpts rather than numbers. Through examining diverse opinions and perspectives, qualitative researchers describe findings within a particular context. Validity and reliability often depend as much on the skill and integrity of the researcher as on the quality of the instrument.

Quantitative methods are distinguished by their emphasis on numbers, measurement, experimental design, and statistical analysis. Interest is in analyzing a large number of cases using carefully constructed instruments that have been evaluated for their reliability and validity. Researchers use predetermined response categories to capture various experiences and perspectives of individuals, often with the goal of examining relationships or patterns among the variables.

Both qualitative and quantitative methods have value. Steinke and Fitch (2011) point out that "there is never one true measure of a complex construct," and they advocate the use of multiple measures (p. 22). At Georgia Institute of Technology (Georgia Tech) (2014), practitioners do not assume that assessment is quantitative. Georgia Tech's assessment website states, "Often the best indicator of student learning can be expressed better as a narrative or a performance than as a number." Numerical scales or rubrics can be useful, but their accuracy depends on a good understanding of the concepts behind the numbers. As Sternberg et al. (2011) point out, it is not clear that rubrics "capture all or even most of the elements that make for a distinguished portfolio, especially because those elements may differ from one portfolio to another" (p. 10).

Quantitative methods can be used to analyze complex issues such as predicting persistence. Knerr (2013) suggests using qualitative measures to understand and create meaning of the world. Qualitative methods can uncover evidence about previously unrecognized or poorly understood circumstances and can help make sense of how and why actual practices differ from stated ones. Several qualitative methods can be used to generate direct as well as indirect evidence of learning and development.

The contrast between quantitative and qualitative methods is an important one. Just as some faculty and staff are more comfortable with descriptive approaches, others are more comfortable with quantitative approaches. In many cases, projects include a mix. As Sternberg et al. (2011, p. 11) conclude, "It is unlikely that there ever will be one perfect measure." But many useful approaches exist and, in many cases, they are best used together. We turn now to classroom assessment techniques that most often are qualitative, indirect assessment methods.

Classroom Assessment Techniques

More than a quarter-century ago, Tom Angelo and Patricia Cross (1993) began to develop and share *classroom assessment techniques* (CATs) as a means to bring assessment issues into closer alignment with faculty interests. Information on these techniques is available on many campus websites, including those at Oakland Community College (2009) and Iowa State University (n.d.). Here we review CATs, including their purposes, methods, and potential.

Rather than relying on informal methods, CATs provide a systematic means for instructors to acquire information from students about how they are learning. Teachers use this information to make day-to-day adjustments in their instruction. Classroom assessment uses small-scale techniques that can be administered in a few minutes at any time during a class period. CATs are usually ungraded and anonymous exercises and are considered formative methods of assessment. *Classroom Assessment Techniques: A Handbook for College Teachers* (Angelo and Cross, 1993) contains complete descriptions of fifty techniques, examples of how the techniques have been used, and the pros and cons of each CAT.

Classroom assessment techniques fall into three broad categories. The techniques in the first group are used to assess course-related knowledge and skills. When using a minute paper, faculty typically ask students to indicate the *most important* thing they learned during that class period and their *most important* unanswered question. The actual questions can vary—any that prompt short written responses from students can work. The background knowledge probe focuses on students' prior learning and enables instructors to find a starting point for presenting material. Faculty ask students to rate their degree of knowledge or understanding of various key course-related areas on a four- or five-point scale. The second group of CATs is used to find out about students' attitudes, values, and self-awareness. Process analysis asks students to keep logs of the steps they use to carry out their assignments and to draw conclusions about their approaches. For example, a biology teacher may ask students to document the procedures they use to carry out an experiment. In punctuated lectures, the instructor actually stops the class and asks students to reflect on their thoughts and activities during the previous few minutes. Students also are asked to write down any insights about how what they were doing helped or hindered their learning.

The third set of CATs is used to assess students' reactions to specific aspects of instruction, including class activities, assignments, and materials, as well as teaching. Faculty on some campuses are using CATs to gather midcourse teaching evaluations. At the University of Nevada, Las Vegas, for example, faculty were dissatisfied with end-of-course faculty evaluations (Bubb et al., 2013). A course evaluation work group found disparity among departments in the types and numbers of questions on the instruments. In addition, paper versions were labor intensive, and electronic versions suffered from low response rates. To see if they could gather more meaningful information, several faculty experimented with midcourse evaluations using CATs. For example, in an educational psychology class, students were asked to indicate a new idea, a question, and a suggestion on an index card. The study found that both student learning and end-of-course teacher evaluations improved when midcourse evaluations were used.

To provide benefits to students, teachers who use CATs must summarize responses and share results with the class. In large classes, teachers can select samples of responses to examine. They must indicate to students how they intend to respond to results and what students themselves need to do to be more successful. Classroom assessment is a three-step process: planning, implementing, and responding.

Classroom assessment has great potential to help faculty improve classroom teaching. Teachers can identify specific problems, such as sequencing issues or unclear concepts. Michael Bridges (n.d.), a faculty member at Carnegie Mellon University (n.d.a), wanted more information about the concepts that his students were having difficulty with in a large-lecture psychology class. In order to assess students' understanding in a timely way and to engage students more actively during the lecture, Bridges used a clicker system to track responses to concept questions relating to the lectures. Multiple-choice questions were administered during the class period, and the software he used provided immediate item analysis showing the percentages of students selecting each response. Although Bridges found that he lost some control of the pace of the lectures, he was able to respond to students' needs by providing additional examples and demonstrations. Classroom assessment techniques can be used in settings other than classrooms. For example, out-of-class learning activities, such as leadership training or community experiences, can be evaluated using these techniques, as can workshops and seminars. Some instructors conduct classroom assessment techniques online. Baepler (2011) suggests using Google Docs. After a classroom assessment form is created, the URL can be sent to students, whose responses can be collected and organized in a Google spreadsheet.

What potential does classroom assessment have to provide helpful information about how programs are working overall? St. John's University (2014) faculty include classroom assessment among a list of indirect measures for assessing student learning outcomes for a program. Because classroom assessment projects are often undertaken on the initiative of individual instructors, it can be challenging to get the results to add up to a coherent picture of what is going on in a program. Nevertheless, a faculty meeting can be a forum for discussing what has been learned. Alternatively, a short questionnaire can be developed for faculty, asking them to reflect on what they learned about critical common goals through the techniques they used during the semester. Faculty could also agree to use a common set of CATs. Care must be taken, however, not to impose so much direction that the ability of individual teachers to frame the questions, select the techniques, and analyze the results for their own use is lost.

CHAPTER 7

ASSESSING LEARNING IN THE MAJOR

Students place great importance on selecting a major. Although they value a broad education, pursuing degrees as preparation for careers is more likely to be considered "very important" by entry-level students. In 2012, 88 percent of respondents to the freshman survey conducted by the Cooperative Institutional Research Program (CIRP) indicated that "to be able to get a better job" was a very important reason for deciding to go to college; about 73 percent indicated "to gain a general education and appreciation of ideas" was very important. At the time we prepared our first edition of this book, the respective percentages for 1997 were 75 and 61, so both reasons have increased in importance, but the gap between them has stayed about the same (Cooperative Institutional Research Program, 2012).

Teaching faculty take on several interrelated roles. They educate students with respect to their specific disciplines; reinforce the knowledge, skills, and values graduates need to function in society; and help prepare graduates for work or further education. In this chapter, we provide examples of how faculty use assessment to examine whether they are accomplishing these multiple purposes. We turn first to some evidence about the workplace skills expected of graduates.

In an aptly titled report, *It Takes More Than a Major: Employer Priorities for College Learning and Student Success*, the results of a 2013 employer survey conducted by Hart Research Associates for the Association of American

Colleges and Universities (AAC&U) were presented. More than 90 percent of respondents agree that a candidate's demonstrated capacity to think critically, communicate clearly, and solve complex problems is more important than the undergraduate major. Furthermore, when asked to choose which is most important, a greater percentage chose graduates having both field-specific and broad knowledge (55 percent) compared to having knowledge of a range of fields (29 percent) or of a specific field (16 percent).

Areas that employers say should receive more emphasis in the curriculum include critical thinking and analytic reasoning (82 percent); ability to analyze and solve complex problems (81 percent); oral and written communication (both 80 percent); application of knowledge and skills to real-world settings (78 percent); locating, organizing, and evaluating information from multiple sources (71 percent); and innovation and creative thinking (71 percent). More than 60 percent would like more emphasis on teamwork (67 percent) and on ethical decision making (64 percent). When asked what might help graduates succeed in the workplace, employers strongly endorse a number of approaches, including developing skills to research questions related to the major, completing a significant project before graduation, and completing an internship or community-based field project. Because campuses cannot possibly do more of everything, assessment helps narrow the choices about what to emphasize and improve.

Here we review approaches that faculty and staff use to examine learning and development in the major. We discuss ways to implement and assess capstone experiences, portfolios, group work, and experiential learning such as internships and service-learning. Several strategies to include employers in assessment activities also are described.

Capstone Experiences and Courses

Capstone experiences for graduating seniors are designed to demonstrate comprehensive learning in the major through some type of product or performance. Many capstone experiences draw on earlier activities, giving students a chance to make connections and integrate what they have learned. In some cases, the capstone experience is the final submission of a portfolio that the student has developed over several years of study. Capstone experiences may also include written projects, research papers, demonstrations, exhibits, or other artifacts. In addition to emphasizing work related to the major, capstone experiences can require students to demonstrate how well they have mastered important learning objectives from the institution's general education program, including critical thinking and problem solving, as well as attitudes and values such as an appreciation of lifelong learning. At the University of LaVerne (Redman, 2013), for example, the goals of general education are embedded in the capstone experience.

Capstone Experiences

Faculty on many campuses have developed challenging capstone experiences that build on students' previous work. At Hampshire College (Wenk and Rueschmann, 2013), the senior capstone is the central activity of the final year, and the curriculum leads purposefully toward this project. At Princeton University (2014), students complete a senior thesis or substantial independent project that allows them to pursue original research and scholarship in a field of their choosing. Seniors work one-on-one with a faculty member who guides development of the project. Planning for the senior thesis starts in the junior year with completion of a junior paper.

At the College of Wooster (2014), all seniors complete a year-long independent study project. Students meet regularly with their advisors to develop topics that require a literature review, lab research, or artistic expression. Students learn how to develop action plans, analyze problems, and communicate results. In the spring, seniors participate in a senior research symposium to celebrate their accomplishments and to which other students, faculty, staff, parents, and community members are invited.

The College of Wooster, Allegheny College, Augustana College, and Washington College were funded by the Teagle Foundation to examine the use of capstone projects at the four campuses (Schermer and Gray, 2012). The project report contains an analysis of capstone experiences in terms of costs and benefits for students, mentors, departments, and institutions. Overall, faculty felt that getting to know students individually and evaluating their performances on capstone projects helped them assess and revise their curricula and teaching practices. The report describes the gold standard for capstone projects, including close mentoring, large scope, high challenge, reflection of students' interests, independence, presentation to others, and peer interaction. Projects should call for opportunities for students to display originality, critical thinking, problem solving, and writing skills. Students mention that these skills, as well as project management, research and inquiry, and lifelong learning skill, are most benefited by participation in a capstone project. Because students worked independently, concentrating on their disciplines, outcomes related to integrating learning across disciplines, using multiple perspectives, and teamwork were not particularly addressed. Data for the research came from surveys and focus groups of students, faculty mentors, and alumni. The results show consistency of reported gains by students and mentors across academic divisions, grade point average levels, and gender. Nearly half of the projects used rubrics for grading, and many involved two raters. One of the report's recommendations is to create a standardized instrument for campus use, as well as an assessment committee to provide oversight.

In her review of research on capstone experiences, Kinzie (2013) concludes that senior projects narrowly focused on the major do not provide much benefit to students in terms of integrating learning, often a goal of such experiences. She suggests explicitly articulating learning outcomes related to integration and developing interdisciplinary capstone experiences. Ferren and Paris (2013) recommend that faculty provide earlier experiences to prepare students for capstone projects. They believe that assessment, including student reflection and interviews, should be used to guide faculty in designing meaningful capstone experiences.

Faculty at California Polytechnic State University San Luis Obispo (2014a) have struggled with making their required senior project a valuable experience across campus. Its purpose is to provide a concluding experience that allows students to integrate what they have learned and demonstrate mastery-level skills, but the requirement was not in place in all departments. In addition, it was not clear if the university's learning objectives were being referenced in the projects, since these were adopted after the senior project was introduced. In preparation for an accreditation visit from the Western Association of Schools and Colleges (WASC), faculty undertook a university-wide assessment of the senior project. The assessment included a department survey to establish basic information about senior projects, including prevalence, form, outcomes, and policies. Surveys of students and faculty with follow-up focus groups to explore results were also included. In addition, all departments were asked to evaluate their capstone experiences using a WASC rubric designed for that purpose. The study revealed a broad emphasis on writing and critical thinking across the senior projects. As a result of the review, campus leaders expect program faculty to improve senior project policies and procedures.

As Berheide (2007) points out in her review of capstone experiences, good assessment practice calls for faculty to analyze student projects systematically for the evidence they provide about program quality and to use the evidence to make curricular improvements. In Berheide's Sociology Department at Skidmore, faculty examined senior seminar papers and found helpful information about students' outcomes with relatively little effort. For example, they found that goals for theory and methods needed some revision and that course sequencing could improve.

Capstone Courses

Completion of a capstone experience may be a specific graduation requirement that exists outside the courses necessary for graduation. In many cases, these experiences are located within capstone courses, usually relatively small classes designed to help students integrate their knowledge. Although a capstone course is valuable in itself, requiring students to complete one does not guarantee that they will have a capstone experience—a well-thought-out project that is comprehensive in nature and allows students to demonstrate a range of abilities. To provide useful assessment information and bring appropriate closure to students' college experiences, capstone projects need to reflect the goals and objectives for learning that have been agreed on for the program as a whole, and they need to be designed and evaluated by faculty responsible for the program, not just the course instructor (Hatfield, n.d.).

In the Department of Political Science and Public Administration at the University of North Dakota, the capstone course is designed around exercises that allow students to learn about and assess their own capabilities in critical thinking and communication (Sum and Light, 2010). Activities include a simulated academic conference in which students present papers written in prior courses and a "learning through teaching" activity in which teams of seniors present key political science concepts to groups of first-year students. Students also learn about and conduct peer-to-peer assessment of learning outcomes, providing useful data for the department to consider as it engages in a cycle of continuous improvement.

Because of the rich, direct information they provide about student learning, capstone projects are valuable for assessment of both individual students and programs. When situated in capstone courses, capstone products become authentic embedded assessment materials, aligned with normal classroom activities. If the desired result is improvement of student learning at the individual, program, and institution levels, Berheide (2007) believes that analyzing capstone projects is an effective method to achieve that result.

In addition to the capstone experience, capstone courses provide an appropriate time and place to collect other assessment information that can be useful in evaluating programs. In some cases, the capstone course is used to administer nationally available or locally developed tests that are focused on learning within the major. Questionnaires also can be administered in the capstone course. Reflecting their widespread acceptance, nearly 70 percent of program directors responding to a 2010 National Institute for Learning Outcomes Assessment survey report using a capstone course, and some 56 percent report using a culminating or final product (Ewell, Paulson, and Kinzie, 2011).

Portfolios

Portfolios, which we described in Chapter 5, are collections of student artifacts and reflections. E-portfolios store information in digital form, such as a video clip of a student teacher in the classroom or a senior engaged in a dance presentation. Program heads reveal that about 30 percent use portfolios in the disciplines. Education programs are most likely to use portfolios (75 percent). Health science, professional, arts and humanities, and computer science programs also report above-average use, with rates between 41 and 33 percent (Ewell, Paulson, and Kinzie, 2011).

The existence of a portfolio does not guarantee that its potential for assessment is being used. Portfolios pose a number of logistical choices about what to collect and how to assess the materials. At the program level, it is particularly important that faculty begin by reaching consensus about overall project goals. Although faculty on many campuses have designed portfolio projects to assess learning in the major, strategies differ with respect to when portfolios are created, what they contain, and how they are used.

In the Department of Political Science at Fort Hays University, students begin creating their portfolios in their orientation class. They add to their portfolios in intensive courses and complete them in the capstone class. For each outcome, students include *required elements*, such as assignments from specified courses. Students may also include *elective elements*, such as information from cocurricular activities, and *change elements*, such as future plans. The portfolio process includes the use of locally developed rubrics that help communicate expectations to students. The portfolios are used for advising students and for decision making at the program level (Mills, Bennett, Crawford, and Gould, 2009).

In the Grand Valley State University School of Social Work, students gather materials throughout their programs, but they create the portfolio itself in their capstone course. At that time, students are asked to choose among their materials and reflect on how their artifacts demonstrate that they have met educational objectives. To reflect new standards introduced by the Council on Social Work Education, faculty spent a year examining courses, identifying where required competences were taught, and designing a common assignment for each course that was clearly linked to competences and rubrics. Then a capstone e-portfolio project was created to house the assignments. The project is introduced at the school's annual orientation when students begin their programs. In the final semester, students create their e-portfolios, including a cover page for each competence. Students provide analysis of how the artifacts they selected demonstrate their mastery of the competence. They also provide self-assessment, a description of their professional development, and a plan for professional growth. Formative assessment is provided through feedback from faculty, and e-portfolio data are aggregated for program assessment (Schuurman, Berlin, Langlois, and Guevara, 2012).

Faculty in the Department of Business Administration at Lewis University designed a project to compare performance of students on entry-level papers with performance on senior portfolios. Focus was on student learning outcomes that "involve using qualitative and quantitative data and technological tools to retrieve, analyze, evaluate, and communicate information" (p. 9). Results, using a carefully developed rubric, showed growth, but the faculty were disappointed that some seniors were performing below acceptable levels. They therefore placed greater emphasis on the required narratives that students must include in their papers to explain the models they are using and added more writing instruction to the entry-level class (Klemic and Lovero, 2011). As these examples illustrate, portfolio strategies to assess learning in the major can differ greatly across campuses and still provide very useful information for assessment.

Some departments gather student assignments using their assessment management systems rather than portfolios. After contending with actual student artifacts that were gathered but not assessed, faculty in the School of Education at Millikin University recently moved to a paper-free environment: all current rubrics and forms are online. Annual faculty retreats are now held in May and August, at the Data Analysis and Review Event, to evaluate collected data. Several training sessions helped launch the updated system. The assessment coordinator visited classes to demonstrate the assessment management system and engage students in conversation about the assignments and their use in demonstrating standards (Magoulias, 2011).

Experiential Education

Experiential education is a general term used to describe academically related work or community experience. Internships, cooperative experiences, student teaching, and service-learning provide these kinds of opportunities, allowing students to be involved with the world outside the classroom.

Employers heartily endorse internships and community-based field projects as ways to connect the classroom to the real world (Hart Research Associates, 2013). And chief academic officers report increasing use of these strategies for assessing student performance (Kuh, Jankowski, Ikenberry, and Kinzie, 2014). Eyler (2009) believes that to justify the inclusion of experiential learning as part of the curriculum, attention needs to be paid to the quality of the intellectual, as well as the work, experience. She suggests several guidelines for creating high-quality experiential education programs: work or service explicitly related to the academic goals of the course or program; well-developed assessments that examine achievement of academic objectives; significant responsibility for the student; academic and site supervisors who understand the learning goals for the student and provide monitoring and feedback; preparation of students for the practical challenges of their placements and learning from the experience; and well-designed reflection opportunities to help students link experience and learning.

Eyler points out that even when professors understand the importance of reflection for linking subject matter and experience, they may find it difficult to design courses that accomplish this.

To determine whether standards such as these are met, experiential education should be assessed by three groups: students participating in the experience, faculty monitoring the experience, and on-site supervisors. Each brings a unique perspective and opportunity to examine how experiential education is functioning.

Internships

The term *internship* is used to describe work experiences that allow participants to explore a profession while they apply their academic skills on the job. Students often earn credit and may receive pay for involvement that will typically require a specified number of work hours. Many internships occur before the senior year in college. Some academic programs, such as journalism, may require all majors to participate in internships; most provide options about participating. *Cooperative education* refers to alternating work and learning experiences related to a specific course of study, with students typically earning pay as well as course credit. Data from the National Association of Colleges and Employers (2013b) indicate that two-thirds of 2013 graduates participated in internships or cooperative education and about half of these received pay.

O'Neill (2010) sees internships as a way for students to sort out connections among their interests, majors, and possibilities for careers. But not all internships fulfill this promise. In fact, compared to other high-impact learning strategies, O'Neill believes that internships have a greater degree of variability in terms of their learning potential. Of millions of definitions available on the Internet, O'Neill finds many differences and some commonalities among those she examined. Commonalities include a reflection component, onsite supervision and guidance, and exposure to a potential career or career interests. Rarely are learning goals mentioned. Standards from the Council for the Advancement of Standards in Higher Education (2012) call for internships that allow students to learn by doing and to reflect on their learning. In fact, reflection, feedback, and deliberation are what distinguish internships from volunteer work. The guidelines of the National Association of Colleges and Employers (2011) specify that internships should provide opportunities for students to apply knowledge gained in the classroom and develop transferable skills, not simply to perform routine work. The internship must have clearly defined learning objectives related to the professional goals of the student's academic coursework. Supervision by an experienced professional who provides routine feedback is also necessary.

AAC&U (2007) investigators attribute variability in the quality of internships to a lack of clarity in design, and O'Neill (2010) urges collegiate faculty to include learning goals as well as career development goals when designing internships. She suggests AAC&U's Liberal Education and America's Promise (LEAP) outcomes as candidates to consider for learning goals. Among career development goals, clarifying work interests, developing contacts, and creating work samples are possibilities she suggests. O'Neil also sees designing and assessing internships as natural areas for academic faculty to partner with student affairs professionals.

To evaluate internships, information must be obtained from students, supervisors, and instructors. Many approaches for student self-assessment and reflection are available and the requirements should be specified as part of the internship course. Interns may start out by completing written statements describing expected learning outcomes. They may be asked to maintain reflective journals or complete weekly reports, or both. At the University of Cincinnati (2014), internship students regularly complete both online learning modules and time logs. Interns may write final reports that summarize and reflect on their growth and experiences, relating their internship experiences to specific themes that are important to the major.

At Rollins College (2013) faculty have designed specific assignments for students that contribute to their grades and must be submitted online. To begin, learning objectives are developed with the site supervisor. Students are reminded that these objectives are statements that clearly define what they intend to learn during the semester. They must focus on new learning and expanded growth, not just work. Student assignments include five reflective journals that address achievement of learning objectives. Specifics about tasks or projects that have been accomplished and any problems encountered are expected. Grading of the journals is based on evidence of thoughtful reflection, critical thinking, and problem solving.

Required online discussions at Rollins (2013) allow interns to reflect collaboratively on and explore topics relating to the work environment. The discussions provide an opportunity for interns to synthesize and connect various theories and concepts to their experiences and for instructors to advise students and facilitate problem solving. In their final reflection paper, students summarize their overall success in achieving the agreed-on learning objectives. They must list each learning objective and discuss the extent to which they met the objective, as well as the tasks they used to accomplish it. Students also respond to a series of questions about how the experience will inform their future learning and how the course has affected their career plans.

Typically on-site supervisors collaborate with students to develop learning goals for the experience. Then, toward the end of the program, they evaluate the student work and performance on the agreed-on goals. Evaluation forms may contain open-ended questions asking about the intern's strengths and weaknesses, specific areas where the intern could improve, and recommendations for improvements in the internship program. The supervisor also may be asked to rate satisfaction with various aspects of the intern's performance, including areas such as problem solving, critical thinking, and communication skills. Faculty coordinators generally approve learning goals and proposed internship experiences, provide general guidance, and make one or more visits to the workplace to observe students on the job.

At Rollins College (2013), a site visit by the internship coordinator gives the student an opportunity to express any concerns. It also allows the instructor to gather feedback on the student's progress, as well as information for continued development of the internship program. Electronic evaluations are used for the site supervisor and student to provide their feedback regarding the internship experience. The site supervisor is strongly encouraged to discuss the evaluation with the student. Both evaluations are required to receive course credit.

Papadimitriou and Mardas (2012) have shared assessment results from the internship program at Aristotle University in Greece. Seniors from the department of economics participate in four-month-long internships and attend seminars on marketing, logistics, and e-commerce to complement their practical training. Participating students were asked for opinions about their internships at the end of the first month and again at the conclusion. About 58 percent of the comments provided at the end of the first month were essentially positive. At the end of the internship, students completed a structured survey using a five-point Likert scale. Students rated their relationships with employers (4.50) quite highly. The mean score for work experience gained was 3.73. Employers, interviewed by phone using a short semistructured instrument, also rated the program highly. For example, their rating for student effectiveness in meeting work requirements was 4.65. In all, "students perceived that they gained extra knowledge to close the gap between theory and practice" (p. 8). In rare cases students indicated problems that the employers did not acknowledge, such as long hours, irrelevant work, or work that was different from what was promised.

After seniors from the Department of Industrial Design at Metropolitan State College of Denver participate in their capstone internship experience, internship supervisors rate their performances on all of the program's student learning outcomes, which are linked to the essential competences of the National Association of Schools of Art and Design (Phillips and Thompson, 2011). Department faculty identified seven outcomes for their graduates, which were subdivided into twenty-two elements for assessment. Outcomes address areas such as performing research, solving design problems, demonstrating technical proficiency, preparing presentations, analyzing current and historical designs, and considering sustainability and cultural influences. All twenty-two elements are included on the supervisor's form and are evaluated if applicable.

Because internships play such a key role in preparing students for the workplace, it is important that information gathered through evaluation activities be shared with others in a department. Assessment information about internships should be an important part of the unit's overall assessment program and included in discussions about how well the unit is achieving its learning goals. In addition to the materials generated through the internship experience itself, many senior or alumni surveys include questions about the availability and usefulness of internships. Focus groups also can address these issues.

Service-Learning

Students at many institutions have opportunities to engage in service-learning experiences. At Portland State University (Kerrigan and Carpenter, 2013), for example, all students complete a senior capstone course that includes community engagement. Faculty build cooperative learning communities made up of students from a variety of majors and backgrounds working as a team with community partners who are considered coteachers in the learning process. Projects include writing grants, creating business plans, designing multimedia products, and serving as advocates for underserved populations.

Across campuses, service-learning experiences range from intensive long-term projects, such as service in a culture abroad, to one-time events, such as cleaning up a neighborhood. Although definitions differ, service-learning is considered a form of experiential education in which students engage in activities that address human and community needs together with structured opportunities intentionally designed to promote student learning and development. Reflection and reciprocity are key concepts. According to Kuh (2008), high-impact service-learning gives students direct exposure to issues they are studying in the curriculum, as well as to community efforts to analyze and solve problems. These programs demonstrate the idea that giving back to the community is an important college outcome and that working in the community provides preparation for citizenship, work, and life.

Several descriptions of good practice for service-learning exist, and all highlight the importance of evaluation as a means to give direction to program improvement. In addition to reflection on the part of students, feedback from those being served, peers, and program leaders also is necessary. At Portland State University (Kerrigan and Carpenter, 2013), assessment of service-learning includes a course e-portfolio containing work samples from students, as well as faculty reflection about the learning goals being addressed in the course.

One-time and short-term learning events can be evaluated through a postevent gathering of participants during which they share reactions and ideas. An additional follow-up session sometime after the event also may be included. Many of the classroom assessment techniques that Angelo and Cross (1993) suggest can be adapted for use with service-learning, such as the minute paper or process analysis. Assessment may involve self-reporting on the part of students and written reports or time sheets signed by students and site supervisors. Interviews, focus groups, contact logs, and reflective journals are other possibilities. Emphasis should be on reflection rather than documentation.

Stoecker and Tryon (2009) explore the relationship between college and community, asking whether the latter benefits as much as service-learning practitioners would like. Interviews with community representatives conducted by service-learning students uncovered several issues, including sending students into the community without the instructor, accepting short-term service-learning as a viable practice, and not setting clear goals for service-learning assignments. The authors endorse a civic engagement model that includes expected community outcomes assessed for achievement. This provides direction for student work in the community and gives evaluators something to measure or document. The authors believe that short-term service-learning should be avoided unless it is part of a project-based model that includes a commitment to an organization for an extended period of time with a faculty person who provides continuity. Stoecker and Tryon applaud year-long course models in this area and believe that training and evaluation systems need to be in place to ensure successful implementation (Maternowski, 2009).

Seifer and Conners (2007) have edited a volume of materials that can be used to address many of the criticisms that Stoecker and Tryon present. Called the *Faculty Toolkit for Service-Learning in Higher Education*, it contains templates to guide faculty in setting learning objectives for service-learning courses in collaboration with the partners who will be served. Multiple useful examples include student self-assessment and reflection materials. Suggestions for reflection techniques include approaches that are grounded in experience and inspire interest—journals, work logs, and digital storytelling, for example.

Experiential learning is strongly encouraged at the University of Cincinnati. Staff have developed the Integrated Learning Experiential Assessment Program (I-LEAP), an online assessment instrument that gathers external reviewers' observations of undergraduate student learning outcomes and skills. The evaluation instrument asks the community partner to rate the student on several learning outcomes, including communication skills, analytic ability, leadership, team work, and professional qualities. Professional qualities include assuming responsibility for actions; exhibiting self-confidence; possessing honesty, integrity, and ethics; and demonstrating a positive attitude toward change (Hall and Palmieri, 2012).

Educators in the Department of Leadership and Civic Engagement at Towson University (2014) present several ideas that can be used to assess service-learning, including asking reflective questions, assigning critical incident journals, and administering a community service attitude scale at the beginning and end of the experience. An available set of criteria for service-learning courses includes connection to discipline, reciprocity, reflection, and assessment.

Steinke and Fitch (2007) believe that service-learning should involve comprehensive student projects or analytic journals that demonstrate critical thinking and problem-solving skills and are assessed for these outcomes. They review many instruments that can be used to assess these skills. The Problem-Solving Analysis Protocol is a direct measure that uses open-ended problems to assess critical analysis and was developed specifically for service-learning (Steinke and Fitch, 2003). The assessment begins with a prompt containing a specific course-related issue with a set of follow-up questions considering consequences, causes, and solutions. The writing protocols are scored using rubrics to measure the use of critical thinking and problem analysis. Fitch and Steinke (2013) continue to develop this measure and encourage faculty and staff to adapt it for their own uses (Central College, 2014).

Other assessment approaches include use of the Problem-Solving Interview Protocol developed by Eyler and Giles (1999). The protocol questions students about the causes, solutions, and action strategies related to a specific social problem both before and after having encountered it in their service-learning experiences. Ash and Clayton (2004) use a reflection process for students that results in "articulated learning": students explain what they have learned, how they learned it, why it was important, and the ways in which it will be used for improvement. The Reasoning About Current Issues Questionnaire can be used to evaluate how students approach solving problems that do not have clear-cut answers. Based on King and Kitchener's reflective judgment model (1994), the questionnaire includes three complex ill-structured problems that cover controversial topics. For each problem, respondents read ten statements and rate the extent to which the statement reflects their own thinking (http://www.reflectivejudgment.org).

Staff at the North Carolina Campus Compact (n.d.) maintain a list of several journals related to civic engagement in higher education. For example, *Partnerships: A Journal of Service-Learning and Civic Engagement*, its peer-reviewed online journal, is hosted by the University of North Carolina at Greensboro. The Center for Community Engagement at Indiana State

University (2014) maintains the online *Journal of Community Engagement and Higher Education,* which focuses on case studies emphasizing community engagement and related learning practices and methods. Center staff also conduct campus reviews of experiential practices across all disciplines using the curricular engagement inventory (CEI). Local inventories of this type can help faculty learn from each other.

Applied Projects

In some departments, students participate in client-oriented project work. In these situations, they are assigned tasks based on clients' needs, allowing students to practice problem-solving skills, communication skills, and if they are working with a group, teamwork skills as well. Faculty in the Department of Management at Miami University of Ohio (2013) focus on experiential education through client-based projects in a program called Crunchtime. Teams of three to five students provide participating companies with an outside evaluation and suggest solutions to existing business problems.

Seniors in the civil engineering technology program at Colorado State University Pueblo (2013) participate in a senior project for external clients. The project includes a final presentation for the clients and the program advisory board, which is evaluated for oral communication skills as well as for design elements. Recent results revealed that students were having difficulty in preparing cost estimates for the project, and faculty have provided additional guidance in this area. Because the project is done in a group, peer and self-evaluations of teamwork are included.

Because applied projects include a product or report that is shared with clients, clients are generally involved in project evaluation. Clients can be asked to complete rating sheets or answer open-ended questions that address various aspects of performance, such as the accuracy and usefulness of student work, as well as student performance on learning outcomes such as critical thinking and problem solving. Generally faculty supervisors also participate in project evaluations.

Faculty at Washington State University have used students' e-portfolios to engage students and area employers in sophisticated assessment processes. E-portfolios were used to document authentic or ill-structured problems, describe research methods, and record findings. Faculty and panels of outside reviewers, including working professionals from the field, reviewed the portfolios using rubrics for guidance. According to Gary Brown, who led the project, e-portfolios allow everyone to learn, including faculty and professionals (Clark and Eynon, 2009).

Group Work and Team-Building Skills

Some two-thirds of employers indicate they would like to see more emphasis on teamwork skills in college curricula, and they routinely rank ability to work in teams as one of the most valuable skills of employees (Hart Research Associates, 2013; National Association of Colleges and Employers, 2013a). In addition to, or as part of, client-related projects, many academic programs include a variety of opportunities for students to work in groups or teams, developing skills that are desirable in the workplace and valued in both general education and major programs. Successful teamwork requires agreement among members about expectations and performance, how decisions will be made and conflicts resolved, and the role of each member (Gardner, 1998.) For faculty to be confident that teams are functioning effectively and students are learning what they should, assessment of group work and team-building skills is necessary.

Hughes and Jones (2011) describe teams as made up of individuals who have a collective identity, a common goal, interdependence on assignments, distinctive roles within the team, and a role in a larger organizational context. Some observers distinguish groups from teams, with members of the former more likely to meet, divide up tasks, and then work independently. Hughes and Jones point out, however, that both groups and teams vary along the dimensions listed above with no specific dividing point. Thus, distinguishing between them is not important. What is important in assessing teamwork is to recognize the difference between the functioning and performance of the team as a whole and the functioning and performance of individual team members. Assessment should focus on the process of working together rather than on the product that is created. As Hughes and Jones note, "Teamwork is not the same thing as team success" (p. 55). Teamwork is the set of cognitive and social skills individuals use to foster success. Regardless of what specific measures are used to assess teamwork, Hughes and Jones call for faculty and staff commitment to teaching what these skills are and to allowing students to practice the skills through appropriate assignments that include meaningful feedback.

One strategy to assess teamwork skills is to give written tests containing various scenarios to which students respond. However, most tests of this kind are designed primarily to help employers select individuals for jobs rather than to help faculty improve their students' team-building skills. More often faculty use rubrics to assess teamwork skills. The AAC&U Teamwork Valid Assessment of Learning in Undergraduate Education (VALUE) rubric can be used to rate the contributions of individual team members to the group rather than the group's performance or product. Teamwork is defined as "behaviors under the control of individual team members (effort they put into team tasks, their manner of interacting with others on the team, and the quantity and quality of contributions they make to team discussions)."(AAC&U, 2014d, p. 29). The dimensions included in the rubric are "contributes to team meetings," "facilitates the contributions of team members," "contributes outside team meetings (completes work and helps others)," "fosters constructive team climate," and "responds to conflict." To gather evidence for use with the rubric, developers recommend that work samples come from students' own reflections about their contribution to a team's functioning, evaluations or feedback from fellow team members, and evaluations of outside observers. As with all other assessment, raters need to be trained to use rubrics they adopt or construct, and students need to be familiar with the criteria that will be applied to teamwork skills.

Students often need some preparation before they can rate themselves or their peers effectively. In fact, they may feel reluctant to do this. Faculty must make it clear to group members how peer evaluations will be used. In many cases, peer evaluations are advisory and used only to supplement the instructor's own judgment. Staff from the Eberly Center for Teaching Excellence and Educational Innovation at Carnegie Mellon University (n.d.b) provide an easy to administer peer- and self-assessment tool that students can use to rate themselves as well as each member of the group. Among others, dimensions include time management and responsibility, adaptability, creativity, technical skills, and communication skills.

Some faculty use classroom assessment techniques (CATs) to detect problems with teamwork early in the semester. Team members can be asked to complete a relevant CAT individually and then to meet as a group to discuss responses. CATs can address specific aspects of teamwork, such as conducting an effective meeting. Using a self-assessment instrument, students can consider the tasks they accomplished at the meeting, the cooperation they exhibited, and the clarity of their goals.

In addition to student self and peer evaluations, faculty or professionals can observe various aspects of the way the team is functioning. For example, group presentations can be evaluated for evidence of teamwork. In some cases, group work can be taped and viewed at a later time to examine interactions among group members. Instructors may ask students to use tools like Google Docs for collaboration; then they can occasionally view documents to gain insight into how group members are working together. To assist in assigning individual grades, faculty may ask students to prepare a final one- or two-page paper describing insights they have gained from working with the group. In some cases, each member is assigned a specific responsibility within a team project or presentation, thus facilitating the instructor's evaluation of individuals' contributions. Staff from CMU's Eberly Center (n.d.a) suggest strategies for assigning and assessing group work. They recommend that faculty ask individual students to demonstrate what they have learned from a group project, perhaps through independent write-ups or journal entries. Staff in the Schreyer Institute for Teaching Excellence at Pennsylvania State University (n.d.c) maintain an online self-paced module on forming and assessing teams.

Employer Involvement

We have described ways that employers contribute to assessment through experiential learning. Here we consider some additional possibilities for employer involvement. Employers can act as assessors or advisors, and they can participate as survey respondents.

Employers as Assessors

Employers often are willing to help collect assessment information from students. Faculty in some departments invite professionals in the field to interview their students about satisfaction with their experiences or to help evaluate their graduates. Professionals may serve on panels or juries as external reviewers. External judges can provide a sense of realism about what the future holds for students ready to graduate, thus helping students envision what will be expected of them on the job.

Faculty from Indiana University's entrepreneurship and corporate innovation curriculum (2014) use a unique approach to drawing on professionals for assessment purposes. All seniors in the independent entrepreneurship program take a new venture creation course that requires each student to complete a business plan. At the end of the semester, students present their proposals to a panel of judges made up of venture capitalists, angel investors, and other successful entrepreneurs. If the plan is judged an acceptable venture, the student receives an A in the course; if the plan is judged unacceptable, the student does not pass. The rationale for this approach is to let students experience the challenge and fear that confront entrepreneurs. If an idea is rejected and the student is a double major, that student can still graduate. Those who are not double majors can take extra courses and graduate the next semester. Some students retake the course to prove to themselves they can do it. Over the years, the initial 5 percent failure level has declined as Donald F. Kuratko, the director of the program, and his team have perfected their counseling of students. For example, students are given a chance to meet with external experts who offer advice on business plans, and faculty are also available to provide support. In addition to grading students based on their plans, the judges provide useful information about how the overall program is working. The panel critiques the class as a whole with respect to communication and planning abilities and provides general feedback about the curriculum. The course has been recognized by *Inc.* magazine as one of the best business courses in the nation and was also featured on the *BusinessWeek* website (Kuratko, n.d.; DiMeglio, 2013).

Employers as Advisors

Community advisory boards can make valuable contributions as faculty assess their programs. At the Farmer School of Business at Miami University of Ohio (n.d.), employers serve as corporate partners in a number of ways. The Business Advisory Council is a resource for students, faculty, and staff in maintaining the quality of the college. At the university's Thomas C. Page Center for Entrepreneurship, an advisory group assists faculty in providing excellent teaching and real-world experience. A Young Professionals Advisory Council comprising alumni members who are future leaders in their companies and communities advises in several areas, including mentorship, experiential learning, and immersion programs.

At Carnegie Mellon University, President's Advisory Boards play important roles in assessment. Each college, department, and school has its own advisory board made up of professionals in the discipline as well as university trustees and alumni. The group visits its respective unit every four or five years and examines quality, evaluates needs, and assesses strengths and weaknesses. The advisory boards have helped foster assessment practices at the university (Kinzie, 2012).

Employer Surveys

Employers can provide valuable insights into workplace needs and the preparation of graduates. Regularly administered surveys for employers gather workforce-related information. In addition to periodic AAC&U surveys, the National Association of Colleges and Employers and the Collegiate Employment Research Institute (CERI) at Michigan State University collect information on recruiting trends. Employers are in the best position to report on the needs of the workplace in terms of both the number of employees they require and the types of skills employees must possess. Employers can provide information about specific expertise needed, including computer skills, communication skills, and personal abilities.

In a recent NILOA study, chief academic officers indicate a substantial increase in the use of employer surveys for assessment at the institution level (Kuh et al., 2014). At the department level, about 20 percent of program heads use employer surveys, particularly in health sciences (60 percent), education (35 percent), and engineering (30 percent) (Ewell et al., 2011). Employers may be asked to rate a list of specific job skills for relevance to the workplace. The list must be well designed. If skill categories are very broad, it is difficult to obtain information that can be used for curriculum improvement (Gardner, 1998). For example, several forms of writing, such as technical writing or correspondence, may be relevant to the work situation and can be included on an employer questionnaire. Employers also can be asked to distinguish between requirements and preparation of technical employees and nontechnical employees because findings can differ for the two groups. An additional distinction is between skills that are required at the new-employee stage and those that are required of experienced employees.

Employer surveys can be focused on particular needs as opposed to a range of topics. For example, faculty may be concerned about experiential education, communication skills, or computer literacy. An employer survey can be developed to focus on any one of these areas of interest. To ensure employer participation, faculty must explain the project's purpose and the uses to be made of employer contributions.

Several strategies can be used to identify employers for assessment surveys. Alumni who receive surveys may be asked to provide their employers' names and contact information. Here, it is particularly important to let alumni know the purpose of the employer survey. For example, employers might be asked general questions about the skills that lead to success in the field, or they could be asked about the preparedness of typical graduates from the institution's program. In some cases, employers are asked questions about specific individuals. If alumni are providing names of their employers, they must be told whether the survey will include questions about their own job performance.

An alternative to obtaining contact information from alumni is to identify employers from existing records of those who have hired graduates in the past. Some departments maintain records based on information supplied by graduates at the time they accept jobs. The institution's alumni or career services office may also have information about employers. Another approach is to obtain contact information from professional organizations. Surveys of employers generally contain some basic questions to help classify their responses, such as the number of professional employees in their firm and the number of entry-level employees they hire in a given year.

Surveys for recruiters of graduates may be helpful in assessing institutional effectiveness. Recruiters can be identified through career services or other administrative units that schedule their visits to campus. These surveys may focus on the recruiters' knowledge of programs and services on the campus and their impressions from interviewing candidates for jobs. Professionals in the Center for Career Development at Babson College reviewed and modified a survey for visiting recruiters that is administered following recruiter interviews of student job candidates (Sharpe, Reiser, and Chase, 2010). To generate feedback on program-level student outcomes, recruiters rate their overall impressions of Babson students on a five-point scale. The questionnaire addresses important student outcomes such as academic training, communication skills, and maturity. Recruiters also rate individual candidates in areas such as rhetoric, quantitative analysis, ethics, and leadership.

Although not used widely, focus groups can be an effective means of obtaining information from employers and can be cost effective if they include employers who are located near the university. Community college personnel may draw on local employers to determine the educational needs of the community. Employers can communicate what they value in employees and provide a rationale for emphasizing certain skills and abilities in the curriculum.

Intentional Learning

Observers have challenged institutions of higher education to examine their roles and responsibilities in preparing graduates for their futures and to recognize that subject matter knowledge and skills are only part of what students need to know. Students also need transferable skills such as the ability to negotiate and compromise and qualities such as adaptability, openness, empathy, and insight. They need to be aware of values and perspectives within their professions, such as the importance of lifelong learning and the ability to question, organize, and connect knowledge. Faculty can assess these attitudes and values in various ways using case presentations, ratings of class discussions, and employer evaluations of graduates' skills in addressing ethical issues.

Staff at the Collegiate Employment Research Institute (2012) at Michigan State University present additional evidence that employers seek skills beyond knowledge of the major. Center staff periodically conduct surveys of recruiters asking them to indicate what type of educational background they seek in new employees. The survey uses a seven-point scale from 1 = very broad educational training to 7 = very specific educational training. The midpoint, 4, represents a balanced student who is liberally educated and possesses knowledge of a discipline. In 2012, the mean of 4.84 suggested that employers lean slightly toward students with specific educational training. According to the report, the increasingly globally networked economy calls for employees who blend deep knowledge in a field with cross-disciplinary skills and an ability to collaborate within and outside the organization. A major requirement for these employees is self-awareness because they must rely on their own inner direction to navigate through their job assignments and manage their careers. Collegiate Employment Research Institute professionals believe that the most desirable employees of the future will be either liberally educated technical (professional) graduates or technically savvy liberal arts graduates.

The authors of AAC&U's 2002 report, *Greater Expectations: A New Vision for Learning as a Nation Goes to College*, recommend a core of knowledge and capacities that all students should acquire. The vision is for students to become intentional learners who are self-aware, adaptable, and able to connect seemingly disparate experiences. Intentional learners are empowered, informed, and responsible for their personal actions and civic values. Central to the vision of the intentional learner are outcomes such as integrative learning (the ability to connect knowledge across fields, experiences, and levels), inquiry learning (the ability to formulate and answer complex questions), global learning (the ability to understand and find interrelations among the world's communities), and civic learning (the ability to understand and participate in decisions that shape and influence a diverse democratic society). Each of these areas is now addressed by the AAC&U VALUE rubrics. AAC&U leaders envision liberal outcomes linked with effective curricular and cocurricular practices, advancing several outcomes simultaneously. They also believe that fostering intentional learners equips students to adapt to their environments throughout their lives (AAC&U, n.d.b).

CHAPTER 8

ASSESSING LEARNING IN GENERAL EDUCATION

E ngaging faculty in outcomes assessment is likely to be more successful if it can be demonstrated that assessment is fundamentally connected with the work they are already doing. Showing faculty colleagues that they can improve the curriculum, their teaching, even student learning, and perhaps even save some time in the process can be persuasive. In this chapter, we address some of the issues and concerns that come into play when examining how programs in general education are functioning. We present an overview of recent thinking about the role of general education in college curricula and discuss some of the many choices involved in assessing these programs.

The Nature of General Education

The meaning of general education and its role in college curricula have long been subject to consideration and debate. Historically, the focus of general education has been on providing broad exposure to skills and attitudes that help graduates function in society rather than on developing specialized knowledge about particular disciplines. However, the notion that general education requirements can be satisfied simply by taking a sampling of courses from a variety of disciplines has been challenged (Gaston, 2010). An initial impetus for rethinking the role of general education came from *Strong Foundations*, an influential and still relevant publication of the Association of American Colleges (1994). *Greater Expectations*, an important undertaking of the Association of American College and Universities (AAC&U) conducted from 2000 to 2006, prompted further conversations about the role of liberal and general education and provided the groundwork for the comprehensive initiative, Liberal Education and America's Promise (LEAP). The 2007 LEAP report, *College Learning for the New Global Century*, contains an explicit statement of the essential learning outcomes of a college education.

The 2013 National Institute for Learning Outcomes Assessment survey of provosts indicates that a large majority of campuses (84 percent) have a common set of intended learning outcomes for their undergraduate students (Kuh, Jankowski, Ikenberry, and Kinzie, 2014). According to the 2009 AAC&U membership survey of chief academic officers, the general education skills most often addressed are writing, critical thinking, quantitative reasoning, and oral communication, and the knowledge areas most likely to be incorporated are humanities, sciences, social sciences, global cultures, and mathematics (Hart Research Associates, 2009).

Questions about general education address not only what students should learn, but how they should learn. In the old view of general education, students could satisfy their distribution requirements by taking one of several introductory courses in various academic departments. Courses were viewed as foundations for more important specialized knowledge, and faculty teaching these courses often believed they were providing a "service" to students majoring in other areas. The Association of American Colleges 1994 work cited above and the efforts of faculty on many campuses confirm that effective general education involves more than exposure to a number of different fields. General education programs should provide students with the opportunity to learn specific thinking and communication skills in courses offered throughout the entire curriculum. Students should study other cultures as well as the diversity in their own culture, be able to integrate thinking and ideas across disciplines, and develop personal qualities characteristic of college graduates. Perhaps of most importance, students should "experience a coherent course of study, one that is more than the sum of its parts" (p. iv).

Nearly twenty years later, Hersh and Keeling (2013) also advocate for coherence in the curriculum. They dispute the notion that students can develop coherence for themselves by selecting individual courses or even a series of courses, stacking them like building blocks. In their view, significant outcomes of higher education are best accomplished cumulatively. They argue for across-the-curriculum approaches to not just writing but critical thinking, problem solving, ethical development, and quantitative reasoning. And they believe all course work should share and reinforce common higher learning outcomes, increasing each year in complexity and sophistication.

Several campuses have introduced innovative approaches. The University of South Carolina's (2013) Carolina Core offers foundation courses in several areas, including communications, scientific literacy, and analytical reasoning and problem solving. It also extends beyond foundation courses to give students the opportunity to develop core competences in an integrative course in their major program. At Lynn University (2014), the curriculum was reenvisioned so that major fields are defined in relationship to the core rather than the opposite. Core areas are presented as dialogues around three themes: self and society, belief and reason, and justice and civic life. The dialogues are structured in three phases of learning, including a foundation phase in the first and second years and transformational and integrative/capstone stages in the third and fourth years. (AAC&U, 2010b).

In responding to the 2009 AAC&U survey, a majority of academic administrators (56 percent) indicated that general education had increased as a priority at their institution, and many were modifying their programs. Although the vast majority of general education programs still use distribution systems, approaches to achieving coherence within these systems differ greatly. On some campuses all students are required to take several core courses, others offer interdisciplinary or thematic courses, and many now require senior capstone seminars (Hart Research Associates, 2009). Regardless of structure, a commitment to assessment is necessary. Assessment plays a vital role in helping to determine whether general education programs are achieving their purposes and, of equal importance, helping these programs evolve and improve. In fact, at Montgomery College (2013), the Collegewide Outcomes Assessment Team sees the assessment process as a way to help ensure that required competences will be embedded, repeated, and combined through interdisciplinary opportunities. Furthermore, by communicating to students where and how they can experience the competences, team members believe the assessment process encourages intentional learning.

Assessment Choices and Issues

The process of assessing general education programs is the same as that for assessing other programs. Once the overall mission and purposes of the program are defined, specific outcomes for learning must be articulated, an approach for organization must be selected, assessment methods must be chosen and administered, and results must be examined and used. Faculty and students should be involved in all aspects of the process. What is particularly challenging about assessment of general education is that in almost all cases, program assessment calls for consensus and agreement among faculty in different academic departments and representing various disciplines. Almost all successful programs for assessing general education outcomes are led by strong interdisciplinary committees that include faculty and staff from across campus. These committees select the approach to assessment, evaluate information, and issue recommendations.

Agreeing on Program Purposes and Learning Objectives

The most important question for faculty to answer with respect to any general education program is: What is the purpose? The answer becomes the foundation for the program and provides the rationale for what and how faculty teach in the program. At many institutions, faculty embrace the view that general education programs prepare students for effective citizenship in a democratic society. However, faculty vary greatly in how this purpose is articulated. At the University of Southern Maine (2013), faculty describe general education as a coherent, integrative, and rigorous liberal education that enables graduates to be world-minded, intentional, lifelong learners. The program involves substantive learning experiences that transcend the perspectives of various disciplines.

Once there is agreement about the purposes of general education, faculty can articulate specific goals for student learning and development and provide opportunities in the curriculum for these outcomes to be addressed. The University of Southern Maine's general education program fosters the values, dispositions, knowledge, and skills essential for students to demonstrate: informed understandings of interrelationships between human cultures and the natural world; analytical, contextual, and integrative thinking about complex issues; effective communication using multiple forms of expression; critical reflection on, and informed action in, their roles as participants in multiple communities; and ethical action to contribute to the social and environmental welfare of local and global communities.

Many campus outcomes statements are based on those described in the AAC&U LEAP initiative. Available on the AAC&U (n.d.a) website, the major categories of essential learning outcomes are knowledge of human cultures and the physical and natural world, intellectual and practical skills, personal and social responsibility, and integrative and applied learning.

California State University has used the LEAP outcomes as the basis for a systemwide initiative, and several campuses in Massachusetts are involved in an interstate vision project supported by the AAC&U and the State Higher Education Executive Officers Association (AAC&U, 2014b, 2014c).

Although differences exist across campuses, common goals include preparing students who can understand and deal with diverse ideas, populations, and cultures and possess a set of competences including critical thinking, creative thinking, oral and written communication, quantitative and information literacy, and problem solving. Important aspects of personal development include abilities to negotiate with others, tolerate ambiguity, be sensitive to the values of others, and evince appreciation for lifelong learning. Because definitions of various competences (such as critical thinking) often differ across disciplines, faculty must clearly define the meaning of their learning outcomes before proceeding with assessment.

Selecting an Assessment Approach for General Education

Once learning outcomes have been articulated, faculty must decide the approach they will use for collecting information. A key decision is whether to use already completed classroom work for assessment or to create special opportunities to assess students outside the course structure. These approaches are not mutually exclusive; in practice, faculty develop or adapt various strategies to serve their own needs. We describe several possibilities here.

Campuswide Approaches Campuswide approaches often focus on individuals or groups of students rather than on courses. General education assessment instruments are administered to all or a sample of students outside the course structure. Often selected on the basis of their class level, students may be invited (or required) to complete online or paper surveys or to attend sessions to complete assessment instruments. Examples include a campuswide end-of-year freshman survey or a junior-level test of writing competence. Instruments may assess specific skills such as computer competence or critical thinking. Alternatively, instruments may cover all or a substantial portion of the learning outcomes addressed in the program. Instruments may be purchased or designed locally.

For convenience, university-wide assessment information may be collected within courses. At Miami Dade College (n.d.b), the general education assessment team has developed tasks that demonstrate student learning in several areas, and the assessment process is focused on "following the student." Near the end of the semester, the director of learning outcomes assessment identifies a sample of students who are close to graduation. Faculty who are teaching courses in which these students are enrolled are invited to administer the tasks in class. Tasks are assessed by the general education assessment team using rubrics, and the results are forwarded to appropriate audiences.

At Truman State University (2011), senior portfolios may be submitted in the capstone course, but provisions have also been made for students to submit at an earlier date. The portfolio project director administers the program with collaboration from faculty and a portfolio committee. Portfolios are scored by teams, and results are summarized in an annual report.

Projects such as portfolios and research papers allow faculty to examine the ability of their students to integrate and apply knowledge. Rather than establishing requirements that exist outside the course structure, capstone or other required courses (in general education or the major) can be used to develop this information, allowing a look at individual students and at courses as well.

Course-Embedded Approaches   Much assessment evidence about student learning is collected within courses, drawing on work that students have already completed as part of their classroom activities. Within this general model, several approaches exist. At Bismarck State College (2014), the general education curriculum is organized around three broad areas—awareness, thought, and communication—that are assessed on a three-year cycle, according to an assessment plan called A-C-T. Each area has a faculty group that meets to discuss and plan assessment activities and create rubrics. The groups also review results and identify needed changes.

Variants of this approach are employed on campuses where general education outcomes are assessed over a period of years. For example, writing and oral communication may be assessed in the first year, quantitative reasoning and critical thinking may be assessed in the second year, and so on. Information is typically collected in classrooms using existing assignments, but focus is on overall learning of the outcome rather than on specific contributions of individual courses. Frequently the material collected is regraded using a rubric. Faculty who are most concerned with the outcome develop the specifics for data collection related to that outcome, and both course-embedded methods and other approaches can be used. McKendree University (2013) faculty have designated 2014–2015 as the Year of Communication. An appropriate subcommittee spent 2013–2014 developing a thoughtful approach for assessment of that outcome.

As a variation of these strategies, assessment approaches may be focused on individual courses. Faculty must demonstrate that their courses are helping students to acquire knowledge, skills, and values associated with one or more general education outcomes. Although course instructors may draw on existing classroom tests and activities, they may also develop new assessment instruments such as writing exercises, exam questions, questionnaires, or even focus group protocols. New instruments may need to be developed for assessment of multiple-section courses if common measures are not in use. Assessment that focuses on individual courses is particularly appealing if there is concern about the value of these courses in the overall general education program. And because most instruction takes place within structured courses, a course-based approach has great potential for making connections between assessment results and needed curriculum improvements. Differences in content coverage across multiple-section courses often become quite clear as instructors plan for and carry out assessment activities.

Binghamton University (2011, 2013) faculty have created a general education assessment process based on course portfolios. Assessment category teams in each of eleven areas of learning are responsible for writing reports on a three-year rotation. Assessment information is collected and analyzed each semester for a randomly selected set of courses in each of the areas. In addition to the course syllabus, a course portfolio must contain a brief description of how the course fulfills the content requirements and meets the learning objectives of the general education category being assessed. It also includes a narrative of strengths and weaknesses in student learning with regard to that area, as well as examples of a range of student work for assignments that measure student achievement of relevant learning outcomes. The portfolio may contain other material at the discretion of the faculty member or the assessment category team. The teams evaluate the portfolios in relationship to achievement of their particular learning goal and make recommendations for improvement. Instructors who do not complete a portfolio when requested may see their course or section removed from the program.

For course-embedded assessment approaches to provide meaningful information about program outcomes, results from individual assignments or courses must be aggregated. This most likely involves additional readings of classroom materials, evaluating reports submitted by course instructors, or both. In several learning areas at Binghamton University (2011), staff from the Office of Institutional Research and Assessment evaluate student work contained in course portfolios using an appropriate rubric and provide results to the assessment category team. As they review aggregated assessment results, faculty must make sure that all of the goals of the general education program are appropriately addressed in at least some courses, and that across all courses, students are achieving learning goals.

In general education programs where outcomes are explicitly stated and linked to individual courses, existing course-embedded activities should be readily available for use, and assessment can proceed in an efficient manner. If existing instruments do not address general education goals explicitly, separate instruments may need to be developed for courses, requiring faculty to work independently or in small groups to design assignments, test questions, surveys, or other assessment instruments.

A criticism of course-embedded assessment is that although it can be used to look at the general education program as a whole, it may not provide a perspective on the overall learning of individual students. Although software systems can aggregate data across courses and students, assignments to demonstrate the cumulative effects of learning still must be carefully designed and administered to students. On some campuses, faculty have developed capstone projects to demonstrate the ability of students to integrate what they have learned. Faculty at Grand Valley State University (Griffin and Burns-Ardolino, 2013), for example, have created an upper-division general education capstone experience that incorporates the goals of integration, problem solving, and collaboration.

Generating, Reporting, and Using Results

Because general education programs usually encompass a broad range of learning outcomes, including critical thinking skills, communication skills, and values and attitudes, faculty must be careful to ensure that the instruments they select address all of their objectives. Creating a matrix to match goals and methods (described in Chapter 4) can be useful for this purpose. Most likely, both direct and indirect methods will be included. In addition to current students, alumni and employers may be asked to provide information. Assessment of general education programs may include creating curriculum maps, reviewing course syllabi, and perhaps documenting classroom assignments. On some campuses, faculty examine whether the curriculum is being delivered as planned. Studies of implementation fidelity can be helpful in understanding assessment findings (Swain, Finney, and Gerstner, 2013.).

Results from campuswide general education assessment activities can be reported in various formats, including project reports or theme reports that concentrate on particular areas of study. Report preparation may be undertaken by members of a campuswide assessment committee or by a faculty member or administrator with assessment responsibilities. Institutional research or assessment office staff may prepare reports, sharing results from questionnaires or other instruments they administer. Reports prepared by staff usually include comparisons and analysis but leave the development of recommendations to a campuswide committee.

If a course-embedded approach is to be implemented, it is important that faculty understand the types of data and analysis they are responsible for generating, the format for reporting their results, and the process that will be used for evaluation. They also must know the possible consequences of the information they provide. Generally an interdisciplinary assessment committee will play a key role. The committee may be primarily a vehicle for faculty discussion and overall problem identification. However, where courses are the focus of assessment, these committees may have the authority to recommend that a course be removed from the general education program if assessment information reveals it is not contributing to program goals. With so much at stake, faculty should have clear directions about their role in the process.

Using Commercial Instruments and the Voluntary System of Accountability

In 2006 Secretary of Education Margaret Spellings's Commission on the Future of Higher Education issued a report calling for ways to publicly compare campuses using value-added measures of student learning (US Department of Education, 2006). In response to this report, education leaders developed the Voluntary System of Accountability (VSA, 2014). As the name suggests, the system is designed to share information about institutional quality from within the higher education community rather than wait for measures to be imposed. The VSA uses a common web report, *College Portrait,* to provide clear, accessible, and comparable information about undergraduate experiences at public four-year institutions. Goals for the VSA include helping campuses identify and implement effective institutional improvement efforts and providing a useful tool for students during the college search process. The VSA is sponsored by the Association of Public and Land-Grant Universities (APLU) and the American Association of State Colleges and Universities (AASCU).

One of several areas included in the *College Portrait* is student learning outcomes. Initially outcomes could be measured using only three instruments: the Council for Aid to Education's Collegiate Learning Assessment (CLA); the ETS Proficiency Profile; or ACT's Collegiate Assessment of Academic Proficiency. In order to examine the technical qualities of the three objective tests and to determine commonalities among the measures, VSA developers undertook a longitudinal study supported by the Fund for the Improvement of Postsecondary Education. The study concluded that scores on the three tests are indeed related but are not equivalent (Klein, Liu, and Sconing, 2009). Thus institutional comparisons cannot be made unless all institutions administer the same test. In addition, the ability to introduce program improvements based on findings from these measures has been questioned. Drawing on responses from a consortium of forty-seven colleges and universities, the Council of Independent Colleges issued a report focused exclusively on the CLA (Paris, 2011). The study indicates that many faculty find it difficult to know what to do to improve their curricula or instruction using CLA results.

An evaluation conducted in 2012 by the National Institute for Learning Outcomes Assessment revealed that the requirement to report value-added statistics derived from standardized tests of generic skills undermines acceptance of the VSA (Jankowski, Ikenberry, Kuh, Shenoy, and Baker, 2012). In response, the VSA advisory board softened the requirement to report student learning outcomes in the *College Portrait,* adding as a measurement option the AAC&U Valid Assessment of Learning in Undergraduate Education (VALUE) rubrics for written communication and critical thinking.

Criticisms of using standardized tests of generic skills to compare institutions include the inability of these measures to test more than a "tiny slice of what a student knows and can do" (Banta, 2012, p. 4), as well as their tendency to reflect knowledge and skills developed prior to college. In addition, differences in student characteristics between institutions introduce differences in scores that are not due to the construct being measured, thus making comparisons across universities a questionable practice. Test groups are rarely true random samples, and testing environments often differ among institutions. For example, tests may be online or proctored (McCollum, 2011). Lack of student motivation to take a test without consequences creates another major source of error (Banta and Pike, 2012).

Faculty from the University of Cincinnati recently participated in an e-portfolio project through the Inter/National Coalition for Electronic Portfolio Research. As part of the research, faculty compared critical thinking scores obtained from CLA performance tasks to rubric scores for critical thinking assignments contained in e-portfolios. Faculty were disappointed to find no statistically significant correlation between the sets of scores and concluded on other bases that rubric-based assessment provides better information for continuous program improvement. In their *College Portrait* report for the VSA, the university submits scores on a 2010 administration of the ETS Proficiency Profile. Justifying their choice, the profile notes that faculty and staff preferred the ETS exam over other options, although no choices were seen as ideal. Although faculty consider the CLA to be an intriguing test, they have concerns about how it is graded (AAC&U, 2010a).

Possin (2013) also believes that scoring of CLA performance tasks is flawed. In reviewing test materials and results, he found that nearly any answer was scored acceptable as long as the student offered a reason to justify it. Possin argues that "graders cannot see the trees for the forest" (p. 9). Because they are taking a holistic view of critical thinking, they are not considering its component skills. Graders are falling for informal fallacies, evasions, and arguments that are not cogent. Possin believes that CLA graders are measuring rhetorical skills rather than critical thinking skills. He asserts that test authors and graders should be experts in the component skills of critical thinking and their application to tasks such as making rational decisions and solving problems. Although the CLA is primarily computer scored, graders confirm computer-assigned scores for 10 percent of the cases. In contrast to the CLA approach that uses holistic scoring of open-ended performance-based tasks, multiple-choice tests such as the ETS Proficiency Profile define critical thinking as a set of discrete subskills that are separately assessed.

In a ten-year retrospective, Hanson and Mohn (2011) report on research to determine whether institutions have changed their primary reasons for using the Collegiate Assessment of Academic Proficiency. In both 1999 and 2009, ACT surveyed its users, and more than 40 percent responded (193 campuses in 1999 and 183 in 2009). In 1999 nearly three-quarters of respondents rated Assessing the Effectiveness of Instructional Programs as very important. In 2009 less than 50 percent rated this very important. By 2009 the greatest percentage of very important responses (70 percent) was for the statement Assessing Student Mastery of Broad Based Competences. This compares to 56 percent in 1999. The percentage of respondents rating Providing Data for Accreditation Purposes very important increased from 51 in 1999 to 65 in 2009. Comparing Performance of Your Own Students with That of Students Nationally also increased in importance. Thus the items that users rated very important shifted to a focus on assessment for external accountability and accreditation and away from seeking direction for program improvement.

In spite of reservations, many institutions administer standardized objective tests, including perhaps as many as one thousand of an estimated forty-five hundred postsecondary institutions (Banta, 2011). The Council of Independent Colleges (2014) continues to work with a consortium of institutions using the CLA to learn about the cognitive growth of their students. And in 2012 Jankowski reported that faculty at St. Olaf College, a council member, used CLA results to suggest improvements in the teaching of critical thinking.

Assessing Specific Aspects of General Education

Here we describe some of the approaches faculty and staff use to define and assess specific areas of general education. We draw heavily on the VALUE rubrics created by faculty teams working with staff from the Association of American Colleges and Universities (AAC&U, 2014d). Several other instruments that can be considered for assessment are presented, and we illustrate their use with examples from many campuses.

Critical Thinking and Problem Solving

A large number of the mission statements of higher education institutions include at least a sentence or phrase about the importance of critical thinking. In fact, among respondents to the 2009 AAC&U survey, nearly three-quarters of those with a common set of outcomes for all graduates included critical thinking (Hart Research Associates, 2009). Only writing skills were included more often (77 percent). Although campus leaders place great value on the ability of their graduates to be critical thinkers, critical thinking is a concept that is difficult to define and therefore difficult to assess. Ennis (2012) describes critical thinking as "reasonably reflective thinking that is focused on deciding what to believe or do." For the VALUE rubric, critical thinking is defined as "a habit of mind characterized by the comprehensive exploration of issues, ideas, artifacts, and events before accepting or formulating an opinion or conclusion." The definition and rubric are designed to be transdisciplinary, recognizing that success in all disciplines requires habits of inquiry and analysis that share common attributes.

The critical thinking VALUE rubric examines five areas: explanation of issues, evidence, influence of context and assumptions, student's position, and conclusions and related outcomes. A description of performance at each of four levels is included in the rubric. In addition to presenting their own rubric, AAC&U developers point readers to other materials, such as the Holistic Critical Thinking Scoring Rubric that is available free from Insight Assessment, the company that produces the California Critical Thinking Skills Test.

Rubrics also may be developed locally. Faculty at the National Technical Institute for the Deaf (NTID), a college of the Rochester Institute of Technology, conducted a study of critical thinking outcomes in their associate degree program. Because the valid assessment of critical thinking skills requires a procedure that separates this construct from the way it is communicated, measurement issues become even more challenging when students have limited English proficiency. A committee of experienced faculty considered several definitions and rubrics before developing their own. The NTID critical thinking rubric contains a four-point analytic rating scale that is used to assess five components of critical thinking. An overall holistic score is also provided (Gustafson and Bochner, 2009).

Tasks and assignments used to assess critical thinking include research papers, presentations, case studies, and simulations. For a small number of students, Ennis (2011) suggests either an open-ended essay test or a multiple-choice test in which students are asked to defend their choices in writing. Some faculty videotape in-class presentations of students and review them later for evidence of critical thinking and other skills. When possible, faculty should take a close look at the processes students use in accomplishing their work in order to determine whether students are employing solid reasoning to answer questions. Students can be encouraged to keep reflective journals or to think out loud as they work through problems. Rubrics used for assessment should be shared with students, and students should be encouraged to use them to evaluate their own work.

Faculty at Tennessee Tech University (2014) have spent several years developing an instrument to assess critical thinking. The Critical Thinking Assessment Test (CAT) has been used on about 150 campuses and is available nationwide. It contains primarily short-answer essay questions scored by faculty on participating campuses. Development of the test was supported by the National Science Foundation. The CAT assesses evaluating information, creative thinking, learning and problem solving, and communication.

Several commercial instruments available to assess critical thinking can be used within particular disciplines as well as in general education programs. The California Critical Thinking Skills Test reflects the 1990 Delphi Expert Consensus Definition of Critical Thinking, which identifies analysis, inference, evaluation, interpretation, and explanation as the five key reasoning skills used to make judgments about what to believe or do. The test is a standardized multiple-choice test that can be completed with paper and pencil or online. Multiple-choice items use everyday scenarios and require test takers to interpret the question using information presented in text, charts, or images. It produces an overall score as well as several subscores.

Because making decisions using critical thinking involves both skills and habits of mind, the test developers recommend use of the California Critical Thinking Disposition Inventory which measures whether a test taker is "willing" to think reflectively. The inventory asks respondents to indicate how strongly they agree or disagree with statements that relate to forming reasoned judgments. The instrument measures attributes that influence an individual's capacity to learn and apply critical thinking skills, including truth seeking, open-mindedness, and anticipation of possible consequences. Systematic thinking and maturity of judgment also are assessed. The inventory can be administered online in thirty minutes or less (http://www.insightassessment.com/Products).

The Watson-Glaser Critical Thinking Appraisal, developed in the 1930s and revised several times, contains five subtests that gauge how well students can reason analytically and logically. The subtests examine inference, recognition of assumptions, deduction, interpretation, and evaluation of arguments. The test is available through Pearson Education.

The *iSkills* assessment from ETS measures the ability to think critically in a digital environment using a range of scenario-based tasks. The online exam measures the test taker's ability to navigate, understand, and critically evaluate information obtained through digital technology. Students are expected to synthesize many different types of data and make informed judgments about what is accurate, relevant, and useful. To motivate students to participate and perform well on the assessment, students can earn a certificate of achievement based on their performance.

Because items on critical thinking tests are often subject to more than one interpretation, faculty should take the test themselves and compare their own answers to those provided in the test materials. Although faculty may not agree completely on answers, the scoring guide should provide answers that can be justified. The difficulty of the test also should be examined. If the test is challenging for faculty, it may be very frustrating for students. Most important, the value of any of these instruments depends on how well the specific content corresponds to the concept of critical thinking shared by faculty teaching in the program.

In addition to critical thinking skills, faculty may expect their graduates to develop skills in problem solving, an outcome that many employers prize. Effective problem solving includes strategies such as developing a clear problem statement and identifying, selecting, and implementing a solution. Although analytical step-by-step approaches may characterize the solution of well-structured problems, the solution of ill-structured problems requires the use of intuition and experience and personal abilities such as patience, persistence, and creativity.

Problem solving is included among the AAC&U VALUE rubrics and is defined as "the process of designing, evaluating, and implementing a strategy to answer an open-ended question or achieve a desired goal." Framing language acknowledges that problem solving covers many activities that vary significantly across disciplines and may range from problems that are well defined to those that are ambiguous. The rubric is designed to measure the quality of a process rather than of an end product. Thus, work samples need to include evidence of the way the individual thinks about a problem-solving task, such as reflections on the process or a record of steps in an assignment. The rubric may be used to score team projects as well as individual projects. Categories in the rubric include problem definition, identification of strategies, proposed solutions, evaluation of solutions, implementation of solutions, and evaluation of outcomes.

The ability of students to solve problems can be assessed using exercises, case study analysis, simulations, and group work projects. Faculty at Miami Dade College (n.d.a) include "problem solving using critical and creative thinking and scientific reasoning" among their expected outcomes. They use a locally developed rubric to evaluate tasks designed to demonstrate achievement of the outcome.

To assess students' problem-solving skills, Harvey and Avramenko (2012) use video "with a pinch of creativity to provide a more interesting and interactive means of assessment" (p. 5). Students are asked to produce a video presentation to reflect problem-solving tasks originating in lectures or case studies. The completed footage is downloaded for review by students and teachers. Using predetermined criteria, students and peers examine the work to identify areas for improvement. (See Chapter 7 for additional strategies that can be used to assess problem solving skills.)

Writing

The way writing is taught and assessed differs greatly across campuses. As the framing language of the VALUE rubric for written communication points out, "The most clear finding to emerge from decades of research on writing assessment is that the best writing assessments are locally determined and sensitive to local context and mission" (AAC&U, 2014d, p. 31). The National Council of Teachers of English/Council of Writing Program Administrators (NCTE/CWPA, n.d.) and the Conference on College Composition and Communication (CCCC, 2009) have prepared position papers on the assessment of writing. Both groups recognize that writing assessment occurs for several purposes, from entry-level placement to graduation requirements, and they recommend that a variety of student work be examined when possible. The CCCC's guiding principles call for assessment to be used for improvement in teaching and learning, undertaken in response to local goals and objectives for writing, and accompanied by professional development opportunities related to assessment. Assessment must be solidly grounded in research on learning, writing, and assessment, and the methods and criteria used for assessment of writing should allow students to demonstrate their writing. Cognizant of benefits as well as costs, the CCCC advocates direct assessment of writing by instructor-evaluators and opposes the use of machine-scored writing. The NCTE/CWPA white paper makes similar points and calls for assessment that recognizes diversity in language, uses multiple measures, and provides feedback to students. Overall, assessment must be appropriate, fair, and valid.

Carleton College (2013) students create a writing portfolio containing work from three departments or programs, as well as a reflective piece demonstrating the student's accomplishments as a writer. At California Polytechnic State University San Luis Obispo (2014b), assessment of writing includes a writing proficiency exam that is holistically scored by two raters using a six-point scale. Combined scores of 8 pass and 6 fail. If the total grade is 7, a third reader grades the paper. Writing is focused on a general topic reflecting societal problems. Students must argue their position and persuade readers to appreciate their analysis.

AAC&U staff offer their VALUE rubric for written communication with the recognition that it should be modified to reflect local circumstances. The rubric contains five areas: context of and purpose for writing, content development, genre and disciplinary conventions, sources and evidence, and control of syntax and mechanics.

Rubrics can be developed to address specific aspects of writing as well. At Rochester Institute of Technology (n.d.), writing faculty introduced assessment of the ability to "revise and improve written products." Portfolios of student writing were collected from several students in the first-year program. The portfolios included the assignment sheet for an essay, the earliest draft receiving peer response, the draft receiving faculty feedback, and the final essay. Faculty at an assessment retreat developed a set of "criteria for assessing revision" to serve as the basis for a scoring guide (p. 4). After numerous improvements, the scoring guide focused on what revisions were necessary, what revisions were made, and what revisions most improved the essay. During reading sessions, faculty envisioned ways to use their assessment efforts to improve their teaching (Martins, 2010).

The Cognitive Level and Quality Writing Assessment Instrument (CLAQWA) is a direct measure that was developed at the University of South Florida to help instructors assess students' writing and cognitive skills (Flateby, 2010). There are two rubrics for scoring, including a cognitive-level skills scale based on Bloom's taxonomy. The rubrics can be applied to an essay assignment that is part of normal course work.

Information Literacy

The Association of College and Research Libraries (2014) defines information literacy as the ability to identify a need for information and then to responsibly and ethically locate, evaluate, and use information to meet that need. Information literacy is recognized by AAC&U leaders as an essential learning outcome and is included in many campus statements of what students are expected to know and do. With respect to information literacy outcomes at Pikes Peak Community College (n.d.), graduates are expected to identify information needed to complete a task, identify potential relevant sources of information, use various search systems to retrieve information in a variety of formats, evaluate the validity of the source, and demonstrate knowledge about the ethical use of materials.

Gilchrist and Oakleaf (2012) believe that more programs should include information literacy in their curricula rather than leaving students to their own initiative in seeking out necessary skills such as strategies for writing research papers. As they describe, at Pierce College, information literacy assignments are developed by faculty within their courses and differ by discipline. However, samples of student work in this and other general education areas are reported to a central database for analysis by an interdisciplinary faculty team using a standard rubric. On many campuses, librarians collaborate with classroom faculty to integrate assessment of information literacy into course assignments, perhaps in the capstone course. In contrast to these approaches, all first-year students at James Madison University (2013a) must pass the Information-Seeking Skills Test, developed by faculty, librarians, and assessment specialists at the university, before they can register for sophomore-level classes. The test examines whether students can conduct a search using a variety of sources, evaluate and cite information, and use information in ethical ways. Students complete an eight-module self-tutorial before taking the web-based fifty-item exam.

Information literacy at Pikes Peak Community College (2011) is assessed using a locally developed measure that includes evaluation of online resources. Recent assessments have found that students need more work with narrowing searches and understanding browser functions. Efforts have been made to help faculty understand what information literacy is and how to address areas that need improvement. As with writing, faculty on several campuses use across-the-curriculum approaches to teach and assess information literacy. Gilchrist and Oakleaf (2012) describe some novel approaches, including a learning community at the University of Baltimore in Maryland, where a history course is paired with an information literacy course.

Rubrics for assessing information literacy (RAILS) are readily available. The RAILS site (http://railsontrack.info/rubrics.aspx) serves as a clearinghouse for information literacy rubrics organized by topic and creator. Topics include defining information needs, evaluating information, locating information, and using information ethically and responsibly. Once logged in, participants can modify or create their own rubrics.

Oral Communication

Rather than requiring a specific set of speaking skills, the National Communication Association presents a document written in 1998 and reaffirmed in 2012 that contains a number of schemes for faculty to consider as they articulate oral communication outcomes for their own graduates. Oral communication skills include both speaking and listening. While basic speaking skills for college graduates include giving directions and expressing a point of view, advanced speaking skills include adapting messages to the demands of the situation or context, using appropriate examples, and using language that maintains audience interest. Listening requires identifying important issues and understanding the messages of others. The framework developed by faculty working with the National Center for Education Statistics includes skills for communicating in interpersonal and group situations (Jones, Hoffman, Ratcliff, Tibbets, and Click, 1994). Rubin (1995) organizes skills in relationship to the purposes of communication: persuading, informing, and relating.

Although outcomes formulated elsewhere can be very helpful, faculty need to consider for themselves which aspects of oral communication they will teach and assess. Many faculty evaluate speaking skills exhibited through individual or group presentations in class, debates, mock interviews, and other assignments. Faculty may develop their own scoring rubrics to assess presentations and performances. Listening skills can be evaluated by asking students to summarize the main points of a group presentation or to judge the appropriateness of presentations for particular audiences. To assess listening skills, Pikes Peak Community College (n.d.) faculty use a locally developed measure that asks students to watch a short video lecture and then answer questions related to its content.

Several faculty recently used a small grant from Indiana University-Purdue University's Program Review and Assessment Committee to assess student interviewing competences demonstrated in a virtual environment provided by Second Life technology. Social work students entered Second Life as avatars of their own creation in order to interview a chatbox avatar, an artificial standardized patient. The patient was programmed with various options allowing students to practice their interview skills. Student reflection papers indicated they found the experience intriguing (Vernon, Lynch, and Tandy, n.d.).

Two AAC&U VALUE rubrics address oral communication and reading. The Oral Communication rubric can be used to evaluate a presentation by a single speaker and addresses organization, language, delivery, supporting material, and central messages. The Reading rubric is concerned with extracting and constructing meaning through interacting with written language. One area considered is the reader's voice in discussing the text. Framing language in the rubric argues that reading is an area that needs more attention.

Ethical Reasoning

In several programs, faculty prepare their graduates to face ethical dilemmas when they enter the workplace. Ethical behavior requires individuals to be able to recognize and articulate the situation, identify important stakeholders, analyze the situation, and develop responsible solutions. Some faculty have developed strategies to examine ethical reasoning, including the use of problem sets, case study analysis, and simulations. Asking students to consider various scenarios and motives for actions such as keeping a job, being promoted, or acting professionally is one approach to gather evidence. A VALUE rubric defines ethical reasoning as reasoning about right and wrong human conduct. Students who exhibit ethical reasoning are able to assess their own ethical values and the context of problems, recognize ethical issues in various settings, think about how different ethical perspectives can be applied to ethical dilemmas, and consider the ramifications of alternative actions. Although it is difficult to ask students to display ethical reasoning, the rubric asks if students have the tools to make ethical choices. The rubric categories are ethical self-awareness, understanding ethical perspectives, ethical issue recognition, application of ethical perspectives and concepts, and evaluation of different ethical perspectives.

The Defining Issues Test (Rest, 1993) is a commercially available instrument that provides an objective measure of moral reasoning. It is based on Kohlberg's (1981) theory of moral development, which moves in stages from adherence to rules, to reasoning based on universal ethical principles. Students are asked to read a set of stories that illustrate moral dilemmas, then indicate their recommendations for what the person described in the story should do. Several scores are generated for the test, the most important of which provides a general index of the development of moral judgment. High values indicate that students emphasize following due process and safeguarding basic rights rather than seeking personal advantage or maintaining approval (Pike and Thomas, 2010).

Values and Attitudes

Most general education programs include intended outcomes that address values and attitudes. Faculty may expect students to be sensitive to the values of others, value lifelong learning, and be able to assess their own learning and development. They can assess whether students possess these values and attitudes by observing student behavior directly, including participation in relevant activities, conduct exhibited in group work, and even body language in focus groups. Students also can be asked to self-report about their preferences and behaviors through questions on surveys, focus groups, and interviews.

Many general education programs, as well as programs in the major, are concerned with developing an appreciation for lifelong learning.

Faculty expect students who exhibit this value to be able to access information, participate in professionally oriented organizations, and report plans for further study after college. Survey instruments often address values with respect to lifelong learning, such as enjoying learning and valuing a broad education. Self-reports included on alumni surveys can address behaviors such as completing additional study after college.

The engineering accreditor ABET (2014) includes recognizing the need for lifelong learning and the ability to engage in lifelong learning among required outcomes for engineers. Faculty in departments seeking ABET accreditation wrestle with how to operationalize the concept. Borgford-Parnell (2006) at the University of Washington uses several criteria to describe graduates who are engaged in lifelong learning: they are self-aware and reflective of their ongoing learning needs, able to self-assess for knowledge and skill deficiencies, and capable of finding appropriate resources and learning opportunities. Lifelong learners understand their learning preferences and know how to adapt them to maximize learning under different circumstances. In addition, they are sufficiently motivated to engage in lifelong learning. Teachers who foster an appreciation for lifelong learning help students understand their learning styles and learning strategies. They require library and web searches and grade on the quality of documentation and the ability to discern the quality of sources.

Faculty in the engineering department at San Jose State University use student work, course reflections, and student surveys to gather evidence on several outcomes, including lifelong learning. Each outcome has a "champion" responsible for examining evidence and making recommendations for that outcome (Mourtos, 2003). The VALUE rubric for Foundations and Skills of Life-Long Learning recognizes all purposeful activity aimed at improving knowledge, skills, and confidence and includes the areas of curiosity, initiative, independence, transfer, and reflection.

General education programs often help students develop a capacity for self-assessment. Indeed, this is one indicator of a successful assessment program. Student capacities for self-assessment can be examined through statements contained in portfolios, through self-assessment of various projects, and by examining the quality of student peer review. To facilitate self-assessment, students should be taught to ask whether their own thinking, as well as the thinking of others, is accurate, relevant, and logical. Alverno College (2006) faculty have incorporated the concept of self-assessment in their curriculum by articulating a developmental framework that guides students as their abilities to self-assess broaden. The framework identifies four components of skills inherent in self-assessment: observing, interpreting/analyzing, judging, and planning. Skills are identified at beginning, intermediate, and advanced proficiency levels. The growth of e-portfolios has increased attention to this ability and has generated research on the topic of student reflection (Yancey, 2009; Eynon, Gambino, and Torok, 2014b).

In addition to valuing lifelong learning and being able to engage in self-assessment, most general education programs contain an expectation that students will develop sensitivity to the values of others, an ability that can be assessed through self-reporting and by observations of student behaviors. Based on the work of Bennett (2008), the relevant AAC&U VALUE rubric defines intercultural knowledge and competence as "a set of cognitive, affective, and behavioral skills and characteristics that support effective and appropriate interaction in a variety of cultural contexts" (AAC&U, 2014d, p. 18). The rubric developers acknowledge that understanding intercultural knowledge is more complex than is reflected in the rubric, which identifies six key areas for assessment. The two knowledge aspects are self-cultural awareness and cultural worldview frameworks, the two skills are empathy and verbal and nonverbal communication, and the two attitudes are curiosity and openness.

McKendree University (2013) faculty emphasize assessment of one student outcome each year, with a second in a carefully designed planning and development stage. The year 2013–2014 has been the Year of Diversity on that campus. Faculty have implemented assessment tools developed by the Diversity Subcommittee and educated the campus community about the diversity student outcome.

At Oklahoma State University, faculty have developed expectations for student learning with respect to knowledge, skills, and attitudes needed to understand and consider diverse points of view (Bowers, 2009). An institutional portfolio containing samples of student work from various courses is used to assess student achievement of the diversity goal. Faculty found few external examples when developing their diversity rubric. Instead, they began to articulate the goal based on university policy documents. Faculty workshops were used to obtain input about initial drafts. The current rubric contains a five-point scale and four criteria. Student work must demonstrate conceptual understanding, a perspective of inclusion, knowledge of historical context, and understanding based on reflection and integration of substantial factual knowledge and personal observation. Samples of student work receive a score on each criterion, as well as an overall score for each paper. Developing the assessment tool has helped faculty focus on diversity as a goal and on creating additional assignments to help students learn about diversity.

As higher education faces demographic and social change, Bringle, Clayton, and Plater (2013) argue for the importance of teaching and assessing knowledge, skills, and dispositions related to the areas of diversity, civic engagement, and global learning. Because these areas are often addressed through service or experiential learning, the authors believe faculty should include as many stakeholders as possible in describing outcomes. They recommend that direct measures be used when feasible. On campuses committed to nurturing the development of civic-minded graduates, they believe work on assessing these three areas, and especially their integration, can provide models for what institutions of higher learning should become.

The Degree Qualifications Profile

In this chapter, we considered separately several of the outcomes that are typically included in general education programs. In reality, students often are exposed to these outcomes simultaneously, and they may be assessed on them simultaneously as well. For example, a classroom presentation describing a historical event may consider aspects of communication, critical thinking, information literacy, perhaps ethics, and other outcomes. A related assignment may ask students to analyze a set of problems using all of these skills. That assignment may then be used as part of a course-embedded assessment process. In this case, assessment reflects that learning is integrated, rather than a separate collection of outcomes.

The Degree Qualifications Profile (DQP) asks faculty to consider alignment of learning, not just within or across individuals but also across institutions. Lumina Foundation principals published the DQP in January 2011 to challenge academic leaders and faculty to think about aligning expectations for student learning across higher education. The DQP articulates a set of specific learning expectations for three degree levels (associate, bachelor's, and master's) in five areas of learning: specialized knowledge, broad integrative knowledge, applied learning, civic learning, and intellectual skills. The last area includes the cross-cutting skills of analytic inquiry, communication fluency, quantitative fluency, engaging diverse perspectives, and use of information resources. Competences are described in action terms appropriate to each of the three levels of study. At the associate level, students may be expected to describe material. At the bachelor's level, they may be expected to explain an idea, and at the master's level, they may be expected to evaluate or create a product. In addition to stating competences, the DQP suggests the kinds of demonstrations that might be relevant for assessing each outcome. The central message of the DQP is the importance of intentionality in the way learning goals, curricula, teaching strategies, and assessment techniques are selected and applied. The DQP competences are statements of what every graduate of a degree program should know and be able to do. The competences are not focused on the average student or a sample of students, but on every student, insisting that all graduates master all competences. Faculty judgment is at the center of this scheme, however, as progressively more challenging exercises, assignments, demonstrations, and other activities are designed (Ewell, 2013).

Lumina Foundation support subsequently was given to organizations willing to experiment with DQP-related projects. Schneider (2013) believes that the DQP faces challenges in being accepted. The tendency to treat college learning as occurring in silos (general education, major, cocurricular) is one obstacle to the approach of intentionality and collaboration implied by the DQP. Fear that common outcomes will lead to common testing also is widespread. Schneider laments that the initial funding of projects was for institutions to examine pieces of the DQP framework, when in fact one of the framework's strengths is its view of education as integrated and applied, with curricula that are designed to connect students' experiences. Schneider concludes that with respect to the DQP, "faculty collaboration across the usual curricular boundaries is indispensible for success" (p. 28). A revised version of the DQP maintains the original framework while addressing some faculty concerns. For example, the language now incorporates the term *proficiencies* rather than *competencies* (Adelman, Ewell, Gaston, and Schneider, 2014).

Assessing General Education Outcomes within the Major

According to the 2002 AAC&U report *Greater Expectations: A New Vision for Learning as a Nation Goes to College,* "the goals of liberal education are so challenging that all the years of college and the entire curriculum are needed to accomplish them. Responsibility for a coherent curriculum rests on the shoulders of all faculty members working cooperatively" (p. 31). In 2004, Gaff noted the challenge in enticing individual departments to incorporate attention to general education goals in their major programs.

Now, faculty in many disciplines endorse outcomes that are traditionally associated with general education. In the philosophy department at the College of Saint Benedict and Saint John's University, faculty took several years before agreeing that excellence in their graduating philosophy majors was reflected in the "capacity to engage in independent and creative problem solving" (Wright, 2011, p. 4). Once on board, faculty agreed on fundamental skills and dispositions consistent with their curriculum. Dispositions include an increased comfort with ambiguity, increased capacity to resist quick and easy answers, and increased pleasure in studying difficult ideas. Drawing on the work of others and based on feedback about earlier attempts, the department assessment coordinator created a "comfort with ambiguity" scale that provides assessment information for the department.

Assessment methods administered in the major often are used for dual purposes. At the same time that faculty examine discipline-specific knowledge and concepts, they also address generic skills such as problem solving and critical thinking. Faculty may assign a project in a capstone course asking students to integrate what they have learned in general education areas with what they have learned in the major.

Approximately 40 percent of provosts report that program outcomes are aligned with institution outcomes on their campuses, and this number can be expected to grow (Kuh et al., 2014). Reinforcing this trend, most professional accrediting bodies specifically address intended outcomes that are descriptive of all college-educated persons.

In the next chapter, we look at assessment in student affairs, another division of the campus that embraces transferable outcomes for learning.

CHAPTER 9

ASSESSING STUDENT LEARNING AND PROGRAM EFFECTIVENESS IN STUDENT AFFAIRS

Just as it has been said that it takes a village to raise a child, it takes the efforts of a campus to produce a graduate. From the time potential students hear about the campus from admissions staff, to registration and orientation, to their first class, through participation in campus activities and leadership development opportunities, students who matriculate are influenced by student affairs personnel. They interact with financial aid counselors and residence hall staff, student activities coordinators in the campus center, and tutors and mentors who meet them outside class. In fact, students spend only about one-third of their time during college attending class and studying and two-thirds engaged in other activities (Kuh, Schuh, Whitt, and Associates, 1991). In the preceding chapters, we described faculty roles in the process of producing a graduate. Now we turn to the responsibilities of student affairs professionals.

Foundations for Assessment in Student Affairs

With extra-class activities playing such an influential role in student learning and development during college, it is as essential that we assess support programs and services as it is to assess pedagogy and curricular effectiveness. Schuh, Upcraft, and Associates (2001) offer several reasons that student affairs leaders should be engaged in outcomes assessment. The first is to survive: declining resources are forcing cuts in both academic programs and student services, so student affairs units must be prepared to demonstrate their worth. Is a unit providing high-quality service? Demonstrating quality may include comparisons with professional standards or with other institutions.

As with academic departments, support units must have goals and objectives against which their performance can be measured. Issues of cost and affordability may arise. Perhaps the services are needed and valuable, but could be offered in a more cost-effective way. Assessment can help service units with strategic planning, focusing on big issues, and preparing for the future, and can assist with immediate decisions, such as how to improve services and reach appropriate audiences.

Student affairs professionals most often begin their work in assessment by gauging awareness and use: How many students know about their programs, and then how many actually participate or take advantage of a program or service? Next, student affairs staff may focus on satisfaction: How satisfied are students who take part in a program or use a service? Students may be contacted days, weeks, or months after their participation to see if their expectations have been met or if they have progressed in desired ways in the interim.

Perhaps even more important, student affairs professionals can contribute to student learning related to classroom experiences. These staff can provide tutors and mentors who know the subject matter and thus can help students with their class assignments. They can set up group activities, such as service-learning or attendance at a play or concert in the community, or study abroad, that extend learning outside the classroom. They can conduct leadership development programs to strengthen that all-important ability employers covet in graduates. In their own programs—those they conduct independent of specific classroom-connected activities—student affairs practitioners can target specific generic skills, such as oral communication and critical thinking. Having a job on campus has been demonstrated to increase student retention to graduation. Serving as a residence hall counselor or helping to staff the student center are jobs that help students acquire skills that will be useful as they pursue careers. Having a student affairs professional as a supervisor can help to ensure that student employees are learning valuable skills on the job.

The Student Learning Imperative developed in 1994 by the American College Personnel Association (ACPA) called for institutions of higher education to create "conditions that motivate and inspire students to devote time and energy to educationally-purposeful activities" (1994, p. 1). The document calls for student affairs professionals to help students connect their out-of-class experiences with their in-class experiences and to focus their efforts on achieving overall institutional goals for learning and development. In addition, it argues for collaboration across all areas of the campus.

Ten years later, in *Learning Reconsidered* (Keeling, 2004) educators were encouraged to view learning as an integrated and transformative act and to seek consensus about the competences and skills that students who complete an undergraduate degree need to possess. Then, educators should map the processes through which students gain these competences and skills and specify ways in which their development can be tracked and evaluated. *Learning Reconsidered* offers a set of seven broad desirable learning outcomes with associated dimensions: cognitive complexity; knowledge acquisition, integration, and application; humanitarianism; civic engagement; interpersonal and intrapersonal competence; practical competence; and persistence and academic achievement. Student affairs professionals are expected to work in partnership with faculty to clarify, define, and achieve these goals. The writers of *Learning Reconsidered* acknowledged that this reconceptualization of learning would bring new responsibilities for student affairs professionals, requiring them to become "full partners in assessing and researching the student experience and college outcomes" (p. 25). Furthermore, "assessment should be a way of life," as student affairs professionals participate in "comprehensive, systematic, and consistent assessment of student learning" (p. 26). *Learning Reconsidered* authors argue for assessment to emphasize student learning rather than satisfaction and to draw on a rich selection of direct and indirect methods, including the use of rubrics.

The Council for the Advancement of Standards in Higher Education (CAS, 2012), a consortium of approximately forty professional organizations that promotes improvement of programs and services to enhance the quality of student learning and development, drew on *Learning Reconsidered* as its recommended outcomes for learning and development were revised in 2008. CAS offers outcomes for learning and development in six domains that correspond roughly to those offered in *Learning Reconsidered*. CAS maintains standards for assessing each student affairs function, as well as general standards that address twelve areas of student affairs practice. Further CAS (2012) revisions in 2011 reflected the work done by ACPA and the National Association of Student Personnel Administrators (NASPA) to define competence areas for student affairs professionals. CAS standards ask student affairs professionals to consider student learning as their primary mission. One of the general standards addresses assessment and evaluation. According to this standard, student support units are to have clearly articulated assessment plans that document achievement of learning outcomes and include evidence of improvement. Direct and indirect methods should be used to demonstrate the degree to which the program's mission, goals, and intended outcomes are being met. Data must include responses from students and other constituents, and these groups must be aware of results and changes made.

In 2006, the ACPA commission directorate for assessment and evaluation released a set of Assessment Skills and Knowledge (ASK) Standards for student affairs professionals with assessment related responsibilities. The standards are illustrated in practice in *Assessment in Practice: A Companion Guide to the ASK Standards,* an edited volume released by ACPA (Timm, Barham, McKinney, and Knerr, 2013). The guide uses a systematic view of assessment to organize its advice. Topics include fundamentals, defining outcomes, collecting data, and using data to direct improvements. Each chapter addresses one or more of the applicable ASK standards. This reference can be helpful as student affairs educators evaluate their assessment approaches.

Pressures for evidence of accountability from accrediting bodies, legislatures, and the public are felt not just by academic administrators and faculty. Many student affairs administrators have responded to these calls by becoming active participants in improving student learning. At the University of Oregon (n.d.), for example, professionals in the division of student affairs engage in assessment in order to improve their roles as educators and achieve their core purpose of transforming and advancing student learning. Assessment at John Carroll University (n.d.) provides an opportunity for reflection and a means to highlight and improve the division's contributions to student learning.

As is true for all divisions of the institution, successfully undertaking assessment in student affairs has three essential stages: planning, implementing, and then improving and sustaining the process (see Chapter 2). Student affairs personnel must articulate purposes, goals, and plans and create foundations and structures that support assessment. Then resources and training must be provided as methods are chosen and carried out. Sustaining assessment requires the use of credible evidence to improve programs, services, and student learning.

To begin designing an effective assessment program, some student affairs divisions offer a definition of student learning. At the University of Alaska (n.d.), Sacramento State (California State University Sacramento, n.d.), and other campuses, definitions are based on those in *Learning*

Reconsidered (Keeling, 2004). Student learning at Sacramento State is described as a "comprehensive, holistic, transformative activity that integrates academic learning and student development, processes that have often been considered separate, and even independent of each other." In the division, "the term learning does not mean exclusively or primarily academic instruction, the acquisition of disciplinary content, or classroom learning." Student affairs leaders also provide definitions for *assessment* and *evaluation*, generally recognizing that both use evidence for improvement (Barham and Dean, 2013). Barham, Tschepikow, and Seagraves (2013) believe having a common language is a key to successful assessment and suggest using a consensus-building process as one way to identify and agree on the meaning of important terms.

Mission, Goals, and Objectives

Assessment begins when campus and division leaders articulate their purposes.

At the Rochester Institute of Technology (2011) a solid, agreed-on set of goals and objectives underlies a successful assessment program. Its vision of student affairs is to develop the nation's most engaged campus community through the design and delivery of high-impact programs and services. The division's strategic goals include enhancing involvement in and commitment to the campus community, initiating innovative practices to strengthen their ability to meet student needs, improving the holistic wellness of all students, integrating assessment results into strategic planning, and advancing the management of information and communication. Using worksheets, each unit within student affairs develops a strategic plan in support of the division plan.

Goals and Objectives

After articulating an overall mission, student affairs leaders can address the specific goals and objectives that will provide direction for assessment. Gettysburg College (2014) professionals provide four cocurricular learning goals that support college goals: citizenship—responsibility to the community; integrity—aligning values and actions; inclusiveness—engaging multiple perspectives; and emotional intelligence—building interpersonal relationships, which involves self-awareness, self-regulation, self-motivation, empathy, and social skill. The goal of citizenship is shared with the college's baccalaureate goal of informed citizenship. At the cocurriculum level, citizenship is demonstrated through using knowledge for the benefit of the community and acting responsibly. In academics, the goal is demonstrated by, for example, understanding other cultures and learning a foreign language. Study abroad, service-learning, and civic engagement provide additional occasions for demonstrating the citizenship goal outside the classroom.

Personnel in the division of Student Success at the University at Albany, State University of New York (n.d.), use a student learning outcomes framework to guide their assessment process. The framework's three learning domains capture the types of learning most valued at the university: balanced life choices, cultural awareness, and university citizenship. A student learning project develops attainable and measurable outcomes at the unit level in each of the division's three domains.

In the division of student affairs at the University of North Carolina Wilmington (n.d.), students are expected to demonstrate learning and development in the following areas: informed reasoning, effective communication, personal responsibility, inclusion and multicultural competence, well-being, and community and civic engagement. University staff recognize that student learning is a dynamic process in motion within individuals. Learning outcomes are viewed as interactive rather than independent. For example, informed reasoning (reasoning about controversial issues) affects multicultural competence (seeing more than one perspective) and shapes how one constructs general well-being (attitudes toward best health practices).

Student affairs professionals use various strategies to develop statements of expected outcomes. Leaders at Louisiana State University (n.d.) engaged in an intensive retreat and reviewed department efforts focused on student learning. They also considered the CAS Standards and NASPA/ACPA publications. Staff eventually selected several student success outcomes (SSOs) that focus on student learning and growth. To develop outcomes for their student affairs division, members of the student learning outcomes task force at Weber State University used a peer-facilitated process. They identified themes from outcomes statements submitted by individual departments. Suggestions were categorized and named as the task force sought consensus (Bresciani, 2013). Members of the student affairs leadership team at the University of Georgia spent a year developing student affairs learning and development objectives (SALDOs), which reflect best practices found in the professional literature, as well as general education goals for the university (Bresciani, 2013).

Mapping Outcomes

The process of mapping outcomes, that is, identifying learning activities that address the outcomes, is strongly recommended in *Learning Reconsidered 2* (Keeling, 2006). Mapping can include intended as well as actual connections and can also show the level of activity involved. Is the outcome introduced or reinforced? Is it a main focus of the program? What level of complexity is involved?

Personnel in the division of student affairs at Ball State University (2014b) present student learning outcomes framed in terms of the related experiences most likely to produce the outcomes. For example, they expect that students will demonstrate leadership competence through involvement in residence hall activities, student organizations, and other cocurricular experiences. Life skills are gained through living/learning communities, career exploration, student employment, and student organizations. The Ball State website presents a completed outcomes map—a matrix with outcomes as row headings and the names of various departments as column headings. Each department is expected to map its own programs and services to the outcomes as part of the planning process.

Leadership and Preparation for Assessment in Student Affairs

As in other divisions, assessment in student affairs benefits from the leadership of senior administrators (Schuh and Gansemer-Topf, 2010) At California State University Sacramento (n.d.), the senior vice president of the division of planning, enrollment management, and student affairs joined leaders of institutional research in academic affairs to launch a comprehensive outcomes-based program in 2005. The vice president encouraged all of the division's twenty or more directors to embrace the program. Each year directors formulate three or four student learning outcomes or objectives to track and measure, at least one of which must be a measurable student learning outcome. With several years of history, the assessment process has helped shape many facets of the division, including strategic planning and budgeting, and it has helped the division thrive in challenging times.

At Gettysburg College (2014), the vice president for student life and dean of students greets all students, parents, colleagues, alumni, and friends with a message on her web page establishing that student learning is the core goal of the college's out-of-class experiences. Students are expected to use their learning to make a difference in their professions, their communities, and the organizations they join. The message describes each of the learning goals adopted for the cocurriculum and establishes their importance.

The commitment to enhancing student learning in the division of student affairs at the University of North Carolina Wilmington (n.d.) is expressed through a statement of good practices for student learning. Good practice in student affairs at the university engages students in active learning (through, for example, structured group experiences and field-based learning); helps students develop coherent values and ethical standards; sets high expectations for student learning that are communicated and assessed; uses resources effectively, including professional staff who can draw on theory and research to improve learning; and forges partnerships across and beyond the campus. The thoroughly referenced list includes an additional aspect of good practice: using systematic inquiry to improve student learning and institutional performance. Good practice begins when student affairs educators ask what their students are learning and how that learning can be improved.

To turn intentions into actions requires support from many sources. Some of the approaches that various student affairs divisions use are described next.

Committees, Offices, and Assessment Teams

To help assessment thrive, student affairs professionals draw on ad hoc and standing committees, internal and external offices, and their own action teams. On many campuses, the student affairs division has its own assessment committee that plays a strong role through providing overall direction, consulting with units, reviewing unit plans and reports, staying current on assessment techniques, and providing resources and training opportunities. Student affairs professionals also may serve on campuswide committees that include academic administrators and faculty.

At Bowling Green State University (2014), a standing Assessment Committee within the Division of Student Affairs includes members appointed by the senior associate vice president. The committee has responsibility for reviewing annual assessment reports. It revises the division's student learning outcomes to ensure that they align with those of the university, and it provides definitions to guide data collection and measurement. Goals for the committee include discussing assessment projects in department leaders' meetings, encouraging departments to develop at least one marketing strategy to share assessment projects and results, training staff on the creation and use of rubrics to measure student learning directly, and collaborating with institutional research concerning the impact of student affairs programs on student retention rates.

Some large divisions of student affairs establish offices that provide support for assessment and research; others employ a single full- or part-time person who assumes assessment responsibilities. Student affairs assessment staff may provide relevant literature and training, as well as furnish usage counts, conduct satisfaction studies, engage in benchmarking, and carry out other projects.

Professionals from Texas A&M University's (2014) Department of Student Life Studies work with clients to plan assessment projects such as developing student learning outcomes, preparing scannable or web surveys and evaluations, and developing ideas for using results. They provide an assessment questions form to guide thinking about projects. The Student Organizations Assessment Center offers similar services to student organizations. For instance, staff assist organizations in developing questionnaires to gather information for planning purposes. Students draft the e-mail cover letter and reminders; then Student Life Studies staff analyze the information and generate a report.

In some student affairs divisions, staff rely for data gathering and analysis on campuswide offices such as assessment, institutional research, strategic planning, or institutional effectiveness. At James Madison University (n.d.), student affairs educators work closely with the university's Center for Assessment and Research Studies. Center personnel help student affairs staff broaden and strengthen their assessment initiatives. At DePaul University (2011), student affairs leaders credit both the Office of Institutional Research and Planning and the Office of Teaching, Learning, and Assessment for helping them design an integrated assessment program that measures day-to-day operations as well as impact on student learning, engagement, and development.

Several student affairs divisions employ an assessment team rather than an assessment committee. At the University of Georgia (n.d.), assessment teams build assessment expertise through a year-long training program. Staff from the Department of Student Affairs Assessment provide the basics of assessment to team members, then draw on that foundation to enhance assessment practice and abilities. Having practitioners throughout the division ensures that the work of assessment does not fall on only unit directors or student affairs assessment staff (Barham et al., 2013). In the Division of Student Affairs at the University of Florida (n.d.), the assessment team is a group of professionals from inside and outside the division. Team members support assessment efforts by planning special events such as assessment boot camps and poster sessions. The team has subcommittees for projects, training, and collaboration.

Resources and Training

Student affairs staff who have earned a master's degree may be better prepared to assess student learning outcomes, as well as the outcomes of their own programs, than the many faculty who have not been trained as teachers. Graduate programs in student affairs or higher education often include courses in statistics, survey methods, and even outcomes assessment. Thus many student affairs professionals can serve as resources to staff and faculty who are new to assessment.

The two major student affairs organizations, ACPA (College Student Educators International) and NASPA (Student Affairs Administrators in Higher Education), have special interest groups focused on assessment. They also sponsor annual assessment conferences and learning communities and maintain lists of assessment-related resources on their websites. Specialty organizations for professionals in areas such as residence life, recreational sports, student health, and advising provide support for assessment as well. In addition, the directors of student affairs assessment have created their own network: Student Affairs Assessment Leaders.

The Assessment Institute in Indianapolis contains a student affairs track, and the Association for Institutional Research also provides relevant conference sessions. Written resources include Upcraft and Schuh's seminal 1996 and 2001 (Schuh and Upcraft) books as well as the more recent Schuh and Associates (2009). These books include specific steps for assessing a number of student affairs functions. ACPA and NASPA offer publications about assessment including *Learning Reconsidered 2* (Keeling, 2006), *Assessment Reconsidered* (Keeling et al., 2008), and the ACPA newsletter *Developments*. Materials from NASPA and ACPA concerning professional competence guidelines that both organizations endorsed in 2010 are also available. ACPA's guide to the ASK Standards (Timm et al., 2013) emphasizes the need to develop assessment skills. Noting in the abstract that "many student affairs professionals are overwhelmed by the idea of assessment," the book covers all aspects of the assessment cycle, beginning with a discussion of the need to clarify and establish a common language for assessment (Barham and Dean, 2013) and to develop outcomes for learning and development (Bresciani, 2013).

Student affairs professionals can find many online resources on their own campuses. For example, guidelines at West Virginia University's site

(2014) establish that the primary purpose of assessment in student affairs is to provide evidence of program quality and student learning and development. Staff at the College of William and Mary (n.d.) provide a statement of values for assessment: assessment should guide decisions, promote collaboration, and help tell the division's story.

At Portland State University (2011), California State University Sacramento (2013), and elsewhere, online assessment guides offer step-by-step processes for designing and implementing assessment projects. Portland State (2014a) leaders provide an activity on how to start an assessment conversation and a planning sheet to help staff align unit goals and activities with division themes and campuswide learning outcomes.

At Ohio State University (2014), Center for the Study of Student Life (CSSL) staff offer workshops and training on topics including qualitative and quantitative research, organizational effectiveness, and assessment. A Resources tab contains information on these topics in the form of presentations, worksheets, and links to helpful websites. CSSL staff also create training videos that are posted on YouTube. Training videos focus on topics like writing student learning outcomes and conducting focus groups.

At the University of Georgia (n.d.), Department of Student Affairs Assessment staff offer training in all areas of assessment, including designing projects, implementing both direct and indirect assessment methods, and using assessment results for improvement. At the University at Albany (n.d.), members of the Assessment Council have developed an assessment education professional development program to help division staff become knowledgeable about assessment planning, design, and implementation. The program provides a mixture of webinars, individual exercises, and projects. In addition to learning about assessment concepts, participants develop practical assessment skills that relate to everyday work in the division.

Division of Student Affairs administrators at the University of Oregon (n.d.) have created a student affairs assessment fellows program for professional staff. Assessment fellows receive specialized training to increase their assessment knowledge and skills. Then, working closely with unit directors, they serve as leaders and consultants within their respective units.

Student affairs leaders may conduct or collaborate on annual assessment-related events. At the University of North Texas (n.d.), assessment teams help with the university's annual student portraits symposium, a campuswide collaboration involving staff from the Divisions of Student Affairs and Academic Affairs. Key issues related to student success and retention are explored using assessment data. An annual conference at

Emory University (2014b) advances assessment knowledge and practice among student affairs professionals.

Assessment Frameworks, Models, and Diagrams

Creating assessment frameworks, models, and diagrams allows student affairs leaders to clarify the process for professional staff and draw attention to what matters most as assessment is carried out.

The assessment framework for the Division of Student Affairs at the University of North Carolina Chapel Hill (n.d.) contains seven components, each accompanied by a related question:

- Strategic goals and outcomes (what to assess)
- Information and data needs of student affairs (what data the leadership team needs)
- The role of the division's Assessment Council (how to work together on the practice of assessment)
- Unit assessment plans (how to practice assessment at the unit level)
- Administrative reviews (how to determine if missions are fulfilled)
- Individual and organizational competences (how to learn about assessment)
- Inside and outside partnerships (how to collaborate on assessment)

The framework illustrates that in implementing assessment, the training needs of individuals and the way they work together are important.

In many student affairs divisions, assessment is conceived as a systematic process represented in a circular flow. At the center of the University of Oregon's (n.d.) circular flow model is the important step of articulating mission, goals, and outcomes. This reinforces the division's core purpose—"to transform and advance student learning"—and signals that all activities must be aligned with this purpose. Each program and unit assesses how it contributes to the division's outcomes, describing methods for delivering the selected outcomes. Next steps are to collect data, interpret findings, and then use the evidence to improve programs and services. Finally the process is repeated to ensure that new programs and improvements to existing programs are accomplishing their purposes. Oregon's model reflects several elements of good practice: it recognizes that programs and strategies need to be in place so that students have an opportunity to learn what is expected of them and it acknowledges that the process should be repeated.

The assessment model at the University of North Carolina Asheville (2014) addresses both student learning and operational objectives and begins with strategic plans, directives, and student learning outcomes. Assessment should help to refine, improve, or change programs, services, and outcomes and to inform the ongoing strategic process. All goals, outcomes, assessment plans, results, and action steps are entered in TracDat. Then Campus Labs technology is used to create surveys, rubrics, and key performance indicator dashboards. Administrators are advised to ensure that their budgets support their goals.

Assessment Plans and Methods

Plans provide direction for actions and important reference points for gauging progress. A carefully constructed plan establishes the purposes for assessment and the questions to be addressed. It identifies the sources or targets of the information, as well as the time-line and resources available. Even as student affairs divisions increase their focus on assessment of learning outcomes, their plans and activities continue to recognize needs for other types of information. Upcraft and Schuh (1996) and Schuh and his coauthors (2009) describe several types of assessment activities:

- Learning outcomes assessment (including student success)
- Tracking who uses the program (including counts and descriptive information)
- Needs assessment (based on student perception and research)
- Student culture and campus environment assessment
- Comparable institution assessment
- National standards assessment
- Satisfaction assessment
- Cost effectiveness assessment

Staff at the University of Alaska (n.d.), the University of Oregon (n.d.), and other campuses use such lists to assist unit planning.

Planning Templates and Guides

Planning templates guide assessment for many student affairs units. At Portland State University (2014a), staff must align mission, goals, objectives, and methods and provide information about when and from whom information will be collected. At Pennsylvania State University (n.d.b), a planning template contains unit objectives and learning outcomes (with a brief description of how they were identified), key findings from recent assessment activities and how they have affected policies or practices, and assessment plans for the coming year or longer. A multiyear assessment matrix helps units plan for the future. In the matrix, outcomes are shown as rows, with semesters as column headings. The matrix can include current and future assessment activities, planning activities, and actual or planned changes in programs.

Student Affairs Division staff at the University of Utah (n.d.) have completed an assessment matrix that shows planned assessment projects for each department categorized by type (general outcomes, learning outcomes, needs, satisfaction, tracking, and other). Many of the assessment projects fit multiple categories. The frequency of the projects and the population to be studied also are reported in the matrix. The matrix allows staff in one unit to be aware of projects in other units.

To guide planning, Weber State University (2014b) staff provide a pyramid for assessment practice. Descriptive data (head counts and demographics) are at the bottom. Satisfaction comes next, followed by performance indicators (cohort tracking data). At the top of the pyramid is evidence about student learning outcomes.

Methods

Once student affairs professionals have determined the types of information they want and from whom, they can make good choices about methods. Chapter 4 contains advice about selecting methods and includes our recommendation to complete an inventory of information that is available internally before planning additional data collection. Saunders and Wohlgemuth (2009) provide a helpful discussion about the use of existing internal and external databases.

In practice, student affairs staff use both direct and indirect methods and both standardized and locally developed instruments. For example, professionals at Prince George's Community College have experimented with e-portfolios in cocurricular programs involving mentoring and advising of students (Ariovich and Antoons, n.d.).

At Weber State University (2014b), the Student Affairs Assessment Committee formulated rubrics for the division's seven learning outcomes. Their rubric for cultural competence addresses knowledge of diversity, cultural awareness, cultural interaction, and cultural attitudes. The rubrics were adapted from those provided by AAC&U and other sources. Staff at Texas A&M (n.d.) have developed resources and rubrics related to student leadership outcomes in their award-winning student leaders outcomes project. Among others, areas addressed include communication skills, delegation skills, and ethical leadership.

To examine their learning outcomes, Sacramento State (n.d.) educators have moved from using indirect methods such as perceptions of increased learning to direct measures such as rubric-scored essays and portfolios of student work. Direct observations of skills exhibited through role playing and other demonstrations also are used. Improving statements of unit-level student learning outcomes through the use of action verbs has facilitated this transition. Some staff are attempting to assess students' changes in behavior. For example, student health and counseling services staff seek to determine if their clients engage in exercise more often after learning about its benefits.

Because they are based on theory and validated empirically, several commercial inventories of student learning and development are used at the University of North Carolina Wilmington (UNCW, n.d.) such as: the Reasoning About Current Issues Questionnaire, the Socially Responsible Leadership Scale, and the Defining Issues Test-2. Professional staff also are developing some of their own instruments to measure learning outcomes. Although it may appear to be more cost-effective to develop home-grown measures, UNCW leaders recommend that locally developed instruments be based on theory and an understanding of psychometrics.

Many student affairs divisions include surveys among their data-gathering strategies. Weber State (2014b) personnel have developed suggested questionnaire items as well as focus group questions for each of seven student learning outcomes. Campus leaders have developed a graduate survey through collaborative effort among career services, alumni services, the academic colleges, and student affairs assessment and research. Studying the survey findings assists faculty and administrators in planning curriculum and advising students. The survey is administered upon graduation and at regular intervals thereafter.

Pennsylvania State University's (n.d.b) well-known survey initiative, Pulse, uses a brief questionnaire focused on a particular topic in both web and phone surveys to gain a better understanding of students' opinions on that topic. The program was initiated in spring 1995 by student affairs professionals at Penn State to gather feedback on student issues, expectations, use of services, and satisfaction. Several Pulse reports are available online.

Staff in each student affairs unit at DePaul University (2011) collect performance data on key activities (cost, magnitude, satisfaction, and learning outcomes) and conduct at least one annual assessment project that focuses on student learning. Departments are recognized for good practice such as assessing students' assignments or writing samples rather than self-reported gains in learning. Using final papers, reflective journals, or action plans as embedded evidence of learning also is applauded. Good practice includes tying results to specific outcomes and grounding the project in literature. Introducing multiple methods, both quantitative and qualitative, is also encouraged.

Staff from the University of South Carolina Columbia (2013) university housing office use several strategies to document the learning and engagement of residents. Expected student outcomes include academic progress, awareness of self, awareness of others, and involvement in community. To examine these outcomes, resident mentors (student staff) use an online form to track the frequency and type of contacts with students. In addition, students use card-swipe machines when they attend planned events. Data are uploaded to identify descriptive information about attendees. Resident mentors also participate in intentional conversations with each resident. Chat questions allow staff to examine student development. Results from the strategies are shared with hall leaders in a timely way. Because community planning for the residential communities involves partners outside the residence hall, data are shared with external stakeholders as well (Falluca and Lewis, 2013).

Student affairs professionals are conducting many comprehensive studies that incorporate assessment data. Based on their individual needs and criteria, or perhaps on a campuswide system that serves academic needs as well, many division leaders are using software systems such as TracDat, WEAVE, Xitracs, CollegiateLink, Campus Labs, and OrgSync to collect and manage data and produce reports. Educational Benchmarking is one example of a firm that offers questionnaires and scale and item averages that can be compared with those of peer institutions. Chapter 6 contains additional examples of assessment projects in student affairs.

Reporting and Sharing Results

Annual reports of assessment findings and their use to guide improvements are required for most student affairs units, usually according to a schedule. Ball State University (2014b) reports are due by June 1 of each year, with highlights presented to the vice president in May. Often a template is provided for annual reports.

Reporting Templates

Student affairs staff at some institutions complete a common reporting template that is used elsewhere on campus. For example, all administrative and student support units at Emory University (2014a) complete an annual report identifying expected outcomes and providing evidence of improvement based on analysis of assessment results. Reports are collected in the university's Office of Institutional Research, Planning, and Effectiveness, where the template and a brief instruction guide were developed. Examples of reports exhibiting good practice are provided on the office website.

At Bowling Green State University (2014), the Student Affairs Assessment Committee expects each unit to submit both an annual report and at least one program assessment report that describes a signature program and indicates the university and division learning outcomes that the program addresses. For example, the program may address the division goal of inquiry—applying knowledge in a practical way. The report includes methods and achievement targets, as well as key results, decisions, and recommendations. Graphs or other visual representations of results are recommended. In contrast to the program assessment report, the annual report contains descriptive information on the unit, such as highlights, collaborations, and awards. Information about program use, performance indicators, and retention initiatives is also solicited.

Evaluating Reports

Two or three Assessment Council members at Oregon State University (n.d.) review the plans and reports submitted by unit staff with emphasis on providing oral and written formative feedback. To help focus on important aspects of assessment, members use a rubric to guide their evaluation. Mission and goals are evaluated according to the criteria of purpose, clarity, and sustainability. Learning outcomes are judged for clarity, measurability, and usefulness, as are operational and business outcomes. Assessment methods must be aligned and appropriate. The results section of the annual report is evaluated for analysis, interpretation, and sharing of findings. Decisions and recommendations are examined for the process of reflection and communication, as well as intended actions. Comments on the reports are meant to improve assessment in the division.

Emory University's (2014a) OIRPE staff facilitate reviews of annual assessment reports using an assessment report evaluation rubric. Each of several areas is evaluated as excellent, acceptable, or needs improvement/clarification. Among the areas evaluated are assessment measures, analysis of results, and planned improvements.

Communicating Results

To highlight their efforts and expertise, Schuh and Gansemer-Topf (2010) believe that student affairs staff "must find mechanisms through which they can communicate their knowledge of student learning and the results of their efforts to enhance student learning" (p. 9). Many student affairs administrators have given priority to sharing assessment information with others, including students. Communication with students is particularly important because it builds support for future projects and credibility for assessment (Dean, 2013). At the University at Albany (n.d.), program initiatives based on assessment results are shared with students through the Your Voice communication campaign. The campaign is made up of visual displays that contain three headings: "Your Voice" (the finding), "We Responded" (what was changed), and "The Result" (e.g., increased satisfaction).

University of North Carolina Wilmington (n.d.) staff use flyers posted around campus; local TV ads; and articles in "SPLASH," a bimonthly newsletter to parents, to share assessment results and changes made to programs and services based on assessment findings. The We've Heard Your Voice campaign demonstrates to students that the time spent taking surveys makes a difference. Oregon State University (2014) staff in the Office of Research, Evaluation, and Planning have published a quarterly newsletter, *OSU Perspective,* for more than ten years that shares assessment advice and results, such as those from the National Survey of Student Engagement.

Student Affairs Research and Assessment Office staff at Pennsylvania State University (n.d.b) use an assessment listserv to communicate assessment-related information to interested parties, including links to office reports on several survey projects. Staff also maintain an online educational programming record to track the programs division staff present each year.

Ethical Behavior

The CAS standards (2012), as well as the ACPA and NASPA joint task force guidelines for professional competence (2010), emphasize ethical professional practice. The influence of these standards and guidelines is evident in student affairs assessment programs. For example, professionals in the Office of Student Life Studies at Texas A&M University (2014) have developed standards of ethical practice to ensure that staff understand and are committed to appropriate performance. They adapted information from the Association for Institutional Research Code of Ethics (2013) and the Texas A&M University institutional review board for human subjects, as well as the CAS standards. Staff at Texas A&M view their standards as a changing document that is shaped by developments in the field and by experience. Among other items, the standards state that staff will work only on assignments for which they have or can acquire expertise and will prepare reports that are accurate and complete. Students also will be informed that they have the right to refuse to participate in a project.

Timm and Lloyd (2013) note the important role of collaboration in ensuring ethical practice. Ethical dilemmas can occur when individuals work in isolation and fail to connect their work to the mission of the institution or the work of others on campus. They suggest cross-department teams as a strategy for avoiding the isolation syndrome. The Department of Student Affairs Assessment professionals at the University of Georgia (n.d.) include collaboration among the principles of good practice they have developed for their assessment initiatives. On their campus, collaboration occurs through partnerships with student affairs staff, students, faculty, administrators, professional organizations, and other constituents in creating and implementing projects that align with assessment plans of others. Department staff also value frequent and open communication among staff, clients, and the university community through several means, including the development of an easy-to-navigate and informative website.

Administrators at the University of Oregon (n.d.) have designed a helpful assessment protocol for student affairs personnel to consider as they develop assessment plans. If staff plan to work with a random sample of students or wish to solicit students for participation who have not previously interacted with a program, a project planning guide must be submitted for a review facilitated by the division's director of assessment. Approval is not needed if participants in the project are solicited because of their participation in a program or access to a service. Students should not receive repeated requests to participate in evaluation or assessment, particularly from the same source, and they should not be oversurveyed. Institutional review board approval is necessary if data or results are to be used for scholarly purposes such as publication or presentations outside the university.

Improving Assessment

Leaders in divisions of student affairs have created thoughtful and challenging strategies to assess their programs and services and to ensure that they are contributing to student learning. Part of the process is to reexamine the assessment program regularly to see what is and is not working (Dean, 2013). Practitioners at California State University Sacramento (n.d.) share some advice about strategies that helped advance the assessment program on their campus, such as referring to assessment as part of staff evaluations, devoting at least one director's meeting or retreat to assessment activities each semester, drawing on internal and external assessment consultants to assist with assessment, and using a systematic annual process to organize assessment activities. The current assessment initiative reflects the division's planned transition from an approach focused on student satisfaction to one focused on student learning.

Annual assessment reporting requirements at California State University Sacramento (2013) continue to evolve. The term *step* has been phased out of the reporting template and replaced by *point* to recognize that research and inquiry do not necessarily follow a particular order or rigid time line. Division staff believe that assessment should tell a story as it answers questions that are important to the various departments. Emphasis should be more on process and less on product. The revised framework allows staff to work more naturally to follow research questions of interest.

Rewards for Assessment

Returning to the framework of the three Rs presented in Chapter 3 as we discussed the involvement of faculty and students in assessment, it is apparent that student affairs professionals have great responsibility for assessing their programs and services. They also have access to many kinds of resources as they learn about and practice assessment. What about rewards? The vision of *Learning Reconsidered* (Keeling et al., 2004) was that student affairs staff would be collaborators, if not leaders, in university-wide assessment. Some opportunities for collaboration have occurred. The excellent assessment practices exhibited by many student affairs professionals should increase these opportunities. Nevertheless, national leaders in student affairs like George Kuh still point out that student affairs staff are "not always encouraged to participate or become directly involved in campus assessment efforts," nor are all staff prepared to design and conduct effective assessment of the out-of-class experiences they provide for students (Kuh, 2010, p. 4). Schuh and Gansemer-Topf (2010) remind student affairs professionals that division mission must support institutional mission. They also suggest learning communities, service-learning, and study abroad as initiatives that by their nature involve assessment responsibilities for student affairs staff, as well as for faculty, and thus provide opportunities for collaboration. Barham et al. (2013) suggest that student affairs professionals take the lead in establishing cross-division teams for large-scale assessment projects sponsored by student affairs. As high-impact practices increase on campuses, opportunities for collaboration should increase as well. Nevertheless, the reward of collaboration with professionals outside the division is perhaps more elusive than it should be.

An alternative benefit or reward from engaging in assessment is to have assessment results valued in broader processes, and this does happen in many student affairs divisions. The function of assessment is often combined with those of program review and planning, greatly increasing the likelihood that assessment results will be used. At Illinois College (n.d.), for example, staff who propose changes to student life programs must identify the anticipated impact of the changes on student learning and development and provide a plan for measuring that impact.

Tangible rewards for assessment work also should be evident. Staff at the University of Southern California (n.d.) who complete seven workshops and a capstone project are awarded a student affairs assessment certificate to recognize their achievement. Rather than being added on, however, assessment responsibilities should be explicitly referenced in job descriptions (Barham et al., 2013). Schuh and Gansemer-Topf (2010) argue that "assessment must be integrated into the work portfolio of all student affairs staff" (p. 3). Negative results should not affect personnel evaluations, but participation in assessment activities should be recognized. As an explicit recognition, student affairs staff can present results from their assessment work at the conferences we have mentioned. And many periodicals in the field of student affairs, including *About Campus*, the *Journal of Student Affairs Research and Practice* and the *Journal of College Student Development*, publish assessment-related articles.

The need for student affairs professionals to assess their effects on student learning is well established. Although they have faced many challenges in introducing the new focus to their evaluation activities, assessment of student learning is thriving in student affairs, and the literature contains many good examples that can be instructive for all units on campus.

CHAPTER 10

ANALYZING, REPORTING, AND USING ASSESSMENT RESULTS

Assessment information is of little value if it is not shared with appropriate audiences and used in meaningful ways. Internal and external assessment expectations have created the need for plans and reports at the institution, department or program, and often the course level as well. In this chapter, we elaborate on how universities and colleges share their assessment results at both the unit and institution levels. And because gathering data is "much easier than using the information to improve student learning," (Blaich and Wise, 2011, p. 11), we begin by describing some strategies that can help faculty and staff use their assessment results.

Helping Faculty and Staff Use Their Assessment Results

In Chapter 2, we offered some advice about helping faculty and staff plan for assessment. In reality, no matter how well assessment plans are designed, putting plans into practice brings significant challenges. Here we provide examples of approaches that campuses use to encourage their faculty and staff to benefit from assessment information.

Encouraging Reflection and Collaboration

To help turn results into actions, faculty, staff, and students need to reflect on assessment information both individually and collectively. Reflection and collaboration are processes that faculty and staff understand to be valuable and encourage in their students. To ensure that assessment will succeed, they must engage in these processes as well. As Love (2012) has noted, for assessment to work, faculty and staff need time to "think out loud with others, to sort through information and ideas, and to come to conclusions that again get tested" (p. 1). This "So what?" part of assessment encourages faculty and staff to consider how the evidence they have gathered can lead to changes in teaching and learning. Love suggests department meetings as one place for discussion but also notes that in these meetings, faculty may be preoccupied with other business or reluctant to talk about change. She also suggests posting results in high-traffic areas with a request for reactions (a faculty break room might do); sending e-mails with a link to an assessment website that contains results and allows for responses; and inviting faculty to meet face-to-face, perhaps with a few important points to ponder. Ewell (2009) also believes that for assessment to work, faculty must have "concrete opportunities" (p. 16) to look at disaggregated data together and engage in collective reflection before any reporting is done. He recommends starting with a few pieces of information for discussion, with additional results provided in answer to questions that are raised. Although faculty and staff may be more interested in discussing results when they have been involved in data collection themselves, conversations about assessment information that has been generated outside classrooms and programs are necessary and possible. At Augustana College, Friday conversations include information about assessment projects, such as the National Survey of Student Engagement (NSSE). The goal is to share data openly, make findings understandable, and generate interest (Provezis, 2011). Discussing results not only builds interest in assessment but also generates support for change (Dean, 2013).

In *Getting Assessment Completed and Reported*, assessment leaders at the University of North Dakota (2014a) recommend that faculty in every discipline have opportunities to discuss assessment results. One suggestion is to plan an annual retreat for this purpose, perhaps using the retreat to review all assessment information collected during the prior year. Notes from previous retreats can be reviewed and individual courses, curricula, and the assessment process itself discussed. Faculty can determine whether previous plans were followed and can prepare a to-do list for the coming year.

All assessment activities and discussions throughout the semester should be documented in notes for electronic filing. This University of North Dakota report concludes with the observation that if faculty are not interested in discussing assessment results, they may need to reexamine their assessment questions.

The University of Iowa (2011) website contains strategies for conducting "painless assessment meetings" focused on moving assessment forward. Meetings should concentrate on a specific assessment question. Current assessment results should be compared to other information a department has collected and put in the context of future assessment plans. Efforts should be documented. A person or working group should be identified to implement any next steps that have been determined and a time line for these actions should be developed.

The assessment reporting process can be used to encourage dialogue among faculty and staff. Emory University's (2014a) department reporting guidelines ask for a description of how faculty were involved in the assessment process, and Seattle University's (2014) reporting template concludes with a "project ownership" section. The individual completing the report needs to indicate if all faculty were involved in the process and also must describe when, how, and by whom findings were discussed and decisions made. Reedley College's (2013) course reporting template contains a checklist asking academic units to characterize the dialogue that occurred while planning assessment, evaluating results, and determining action plans. The options include "with others during department/division meetings," "during an on-campus workshop," "by email, with colleagues from other campuses," and "with my dean/colleagues." If the final option, "no dialogue occurred," is chosen, a reason for this must be entered as text. Marquette University's (2014) assessment process calls for faculty and staff to discuss their results. Program assessment leaders coordinate program assessment on that campus.

Blaich and Wise (2011), from the Center for Inquiry at Wabash College, worked with dozens of institutions during the Wabash National Study of Liberal Arts Education, a longitudinal investigation of the impact of liberal arts practices on student outcomes. In an occasional paper for the National Institute for Learning Outcomes Assessment (NILOA), *From Gathering to Using Assessment Results*, Blaich and Wise conclude that faculty, staff, and students need to have the opportunity to respond to assessment information before it is distributed, and they recommend that resources be set aside for this purpose. Rather than leaving communication to chance, they recommend developing a communication plan so that a wide range of campus representatives is involved in discussing results and helping to identify one or two outcomes on which to focus improvement efforts. Campuses that participate in the continuing Wabash Study develop plans for conversations about results that are akin to a campaign rather than a series of reports on a website. Conversations may begin before the data are available and can consider what might happen if results are negative. Important individuals, constituents, and governance structures are included in the plans, as are students. Blaich and Wise believe that meeting informally with students and asking them to reflect on their experiences is a particularly helpful way to understand how to interpret and use results.

Providing Mentors

On several campuses, faculty and staff can draw on colleagues with special knowledge as assessment mentors or consultants to help them with assessment responsibilities. To support assessment and program review and to close the loop for continued improvement of student learning at California State University Stanislaus (2013), assessment mentors help faculty interpret assessment findings and decide how to use them for improvement. The Office of Assessment facilitates the mentor program, asking for brief descriptive reports as consultations are completed. Mentors are paid $250 per day. The Professional Resources and Opportunities for Faculty Center at Texas A&M International University provides "assessment champions" to mentor faculty and staff on assessment issues (Baker, 2012b).

Sharing Materials

Providing targeted assessment materials to help faculty and staff think about reporting and using their results is another helpful strategy. If rubrics are used to assess unit reports, these should be shared with faculty and staff to guide them as they carry out their assessment responsibilities. At Cochise College (2009) an assessment checklist encourages faculty and staff to ask thoughtful questions—for example: Is the rationale for selecting the assessment task clear? Are results analyzed in ways consistent with the plan? Is it clear what was learned? Will the action plan close the loop? What steps will be taken to improve student learning?

Assessment leaders may provide lists or tables containing specific suggestions for possible changes faculty can consider as they think about using their assessment results. After suggesting that faculty reflect on results together, Triton College (n.d.) leaders present a list of ideas to consider, including staff development, new teaching materials, an additional assignment, revised prerequisites, and more time on a topic. Office of Institutional Accreditation and Program Assessment personnel at the University of Texas at Austin (2013b) applaud the use of evidence to guide decisions and suggest changes for faculty to consider in using their results. The "Making Changes Based on Evidence" chart organizes possibilities into four categories: program, curriculum, operations, and assessment plan or process. Possibilities to consider in the first category include new program direction or purposes, aligning outcomes with mission, adjusting admission standards, and improving advising processes.

At the Community College of Allegheny County (2011), an online collection of helpful advice prepared by the Assessment Advisory Committee is presented as a tip-of-the-month series. One tip explains the importance of closing the loop, defined as using assessment results to improve student learning, and provides several examples. For example, Art Department faculty recognized that students were having trouble understanding linear perspective and used the finding to make helpful changes in the classroom.

Communicating about How Assessment Results Have Been Used

Barham, Tschepikow, and Seagraves (2013) argue that to embrace assessment, faculty and staff must believe it is worthwhile. One of the best approaches to demonstrate assessment's value and encourage faculty and staff to use their own assessment results is to share what other departments are doing. California State University Stanislaus (2013) educators conduct the annual Assessment Spotlight, a half-day event during which members of the university community present briefings lasting fifteen to twenty minutes on an assessment or continuous improvement project conducted in the current year. University of Central Florida (n.d.) staff have compiled a report of success stories available through the web pages of the Office of Operational Excellence and Assessment Support. Each story contains assessment methods, results, actions taken, and resulting improvements. For example, faculty teaching in the political science master's program used a rubric to grade accomplishments in quantitative research techniques. After results were discussed, faculty decided to bring the course objectives and the rubric into closer alignment, a change that has improved learning. At Portland Community College (2014), award-winning assessment reports are recognized on the website. Reports can be acknowledged in any one of several categories: changes introduced based on prior assessment, assessment design, presentation of results, planned improvements to student achievement of outcomes, or planned improvements to assessment methods or tools.

On the assessment website of the University of North Dakota (2014b), a sidebar enables viewers to scroll through to see how several departments use assessment results to make changes. For example, chemistry faculty integrated topics across courses with good results, and social work faculty introduced new assignments.

At LaGuardia Community College, mini-grants help program faculty implement changes suggested by their assessment results. Those who receive a grant are invited to present their projects as case studies of effective assessment (Provezis, 2012). Barham et al. (2013) suggest several ways to celebrate assessment successes, including acknowledging them in meetings, giving listserv recognition, and providing annual awards. At Northern Arizona University (2014b), Seals of Assessment Excellence, electronic logos, are awarded to programs whose faculty are doing outstanding assessment work (Paradis and Hopewell, 2010).

Dean (2013) recommends that faculty and staff let students know when assessment changes are based on information the students took time to share. At the University of North Dakota (2014b), a web page titled "For Students—You Said, We Did . . .," describes several changes to the freshman-year experience program that were based on assessment results, including increased opportunities for student involvement and reflection. The "For Students—What Surveys Tell Us" page highlights findings from several surveys and explores changes taking place.

Just as it can be used to encourage discussion, the assessment reporting framework can address and encourage communication. Casper College (2014) faculty are asked to describe how assessment feedback is provided to students, faculty, and staff. Suggested possibilities include reports for faculty or the dean, web pages, alumni newsletters, and discussions with students or others.

Linking Assessment Results to Important Processes

Regional accreditors, professional accreditors, and state governments all have specific requirements that affect the assessment process. However, usually internal needs play the biggest role in shaping assessment requirements for units and the institution as a whole. Assessment results can and should be included in annual processes such as strategic planning, budgeting, and program review. Barham et al. (2013) argue that infusing assessment into these processes is "a relatively effortless task" and greatly affirms the value of assessment (p. 78). Asking for assessment information in planning documents, annual reports, program reviews, and budget requests is all that is needed. The assessment plan for the Community College of Allegheny County (2009) contains such linkages, and an example from Indiana University-Purdue University Indianapolis (IUPUI) is presented in Chapter 11. As at St. Olaf College, assessment results also should be considered in curriculum review and faculty development efforts (Jankowski, 2012). And linkages to teaching and learning should be apparent. At the University of Cincinnati, faculty leaders stress that "assessment is pedagogy. It's not some nitpicky, onerous administrative add-on. It's what we do as we teach our courses, and it really helps close that assessment loop" (Association of American Colleges and Universities, 2010a).

Assessment Reporting by Departments and Programs

On most campuses, academic and student affairs units have guidelines or templates to follow in completing assessment reports. These may address learning in general education or in the major, or they may capture information about student programs and services. Often the guidelines and templates mirror those provided for planning. Across campuses, similarities exist in the information that is expected, but variety exists as well in both the content expected and reporting cycles. Guidelines for assessment reports often reflect the campus philosophy of assessment and therefore send messages to faculty and staff about what is considered important. As a result, requirements for assessment reporting influence the approaches that faculty and staff take, not just to fill out reports but to the way they conduct assessment.

On an Annual Assessment Update form, Casper College (2014) leaders recommend that faculty use their updates to celebrate achievements in student learning. In fact, one of the five questions on the report asks faculty to identify ways in which they have used assessment findings to celebrate student success—such as prizes to students or hosting student parties. Updates also provide information about the progress made in each program with respect to assessment and identify areas for future curriculum improvements.

Reporting formats usually begin with some background information, such as the program or course that is the basis for the report. Then reports include a statement of outcomes that have been assessed; a description of methodology along with targets or benchmarks; results; planned or actual actions; and, in many cases, observations about the process. Although some reports have tables and grids, many include questions for faculty and staff to consider as they complete their reports. Regardless of specifics, the reporting process should be used to encourage best practice in assessment.

Outcomes

In addition to indicating the student outcomes that are the basis of the report, faculty may need to establish the relationship of the outcomes to those of the institution, division, or college. On its *Student Learning Assessment Report*, Marymount University's (2012) template asks faculty to describe how the program's outcomes support the institution's mission, strategic plan, and school plan. Because outcomes are most useful when they are distributed widely (Ewell, 2009), faculty may be asked to describe how expected learning outcomes are shared with others. St. Olaf College (2012) faculty who are assessing general education courses indicate how they share outcomes with students. Faculty may include outcomes, or a link to them, on the course syllabus, refer to the outcomes in a course assignment, or discuss outcomes in class.

Methods

Nearly all unit reporting guidelines ask for a description of methods, although the level of detail varies. At Portland Community College (2013), faculty include a description of the group of students who were assessed, the specific methods used to collect information, and benchmarks if appropriate.

Faculty at Reedley College (2013) use Blackboard to complete a separate online Course SLO Assessment Report Form for each course. The assignments or instruments used to assess the course student learning outcomes (SLOs) are entered using a checklist with a wide range of possibilities, including tests, rubrics, performance observations, and group work. Then faculty describe the expected level of achievement on the instruments.

At Seattle University (2014), *Assessment Project Reports* include a section on project design and coherence. Faculty must describe how the student product is scored (e.g., course instructor, judging panel). Efforts to establish interrater reliability must be described when rubrics are used. Faculty are asked to explain the alignment between SLOs and the student products, such as test items, used to assess them.

Findings

To report findings. Pennsylvania State University (2012) faculty include a summary of results using prose, tables, charts, or graphs and a brief description of what was learned from the analysis. At Casper College (2014) faculty describe specific findings in relationship to student learning outcomes and provide any context. For example, if a rubric was used for the first time, that might be noted in the report. Seattle University (2014) faculty are asked to indicate the percentage of students meeting the program's aspirational goals and the percentage that did not meet minimum standards.

Action Plans

One of the most important aspects of assessment is the actions or plans that faculty and staff implement based on assessment findings. As such, nearly all assessment reporting formats ask faculty and staff to include action plans. At California State University Stanislaus (2013) assessment reports include a manageable number of specific action plans that are directly related to the outcomes and results of assessment. The individuals responsible for implementing the actions, as well as needed resources, must be identified. Emory University (2014a) faculty describe how they will use their findings to strengthen student learning in the future, including a target date for implementation, a responsible person to oversee the implementation, and resources needed.

On a course assessment report form, Reedley College (2013) assessment leaders ask for an action plan indicating anticipated changes and when they will be implemented. Faculty can choose from a checklist of possibilities that results are positive, so no changes are to be made, or they can indicate that they will conduct further assessment related to the issue or outcome. Several other possibilities are new or revised teaching methods, changes to syllabi or course sequencing, new methods of evaluating student work, and modification to staffing.

Follow-Up

Because action plans are often developed at the end of one academic year for implementation during the next academic year, some follow-up is necessary to determine if reported plans are actually put in place. Schuh and Gansemer-Topf (2010) note that plans are often developed and not always carried out.

To ensure that department and program assessment plans are implemented, Rice University (n.d.) staff use a two-year reporting process for any set of outcomes. In year 1 of the Rice Outcomes Assessment Reporting System (ROAR), faculty in academic units complete an initial report with results, conclusions, and a plan to act on the conclusions. In the second year, the implementation of the plan is described, including evaluation activities, additional plans for action, and budget implications. The second year of the cycle is called the RIPE (Report of Improvement Plan's Effectiveness). In practice, each academic faculty will be working with both stages of the cycle in any year as various outcomes are identified for assessment.

Using a similar approach, Triton College (2014) assessment plans are submitted in the fall of each year and assessment reports summarizing results in the spring. Based on results, faculty provide a plan of action containing specifics about what they will do to improve student learning. By the end of the following fall semester, they submit an assessment implementation report containing a detailed description of efforts used to improve student learning based on the previous year's assessment activities and reflecting the plan of action submitted in the spring. Faculty also describe how and when the assessment effort described in the implementation plan will be assessed if necessary.

Closing the Loop

To successfully complete the loop of assessment, faculty and staff should not only indicate that changes were implemented, but also provide information about the effects of the changes on learning. The assessment report faculty complete at the University of North Dakota (2012b) asks about any initiatives undertaken to find out if changes made in the previous year worked and for a description of these loop-closing efforts. DePaul University (2014) faculty begin their annual report with a follow-up on the previous year's planned actions, discussing how they implemented their plans, as well as the results of these actions.

Reflections on the Process

To improve assessment, faculty and staff on many campuses are asked to reflect on the approaches they are using. St. Olaf (2012) faculty who have assessed general education courses are asked if their assessment activity was useful for reflecting on teaching. Those who did not find it useful are asked to suggest changes to the process. Faculty also are asked to provide suggestions for the curriculum committee concerning the content or wording of the outcome they have assessed. Suggestions for campus conversations or faculty development prompted by assessment activities are solicited as well.

Wehlburg (2013), who writes that the reporting structure itself should be used to encourage faculty and staff to use their assessment results for improvement, questions the value of reports that do not do much to change the status quo. Wehlburg recommends that leaders reward faculty who can demonstrate that they have effectively used their assessment results to enhance learning.

Summarizing Reports

On many campuses the results of individual course or program reports are summarized to get a sense of the activities that are occurring, aggregate specific findings, identify best practices, or gather recommendations for various committees.

At St. Olaf (2012), Office of Institutional Research and Evaluation staff summarize course reports that assess general education outcomes. Summaries are prepared by outcome, not by course. Staff then share outcome reports with the Curriculum Committee. Suggestions for faculty development are shared with faculty development leaders.

Reedley College (2012) staff use data entered on SLO assessment reporting checklists to summarize the action plans of units. On average about 65 percent of course reports indicate positive results, with no changes needed. The remaining reports indicate multiple planned actions such as conducting further assessment (20 percent), introducing new or revised teaching methods (20 percent), developing new methods to evaluate student work (18 percent), and revising course syllabi (13 percent).

Assessment and Evaluation Committee members at St. Ambrose University (2014) summarize their evaluations of unit assessment reports and share a "state of assessment" report with the vice president of academic and student affairs. Illinois College (n.d.) vice presidents complete an annual vice president assessment synthesis report that summarizes and analyzes assessment activities in their divisions. The vice presidents indicate whether their expectations have been met. Any deficiencies are noted with suggestions for remediation. The reports are submitted to both the faculty or staff in the division and the chair of the campuswide Assessment Committee.

Managing Data

At many institutions, data management systems have been developed or purchased to help with the storage of assessment materials. As noted above, Blackboard is used at Reedley College. Since 2006, St. John's University (2014) has used WEAVE, a planning management system that helps faculty and administrators write outcomes and assessment criteria as well as develop and track assessment plans. St. John's personnel describe WEAVE as a living database—a place where activities related to assessment can be monitored. WEAVE contains sections for goals, outcomes, and objectives; measures; achievement targets; and findings. It also includes action plans, achievement summaries, annual reports, and a document repository. St. John's department representatives submit annual summaries of their activities using WEAVE. Reports are expected to be accurate, detailed, and honest.

Data storage is necessary at all levels of a campus. Although Blackboard is used at Marymount (2012), the required Student Learning Assessment Report still asks faculty to describe where and how data and documents used to generate their reports are being stored. At the University of North Dakota (2014b) faculty are urged to keep track of their internal documents.

Although many campus administrators have purchased assessment management systems, others have not. Those investigating which system to buy often find the choice difficult. Systems differ in their purposes: some are focused on document management, others on collecting data about student performance. Faculty at Prince George's Community College (Ariovich and Richman, 2013) have used Tk20 software to integrate grading and program assessment for individual students (we share some highlights of their work in Chapter 5). Other campuses use Chalk and Wire, ExamSoft, or LiveText to store artifacts and rubrics. As in all other areas of assessment, the questions faculty want to answer provide the best direction for choosing a system. Once specifications have been identified, several resources can be helpful in making the decision to purchase a particular system (Borden and Kernel, 2012; Damsgaard and Karlsbjerg, 2010; New Media Consortium, 2014; Oakleaf, Belanger, and Graham, 2013).

Assessing Unit Reports

One way to encourage good assessment practice is to assess reports submitted by units and provide faculty and staff with feedback. Fulcher and Good (2013) from James Madison University argue for the "surprisingly useful practice of meta-assessment," the evaluation of assessment processes and reports. As they point out, the easy part is checking to see if all departments and units are submitting reports. The difficult part is determining their quality. Using a rubric to evaluate reports helps to identify aspects of assessment that need improvement.

At James Madison University, reports are strong in most areas, with the exception of using results for improvement, so assessment leaders there are developing strategies to help faculty in this area. Assessment office personnel are working with faculty development leaders to help faculty align assessment instruments with curriculum and pedagogy.

At Marquette University (2014), faculty have developed a peer review process that involves more than one hundred program assessment leaders (PALs) and provides an opportunity for face-to-face interaction with peers. The goal is formative feedback, so no scoring sheet is used. However, an assessment cycle rubric is available to guide peer reviewers. The rubric contains four levels of completion for each of five components of the assessment cycle. Program assessment peer reviews are conducted once a year at a half-day assessment working seminar. The session starts with a general program about the components of the rubric, the characteristics of good assessment, and a mock peer review. During the three-hour peer review portion of the session, each participant works in an assigned group of three or four PALs per table. To help with sharing ideas, table assignments include faculty from unrelated disciplines. After the event, each program faculty receives a copy of the relevant completed peer review form and results also are shared with the appropriate chair and dean. Aggregate results have improved over three iterations of this process. Initially fewer than half of the reports met or exceeded expectations for "assessment measures." After follow-up visits from the vice provost and assessment director, the percentage increased to 82 (Bloom, 2010).

In some cases, academic units are asked to respond to the information they receive from the review process. For example, Marymount University (2012) faculty need to reply to the previous year's University Assessment Committee review of their unit's report. On the current report, each recommendation from the previous year's review must be listed with a specific response. At Northern New Mexico College (2011) faculty have used an improvements report form to gather feedback on peer review. In addition to listing improvements made, the form asks faculty to rate the feedback from peer review for its accuracy, ease in understanding, and helpfulness.

At the University of North Dakota (n.d.), the University Assessment Committee reviews all assessment plans and reports. To provide advice, the committee makes notes in the form of "assessment reviews" that are returned to the department. One of the University Senate's assessment web pages (Understanding Your Review) answers questions, noting that any suggestions offered in the reviews are genuine suggestions, not rules. The process of reviewing reports is focused on improving the assessment process and making it more rewarding for faculty, staff, and students. At Augustana College, the role of the Assessment Review Committee has evolved from one of grading reports to one of guiding assessment. Committee members act as consultants, helping faculty create questions that are important to them and consider how data can be used. Because all members of the committee look at program reports, they can learn about other perspectives and take information back to their own departments (Provezis, 2011).

Making the Process Transparent

Pikes Peak Community College (n.d.) is one of many institutions where administrators have attempted to make assessment processes transparent, an effort that many observers encourage (Baker, Jankowski, Provezis, and Kinzie, 2012). Staff at NILOA have developed a transparency framework to help institutions share evidence about student learning. Faculty and staff can use the framework to examine how well their websites communicate assessment information. Each of six components of the assessment process can be evaluated. Basic web communication is assumed, such as providing information that is meaningful to multiple audiences and allowing users to provide feedback and comments. Many campuses have benefited from the framework, with several seeking permission from NILOA to use the image and design of the transparency framework on their own websites.

The "Use of Student Learning Evidence" component of the framework encourages campus leaders to prominently display the ways they use assessment results for improvement and to update information regularly to reflect current activities and future plans. On their website, assessment leaders at Pikes Peak Community College (n.d.) share information about improvements they have made based on assessment information. For example, they have embedded resources about information literacy in English and computer science classes.

George Kuh (2013), one of NILOA's co–principal investigators, argues that college leaders should be more forthcoming about what they know about both student and institutional performance and about how they use this information. To increase awareness, various reporting formats should be tried. The Voluntary System of Accountability (VSA) is a transparency framework that publishes college portraits for member schools (see Chapter 8). Kuh believes that the VSA and other initiatives of this type (the private sector's U-CAN and the American Association of Community College's Voluntary Framework of Accountability) face several challenges in making their frameworks more useful for encouraging improvement— for example, presenting targeted information to different audiences in clear and meaningful language, presenting information at the program as well as the institution level, and adopting a qualifications framework, such as the Degree Qualifications Profile, to provide coherence and continuity across institutions.

The 2013 NILOA survey of chief academic officers indicates that administrators on 90 percent of campuses share assessment information such as learning outcomes with external audiences using websites or publications, but only 35 percent share assessment results (Kuh, Jankowski, Ikenberry, and Kinzie, 2014). A number of institutions, such as Appalachian State University (2014), make NSSE or testing results available online. In addition to institutional data, some websites contain assessment reports completed by department or program faculty, but often these are password-protected.

Institutional Assessment Reporting

In the Wabash National Study, campus faculty and staff collected extensive data that were carefully analyzed and presented in reports (Blaich and Wise, 2011). When the study authors discovered little interest in the documents at many institutions, they concluded that discussion and reflection are needed before reports are written. But written reports are still an important part of any communication plan. Schuh and Gansemer-Topf (2010) argue that an annual assessment cycle, including preparation of written reports, is necessary to demonstrate an institution's commitment to assessment.

Communication plans typically focus on conveying a message. Reporting is a subset of communication that is often structured and formalized. Reports such as status updates or meeting minutes provide the formal record of what has taken place, including decisions made and actions taken. Discussing results and issues before reports are completed helps to ensure that the written record will convey an accurate picture of a project (Kabik, 2013).

Guidelines and templates provide structure for required assessment reporting at the unit level. But other assessment reports must be written as well. Assessment activities conducted at the institution level must be documented and shared. The concept of a report no longer means just a paper copy that is sent through campus mail. Knerr and Gold (2013) define assessment reporting as "the way in which information gathered in assessment activities is shared with constituents and audience members" (p. 47). A plan for distributing reports includes a list of the individuals and groups that can or should benefit from the information, the types of reports that will be included, and methods for delivery.

Schuh and Associates (2009) recommend that audiences for assessment reports be identified and their needs taken into account. Considerations include stakeholders' expectations for timely information, their familiarity with the projects, and their interest in results. Very few individuals want to read long reports, so several approaches may be necessary. Among others, possible formats include summary reports, theme reports, and comprehensive reports. Written reports can be delivered through paper or electronically and often are presented both ways. Much assessment reporting is created for online delivery, including electronic newsletters or data dashboards. Oral presentations are another possibility and typically require the creation of new materials such as handouts or visual displays.

Vanderbilt University (n.d.) administrators provide some advice about writing an assessment report. To begin, a report should identify the author, the originating office, and the date. Many reports found online are not dated and are not attributed to an individual or office, making it very difficult to determine if they are current or credible. Vanderbilt personnel recommend synthesizing data from several sources in order to tell a story with a meaningful point. Here we consider some potential types of reports.

Theme Reports

With respect to institutional data, faculty and staff may be more interested in certain issues than in seeing all results at once. Thus, extracting information from a larger project that focuses on a particular theme is helpful. For instance, a survey of seniors may include several questions about students' plans for the future and other career issues such as self-ratings of preparation for work and satisfaction with advice about careers. Responses to these questions can be combined in a single newsletter or note that focuses on a career theme. Evidence about a particular skill such as critical thinking or writing could also be the focus of a theme report.

Rather than selecting information from one assessment project such as a senior survey, information for a theme report may come from several projects. At St. Olaf (2013), the Office of Institutional Research and Evaluation staff bring together assessment findings from several sources to create reports that are organized around specific outcomes or topics. A recent report addressing learning in the fine arts captures findings from three surveys: the Higher Education Data Sharing Consortium Alumni Survey, the NSSE, and the Essential Learning Outcomes Assessment. The last was developed by a team of St. Olaf faculty and staff to examine perceptions about learning outcomes. At George Mason University (2014) assessment leaders create condensed *In Focus* reports that use data from various sources. They also distribute the *Eye on Assessment* newsletter to share assessment results.

A University of Iowa (2013a) assessment review drew on unit reports to create an overview of the assessment activities going on across the campus. The writer considered each of several possible approaches to assessment, then provided two or three examples of departments using the approach. For instance, the departments of biochemistry, sociology, and political science use final projects for assessment, while several other departments use student surveys.

Extracts for Colleges and Departments

Assessment leaders often provide extracts from one or more institution-wide studies that include specific results for colleges and departments. Generally each department receives its own results as well as campus-wide averages. Extracts can provide overviews of an entire study or can concentrate on particular themes. Reports may include qualitative as well as quantitative information. For example, many senior and alumni surveys ask students to provide overall comments. The reflections provided by students about experiences in their majors are most useful if they are categorized and provided to the relevant departments.

Oral Reports

Although Banta and Blaich (2011) warn against giving presentations in which data and conclusions are simply handed out to faculty without any prior discussion, oral reports, used thoughtfully and timed correctly, can be a valuable way of sharing information. In fact, chief academic officers indicate that presentations at faculty meetings and retreats are the most effective way to share assessment information internally (Kuh et al., 2014).

Oral reports can be presented informally at brown bag lunches or with brief presentations at open forums. At the Massachusetts College of Liberal Arts, an informal presentation for faculty reviewed findings from two recent survey projects (Bendikas, 2013). Results from the Cooperative Institutional Research Program (CIRP) freshman survey were used to emphasize the high proportion of first-generation college students on campus and the importance of well-designed syllabi for this group. NSSE results were used to highlight the importance of active learning.

On some campuses, poster sessions, which combine elements of both written and oral reports, are staged to share assessment activities and findings. At these sessions, faculty summarize the highlights of their assessment work in outline form, then make themselves available to answer questions and engage in informal conversation. In 2013, assessment administrators and the Assessment Coordinators' Network at the University of Texas at Austin (2013a) hosted a poster session and panel discussion to highlight the assessment activities taking place across their campus. The posters displayed assessment projects from academic, administrative, and student support services units.

Comprehensive Reports

Comprehensive reports of campuswide activities generally include descriptions of purposes, methods, results, and conclusions—categories that are typically contained in unit reports. Although time-consuming to prepare, these reports help to establish the importance of campuswide assessment projects. They also provide a permanent record that can be used for reference purposes.

To emphasize their value and generate interest, comprehensive reports begin with an explanation of objectives—a narrative explaining important reasons that a project was undertaken. If the project is focused on demonstrating student learning, goals and objectives for learning must be described in either the body of the report or an appendix. The methodology section should explain which objectives were examined by which methods and why these methods were chosen. The methods themselves should be described. What exactly was collected in student portfolios? How were portfolios evaluated? Protocols for focus groups or interviews should be included too. To establish credibility, the methodology section should describe the target groups studied, including sampling techniques and a comparison of those who were included in the study with those who were eligible. Then specific findings should be shared. What were scores on a test? How well did students do on a writing assignment? If standards are in place, this section of the report should indicate how well students performed compared to the standards. For survey projects, the writer can share enough information to clarify major points and put additional details in an appendix or technical report. To provide a complete picture, negative results must be reported with the positive. Personal visits with those who could be affected by findings is a good strategy (Dean, 2013).

In addition to presenting results, some evaluation should be included. What can be concluded from the evidence? How well are goals being achieved? Answers to these questions should reflect faculty discussion and consensus, not just the opinion of the report writer. Prior research and findings should be considered, but Vanderbilt (n.d.) assessment leaders warn not to include analysis that goes beyond the data. A section about conclusions can be followed with a section of recommendations. Recommendations may indicate the actions that those responsible for planning the assessment project will take themselves, as well as the actions they will ask others to take. According to Schuh and Associates (2009), recommendations should be realistic and timely, as well as understandable and specific.

A thorough assessment report will contain some observations and recommendations about the assessment methods that were used. Was the survey instrument easy to understand? Did rubrics work? Future plans for assessment should also be included. The type of extensive report just described benefits greatly from an executive summary that provides an overview. An executive summary should contain one or two pages that capture main points and should be able to stand alone as a brief review of the project.

Institutional Data and Dashboards

Many campuses have "a plethora of data" waiting to be used (Tweedell, 2011). In addition to posting student facts, institutional profiles, and report summaries on their websites, institutional research office personnel often are willing to provide other information and analysis. Assessment leaders at Arkansas State University employ student interns to help analyze masses of unused data stored in department offices (Welsh, 2013). Blaich and Wise (2011) ask institutions participating in the Wabash Study to begin by doing a data audit including not only surveys, but also data from their student information systems and student assignments. The intent is to help faculty and staff become more aware of the evidence they already have.

Many institutions now are sharing information in efficient graphical formats. In what has been called "dashboard fever" (Lederman, 2009), data historically stored in separate places have been aggregated in dashboards created to monitor key performance indicators and to examine issues in an efficient way. Seybert (n.d.) defines a *dashboard* as "a brief document that graphically displays critical institutional information in a succinct, easily understood, and visually appealing format" (p. 1). He notes that for dashboards to be most useful in evaluating performance, benchmarks need to be in place. Del Mar College (2013) administrators describe their online dashboard as "a way to view data from several different reports with one simple click." It shows student characteristics, enrollments, and contact hours, as well as budget and staff information. Data are displayed in graphs and tables and include historical trends as well as projections.

Typically campuses use dashboards to share information about student success, such as retention and graduation. Information on outcomes and satisfaction also is commonly included. Buena Vista University's (2014) assessment home page features dashboard results for several of its expected learning outcomes, including written and oral communication, and integrative learning.

Analyzing Assessment Information

Faculty and staff need to think about how different kinds of information can be used as they develop their assessment questions and design their assessment processes. Ewell (2009) encourages participants to engage in expectation exercises, asking what they expect data to reveal. How can the data be analyzed? What kinds of comparisons are possible? Answering these questions helps to identify the appropriate methods and sources for obtaining the information. Perkins and Fifolt (2013) define analysis as breaking information down, making sense of it, and then reorganizing it in useful ways. Here we describe some approaches to accomplish this.

Descriptive and Comparative Information

Faculty often are interested in the basic descriptive information generated from assessment projects. This includes percentage distributions showing responses to various questions on surveys, means on assessment exams, and summaries of scores assigned to various products and performances. Descriptive information about those who participated in the study and their representativeness is also important. As they review their results, assessment administrators at the University of Texas at Austin (2013a) encourage faculty to look for patterns and ask if the data reveal something new or just tell them what they already know. Hatfield (n.d.) recommends that faculty look for surprises.

In the data they examined for the Wabash National Study, Blaich and Wise (2011) found that the variability within campuses "dwarfs the difference between institutions" in measures such as growth in outcomes and student experiences (p. 10). As Ewell (2009) notes, overall measures of central tendency (means, medians, and modes) for an entire institutional sample do not show strengths or weaknesses across types of students—information that is needed to guide intervention. Thus, disaggregating results to find out why some students differ so much from others is important assessment work (Blaich and Wise, 2011). Comparisons among various groups of students, comparisons to previous findings, and, in some cases, more sophisticated analyses that examine factors related to performance and satisfaction can help guide decisions about how to use assessment information.

Many reports compare student outcomes according to personal characteristics such as gender or race/ethnicity; others concentrate on educational backgrounds. Parents' education may be examined to identify first-generation college students, and high school class rank is often of interest. Assessment results frequently are examined based on students' current classification levels or across majors. George Mason University's (2014) graduating senior survey report shows results by college. Results based on participation in various programs such as distance education or freshman learning communities may be examined.

In addition to comparing results across subgroups of students, other kinds of comparisons can be made. Some studies compare student performance across multiple measures of the same outcome to see if results are similar. Scores also can be compared across outcomes. Results on a writing examination may be contrasted with those on a critical thinking inventory. This allows faculty to identify areas of strength and those that need attention.

Comparing results on one or more instruments across a period of years can be helpful in determining consistency of findings (Hatfield, n.d.). Comparisons can be made for cohorts of students or for the same students at different times. For example, life goals that students endorse when they are freshmen can be compared to those they later endorse as seniors. When external norms are available, local students can be compared to students elsewhere.

Many unit assessment reports contain comparisons of assessment results to agreed-on targets or standards. This enables faculty to determine if students are achieving at acceptable levels and if targets are appropriately set. Staff at George Mason University (2014) recommend that faculty look for strengths and weaknesses even when targets are met. Emphasis should be on improving student learning rather than getting good scores.

Assessment studies may collect information from groups other than current or previous students. Recruiters, employers, and professionals in the field often participate in assessment projects, allowing comparisons among these groups. Responses of employers about the types of knowledge and skills they consider important on the job can be compared with responses from alumni to these same questions. Background questions on employer surveys allow comparisons of their answers within groups. For example, responses of firms can be compared based on the number or types of individuals they employ.

Impact of Various Response Scales on Analysis

The specific assessment measures faculty use shape subsequent analyses. Certain response scales limit the types of descriptive statistics that can be calculated. Responses that are expressed in categories such as gender and race can be reported in tables showing the number or percentage of cases in each group, but do not allow researchers to calculate means or medians. This is because the data have no natural order. For example, analysts could report on the percentage of women first and then the percentage of men, or the reverse. However, the mode can be used to illustrate the category that is represented most frequently. Content analysis applied to open-ended questions on surveys or comments from focus groups represents one way to generate categorical data. Comments are coded and sorted into various categories. Then researchers can report on the number or percentage of cases in each of the categories.

Both medians and modes can be calculated for response scales that capture ranks or orders, such as Strongly Disagree to Strongly Agree. Occasionally analysts report means for this information, but need to remember that applying numbers such as 1 to 5 to these responses implies an assumption that the distance between the categories is equal. Scaled or interval data such as age and height are expressed in meaningful numbers. Thus, these data lend themselves to descriptive statistics such as means, medians, and modes, and multivariate analysis such as regression and analysis of variance.

Scoring scales used for performance assessment and portfolios represent rank or order data. Although they can be used to calculate means, the difference between 1 and 2 is not necessarily the same as the difference between 5 and 6. However, correlation statistics are routinely used to report interrater reliability using tests for ranked variables. Although judgment is applied in deciding the weights to be assigned to various questions, scores on multiple-choice and other objective tests are treated as interval data and can be used in multivariate analyses.

As suggested, possibilities for further analysis of comparative data depend on the type of information collected. For example, in a comparison of results for males and females on a survey item that asks for reasons that students have chosen to study on the campus, cross-classification tables can be used to display results in categories. Then researchers can use chi square analysis to see if the distribution of responses across categories differs significantly by gender. If, however, researchers are comparing test scores for students taking distance education classes with those of students on campus, they will be able to calculate means and use t-tests to see if scores differ significantly. For a comparison of test scores across several sites, analysis of variance can be used rather than t-tests.

Qualitative Analysis

Qualitative analysis involves immersion in data as researchers search for relationships. Emphasis is on a particular topic for a specific group rather than on generalizing results. Perkins and Fifolt (2013) review several approaches for analyzing qualitative data, including the constant comparative method in which comments are compared and coded based on the participants' original language, as well as on categories that emerge. Thematic coding can then be used to combine categories into overarching themes. Ethnography (participant observation through prolonged immersion) and narrative analysis (use of storytelling methodology) are other approaches. Triangulation is used to analyze research questions from multiple perspectives including data, methods, investigators, and theories. Many researchers use both surveys and focus groups for this reason. Credibility of qualitative data calls for checking of study approaches and findings by the individuals who participated in the study and, perhaps, seeking an external review. The investigator also needs to keep an audit trail of decisions made throughout the project to demonstrate that decisions were appropriate, consistent, and confirmable. Readers of the study can decide for themselves whether they think results are transferable.

Multivariate Analysis

A number of investigators use multivariate analysis to examine assessment-related issues, perhaps to determine the effectiveness of a particular program on an outcome variable such as grade point average (Cooper and Shelley, 2009). Researchers may examine a model that relates GPA to academic and social experiences, as well as to a set of background characteristics. Independent variables, such as age, time to degree, and hours typically spent studying, working, and on other out-of-class activities can be included. Participation in the program of interest can be reflected in the model by creating a dummy variable. Students can be assigned a value of 1 if they were in the program and 0 if not. Including this variable allows investigators to determine the average increment to GPA of program participation. Various techniques can be used to examine the relationship between GPA and the set of independent variables that has been identified.

Professionals on several campuses examine models to explain persistence in college and other categorical variables, and Astin and antonio (2012) have reviewed much of this work. Although inferences can be made, Perkins and Fifolt (2013) remind researchers that multivariate techniques examine strength of relationships and do not determine causality. In addition, practical significance (value of findings) is more important than statistical significance (differences not due to chance).

A common use of multivariate analysis is to compare test scores. Rather than directly comparing pretest scores to posttest scores, predicted posttest scores are developed based on pretest scores and background educational characteristics such as high school class rank and entry-level test scores. Actual posttest scores are then compared with predicted posttest scores. Pike (2009) discusses some issues in using gain scores and value-added approaches. Bowman (2013) describes approaches that use self-reported gains in skills from high school as a control variable when analyzing survey data about self-reported gains in college.

Data Mining and Learning Analytics

Generally the term *data mining* means exploring large data sets to discover something new. Institutional research staff may offer data-mining services. At the University of Utah (2012a), staff in the Office of Assessment, Evaluation, and Research in student affairs list data mining among the types of services they provide. These professionals conduct different types of analysis on existing data, such as those they collect and those held in the university's Office of Budget and Institutional Analysis.

The terms *descriptive analytics* and *predictive analytics* may be used in place of *data mining*. *Learning analytics* refers to these approaches when used to optimize learning in higher education. An adaptation of "big data," a branch of statistical analysis first used by businesses to predict consumer behavior (New Media Consortium, 2014), learning analytics employs statistical analysis to evaluate data sources about students in order to determine patterns that can lead to informed decision making. Web tracking of the frequency and sequence of activities can be used to predict behavior. Data may include items such as time spent using library resources, clickers, or online discussions. Learning analytics has been used to identify students at risk of failing a course or leaving an institution. Intervention can help the student at the individual level and can improve retention and graduation rates at the institution level. Booth (2012) believes that well-established principles of good practice in assessment should inform the application of learning analytics to higher education, ensuring that the power of analytics serves learning in a meaningful way.

Purdue University (2013) specialists have developed the Signals Project to increase student success in the classroom. The project identifies early warning signs (e.g., course log-ins, grades) and intervenes with academically at-risk students before they reach a critical point. Students are assigned to risk groups based on a predictive student success algorithm. One of three stoplight ratings corresponding to the risk groups can be released on the Blackboard home pages of students, and e-mail messages from instructors can be sent to at-risk groups. Signals encourages students to use available resources on campus to increase their academic success.

Souza (2013) asserts that the promise of learning analytics is already being recognized on her campus. At the Wegman School of Pharmacy at St. John Fisher College, faculty use ExamSoft to tag every question on all course-level exams with multiple codes that correspond to program outcomes, course outcomes, and level of Bloom's taxonomy. This provides outcome data at the program level. And at the student level, faculty can see across courses if a student is having difficulty with a particular area of study (also see Chapter 5).

Displaying Results

Most reports include graphic displays. For example, pie charts can be used to show how parts of a whole are distributed, such as the percentages of students who are working in jobs categorized as in their major, related to their major, or not in their major. Pie charts are useful if results fall into no more than five or six (generous) slices. Categories represented by very small percentages do not show well on a pie chart. Vertical or horizontal bar charts also are used to show percentages or counts of cases in various categories such as years, majors, or classification levels. Line graphs are popular for displaying trend data. Several line graphs can be shown on the same display. Trends in scores for freshmen on a test could be represented by one line, with a second line showing trends for juniors. All charts and tables must be clearly labeled if they are to be useful to readers. Current survey software allows faculty and staff to explore possibilities for graphical presentation. At Columbia College Chicago (2014), staff in the Office of Evaluation and Assessment offer to help faculty "transform data into visuals that emphasize patterns." Vanderbilt's (n.d.) assessment website offers good advice about displaying data in graphs and tables.

Other Considerations

As we have seen, faculty and staff on many campuses take appropriate actions to encourage collaboration and use their results to improve learning in the major, in general education programs, and in student affairs programs and services. Some observers believe that more change is actually going on than is documented (Hatfield, n.d.; Baker et al., 2012). But some warn against a rush to change. Changing curriculum does not necessarily mean improving learning, although some individuals may assume that it does. Banta and Blaich (2011) point out that state mandates or campus leaders may advocate for immediate action and that forcing change can lead to disappointing results. Others avoid change. As Blaich and Wise (2011) point out, many faculty and staff conclude that it is "far less risky and complicated to analyze data than it is to act" (p. 13). Finding the right balance can be a delicate process. Faculty and staff at the Community College of Baltimore County (2011) make the assumption that assessment is "neither precise, nor perfect, and its data are interpreted with that in mind." They approach assessment with an open and creative mind as they use its results to improve student learning.

CHAPTER 11

ASSESSING INSTITUTIONAL EFFECTIVENESS

In previous chapters, we have outlined the assessment essentials for an effective campus approach to continuous improvement of curriculum, instruction, and student services:

- Engaging stakeholders
- Agreeing on definitions of terms
- Developing an overall plan
- Selecting methods
- Administering instruments, collecting and storing data, analyzing data, and interpreting findings
- Communicating findings to stakeholders
- Using the findings to improve processes

We have suggested how these steps may be carried out in assessing outcomes in general education, major fields, and student affairs. Now we consider how all of these processes may be brought together at the campus level to assess institutional effectiveness. It takes a campus to develop a graduate. While student learning as a result of faculty efforts is at the heart of the process, learning is most efficient and effective when admissions officers ensure student-campus fit by presenting the institution clearly, financial aid is administered in a way that maximizes the number of students who receive the aid they truly need, buildings are planned to provide a variety of spaces conducive to teaching and learning, and all facilities are maintained at a level that provides a comfortable and attractive environment for learning.

Linking Assessment and Institutional Planning: An Example

Banta uses the cycle depicted in figure 11.1 to describe the approach to assessing institutional effectiveness that is used at Indiana University-Purdue University Indianapolis (IUPUI). First we provide a brief overview of the cycle, then more details in later sections of this chapter.

Outcomes assessment is connected with strategic planning at the institution level at IUPUI. As the academic plan for the campus develops and evolves, performance indicators are derived from the content that will help to determine if the goals and objectives of the plan are being achieved. Banta's staff collect the performance indicator data from a variety of internal and external sources and produce reports for the campus, the community, the state, and the regional accreditor, the Higher Learning Commission of the North Central Association of Colleges and Schools.

At IUPUI (n.d.b), a web-based reporting template (www.planning .iupui.edu/apbrv2) used by every academic and administrative unit asks deans and vice chancellors to enter their goals and related objectives and then note, for each objective:

- Actions taken to date
- Indicators of progress
- Activities planned

The template includes a tagging system that helps to guarantee that each unit goal is connected to a campus goal. Thus, each unit is conducting activities that will further achievement of institutional goals.

Performance indicators produced and aggregated at the campus level assist in charting campus-level progress. And when they are disaggregated, they also can give units information helpful in gauging their own progress and comparing that with campus averages and with those of other campus units they consider peers. For example, a campus goal to increase the effectiveness of undergraduate advising can be assessed by tracking the number

FIGURE 11.1 PLANNING, EVALUATION, AND IMPROVEMENT AT IUPUI

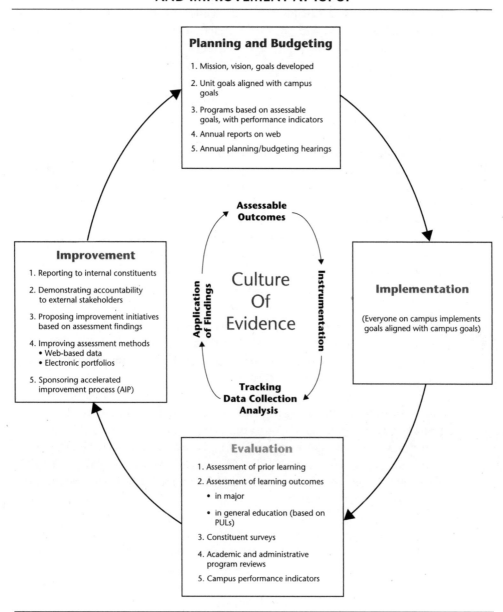

Planning and Budgeting

1. Mission, vision, goals developed
2. Unit goals aligned with campus goals
3. Programs based on assessable goals, with performance indicators
4. Annual reports on web
5. Annual planning/budgeting hearings

Improvement

1. Reporting to internal constituents
2. Demonstrating accountability to external stakeholders
3. Proposing improvement initiatives based on assessment findings
4. Improving assessment methods
   • Web-based data
   • Electronic portfolios
5. Sponsoring accelerated improvement process (AIP)

Assessable Outcomes

Culture
Of
Evidence

Application of Findings

Instrumentation

Tracking Data Collection Analysis

Implementation

(Everyone on campus implements goals aligned with campus goals)

Evaluation

1. Assessment of prior learning
2. Assessment of learning outcomes
   • in major
   • in general education (based on PULs)
3. Constituent surveys
4. Academic and administrative program reviews
5. Campus performance indicators

© Trudy W. Banta, Indiana University-Purdue University Indianapolis.

of faculty engaging in professional development designed to improve their skills in both academic and career advising. Additional indicators include measures of student satisfaction with academic advising and career advising. Campuswide tracking of faculty participation and an institution-wide questionnaire yield unit-specific data and campus averages for use in making comparisons. IUPUI's (n.d.a) campuswide student satisfaction data may be viewed at http://www.imir.iupui.edu/.

Faculty and staff in every unit implement planning goals. Banta's staff provide a suite of evaluative activities that includes assessment of learning, gauging satisfaction through stakeholder surveys, conducting program evaluations, and supporting peer review (campuswide program review) for academic and administrative units. Banta's staff also provide information and consultation to support disciplinary and institutional accreditation for academic and administrative units.

Banta and her staff members attend the meetings of many ad hoc and standing campus committees in order to listen for information needs and provide appropriate information already collected or, in some cases, to offer to collect new data. In addition to committee service as an avenue for identifying ways in which evaluative data may be put to use, program review and accreditation also provide these opportunities.

One common use of data is to improve assessment strategies and instruments. For example, the electronic portfolio as a medium for collecting evidence of student learning has emerged at IUPUI as an improvement in data-gathering tools over the past decade.

Finally the use of assessment-generated information to guide resource allocations aimed at improving campus programs and processes may suggest new planning initiatives or modification of existing goals or objectives. And the assessment process itself must be evaluated periodically. These steps complete an institutional effectiveness cycle at IUPUI and begin the process anew to see if changes undertaken achieved their goals and if continuous improvement is realized.

Incorporating assessment within a cycle of ensuring institutional effectiveness is an important way to guarantee that assessment information will be used to guide improvement. To contribute to improvement, the assessment process itself must be well designed and functioning appropriately. Here we elaborate on several strategies that campus leaders use to develop strong assessment programs at the institution level. These strategies help to encourage and support faculty and staff as they carry out their assessment responsibilities.

Organizing to Assess Institutional Effectiveness

Assessment programs that lead to improvement have key players, commit-tees, and structures in place that support assessment efforts. Much variety exists in the way campuses are organized, although common threads are evident. Here we elaborate on some of the ideas about organizing for assess-ment that we introduced in Chapter 2.

Assessment Leaders

On campuses where assessment is successful, one or more key individu-als provide direction for the campuswide assessment process by commu-nicating the institutional priority of assessment, committing resources to support assessment initiatives, and including assessment results in public statements. In some cases, the president of the institution takes this role. In others, the academic vice president or the vice president for planning becomes the person most identified with nurturing the assessment process. At IUPUI a vice chancellor or senior advisor—a member of the chancel-lor's cabinet—coordinates assessment efforts. At Samford University (2013) an associate provost facilitates assessment. Leaders keep faculty atten-tion focused on assessment by routinely using data in conversations and speeches about campus strengths and weaknesses, new program initiatives, and goals for the future.

The key leaders may assign day-to-day responsibility for coordinating the assessment program to a respected member of the faculty. However, in order to draw on professional expertise, the director of an institutional research, planning, or assessment office often assumes operational respon-sibility for assessment, facilitating the assessment work of faculty and staff in various campus units, and serving as a regular or ex officio member of a campuswide assessment committee.

Assessment Committees

Assessment must not be seen as the exclusive concern of administrators or experts. In order to reflect a variety of interests, most institutions appoint a committee or task force of faculty, staff, and students that assumes responsi-bility for assessment. Some institutions use an existing senate, curriculum, or planning committee for this purpose. Linking assessment to existing structures can increase the likelihood that assessment information will be used. At Butte College (2013), assessment is led by faculty through the Academic Senate and the Curriculum Committee. These groups provide general standards for assessment. At IUPUI the campus assessment process is guided by the Program Review and Assessment Committee (PRAC), which includes two faculty members from each academic unit, appointed by the dean of that unit; a librarian; student affairs professionals; and several staff members who conduct assessment for other campus units, such as the faculty development office (the Center for Teaching and Learning) and the Center for Service and Learning. Representatives of a local community college and a nearby private university also attend PRAC meetings.

Assessment committees contribute in a variety of ways to planning and carrying out the assessment process. For example, committee members may create definitions, issue guidelines, and develop goals and objectives for learning. They likely will create and oversee implementation of a campuswide assessment plan that has approval of the institution's governance structures. In many cases, the assessment committee acts as an oversight body that receives assessment information from campus units and issues summary and evaluative reports. Committee members may review assessment reports to determine whether they meet specific criteria; as at IUPUI, they may assign ratings to the reports using an agreed-on rubric. Thus, committee members become familiar with factors that lead to successful assessment and can help other faculty and staff become knowledgeable about the assessment process.

Leadership in Units

Assessment at the division, college, and department levels also needs key players, committees, and structures. The dean or department chair may see his or her role as helping develop the general framework for assessment and encouraging faculty to develop the specifics of the program. An undergraduate or graduate program coordinator may furnish administrative support for faculty and staff. In the School of Arts and Humanities at Lehman College (2013), professionals in the dean's office oversee assessment, making sure that each department has an assessment coordinator or committee, as well as an up-to-date assessment plan.

Central Offices

Many institutions have central units such as the Office of Planning and Institutional Improvement (PAII) at IUPUI that provide continuity and support for the assessment process. Typically, office staff act as facilitators and consultants rather than as monitors of assessment. Macalester College's (2012) Office of Assessment provides a forum for continuous dialogue about institutional objectives and engages "assessment as a focus of faculty development" designed to help faculty increase the effectiveness of their approaches to assessment and evaluation.

Central office staff often coordinate large-scale assessment projects, such as senior surveys or standardized testing, that are beyond the scope of individual divisions and departments. If so, they may use web pages or other approaches to make the results available and useful to colleges and departments. Professionals from the Office of Assessment and Planning at Lehman College (n.d.) serve as a general resource on assessment issues and work closely with the college assessment council to provide development opportunities for faculty and staff. They also include keeping abreast of good practices and investigating technological resources for assessment among their objectives.

The existence of a central assessment office demonstrates the institution's continuing commitment to assessment, but it may increase the risk that assessment will be seen as "something the administration does." Central offices combat the view that assessment is strictly an administrative concern by encouraging and supporting assessment in the disciplines. For example, staff provide consulting services to faculty who are designing their own assessment projects. Lewis and Swerdzewski (2009) advocate for an internal consultant model of assessment. This approach calls for an experienced assessment practitioner to work with a designated faculty representative from each academic department. James Madison University (n.d.) has developed the Program Assessment Support Service to facilitate this approach.

Assessment is often combined with other functions such as institutional research, institutional effectiveness, or planning. At Ball State University (2014a), the Office of Academic Assessment and Institutional Research was repositioned as the Office of Institutional Effectiveness in 2012. In addition to supporting assessment, the office provides information for planning and decision making. It also manages Digital Measures Activity Insight, an online system for reporting of faculty activities. At the University of Texas at Austin (2013a), Office of Institutional Accreditation and Program Assessment staff coordinate program and general education assessment and advance institution-wide assessment and resources. Office members collaborate with faculty and staff "to build an integrated system for institutional improvement using assessment, strategic planning and program review."

Planning and Institutional Improvement at IUPUI

The Office of Planning and Institutional Improvement (PAII) at IUPUI has the following units:

- Testing Center
- Office of Institutional Effectiveness
- Office of Institutional Research
- Office of Program Review
- Office of the Economic Model

Testing Center

Testing Center (TC) personnel conduct assessment of prior learning, or evidence-based assessment. In an era when public attention is focused on the cost of higher education and the need to produce more college graduates more quickly, ways to give students credit for their learning outside college are being sought. Electronic portfolios provide an excellent mechanism for submitting evidence of prior learning. CLEP, DANTES, and DSST, which are administered in the TC, exemplify nationally distributed instruments for assessing prior learning. TC psychometric consultants also assist faculty in developing local tests for the purpose of permitting students to demonstrate that they already possess the knowledge and skills imparted in a particular course or course sequence. Assessing student learning for the purpose of placing students in appropriate courses represents an important function that contributes to ultimate student success.

TC personnel have been instrumental in offering faculty development for designing classroom tests and for revising end-of-course evaluations to focus more on the experience of the learner than on the behavior of the instructor. For example, some of the typical items about whether the instructor starts each class on time or knows the subject well (which is hard for a novice in the field to judge) are being replaced by lists of course outcomes for which students self-report the effectiveness of the class in helping them learn.

The TC director, Howard Mzumara, is trained in program evaluation and often serves as an outside evaluator on externally funded grants. Working with School of Science faculty in this capacity, Mzumara has been able to convince some faculty members skeptical of outcomes assessment that the evaluation of instructional innovations funded by the National Science Foundation constitutes valuable assessment information which can be used to guide improvements that enhance learning.

Office of Institutional Effectiveness

Office of Institutional Effectiveness (OIE) personnel convene a subgroup of the Program Review and Assessment Committee (PRAC) to apply a rubric in evaluating unit annual assessment reports and report their findings and recommendations to each unit. Members of this subgroup also report annually at a PRAC meeting on the improving state of PRAC reports. OIE personnel prepare an annual report summarizing all assessment activities underway at IUPUI (see http://planning.iupui.edu/2 .html#campusAssessmentReports, IUPUI Campus Assessment Reports).

OIE principals Susan Kahn and Susan Scott lead IUPUI's electronic student portfolio initiative. Using a small budget for seed money, Kahn and Scott have succeeded in enabling faculty members in seventeen of twenty colleges to develop technical expertise in using e-portfolios, planning a project, and applying their new expertise in deepening student learning. Several IUPUI faculty have adopted or adapted AAC&U Valid Assessment of Learning in Undergraduate Education (VALUE) rubrics to assess student work in the e-portfolios.

The most comprehensive assessment work of OIE personnel is the annual *IUPUI Performance Report* (see www.iport.iupui.edu) for which unit annual reports are scanned for evidence related to campus planning goals. Achievements of academic and administrative units related to each planning goal are described in a narrative. Relevant performance indicators are summarized in tables and charts in the printed report and on the web. Performance data are considered in an annual review session by a group of stakeholders for each goal; for instance, the campuswide Graduate Affairs Council performs the annual review for the goal of improving graduate education. The stakeholders assign a green, yellow, or red "traffic light" to their goal to indicate outstanding, moderate, or little to no achievement for that year. The appropriate colored traffic light appears next to each goal in the performance report, which is distributed by the chancellor both inside IUPUI and in the Indianapolis community at the annual "Chancellor's Report to the Community" every spring.

Office of Institutional Research

Primary responsibility for collecting, aggregating, analyzing, and reporting performance indicator data for the campus belongs to OIR personnel. Surveys of enrolled undergraduate and graduate students, undergraduate and graduate alumni, faculty and staff, and some employers are designed and administered by Office of Institutional Research (OIR) personnel. They also analyze and interpret the findings and disseminate reports in person, in writing, and on the web.

Working closely with academic deans over a period of years, OIR principals have developed a series of management indicators that are made available to the deans at the time they begin work on their annual reports. These indicators comprise enrollment, persistence, and graduation statistics. They also include research income per faculty member and student, alumni, faculty, and staff survey responses for each unit, as well as for the campus as a whole (see http://imir.iupui.edu/ and scroll down to "Survey Summary Reports").

OIR's director, Larry Miles, meets with the chair of each department engaged in self-study for program review to present relevant data about students, faculty, and staff. If the data in the prepared template raise additional questions, Miles responds to those questions in subsequent reports. The aim is to supply sufficient information for the department undergoing review to construct a detailed and accurate portrait of its achievements and challenges for a visiting team of reviewers.

IUPUI has not elected to purchase a commercial software system such as those offered by LiveText, Tk20, WEAVE, or Nuventive. Instead faculty and staff in most departments use OnCourse, Indiana University's open source learning management system, as they collect and aggregate assessment data. The registrar has added to the site for recording undergraduate course grades a separate site for faculty to use in recording for each of their students a level of effectiveness—Very Effective, Effective, Not Effective—in mastering one or two generic skills such as written communication, information literacy, and critical thinking emphasized in a given course.

A business intelligence initiative has produced a complex data storage and management system that promises to facilitate the generation of reports and the sharing of institutional data. OIR staff now will be in a better position to conduct learning analytics, including a planned study of the effectiveness of various levels of financial aid in influencing student persistence.

Office of Program Review

Peer review, or program review, is the most comprehensive evaluative process undertaken at IUPUI. Program review was initiated in 1994 by Banta and colleagues in response to requests from the deans of liberal arts and science colleges, where the opportunity for disciplinary accreditation is rare. While designed primarily to look comprehensively at the teaching, research, and engagement activities of programs without accrediting bodies, every academic and administrative unit is invited to undergo peer review. In accredited programs such as education, nursing, and social work, the review may be of the entire unit (e.g., allied health, with ten separately accredited departments) or focused on a single function such as career advising (business), fundraising (dentistry), the admissions process (law), readiness to offer a new PhD program (rehabilitation sciences), or a graduate program not subject to disciplinary accreditation (PhD in nursing).

To avoid the perception that units are targeted for review if they are in trouble, Office of Program Review (OPR) director Karen Black maintains an eight-year schedule of reviews. Deviations from the schedule are rare but have been made if, for instance, key faculty would be on sabbatical or an interim department chair would be in place during the scheduled year.

All student affairs units are on a schedule for review, and other support units, such as human resources and the library, have been reviewed.

Review teams of five individuals reflect IUPUI's principal planning themes of Teaching and Learning, Research and Scholarship, and Civic Engagement. Two reviewers from the given discipline or administrative function can assess all of these areas, including student learning and the status of outcomes assessment. Two IUPUI reviewers from related areas assess campus contributions of the unit, convey the reality of institution-wide resource constraints, and are invited to identify for the unit under review potential cross-disciplinary opportunities in teaching, research, and community engagement. Finally, a local community representative assesses the standing of the department in Indianapolis and identifies additional ways for the unit to contribute knowledge and expertise in the community.

After reviewing the unit's self-study, review teams typically spend two and a half days on campus meeting, as appropriate, with the responsible vice chancellor (academic, student affairs, or administrative support); the appropriate dean or director; and faculty, staff, students, and alumni. The self-study contains a brief list of questions for the reviewers to address in particular, though they are encouraged to adopt their own reporting framework. An exit briefing with the relevant administrators, not including the unit head, takes place as the campus visit is concluded. The visiting team of peer reviewers is asked to submit a final written report within a month.

Once the final report of the review team is received, the department chair and faculty and staff in the unit may take up to six months to consider the report's conclusions and recommendations and produce a written response. Then a meeting with the unit chair, the dean or director of the division under review, and campus administrators takes place. The purpose of this meeting is to guarantee that review recommendations are at least considered by department leaders as well as faculty and staff. If campus-level support is needed, this is the opportunity to make this request. Often recommendations for academic units involve strengthening the assessment of student learning, so the participation of OPR principals makes it possible to seize this opportunity to offer assistance with outcomes assessment.

Office of the Economic Model

Activity-based costing offers a fresh approach within higher education to determining how much certain functions cost to deliver as compared with other functions. Activity-based costing requires estimates of the amount of time faculty or staff expend in accomplishing certain tasks. If one knows how many hours an individual worked on a project, one can multiply that number by the per hour wage of the individual and add estimated costs of such resources as space, equipment, utilities, and staff support to obtain a cost for the function. Costs for various functions, such as advising or offering a course online, can be compared with alternatives. Cost is but one indicator of effectiveness, but it is sufficiently important to be persuasive in decision making. Over the years, looking at the costs of administration has led to departmental consolidation in several areas at IUPUI.

Administering an Assessment Plan

Planning is the establishment of a readiness to act on the basis of shared understanding. Here we describe several aspects of assessment that faculty and staff need to consider as they develop and carry out their assessment plans.

Planning Levels

Assessment planning and activities occur at multiple levels of a campus. Generally institutional planning will be concerned with selecting campuswide assessment activities, developing the process for assessing general education outcomes, and establishing requirements for unit plans. In addition to gathering information about student learning, educators may examine issues of program completion, student satisfaction, and success after graduation. Faculty and staff at Old Dominion University (2014) and Oklahoma State University (n.d.) address these areas as they develop their plans for assessment.

In an institutional assessment plan, leaders describe assessment activities that are carried out at the campuswide level, such as surveying alumni who graduated five years ago or administering a standardized test of critical thinking to a sample of sophomores. These activities generally concentrate on learning goals that cut across disciplines.

Institutions differ both in who writes the campuswide plan for assessment and who carries it out. In most cases, a committee like PRAC at IUPUI creates the plan and has continued responsibility for its administration. A PRAC subcommittee reviews unit reports and makes recommendations for improvements to the reports. Based on their review of campuswide data, PRAC members also make recommendations for improving programs (e.g., the approach to general education).

Separate provisions may be made for carrying out various activities described in the plan. For example, a director of writing competence may be appointed to administer campuswide writing examinations or, as at Truman State University (2011), a director may administer a portfolio program. Likewise, a committee member or professional staff may need to support assessment by analyzing data and writing reports, particularly for large-scale projects.

In addition to institutional planning for assessment, planning occurs at other levels as well. In fact, much of the material shared on assessment web pages is designed to help faculty develop their own program- or course-level plans for assessment. The institutional plan may call for specific actions on the part of program faculty or may allow them to develop their own assessment approach. Assessment leaders at Cochise College (2014) have designed a new assessment process for departmental planning and actions, the Cochise Learning Improvement Project, which has three phases. In the investigation stage, department faculty design and carry out their initial assessment plans. Based on their results, faculty develop an action plan to improve student learning. In the experimentation phase, faculty introduce and evaluate these planned actions. If implementation of their actions proves successful, they move to the final stage, integration, permanently introducing the new strategies into the curriculum. This new system encourages faculty and staff to introduce improvements. It also is designed to make the reporting and approval process more convenient.

The web pages for Southern Illinois University Edwardsville (n.d.) contain specific guidance with respect to assessment planning. Faculty in undergraduate programs are required to use senior assignments as one of their performance indicators or assessment measures. Faculty in graduate programs must align their outcomes with the goals of graduate learning defined by the university's Graduate Council. And they must use theses, final projects and performances, exams, or portfolios for assessment. If course grades are used as one of the assessment measures, specific guidelines must be followed.

In addition to institutional guidelines, unit planners must recognize the needs of discipline-specific bodies, as well as their own mission statements. Undergraduate programs, minors, or graduate programs may need to be evaluated. Faculty may also need to participate in assessment of general education, perhaps collecting assessment information at the course level.

In their unit plans, faculty at St. Ambrose University (2014) must include at least two instruments for each student learning outcome. To ensure that inferences made from the data are valid, faculty are to document and evaluate the quality of the instruments they are using. The plan must include both methods used to assess outcomes and those used to ensure the quality of assessment tools. Faculty at Rice University (n.d.) need to collect as much information as is necessary to make valid programmatic decisions. They are advised to ask important and relevant questions and to involve all faculty including adjuncts and graduate assistants if applicable so that everyone contributes.

Using Assessment Information

Before assessment results can be shared and acted on, the information that is collected must be summarized and analyzed. An assessment plan should specify the way assessment results will be reviewed and the types of analysis that will be provided. Planners from the University of California Irvine (n.d.) recommend identifying who will participate in reviewing evidence, when the review will take place, and what will happen at the review. For example, assessment plans may call for a grading day for faculty to evaluate artifacts selected from general education courses.

As faculty plan for assessment, they should consider how assessment information will be shared, including types of reports that will be prepared, and intended audiences. It is particularly important to develop internal processes for discussion, review, and decision making. Love (2012) argues that talking about assessment results is part of the data analysis process and should be encouraged. Baker, Jankowski, Provezis, and Kinzie (2012) believe that time to reflect on results or evidence is an "important stage in the assessment cycle that is often glossed over" (p. 9).

An assessment plan should specify how assessment results will be linked to other important processes. Developing an organizational map that shows the results that will be distributed to various units for further action can be helpful. Perhaps recommendations for improvements and new initiatives will be prepared by an assessment committee and forwarded to organizational units such as a curriculum committee or a faculty development group. At Cabrillo College (n.d.), the annual summary report prepared by members of the assessment committee is shared with the Faculty Senate, the governing board, the College Planning Council, and faculty unions.

Some administrators explicitly link the assessment process to their internal budgeting process, setting aside a block of funds for initiatives to improve student learning based on recommendations from assessment activities. Leaders at Queens University of Charlotte believed that linking assessment and budgeting would "go a long way toward making a fledgling culture of evidence truly sustainable, meaningful, and expected" (Slater, Burson, and McArthur, 2011, p. 9). In a demonstration project, Queens Assessment Committee members developed funding recommendations based on compelling assessment results received from five academic programs. In addition, the university's assessment reporting template was modified to allow easy reporting of data that support budgeting needs.

Leaders at Colorado State University have been particularly successful in organizing and using assessment information for program review and other purposes (Kinzie, 2011). The university uses PRISM, an online planning infrastructure that supports decision making. One aim of PRISM is to provide faculty with continual feedback on assessment. Interactive assessment plans allow trained peer reviewers to provide ratings and comments online. The system contains entry points customized to various audiences allowing for highlighting of results most likely to interest them (Baker et al., 2012).

Faculty at Calvin College use what is called a horizontal approach to assessment planning. They identify one or more outcomes that are particularly important. After clarifying the outcomes and identifying appropriate measures, data are collected, discussed, and used to make teaching adjustments in a cycle that takes a few months to a year. Bradley (2009) likens this horizontal assessment approach to the undergraduate research model where students probe a small area in sufficient depth to enjoy discovery.

To ensure that assessment will be successful on their campus, Palo Alto College (2013) leaders present assessment plans for the academic year along a time line. In 2012–2013, the process for assessing critical thinking and quantitative skills at this two-year institution began during the August Convocation Week, when faculty were given an assessment calendar. In late September, faculty selected artifacts from their classes that demonstrated achievement of the relevant outcomes. In February, graders used a rubric to assess the artifacts with time allowed for discussion and evaluation of results. In spring, chairs and lead assessors met with faculty to share a summary of results.

Assessing and Facilitating Assessment

At both the institutional and unit levels, a thorough plan will include provisions for evaluating the assessment program itself. In fact, the goal of refining the assessment program should be established from the start of planning, and clear means to evaluate the program should be identified. The most important consideration is whether the assessment process is leading to improvements in academic and cocurricular programs. A key factor is how closely assessment methods are linked to learning outcomes. Leaders at Texas A&M University-Corpus Christi found several issues when evaluating program assessment reports prepared on their campus, including goals that were too broad and poor alignment between goals and measures (Hardin, 2012).

Regional accreditation provides an external review of campuswide assessment activities but cannot substitute for the timely review that must happen internally. The assessment plan should include specific opportunities to reflect on the assessment process. For example, the plan may call for the assessment committee to devote a regular meeting to this discussion each year, asking if any problems have been identified, whether activities need to be modified or expanded, and whether information is being made available to appropriate audiences. However, any issues about the assessment process should be considered as they arise, not postponed to an annual meeting. Voices other than those on the assessment committee also need to be heard. Students should be given opportunities to critique assessment projects as they participate in them, and focus groups of assessment audiences can be held at any time.

Rather than simply revising strategies and methods that are already in place, Banta and Blaich (2011) argue that any review of assessment should focus on fundamental questions, asking whether the assessment program is reflecting the core values of faculty and staff and if it is actually improving learning. A review of an assessment program should focus on the resources available to support faculty, staff, and students as they discuss assessment results and proposed changes. The effectiveness of the communication plan in creating a common understanding among stakeholders of a program's strengths and weaknesses should also be examined.

Faculty and staff need support if they are to plan and carry out successful assessment programs. Assessment web pages with links to required or suggested templates and other materials are helpful to those who are preparing plans for department or course assessment. Assessment rubrics developed for evaluating reports can provide guidance for planning as well. Faculty may also benefit from a list of items to include in a good assessment plan such as those shown in exhibit 11.1.

Although it must reflect a great deal of thought, an assessment plan need not be lengthy. It needs to be sufficiently specific that all those involved know who is going to do what, when they will do it, and how they will use the information that is generated. However, having a well-written plan does not guarantee successful assessment. The plan must reflect discussion and consensus among those charged with developing the plan and must be seen as a starting point for assessment, not the final word. The planning process must be flexible enough to move forward if problems occur or if promising opportunities become available. Assessment plans often need to be revisited as programs mature.

EXHIBIT 11.1 ASSESSMENT PLAN OUTLINE

1. *Departmental goals:* Describe what the department intends to accomplish, how the department's goals relate to campus mission, and purposes for assessment.
2. *Learning outcomes:* Describe what students must know, do, and value.
3. *Techniques and target groups*: Indicate how you will determine whether learning outcomes have been met, including methods, standards, target groups, and any potential impact on students.
4. *Analysis of results:* Indicate how you will review and present what you have learned from your assessment activities.
5. *Provisions for administration:* Specify who has responsibility for seeing the plan is carried out, who will collect and analyze data, and who will summarize and report results.
6. *Use of information:* Describe provisions for sharing information with internal and external audiences and for making recommendations and decisions.
7. *Time line:* Indicate when data will be collected and analyzed, when reports will be available, and when recommendations will be made.
8. *Assessment evaluation:* Indicate how the assessment program itself will be evaluated.

Considering Costs

Although specific figures ordinarily do not appear in the assessment plan itself, meaningful planning requires some consideration of costs. Assessment of institutional effectiveness takes a great deal of effort by many individuals. In several cases, new positions are created in order to carry out assessment. As might be expected, salaries and stipends for assessment personnel constitute the largest expenditure category (Cooper and Terrell, 2013). In addition to stipends for participating in assessment activities, small grants for carrying out assessment projects may be awarded. At IUPUI, PRAC grants for innovative work in assessment are capped at twenty-five hundred dollars. In many cases, faculty and staff time is reallocated from other efforts, thus realizing an opportunity cost of using faculty time on assessment rather than on something else.

Cooper and Terrell (2013) provide useful information from a survey asking what institutions are spending in several broad categories. For example, campuses paying for assessment software averaged an expense of about ten thousand dollars a year. However, about 35 percent of respondents indicated that they do not use software to manage their assessment data. An additional 11 percent reported that they do not pay for the software they use (perhaps relying on widely available software programs like Excel). The authors note that all assessment expenditures should be evaluated in terms of their ability to contribute to useful results.

Ewell, Paulson, and Kinzie (2011) believe that assessment at the institution and program levels is undercapitalized, pointing to the array of assessment activities that are conducted with "virtually no budget and rarely with support such as course release time" (p. 21). For faculty faced with limited resources, Cynthia Tweedell (2011) proposes using home-grown tests rather than standardized tests that "may have only a limited relationship with improving learning outcomes on a particular campus" (p. 4). Using authentic assessment that draws on assignments students have already completed is another cost-effective measure.

To use assessment resources efficiently, faculty need to set priorities and concentrate on their most important questions. Perhaps they are most concerned about internships or study-abroad experiences, or they have introduced a new program that needs attention. They may be able to alternate their activities. Everything does not need to be done every year. Doing a pilot study may help faculty decide which direction is best. For example, portfolios may be tried out with a sample of students before being widely used. Taking advantage of campuswide assessment or institutional research information can help conserve unit resources. Sometimes the best approach is to strengthen an activity already in use, such as an alumni questionnaire that could be expanded from a short survey instrument concentrating on employment questions to a longer questionnaire asking about preparation in important areas of learning. Using naturally occurring data collection points such as orientation, required courses, or application for graduation is an additional strategy. A short questionnaire may even be administered on graduation day. The overall assessment questions and needs of faculty and staff provide the best direction about what to emphasize.

As institutions examine assessment costs, Swing and Coogan (2010) advise planners to remember: start-up costs will be highest, costs vary with circumstances such as a new general education program, locally developed instruments are not free and may not necessarily lead to change, existing data should be used first, and sampling can work.

Linking Assessment to Other Valued Processes

For assessment to be valuable, it must be linked to other important processes. Leaders at several campuses place assessment at the center of their information-gathering activities. Here we provide some examples of campuses that have successfully incorporated assessment into various systems and procedures such as institutional effectiveness, strategic planning, and program review.

As at IUPUI, planners at the University of Texas at Austin (2013a) feature assessment in their institutional effectiveness cycle. Assessment plans are aligned with strategic plans allowing for assessment information to contribute to resource decisions and to continuing improvement. UT Austin leaders engage in assessing institutional effectiveness because it allows the campus to obtain better information for evaluating policies and practices and making decisions. Staff from the Office of Institutional Accreditation and Program Assessment collaborate with others to create an integrated system for improvement that brings together strategic planning, program review, and assessment. Office staff also coordinate program and general education assessment and advance institution-wide assessment.

Leaders at Troy University (2012) have introduced a new online institutional planning and effectiveness system in which all academic and nonacademic programs submit annual plans and reports. Unit faculty and staff build plans for improvement for outcomes not met. Outcomes that have been met can be captured in the system and included in annual achievement reports. The Institutional Effectiveness Committee reviews existing programs over a three-year period. It also reviews all revised programs, new programs, and substantive change proposals to verify that institutional effectiveness requirements are being met.

Campus leaders incorporate assessment information into their planning and decision- making processes in various ways. At St. Olaf College (Jankowski, 2012), responsibility for assessment resides in the Curriculum Committee and its Assessment Subcommittee. At St. Ambrose University (2013), educators have developed specific strategies to include assessment information in both program review and curriculum processes.

The Educational Policies Committee at St. Ambrose (2014) conducts formal program reviews that feature assessment activities and findings. Faculty offering programs reviewed in the 2013–2014 academic year were required to submit a letter of support from the Assessment and Evaluation Committee indicating that they are conducting appropriate assessment and identifying areas to strengthen. Faculty from programs being reviewed submit all annual assessment forms completed since the last program review. Documentation of the assessment process, including how faculty share responsibility for student learning and assessment, analyze and use evidence, and improve both student learning and assessment efforts, is required.

St. Ambrose (2013) leaders also have linked assessment to the curriculum review process. Faculty who propose a new general education course must identify the general education outcomes included in the course and align the course outcomes with those of the general education program. In the proposal, faculty also must indicate how each outcome will be assessed and the percentage of students' grades that will be determined by achieving each outcome. At St. Ambrose, assessment is guided by the university's Institutional Assessment and Evaluation Plan.

At Butler University (2013), assessment support is housed in the Office of Institutional Research and Assessment and assessment information is featured prominently in program review. The goal of program review is to improve academic programs by providing an opportunity for faculty to reflect on their educational practices and institutional priorities. Butler faculty submit annual assessment reports and regularly examine their student learning outcomes (SLOs) for continuing relevance. All SLOs must be measured quantitatively over a three-year cycle. Program reviews are conducted every five years and include previous annual assessment reports. In addition to assessment information, the self-study must include statements of program changes; faculty productivity analysis; resource needs; and analysis of strengths and weaknesses. At least one external reviewer with expertise in education and assessment must be involved in the process.

At Northeastern Illinois University (2012), funding requests are based on data analysis and review of assessment results. Assessment results are linked to the internal budget cycle, grant support, and strategic planning processes. Curricular and cocurricular program redesign is also based on assessment evidence. Office of Assessment and Program Review (OAPR) staff provide guidance for the program review process. New academic programs are reviewed three years after they have been approved and implemented. Other programs are reviewed within eight years.

Assessment information is at the core of the Northeastern Illinois University (n.d.a) self-study, which must include the program's rationale, mission, and distinguishing features. Figures on enrollment and completions for the previous five years are necessary, as are numbers of faculty and staff. Then program faculty must include their operational goals and goals for student learning. Each learning goal must include two student learning outcomes, and faculty must indicate the specific courses or activities where the outcomes are achieved. Both direct and indirect evidence of student learning must be presented. As part of external scanning, faculty compare their program to a similar program at a peer institution in terms of goals, offerings, number of participants, outcomes, and organizational support and structure. The scan can help faculty identify national or regional trends in program offerings, student demand, and economic considerations. Faculty can indicate if they have sufficient resources with respect to instructors, staff, and space. The self-study includes a summary of findings as well as recommendations, which can include changes in the curriculum or in assessment or instructional practices. Resource needs also can be presented. Faculty must develop a plan to achieve needed improvements identified in the self-study.

The review process includes a visit and brief report from an external reviewer. After the self-study is completed, the provost consults with the president, deans, and executive director of OAPR to decide whether the program should be found in good standing. If not, the program is flagged for annual review or its enrollments are suspended. Flagged programs must submit annual progress reports (NEIU, n.d.b).

It is clear from these examples that leaders on several campuses have successfully incorporated assessment into processes such as planning, budgeting, program review, and curriculum revision. These linkages allow assessment information to make valuable contributions to decision making; without these linkages, the usefulness of assessment information is limited. As Ewell (2009) has stated, goals for learning and evidence about them should be apparent throughout higher education.

CHAPTER 12

SUMMING UP

A Time of Transition

A s we send this book to press, it is difficult to predict a precise path for the evolution of outcomes assessment. We are in a time of significant transitions in a number of areas. Clearly the demands for accountability in higher education will not diminish, so there will be a continuing need for effective direct and indirect measures of individual and institutional performance.

Since the Spellings Commission report in 2006 (US Department of Education), there has been some pressure to measure student learning using a standardized test of generic skills. But many faculty and administrators have countered this pressure on the basis of their negative experience with these tests, and the press to assess with a test seems to be receding nationally, though it is still on the agenda in some state legislatures. Now some public officials in the United States are advocating the use of completion rates, graduates' earnings, and graduates' advanced degrees as accountability measures (Kington, 2012). And the European Commission (2014) has issued a report recommending that quality assurance be used to assess whether the skills college students acquire really meet labor market needs. If measures of completion and employability become the coin of the realm, will this shift attention from the assessment undertaken for improvement purposes that we have been describing in this book?

The 2014 revision of the Lumina Foundation's Degree Qualifications Profile (DQP) has just been released. Faculty at more than four hundred colleges and universities have used this "framework for defining the high quality learning that college degrees should signify" (Adelman, Ewell, Gaston, and Schneider, 2014) since the first version was published in 2011. The authors of the DQP have insisted that it is not aimed at standardizing curricula in US colleges and universities. Yet some observers have worried that widespread adoption of the DQP could have that effect. More agreement on the knowledge and skills college graduates should attain could have an important effect on outcomes assessment, but it is difficult to identify that effect. Such agreement could bring colleagues from various disciplines on campuses or from various institutions across the country together to create more valid and reliable assessment instruments than any single group could develop alone. But increased standardization of assessment measures could encourage their use to make unwarranted comparisons among institutions and could even narrow curricula and course content if faculty begin to teach to the test, which many in K–12 education decry.

The difficulty young people had finding employment during the Great Recession and the desire to increase the percentage of college graduates are global phenomena that have given rise to learning outcome-based qualification systems and more ways to validate competence acquired outside the classroom (CHEA International Quality Group, 2014). Digital badges, massive open online courses (MOOCs), and competence-based assessment are examples of these developments. Competence-based degree programs are being offered by Western Governors University and Southern New Hampshire's College for America and through the "flexible option" of the University of Wisconsin System. These options can increase access and college completion and call ever more attention to the need for outcomes assessment. But do they give students such broad opportunities to develop their own pathways to credentials that they sideline college educators' influence in organizing an effective educational experience? Do they advantage preparation for today's jobs at the expense of general education?

In the past two decades, regional and disciplinary accreditors have exerted the most powerful external influences on outcomes assessment at the campus level. But as members of Congress debate changes proposed for the next reauthorization of the Higher Education Act, accreditation is under fire. Accrediting agencies are viewed by some as poor stewards of federal financial aid for students, setting only minimum standards for institutions, conducting some actions in secret, and permitting conflicts of interest to affect the accreditation process (Kelderman, 2014). One possibility is that accreditors could be stripped of their role as gatekeepers of student financial aid. Since that has been the big stick with which accreditors have wielded power over institutions in the past, if the ability to cut off financial aid disappeared, would accreditation still have an important role in encouraging campus participation in assessment activities—or in any campus activities for that matter?

These are but a few of the many changes influencing assessment that have occurred since we published our original version of *Assessment Essentials* in 1999. In that edition, we described several choices for faculty and staff to consider as they implemented their assessment programs. Some of the questions we examined then are still being discussed. Does accountability shape assessment choices or does the aim to improve (Ewell, 2009)? Do we need to use standardized measures, or will using local measures suffice (Benjamin, 2012)? What methods or designs should we use? What role will technology play? Can we build a culture of assessment?

Over the years, these questions have been addressed, if not answered, and progress has occurred in many directions. Faculty and staff have created a common vocabulary with shared understanding of concepts such as outcomes and rubrics. They have developed assessment models in addition to assessment plans. Seasoned assessment practitioners share their advice, and rubrics are used to assess assessment. While we cannot make accurate predictions about the way forward for outcomes assessment during this period of significant transitions, we can offer some observations about the current practice of assessment.

Current Practice

Purposes

Accountability matters, but so does improvement. Although methods differ greatly across departments, these overriding reasons for undertaking assessment do not. Regardless of discipline group, at least 74 percent of program heads endorse institutional accreditation as a reason for undertaking assessment and 77 percent endorse program improvement (Ewell, Paulson, and Kinzie, 2011).

Clearly assessment activity intensifies as accreditation visits approach. And as might be expected, it may diminish immediately after. Hardin (2012), at Texas A&M University-Corpus Christi, notes that assessment momentum on her campus seemed to stagnate in the year after the reaffirmation process was complete, particularly for programs that had felt compelled to do assessment. This is a time when leadership is particularly important. For example, after a successful accreditation visit on her campus, Jo-Ellen Asbury (2010), assistant vice president for academic affairs at Stephenson University, considered how to reenergize assessment efforts. The Office of Institutional Research and Assessment followed the advice of its advisory group and planned a Putting Your Best Foot Forward event that included roundtable discussions about how faculty use assessment to improve learning.

Assessment Approaches

A notable development in assessment practice has occurred as the field has matured. In 1999 a survey was often the method of choice. Today faculty routinely use course-embedded methods including rubrics, performance assessment, capstone courses, and comprehensive projects (Kuh, Jankowski, Ikenberry, and Kinzie, 2014).

The need to include direct assessment measures, whether quantitative or qualitative, in credible assessment programs is now well established. Accreditors expect institutional assessment plans to include direct measures of learning and, in turn, campus leaders ask their units to include this kind of evidence. Still, some observers are reminding faculty and staff that indirect measures have value too. Spangehl (2007) includes disregarding satisfaction and other indirect measures of learning as one of several mistakes assessment practitioners have made. Shirley M. Tilghman (2012), past president of Princeton, has argued against using nationally available standardized tests for assessment and concluded that indirect measures such as student and alumni surveys, as well as retention, graduation, and job placement rates, are "arguably the most meaningful" ways to determine student outcomes. She reasons that the ultimate goal of college is to produce productive citizens, and indirect measures provide evidence that institutions are doing this. AACSB International has recently reaffirmed the value of indirect measures for business schools it accredits. In a revised white paper issued in 2013, AACSB leaders encouraged institutions to include indirect measures as part of their accreditation portfolios in order to capture the important information and insights these instruments provide. One significant message here is that the voices of students matter (see Chapter 6).

Kyllonen (2013) notes the emerging recognition that noncognitive factors such as work ethic, motivation, teamwork, and cultural awareness play an important role in student success. If, as Kyllonen suggests, the twenty-first century is an era when soft skills are becoming prominent, assessment methods will need to provide evidence that students possess them (see Chapters 7 and 8).

Stakeholder Involvement

Assessment practitioners often point to engaging additional faculty in assessment as a major challenge. Program heads are less concerned. They would prefer to see better measures and improved faculty expertise (Ewell, Paulson, and Kinzie, 2011). If faculty are to be involved in assessment, they need to be supported. The good news is that on many campuses, significant ways to do this are underway. At the University of North Dakota (2014b), for example, faculty mentors are available to help other faculty as they undertake assessment responsibilities. Ewell (2010) writes that not everyone needs to be on board to have a successful program, but it does take more than a small core (see Chapters 3 and 10).

Enlisting student affairs professionals to focus their assessment efforts on student learning is a noteworthy development. Staff in many student affairs divisions have developed statements of learning outcomes for their graduates. At Chapman University (2014), student life learning outcomes include a healthy sense of self, a framework for personal ethics and values, and an ability to develop and sustain meaningful relationships. Collaboration between faculty and staff is also important. Professionals in the student affairs division at California State University, Long Beach (n.d.a) attribute the strength of their assessment program to the partnership of Student Services and Academic Affairs. More of these initiatives are needed and welcome (see Chapters 6 and 9).

Faculty and staff on several campuses have found interesting and challenging roles for students. At North Carolina A&T State University students conduct focus groups and participate in other assessment research (Baker, 2012a). Northern Illinois University leaders have created a student advisory council to help with assessment (Niemi and Douglass, 2013). Arkansas State University's assessment director asks students to help analyze departmental data that might be neglected otherwise (Welsh, 2013).

Assessment leaders on several campuses, such as the University of North Carolina Wilmington (n.d.), make a point of sharing assessment results with their students. But many others do not. Among respondents to a survey of department chairs at Kansas public universities, nearly 50 percent indicate they do not share assessment results with prospective or current students (Crawford and Gould, 2012). Actively engaging students in the assessment process also remains a largely untapped opportunity. Fewer than 10 percent of rubrics that evaluate assessment reports include "participation of students in the assessment process" as a criterion (Fulcher, Swain, and Orem, 2012).

Megan Rodgers (2011) was correct when she noted the great interest students have in seeing their institutions do well—the ultimate student reward for participating in assessment. As a graduate student at the Center for Assessment and Research Studies at James Madison University, Rodgers lamented that students are largely left out of the process of convincing others about assessment's value even though they could be very effective in spreading this message. Rodgers believes that students have a common goal with faculty and administrators: to improve the quality of education (see Chapters 3 and 6).

Technology

Much of the technology in use today was available in 1999, but options for applying it were limited. Now, faculty and staff have many choices. In her 2009 review in *Change*, Pat Hutchings described for-profit assessment providers as the new guys in town. The technology tools they supply support a wide range of assessment-related processes, including formulating student learning outcomes; developing rubrics; creating electronic portfolios; and, most frequently, managing, maintaining, and reporting assessment data. Some one-third of campuses have yet to introduce assessment software (Cooper and Terrell, 2013), and, as several of our examples illustrate, faculty and staff often change the system they are using. Selecting and preparing to use technology takes time and money as well. Hutchings considers whether technology solutions will increase the emphasis on data and reports and overshadow the deliberations that should be the foundation of assessment. We hope instead that the availability of timely data will lead to more informed discussions and better decisions.

Continuing Challenges

Many of the recent changes to assessment were visible in 1999. Challenges continue and choices must be made. Here we consider some areas of assessment that are provoking much thought.

Assessment's Effect on Individual Students

To avoid possible harm to students, an early notion about outcomes assessment was that it should have no effect on individual students—that assessment results should be used only to evaluate programs. Now practitioners believe assessment should help faculty and staff fulfill their obligation to help every student learn. Good assessment "can and should support learning," according to Hersh and Keeling (2013, p. 4). These authors argue that formal and informal feedback should be frequent and formative, criterion-referenced standards should be high and clear, and assessment should encourage students to integrate their learning across their experiences. They advocate coherent programs that support the intellectual growth of students throughout their undergraduate programs.

The Degree Qualifications Profile provides a framework to achieve coherence across programs and degree levels (Adelman et al., 2014). In addition, it contains competences that describe "what *every* graduate of a degree program at a given level ought to know and be able to do" (Ewell, 2013, p. 7). Rather than examining performances of representative samples of students, the expectation of the DQP is that the competence of each student will be demonstrated. Ewell (2013) describes this approach as a "significant shift in the underlying philosophy of assessment," which has centered largely on "periodic inspection of samples of students" (p. 8). Jankowski, Hutchings, Ewell, Kinzie, and Kuh (2013) consider the DQP "not as a document but as a call to action" (p. 9) and an opportunity to create a shared understanding among faculty, staff, students, and the public of the meaning of a degree.

Technology is making it possible to efficiently aggregate information about individual students to the program level. For example, faculty and staff at Prince George's Community College have developed a unique assessment approach called the All-in-One. Using rubrics embedded in software, faculty assess whether students have mastered expected competences. Results are recorded and cumulated to course and program levels (Ariovich and Richman, 2013). In this case, information about individual student accomplishments provides the basis for holistic information about academic programs (see Chapter 5).

For systems such as these to work, assignments and standards must be carefully developed. Ewell (2013) describes assignment templates as a way to elicit students' best work. Creating appropriate standards is an additional challenge. Staff from the Assessment Office at the University of Hawaii at Manoa (2012) present a workshop, "What's Good Enough," on setting standards. They note the importance of information from employers, colleagues, and disciplinary associations in setting standards. The topic of standards was recently discussed by faculty and staff on the University of Kentucky's ASSESS Listserv. Questions revolved around the basis for setting standards and whether thresholds for individual assignments should exist outside the acceptable passing rate for a course.

Alternative Ways to Credential Students

Competence-based education (CBE) programs are generating increased interest as issues of educational quality and cost come into play. As Rebecca Klein-Collins (2013) explains, CBE focuses on what students know and can do rather than on course completion. Many CBE models are based on self-paced online formats and often function apart from credit-hour generation. Western Governors University (WGU), for example, has no traditional courses. Students are on a subscription plan. They pay a fee and can take as many assessments as they like during the subscription period.

What does this imply for assessment? As Klein-Collins points out, assessment is the core of the CBE framework. CBE approaches depend on essential elements of assessment, including clearly defined learning outcomes and appropriate standards for performance. Online learning appears amenable to traditional assessment approaches. For example, Merilee Griffin (2010) studied whether faculty teaching a first-year composition course could work together in an online setting and still develop an interpretive community that would score student writing in similar ways. The study produced high rates of interrater reliability and Griffin concluded that communicating online "can produce shared perspectives" (p. 16).

Rather than drawing on standard assessment methods, however, Prineas and Cini (2011) believe that innovative approaches to online learning will energize assessment in interesting ways. Self-paced online learning programs allow assessment to occur without any additional data collection, rubrics, or rescoring. Students advance from one module to the next when they successfully complete authentic tasks designed to demonstrate their mastery. Carnegie-Mellon's Open Learning Initiative (OLI) provides feedback to students during the problem-solving process. In addition, timely and effective feedback to instructors empowers them to intervene effectively.

Prineas and Cini (2011) project that what is now called learning analytics based on tracking students' interactions with online texts and courseware will eventually be used at the program level in real time so that students quickly benefit from adjustments such as changes in course sequences and academic requirements. In fact, the authors see the day when no course will be completely face-to-face without any online practice and assessment. Student learning will be self-paced and faculty will recognize that effective teaching "takes a village" (p. 12). If they are correct, the impact of technology on assessment is only beginning. (Learning analytics is further described in Chapter 10.)

The concept of digital badges is a recent alternative for recognizing student competence that originated as a way to acknowledge and motivate learners in MOOCs. Typically learners encounter module-based instruction and are rewarded with the image of a digital badge on completion. Badges can be displayed in electronic portfolios and listed on résumés, so employers can quickly verify that an individual has developed specified competences. Badges also can be incorporated in traditional courses. Alan Reid and Denise Paster (2013) incorporated a badge system they designed themselves using available web technology for the first-year composition course at Coastal Carolina University when they added digital modules to the curriculum.

Faculty and staff associated with the newly created interdisciplinary major in sustainable agriculture and food systems at the University of California at Davis caused a stir with their award from the Mozilla Foundation for developing a unique open badge. Faculty at UC-Davis note that their badge system works well with their hands-on curriculum and its seven well-defined core competences (Fain, 2014). Kevin Carey (2012) sees the potential of badges to "fundamentally redefine the credentials that validate higher learning," making the standard college transcript look "like a sad and archaic thing" (pp. 1–2). Of course, just as a college degree depends on the authority of the granting institution, badges need to be issued by a credible authority as well. In 2013 Mozilla created an open standard for badges that recognize educational or professional achievement, and Pearson also offers diplomas, certificates, and other credentials based on Mozilla's standards (Biemiller, 2014).

Whether based on traditional credit-hour courses, self-paced modules, or open badges, any system that involves learning necessarily involves assessment. In all of these cases, materials gathered from individual students can be used to ensure that academic programs are functioning well and improving.

Sharing Assessment Information and Results

At hundreds of universities and colleges, campus leaders maintain assessment websites that share information with their stakeholders. Many sites are interactive, containing links to other universities' web pages and to assessment resources such as reporting forms and workbooks. Several sites provide a direct link to Internet Resources for Higher Education Outcomes Assessment, the helpful meta-site Ephraim Schechter maintains at North Carolina State University. Schechter has created an online annotated bibliography for the assessment web pages of approximately five hundred colleges and universities. (http://www2.acs.ncsu.edu/UPA /Archives/assmt/resource.htm). Links also are provided to the website of the National Institute for Learning Outcomes Assessment, which contains valuable resources, including thoughtful occasional papers written by assessment practitioners and a Featured Website series (http://www .learningoutcomesassessment.org/).

To see what institutional websites generally reveal about outcomes assessment activities, Jankowski and Makela (2010) reviewed the websites of 725 randomly selected accredited institutions. Only about one-third of these websites returned results for search terms such as *learning outcomes* and *outcomes assessment*. Assessment information was most often found on the web page of the provost or chief academic officer or the institutional research office—pages that target internal audiences such as faculty and staff. The authors encourage institutions to post student outcomes statements and resources in multiple places and to help various audiences understand the information.

In our own review, we found many assessment websites that creatively present the work of faculty and staff, including student learning outcomes, resources, and methods. In some cases, campuswide assessment results are included, particularly for national surveys. Several websites contain candid discussions of assessment issues that faculty and staff face. Assessment leaders on these campuses explain the reasons for their decisions, revealing problems but also solutions. Faculty leaders at the University of Iowa (2013a), for example, recognized that assessment practices were sporadic across the campus and embarked on a four-year plan to improve.

Faculty and staff writing on the ASSESS listserv have discussed whether departments should be required to publicly report their assessment results. Many of the respondents spoke against this practice, worrying that standards would decline in order to report good results. But others suggested that reporting on actions taken on the basis of assessment findings constitutes a safer approach. Administrators on most campuses give program faculty a choice in what they share.

As with all other aspects of assessment, campus leaders differ in their approaches to reporting. At the University of Arizona, exemplary assessment web pages for both undergraduate and graduate programs are identified on the assessment office website. Viewers can click through to lists of activities and reported results (http://assessment.arizona.edu/). At Arkansas State University, online unit reports follow the format: Data Say; So What; How We Changed; and What We Got. This framework shares enough information to give viewers some understanding of how assessment information is collected and used (http://www.astate.edu/a/assessment /action-reseach/). In contrast, all department information at Colorado State University Pueblo (2014) is publicly available on the university's assessment website through a link to program assessment results and reports. Using the required reporting format, faculty describe results and related conclusions about student performance, as well as planned changes.

Choosing how much information to reveal and in what format is an important decision. As discussed in Chapter 10, the National Institute for Learning Outcomes Assessment (NILOA) has taken the lead in the area of transparency, describing what it means and highlighting institutions that are doing a good job of presenting assessment information.

Assessment Costs and Benefits

In an era when the overall cost of higher education is under constant scrutiny, assessment proponents need to consider the costs and benefits of the programs they administer. Although campus leaders recognize that undertaking assessment involves expenditures, little information about costs and benefits is available. To complicate matters, no acceptable methods exist to assign dollar values to such benefits of assessment as improved student learning.

The 2013 NILOA paper by Tammi Cooper and Trent Terrell provides some specific cost information gathered through an online survey about assessment spending. Across responding institutions, the average spending on assessment was $160,000, with the largest portion ($108,000) for salaries of faculty or administrators with assessment responsibilities. The vast majority of institutions spent $25,000 or less per year on assessment resources and less than $10,000 per year on faculty development. A majority of respondents did pay for assessment software and usually spent less than $10,000. More than 70 percent of respondents agreed that the benefits of assessment were worth the expenditures. In general, perceived benefits were related to the usefulness of assessment results rather than to the amount of money spent. The authors urge campus practitioners to compile their annual expenditures and determine those that are most useful.

Randy Swing and Christopher Coogan (2010) urge faculty and staff to consider the ratio of assessment costs to assessment benefits in order to make better decisions. Because assessment results that are not used have costs but no benefits, assessment should begin with a clear purpose and a way to achieve that purpose. In the absence of better measures, faculty and staff can make comparative judgments about the value of various methods. The challenge of measuring benefits may be greater than that of measuring costs, but will need to be addressed if institutions are to make sound decisions about assessment (see Chapters 4 and 11).

Finding a Home for Assessment

The tension between improvement and accountability that exists externally is mirrored on college campuses. To be successful, assessment must contribute to administrative processes such as planning and budgeting. But successful assessment also requires a close link with classroom processes. On its web pages, the NILOA features nine campuses as institutional examples of good assessment practice. Of these, several stand out for the close association that faculty and staff have developed between assessment of student learning and evidence-based teaching.

Faculty at Juniata College have an active interest in the scholarship of teaching and learning (SoTL) (Jankowski, 2011a). They examine literature and collect data to answer questions about learning in the classroom. Assessment concentrates on these questions as well. The SoTL center, created in 2009, provides brown bag lunches and learning communities focused on various aspects of teaching and assessment, such as writing assignments and portfolios. Elsewhere on campus, staff have created the Just the Facts website to help make student learning outcomes transparent (Juniata College, n.d.b). Viewers can click on a particular program and view various kinds of information, including outcomes. The college has participated in the National Survey of Student Engagement and the Collegiate Learning Assessment, and information from these studies is available online through the Institutional Research Office site (Juniata College, n.d.a).

St. Olaf College leaders frame assessment as "inquiry in support of learning" (Jankowski, 2012). The Center for Innovation in the Liberal Arts (CILA) on that campus focuses on the scholarship of teaching and learning, providing learning communities and other resources for faculty. CILA's active support in this area has helped create a more receptive atmosphere for assessment. Placing responsibility for assessment within the Curriculum Committee also visibly links assessment to classroom issues. At St. Olaf, assessment has benefited from leadership from the Office of Institutional Research and Evaluation. Jo Beld, director of evaluation and assessment, has encouraged faculty to conceptualize assessment as a resource to help them accomplish their work (Jankowski, 2012).

Assessment programs at large research universities also benefit from the support of teaching and learning centers. Staff at Carnegie Mellon University's Eberly Center for Teaching Excellence and Educational Innovation actively reinforce a connection between assessment of student outcomes and improvements in teaching and learning. They focus on solving problems using a research approach (Kinzie, 2012). The center's website provides multiple examples of useful assessment projects (see Chapters 5 and 6). Carnegie Mellon's Office of Institutional Research and Analysis (n.d.c) also provides consulting support for assessment.

At Cornell University (n.d.a), the Core Assessment Committee is the primary organizational structure responsible for promoting assessment and is chaired by the senior vice provost for undergraduate programs. The chair's online message contains the hope that the teaching goals of faculty will be enhanced through systematic assessment of student learning (Brown, n.d.). Both the Center for Teaching Excellence and the Institutional Research and Analysis office also contribute to assessment.

One could conclude from these examples that successful assessment needs to be infused into many campus processes. Faculty questions may be different from those of staff in a budget or planning office, but their questions are just as important. Early in its history, outcomes assessment was deliberately separated from classroom processes, especially grading (Ewell, 2009; Spangehl, 2007). If assessment practitioners were reluctant to include faculty grades as an assessment measure, teaching centers had little interest in the language or processes of institutional assessment (Hutchings, 2010). Now, the information used to assess learning outcomes often comes from efforts that are embedded in the classroom. As Hutchings points out, teaching and learning centers are positioned to increase faculty involvement in assessment through emphasizing research and evidence; providing grants to explore new classroom approaches that then are assessed; engaging in faculty development on topics related to assessment, such as e-portfolios; and helping faculty document and share the work they do that is related to improving student learning. The Eberly Center at CMU provides a model in this regard.

Hutchings (2010) and others suggest reframing the work of assessment as scholarship (Banta and Associates, 2002), and the Northern Illinois University

(2014) website contains a web page of assessment scholarship created by its faculty. Hutchings notes that the rising profile of pedagogy has increased faculty interest in assessment as it relates to student learning. Increasing interest in the scholarship of teaching and learning and its focus on inquiry has also benefited assessment. To the extent that teaching centers emphasize evidence, they strengthen assessment. Assessment needs to reside in multiple areas of a campus if its benefits are to be tapped for multiple purposes.

Creating a Culture of Assessment

According to Barham, Tschepikow, and Seagraves (2013), an organization that has created a culture of assessment is one "whose values, beliefs, norms, and behaviors reflect a shared appreciation of assessment practice and its value to institutional advancement" (p. 73). Faculty, administrators, staff, and students act on the common understanding that assessment can improve the campus. Building a culture of assessment involves delineating roles and responsibilities, providing training so that individuals can fulfill their responsibilities, and supporting and using assessment throughout the campus.

Creating a culture of assessment takes time. Agreeing on language and terms is a key element, as is support from campus leadership. Miami Dade Community College faculty became interested in becoming a "learning college" in 2005. College faculty and staff attended multiple conferences and invited experts to campus as they sought to rewrite what were outdated and neglected college goals. The culture of assessment really began to take root, however, when the college president pointed out that the word *goal* was not working. He argued that the college was developing a set of institution-wide *learning outcomes*, not a set of general education goals. After ten essential learning outcomes were adopted, the entire campus—including faculty, staff, and students—took part in a "Covenant of Engagement" ceremony to support the outcomes. Later, authentic assessment activities were created to examine attainment of the outcomes and the campus commitment to assessment has continued (Reed, 2011b).

Campuses vary in mission and values, and faculty and staff therefore approach assessment with unique perspectives. In 2012, Christopher Eisgruber, then provost, now president, of Princeton University argued for promoting a "culture of engagement" rather than a "culture of assessment." Although leaders at Princeton believe emphatically in the importance of learning and endorse assessment, they believe that their unique senior thesis requirement, a rich capstone experience requiring in-depth independent work, benefits students but does not yield evidence that can be compared with results from other institutions. Princeton's campus leaders believe that assessment should focus on promoting faculty and student engagement with learning because engagement enhances learning. At Duke University's Trinity College, faculty and staff view assessment as integral to their "culture of evidence." The campus tracks progress of individual students and uses both direct and indirect measures to assess student learning (Reed, 2011a).

Regardless of specifics, a campus commitment to improvement is the foundation of an assessment culture. Leaders who are willing to encourage faculty to try to achieve learning goals, even if they fail at first, create conditions where assessment can thrive. The provost at Juniata College acknowledges that failing to achieve goals is not necessarily a bad thing if it helps faculty rethink their approaches and improve what they do (Jankowski, 2011a).

Some campus leaders are reluctant to publicly share assessment information, but we believe that telling assessment stories is an important way to build an assessment culture. *Assessment Update* is a valuable source for detailed accounts about the issues faculty and staff face on their campuses and the solutions they develop to address these issues. Faculty and staff reflect on assessment challenges in their own words, provide a narrative record of their progress, and reveal their commitment to improving learning on their campuses. The NILOA examples of institutional best practice provide similar stories of campus efforts to create sustainable assessment programs that are of value to the institution. Written by NILOA professional staff, the descriptions are based on various campus resources, including interviews with campus leaders.

Schuh and Gansemer-Topf (2010) make the very important point that "sustainability of assessment is most at risk when it is the sole responsibility of one person" (p. 11). One defense against this problem is to make sure that there are overlapping points of commitment and expertise throughout the campus. Just as shared stories are important, so are shared responsibilities. At Juniata College, leadership of the SoTL center rotates through faculty who serve a three-year tour, first as designated director, then director, and finally past director. This ensures continuity of efforts (Jankowski, 2011a).

Throughout this book, we have provided many examples of faculty and staff who use assessment results to improve curriculum and teaching practices, as well as to improve assessment. To truly sustain assessment, the results of assessment activities must lead to improvements. In fact, using results effectively is the most important way to build a culture in which *assessment is essential.*

REFERENCES

AACSB International. (2013). "Assurance of Learning Standards: AACSB White Paper No. 3." http://www.aacsb.edu/publications/whitepapers/assurance-of-learning-standards.pdf

ABET. (2013). "History." http://www.abet.org/History/

ABET. (2014). "General Criterion 3: Student Outcomes." http://www.abet.org/eac-criteria-2014–2015/

Adelman, C., Ewell, P. T., Gaston, P., and Schneider, G. C. (2014). "The Degree Qualifications Profile 2.0: Defining U.S. Degrees through Demonstration and Documentation of College Learning" (Draft). Indianapolis, IN: Lumina Foundation.

Alverno College. (2006). "Self Assessment." http://depts.alverno.edu/saal/selfassess.html

Alverno College. (2011). "Our Ability-Based Curriculum." http://www.alverno.edu/academics/ourability-basedcurriculum/

Alverno College. (2013). "Workshops." http://www.alverno.edu/academics/resources foreducatorsresearchers/workshops/

American Association of Community Colleges et al. (2013). *Principles for Effective Assessment of Student Achievement.* July 19.

American Association of Community Colleges. (2014). "What is the VFA?" http://www.aacc.nche.edu/Resources/aaccprograms/vfa_archive/Pages/default.aspx

American Bar Association. (2013). "Standards for the Approval of Law Schools. 2012–2013." www.americanbar.org/content/dam/aba/publications/misc/legal_education/standards/

American College Personnel Association. (1994). *The Student Learning Imperative: Implications for Student Affairs.* http://www.acpa.nche.edu/student-learning-imperative-implications-student-affairs

American College Personnel Association. (2006). *Assessment skills and knowledge content standards for student affairs practitioners and scholars.* [Brochure]. Washington, DC: Author.

American College Personnel Association and National Association of Student Personnel Administrators. (2010). "Professional Competence Areas for Student Affairs Professionals." Washington, DC: Author.

American University. (2014). "Learning Outcomes and Assessment." http://www .american.edu/provost/assessment/

Anderson, L. W., and Krathwohl, D. R. (Eds.). (2001). *A Taxonomy for Learning, Teaching, and Assessing: A Revision of Bloom's Taxonomy of Educational Objectives.* New York: Longman.

Anderson, T. (2013). "Building a Culture of Assessment in the Arts and Sciences." *Assessment Update, 25*(1), 3–4,14.

Andrade, M. S. (2013). "Launching E-Portfolios: An Organic Process." *Assessment Update, 25*(3) 1–2, 14–16.

Angelo, T. A., and Cross, K. P. (1993). *Classroom Assessment Techniques: A Handbook for College Teachers* (2nd ed.). San Francisco: Jossey-Bass.

Anoka Ramsey Community College. (2014). "Program Goals and Competencies." http://www.anokaramsey.edu/en/about/Information/Assessment/Program Goals.aspx

Appalachian State University. (2014). "Potential Assessment Data." http://irap .appstate.edu/assessment/potential-assessment-data

Ariovich, L., and Antoons, I. (n.d.). "Using E-Portfolios for Learning and Assessment in Co-Curricular Programs." http://www.pgcc.edu/uploadedFiles/Pages/ About_PGCC/opair/Using%20Portfolios%20for%20Learning%20and%20 Assessment%20in%20Co-curricular%20Programs.pdf

Ariovich, L., and Richman, W. A. (2013). *All-in-One: Combining Grading, Course, Program, and General Education Outcomes Assessment.* Urbana: University of Illinois and Indiana University, National Institute for Learning Outcomes Assessment.

Asbury, J. (2010). "Building a Culture of Assessment." *Assessment Update, 22*(4), 10–11.

Ash, S. L., and Clayton, P. H. (2004). "The Articulated Learning: An Approach to Guided Reflection and Assessment." *Innovative Higher Education, 29*(2), 137–154.

Association of American Colleges. (1994). *Strong Foundations: Twelve Principles for Effective General Education Programs.* Washington, DC: Author.

Association of American Colleges and Universities. (2002). *Greater Expectations: A New Vision for Learning as a Nation Goes to College.* Washington, DC: Author.

Association of American Colleges and Universities. (2007). *College Learning for the New Global Century: A Report from the National Leadership Council for Liberal Education and America's Promise.* Washington, DC: Author.

Association of American Colleges and Universities. (2008). *Our Students' Best Work: A Framework for Accountability Worthy of Our Mission* (2nd ed.). Washington, DC: Author.

Association of American Colleges and Universities. (2010a). "News Feature: AAC&U Member Innovations. Assessing Learning Outcomes at the University of Cincinnati." http://www.aacu.org/aacu_news/aacunews10/april10/feature.cfm

Association of American Colleges and Universities. (2010b). "News Feature: AAC&U Member Innovations. What's in a Dialogue? Lynn University's Core Explores Big

Questions." http://www.aacu.org/aacu_news/aacunews10/February10/feature
.cfm

Association of American Colleges and Universities. (2014a). "Critical Thinking
Assessment." http://www.aacu.org/resources/assessment/critical_thinking.cfm

Association of American Colleges and Universities. (2014b). "LEAP California."
http://www.aacu.org/leap/LEAPCSUInitiative.cfm

Association of American Colleges and Universities. (2014c). "LEAP State Initiative
Massachusetts." http://www.aacu.org/leap/massachusetts.cfm

Association of American Colleges and Universities. (2014d). "VALUE: Valid
Assessment of Learning in Undergraduate Education." http://www.aacu.org/
value/rubrics/

Association of American Colleges and Universities. (n.d.a). "The Essential Learning
Outcomes." http://www.aacu.org/leap/documents/EssentialOutcomes_Chart.pdf

Association of American Colleges and Universities. (n.d.b). "The Intentional
Learner." http://leap.aacu.org/toolkit/wpcontent/files_mf/purposeful_
pathways_excerpt.pdf

Association of American Colleges and Universities and Council for Higher Education
Accreditation. (2008). "New Leadership for Student Learning and Accountability:
A Statement of Principles, Commitment to Action." Washington, DC: Author.

Association of College and Research Libraries. (2014). "Information Literacy
Standards for Higher Education." http://www.ala.org/acrl/standards/
informationliteracycompetency

Association for Institutional Research. (2013). "Code of Ethics and Professional
Practice." http://www.airweb.org/Membership/Pages/CodeOfEthics.aspx

Astin, A. W. (1985). *Achieving Educational Excellence: A Critical Assessment of Priorities and
Practices in Higher Education.* San Francisco: Jossey-Bass.

Astin, A. W. (1991). *Assessment for Excellence: The Philosophy and Practice of Assessment
and Evaluation in Higher Education.* New York: American Council on Education/
Macmillan.

Astin, A. W., and antonio, a. l. (2012). *Assessment for Excellence: The Philosophy and
Practice of Assessment and Evaluation in Higher Education* (2nd ed.). Lanham, MD:
Rowman & Littlefield.

Axelson, R. D., and Flick, A. (2009). "Sustaining Assessment: A Post-Epidemiological
Approach to Using *the Program Evaluation Standards.*" *Assessment Update, 21*(3), 5–7.

Baepler, P. (2011). "Alternative Assessment in the Cloud." *Assessment Update, 23*(2),
1–2, 13–14.

Baker, G. R. (2012a). *North Carolina A&T State University: A Culture of Inquiry.* Urbana:
University of Illinois and Indiana University, National Institute for Learning
Outcomes Assessment.

Baker, G. R. (2012b, April). *Texas A&M International University: A Culture of Assessment
Integrated.* Urbana: University of Illinois and Indiana University, National Institute
for Learning Outcomes Assessment.

Baker, G. R., Jankowski, N. A., Provezis, S., and Kinzie, J. (2012, July). *Using Assessment
Results: Promising Practices of Institutions That Do It Well.* Urbana: University of Illinois
and Indiana University, National Institute for Learning Outcomes Assessment.

Ball State University. (2014a). "Institutional Effectiveness." http://cms.bsu.edu/
about/administrativeoffices/effectiveness

Ball State University. (2014b). "Student Affairs Assessment Plan." http://cms.bsu.edu/about/administrativeoffices/studentaffairs/studentaffairsassessmentplan

Ball State University. (2014c). "Writing Proficiency Exam." http://cms.bsu.edu/academics/collegesanddepartments/universitycollege/writingproficiency/exam

Banta, T. W. (1984). NCME award. *Educational Measurement, 3,* 23–24.

Banta, T. W. (2000). "Seeing Ourselves as Others See Us." *Assessment Update, 12*(6), 3, 13, 16.

Banta, T. W. (2009). "Sour Notes from Europe." *Assessment Update, 21*(6), 3, 7.

Banta, T. W. (2011). "Will We Just Stand By and Watch This Happen?" *Assessment Update, 23*(5), 3, 8.

Banta, T. W. (2012). "Addressing a Question of Credibility." *Assessment Update, 24*(6), 3, 15.

Banta, T. W. (2013). "Parallel Paths to Progress in Assessment in Europe and the United States." *Assessment Update, 25*(6), 3, 15.

Banta, T. W., and Associates. (2002). *Building a Scholarship of Assessment.* San Francisco: Jossey-Bass.

Banta, T. W., and Blaich, C. (2011). "Closing the Assessment Loop." *Change: The Magazine of Higher Learning, 43*(1), 22–27.

Banta, T. W., Griffin, M., Flateby, T. L., and Kahn, S. (2009, December). *Three Promising Alternatives for Assessing College Students' Knowledge and Skills* (NILOA Occasional Paper No. 2). Urbana: University of Illinois and Indiana University, National Institute for Learning Outcomes Assessment.

Banta, T. W., Jones, E. A., and Black, K. E. (2008). *Designing Effective Assessment: Principles and Profiles of Good Practice.* San Francisco: Jossey-Bass.

Banta, T. W., and Pike, G. R. (2012). *Making the Case Against—One More Time.* Urbana: University of Illinois and Indiana University, National Institute for Learning Outcomes Assessment.

Barham, J. D., and Dean, L. A. (2013). "Introduction: The Foundation." In D. M. Timm, J. D. Barham, K. McKinney, and A. R. Knerr (Eds.), *Assessment in Practice: A Companion Guide to the ASK Standards.* Washington, DC: American College Personnel Association.

Barham, J. D., Tschepikow, W. K., and Seagraves, B. (2013). "Creating a Culture of Assessment." In D. M. Timm, J. D. Barham, K. McKinney, and A. R. Knerr (Eds.), *Assessment in Practice: A Companion Guide to the ASK Standards.* Washington, DC: American College Personnel Association.

Baruch College. (2014). "Assessment at Baruch." http://www.baruch.cuny.edu/assessment

Bass, R. (2014). "Social Pedagogies in ePortfolio Practices: Principles for Design and Impact." http://c2l.mcnrc.org/wp-content/uploads/sites/8/2014/01/Bass_Social_Pedagogy.pdf

Beld, J. M. (2013). "Actionable Assessment for Academic Programs: Principles and Practices for Usable Results." http://www.aacu.org/meetings/ild/documents/Beld-Actionableassessment-ILD2012.pdf

Bendikas, Khris. (2013). "Listening to What Our Students Are Telling Us about Their Learning and Using It in the Classroom." http://www.mcla.edu/Academics/uploads/textWidget/3241.00087/documents/Brown_Bag_Lecture_Feb_22_MCLA.pdf

Bengiamin, N. N., and Leimer, C. (2012). "SLO-Based Grading Makes Assessment an Integral Part of Teaching." *Assessment Update, 24*(5), 1–2, 15–16.

Benjamin, R. (2012). *The Seven Red Herrings about Standardized Assessments in Higher Education.* Urbana: University of Illinois and Indiana University, National Institute for Learning Outcomes Assessment.

Benner, J., and Kapcsos, K. (2010). "From Consensus to Performance: Formative Course Assessment in Elementary Algebra." *Assessment Update, 22*(6), 8–10.

Bennett, J. M. (2008). "Transformative Training: Designing Programs for Culture Learning." In M. A. Moodian (Ed.), *Contemporary Leadership and Intercultural Competence: Understanding and Utilizing Cultural Diversity to Build Successful Organizations* (pp. 95–110). Thousand Oaks, CA: Sage.

Berheide, C. W. (2007, Spring). "Doing Less Work, Collecting Better Data: Using Capstone Courses to Assess Learning." *Peer Review, 9*(2), 27–30.

Berry, C. (2013). "The Use of AAC&U Value Rubrics at Winston-Salem State University." http://www.aacu.org/value/casestudies/

Biemiller, L. (2014, February 13). "Quickwire: Pearson Offers a Badge Platform." *Chronicle of Higher Education: Wired Campus.* http://chronicle.com/blogs/wiredcampus/quickwire-pearson-offers-a-badge-platform/50469

Binghamton University. (2011). "Assessment of General Education." http://www2.binghamton.edu/academics/provost/documents/gened-assessment-revised-051711.pdf

Binghamton University. (2013). "General Education Assessment." http://www.binghamton.edu/academics/provost/other-resources/assessment/gened.html

Bismarck State College. (2014). "Academic Assessment." http://www.bismarckstate.edu/about/institutional/academicassessment/

Blaich, C. F., and Wise, K. S. (2011). *From Gathering to Using Assessment Results: Lessons from the Wabash National Study* (NILOA Occasional Paper No. 8). Urbana: University of Illinois and Indiana University, National Institute for Learning Outcomes Assessment.

Bloom, B. S. (Ed.). (1956). *Taxonomy of Educational Objectives, Handbook I: Cognitive Domain.* New York: McKay.

Bloom, M. F. (2010). "Peer Review of Program Assessment Efforts: One Strategy, Multiple Gains." *Assessment Update, 22*(5), 5–7, 16.

Booth, M. (2012). "Learning Analytics: The New Black." *EDUCAUSE Review, 47*(4). http://www.educause.edu/ero/article/learning-analytics-new-black

Borden, V.M.H., and Kernel, B. (2012). "Measuring Quality in Higher Education: An Inventory of Instruments, Tools, and Resources." http://apps.airweb.org/surveys/Default.aspx

Borgford-Parnell, J. (2006). "Teaching and Assessing Lifelong Learning." http://depts.washington.edu/celtweb/teaching/workshops.html

Boughton, D. (2013). "Assessment of Performance in the Visual Arts: What, How, and Why." In A. Karpati and E. Gaul (Eds.), *From Child Art to Visual Culture of Youth—New Models and Tools for Assessment of Learning and Creation in Art Education.* Bristol, UK: Intellect Press.

Bowers, P. (2009). "Diversity as a Learning Goal: Challenges in Assessing Knowledge, Skills, and Attitudes." *Assessment Update, 21*(5), 3–5.

Bowling Green State University. (2013). "Selection of Canvas." http://www.bgsu.edu/offices/provost/page116100.html

Bowling Green State University. (2014). "Divisional Assessment." http://www.bgsu.edu/offices/sa/vp/priorities/page68710.html

Bowman, N. A. (2013, Winter). "Understanding and Addressing the Challenges of Assessing College Student Growth in Student Affairs." *Research and Practice in Assessment, 8,* 5–14.

Bradley, W. J. (2009). "Horizontal Assessment." *Assessment Update, 21*(3), 10–11.

Brandeis University. (n.d.a). "First Year Reflective Guide." http://www.brandeis.edu/assessment/docs/first_yr_reflective_guide.pdf

Brandeis University. (n.d.b). "Overview." http://www.brandeis.edu/assessment/overview.html

Bresciani, M. J. (2013). "Developing Outcomes." In D. M. Timm, J. D. Barham, K. McKinney, and A. R. Knerr (Eds.), *Assessment in Practice: A Companion Guide to the ASK Standards.* Washington, DC: American College Personnel Association.

Bridges, M. (n.d.). "Using a Clicker System and Concept Questions to Assess Student Understanding During Class." http://www.cmu.edu/teaching/assessment/examples/courselevel-bycollege/hss/course_clickersConceptQuestions-psychology.html

Brigham Young University. (2014). "Expected Learning Outcomes Evidence and Assessment." http://learningoutcomes.byu.edu

Bringle, R. G., Clayton, P. H., and Plater, W. M. (2013). "Assessing Diversity, Global, and Civic Learning: A Means to Change in Higher Education." *Diversity and Democracy, 16*(3). https://www.aacu.org/diversitydemocracy/vol16no3/bringle_clayton_plater.cfm

Brown, L. (n.d.). "Message from the Vice-Provost." http://www.cornell.edu/provost/assessment/docs/message_from_laura_brown.pdf

Bubb, D. K., Herzog, M. B., Terry, P., and Geithner, C. A. (2010). "Bottom Up: Institutional Collaboration and the Creation of an Assessment Culture." *Assessment Update, 22*(3), 6–8.

Bubb, D. K., Schraw, G., James, D. E., Brents, B. G., Kaalberg, K. F., Marchand, G. C., Amy, P., and Cammett, A. (2013). "Making the Case for Formative Assessment: How it Improves Student Engagement and Faculty Summative Course Evaluations." *Assessment Update, 25*(3), 8–9, 12.

Buena Vista University. (2014). "BVU Objective Data Dashboard." http://www2.bvu.edu/academics/assessment

Buffalo State University. (n.d.). "Principles of Student Outcomes Assessment." http://www.buffalostate.edu/academicaffairs/x585.xml

Burton, A. (2012). "A 'Wisdom of Crowds' Approach to Outcomes Assessment." *Assessment Update, 24*(3), 1–2, 14–16.

Butler University. (2013). "Assessment Protocol." http://www.butler.edu/institutional-research/assessment-review/protocol/

Butte College. (2013). "Student Learning Outcomes Philosophy Statement." http://www.butte.edu/slo/

Cabrillo College. (n.d.). "Student Learning Outcomes." https://sites.google.com/a/cabrillo.edu/student-learning-outcomes/home

California Lutheran University. (2014a). "Assessment System." http://www.callutheran.edu/assessment/cycle/

California Lutheran University. (2014b). "Signature Assignments." http://www.callutheran.edu/assessment/student_learning_outcomes/SignatureAssignments.php

California Polytechnic State University San Luis Obispo. (2014a). "Academic Assessment." http://www.academicprograms.calpoly.edu/content/assessment/index

California Polytechnic State University San Luis Obispo. (2014b). "Writing Proficiency Exam Scoring." http://writingcenter.calpoly.edu/content/gwr/wpe/wpe

California State University Fresno. (2007). "Voices of Experience: Assessment Advice from Cal State Fresno's Veteran Assessment Coordinators." http://www.fresnostate.edu/academics/oie/documents/assesments/assesstipsf07acmtg2.pdf

California State University Long Beach. (n.d.a). "Assessment." http://www.csulb.edu/divisions/students/assessment/

California State University Long Beach. (n.d.b). "Assessment Definitions." http://www.csulb.edu/divisions/aa/grad_undergrad/senate/committees/assessment/dev/info/what/

California State University Sacramento. (2013). "Assessment Guide 2012–2013." http://www.csus.edu/student/assessment/Assessment%20Guide/assessmento-guide—pdf.pdf

California State University Sacramento. (n.d.). "Assessment PEMSA." http://www.csus.edu/student/assessment/index.html

California State University San Bernardino. (2014). "Collegiate Learning Assessment FAQ." http://www.ugs.csusb.edu/testing/clafaq.html

California State University Stanislaus. (2013). "Office of Assessment." http://www.csustan.edu/oaqa/

Cambridge, D., Cambridge, B., and Yancey, K. B. (2009). *Electronic Portfolios 2.0: Emergent Research on Implementation and Impact.* Sterling, VA: Stylus.

Carey, K. (2012, April 8). "A Future Full of Badges." *Chronicle of Higher Education.* https://chronicle.com/article/A-Future-Full-of-Badges/131455/

Carleton College. (2013). "The Writing Program." http://apps.carleton.edu/campus/writingprogram/carletonwritingprogram/portfolio

Carnegie Mellon University. Eberly Center. (n.d.a). "Assess Teaching and Learning." http://www.cmu.edu/teaching/assessment/

Carnegie Mellon University. Eberly Center. (n.d.b). "Group and Self-Assessment Tool." http://www.cmu.edu/teaching/assessment/assesslearning/tools/groupselfassessmenttool.pdf

Carnegie Mellon University (n.d.c). "Institutional Research and Analysis. University Assessment Plan." http://www.cmu.edu/ira/assessment/index.html

Casper College. (2014). "Program Assessment Plan Template." http://www.caspercollege.edu/assessment/

Casper College. (n.d.a). "Best Practices in Assessment." http://www.caspercollege.edu/assessment/downloads/best_practices.pdf

Casper College. (n.d.b). "Institutional Review Board Guidelines for Casper College Assessment Activities." http://www.caspercollege.edu/assessment/downloads/IRB_assessment.pdf

Catalyst for Learning. (2014). "ePortfolio Resources and Research." http://c2l.mcnrc.org/

Central College. (2014). "PSIP." http://departments.central.edu/psychology/faculty/psap/

Chaffey College. (2013). "Outcomes and Assessment." http://www.chaffey.edu/slo/index.html

Chapman University. (2014). "Student Life Learning Outcomes." http://www.chapman.edu/academics/learning-at-chapman/student-life-learning-outcomes.aspx

CHEA International Quality Group. (2014, January). *Higher Education Outside Colleges and Universities: How do We Assure Quality?* (Policy Brief 2). Washington, DC: Author.

Cherry, M., and Klemic, G. (2013). "Focus on the Bottom-Line: Assessing Business Writing." *Assessment Update, 25*(2), 5–6, 14.

Clark, E. J., and Eynon, B. (2009). "E-Portfolios at 2.0—Surveying the Field." *Peer Review, 11*(1), 18–23.

Clemson University. (2014). "Welcome to the e-Portfolio Program." http://www.clemson.edu/academics/programs/eportfolio/index.html

Cluphf, D. J., and Lox, C. L. (2009). "Journals and Program Assessment." *Assessment Update, 21*(4), 5–7.

Cochise College. (2009). "Cochise College Assessment Handbook." https://my.cochise.edu/c/document_library/get_file?uuid=86976 ed1-dce8–417e-b66d-e8d25b98b74d&groupId=216207

Cochise College. (2014). "Learning Improvement." http://www.cochise.edu/instruction/learning-improvement/

College of William and Mary. (n.d.). "Our Vision for Student Affairs Assessment" http://www.wm.edu/about/administration/senioradmin/studentaffairs/about/assessment/index.php

College of Wooster. (2014). "Undergraduate Research." http://www.wooster.edu/academics/research/

Collegiate Employment Research Institute. (2012). "Liberally Educated Versus In-Depth Training: Employers' Perceptions of What They Look For in New Talent: CERI Research Brief 2012.4." http://www.ceri.msu.edu/wp-content/uploads/2010/01/CERI-Research-Brief-2012–4-Liberally-Educated-Versus-In-Depth-Training.pdf

Colorado State University Pueblo. (2013). "Civil Engineering Program Assessment Report 2012–2013." http://www.colostate-pueblo.edu/Assessment/Results AndReports/Documents/2013%20Reports/CET.pdf

Colorado State University Pueblo. (2014). "Institutional and Academic Program Results and Reports." http://www.colostate-pueblo.edu/Assessment/ResultsAndReports/Pages/default.aspx

Columbia College Chicago. (2014). "Evaluation and Assessment." http://www.colum.edu/Administrative_offices/Academic_Affairs/evaluation_and_assessment/.

Community College of Allegheny County. (2009). "Plan for Assessment of Institutional Effectiveness." http://www.ccac.edu/files/PDF_Document/1816e35e c28b4797969f2eaca59b99d4.pdf

Community College of Allegheny County. (2011). "Closing the Loop. What Does It Mean?" http://www.ccac.edu/files/PDF_Document/4f40fcec9d7e4b16852a56be5 2c408de.pdf

Community College of Baltimore County. (2011). "CCBC Assessment." http://www
.ccbcmd.edu/loa/loaindex.html

Conference on College Composition and Communication. (2009). "Writing
Assessment: A Position Statement." http://www.ncte.org/cccc/resources/
positions/writingassessment

Cooper, R. M. (2009). "Planning for and Implementing Data Collection." In J. H. Schuh
and Associates, *Assessment Methods for Student Affairs.* San Francisco: Jossey-Bass.

Cooper, R. M., and Shelley II, M. C. (2009). "Data Analysis." In J. H. Schuh and
Associates, *Assessment Methods for Student Affairs.* San Francisco: Jossey-Bass.

Cooper, T., and Terrell, T. (2013). *What Are Institutions Spending on Assessment? Is It
Worth the Cost?* Urbana: University of Illinois and Indiana University, National
Institute for Learning Outcomes Assessment.

Cooperative Institutional Research Program. (2012). "The American Freshman:
National Norms Fall 2012." http://www.heri.ucla.edu/monographs/the
americanfreshman2012.pdf

Cornell University. (n.d.a). "Assessment of Student Learning." http://www.cornell
.edu/provost/assessment/

Cornell University. "Setting Learning Outcomes." (n.d.b). http://www.cte.cornell
.edu/teaching-ideas/designing-your-course/setting-learning-outcomes

Cornell University. (n.d.c). "So You Want to Survey Cornell Students." http://irp.dpb
.cornell.edu/surveys/you-want-to-survey

Cosgrove, J. J., and McDoniel, L. J. (2009). "Creating a Culture of Action Using
Mission-Based Assessment." *Assessment Update, 21*(4), 11–14.

Council for the Advancement of Standards in Higher Education. (2012). *CAS
Standards for Higher Education* (8th ed.). Washington, DC: Author.

Council of Independent Colleges. (2014). "CIC/Collegiate Learning Assessment
(CLA) Consortium." http://www.cic.org/Programs-and-Services/Programs/
Pages/Collegiate-Learning-Assessment-(CLA).aspx

Crawford, C. B., and Gould, L. (2012). "Department Chair Perspective on Learning
Outcomes Assessment at Kansas's Public Universities." *Assessment Update, 24*(1), 9,
13–14.

D'Allegro, M. L. (2011). "Any Questions?" *Assessment Update, 23*(4), 6–8.

Damsgaard, J., and Karlsbjerg, J. (2010). "Seven Principles for Selecting Software
Packages." ACM Digital Library. http://queue.acm.org/detail.cfm?id=1787252

Davis, A. P., and Ohlemacher, J. L. (2013). "Holistic Assessment of General Education
at Carroll Community College." http://www.aacu.org/value/casestudies/

Dean, K. L. (2013). "Politics in Assessment." In D. M. Timm, J. D. Barham,
K. McKinney, and A. R. Knerr (Eds.), *Assessment in Practice: A Companion Guide to the
ASK Standards* Washington, DC: American College Personnel Association.

Del Mar College. (2012). "Assessment Manual. Appendix D. Role of Stakeholders
in Assessment of Learning Process." http://www.delmar.edu/WorkArea/
DownloadAsset.aspx?id=2147483694

Del Mar College. (2013). "Dashboard." http://www.delmar.edu/spir/db.aspx

Del Mar College. (n.d.). "Timeline for Assessment of Student Learning." http://
dmc122011.dlmar.edu/cmmittee/assessmentslc/docs/timeline.pdf

DePaul University. (2011). "Division of Student Affairs Assessment." http://
studentaffairs.depaul.edu/assessment.html

DePaul University. (2014). "Annual Assessment Report." http://condor.depaul.edu/ tla/Assessment/AssessmentTemplates.html#apr_templates

Diamond, R. M. (2008). *Designing and Assessing Courses and Curricula: A Practical Guide* (3rd ed.). San Francisco: Jossey-Bass.

DiMeglio, F. (2013). "Risky Business: Indiana U's Spine 'Sweat Experience.'" http:// www.businessweek.com/articles/2013–04–12/risky-business-indiana-us-spine-sweat-experience

DiPietro, M. (n.d.). "Journals to Monitor Student Learning in Statistics." http://www .cmu.edu/teaching/assessment/examples/courselevel-bycollege/hss/course_ journals-statistics.html

Eastern Connecticut State University. (n.d.). "Assessment Activity around Eastern." http://nutmet.easternct.edu/assessment/activity.htm

Ebersole, T. E. (2009). "Postsecondary Assessment: Faculty Attitudes and Levels of Engagement." *Assessment Update, 21*(2), 1–2, 13–14.

Edmonds Community College. (n.d.). "SIMPLE Plan." http://www.edcc.edu/grants/ SIMPLE_plan.html

Ehrmann, S. C., and Peterson, N. S. (2010), "Matrix Surveys: A New Tool for Evaluation and Research." *Assessment Update, 22*(3), 3–5.

Eisgruber, C. (2012, October 23) "Promoting a 'Culture of Engagement' not a 'Culture of Assessment.'" Remarks prepared for delivery to presidents of the American Association of Universities, Princeton, NJ. http://www.princeton.edu/ president/eisgruber/speeches-writings/archive/?id=10613

Emory University. (2014a). "Outcomes Assessment at Emory." http://www.oirpe .emory.edu/Assessment/

Emory University. (2014b). "Student Affairs Assessment Conference." http:// assessmentconference.emory.edu/

Ennis, D. J. (2010). "Contra Assessment Culture." *Assessment Update, 22*(2), 1–2, 15–16.

Ennis, R. (2011). "Critical Thinking Assessment." http://www.criticalthinking.net/ testing.html

Ennis, R. (2012). "Definition of Critical Thinking." http://criticalthinking.net/ definition.html

Eubanks, D. A., and Royal, K. D. (2011). "A Survey of Attitudes about Methods of Assessment." *Assessment Update, 23*(3), 1–2, 13–15.

European Commission. (2014, January 28). "Member States Urged to Improve Quality Checks in Universities and Vocational Colleges." http://europa.eu/rapid/ press-release_IP-14–83_en.htm?locale=en

European Students' Union. (2014). "European Students' Union." www.esu-online.org

Ewell, P. T. (1984). *The Self-Regarding Institution: Information for Excellence.* Boulder, CO: National Center for Higher Education Management Systems, 1984.

Ewell, P. T. (2004). "Tomorrow the World: Learning Outcomes and the Bologna Process." *Assessment Update, 16*(6), 11–13.

Ewell, P. T. (2009, November). *Assessment, Accountability, and Improvement: Revisiting the Tension* (Occasional Papers No. 1). Urbana: University of Illinois and Indiana University, National Institute for Learning Outcomes Assessment.

Ewell, P. T. (2010). Foreword to P. Hutchings, *Opening Doors to Faculty Involvement.* Urbana: University of Illinois and Indiana University, National Institute for Learning Outcomes Assessment.

Ewell, P. (2012). Foreword to R. Benjamin, *The Seven Red Herrings of Standardized Assessments in Higher Education.* Urbana: University of Illinois and Indiana University, National Institute for Learning Outcomes Assessment.

Ewell, P. (2013, January). *The Lumina Degree Qualifications Profile (DQP): Implications for Assessment* (Occasional Paper No. 16). Urbana: University of Illinois and Indiana University, National Institute for Learning Outcomes Assessment.

Ewell, P., Jankowski, N., and Provezis, S. (2010). *Connecting State Policies on Assessment with Institutional Assessment Activity.* Urbana: University of Illinois and Indiana University, National Institute for Learning Outcomes Assessment.

Ewell, P., Paulson, K., and Kinzie, J. (2011, July). *Down and In: Assessment Practices at the Program Level.* Urbana: University of Illinois and Indiana University, National Institute for Learning Outcomes Assessment.

Eyler, J. (2009). "The Power of Experiential Education." *Liberal Education, 95*(4). http://www.aacu.org/liberaleducation/le-fa09/le-fa09_Eyler.cfm

Eyler, J., and Giles, D. E. (1999). *Where's the Learning in Service-Learning?* San Francisco: Jossey-Bass.

Eynon, B., Gambino, L. M., and Torok, J. (2014a). "The Difference ePortfolio Makes: The Value of Integrative ePortfolios in Higher Education." http://c2l.mcnrc.org/wp-content/uploads/sites/8/2014/01/C2L_Propositions.pdf

Eynon, B., Gambino, L. M., and Torok, J. (2014b). "Inquiry, Reflection, and Integration." http://c2l.mcnrc.org/wp-content/uploads/sites/8/2014/01/C2L_Design_Principles1.pdf

Fain, P. (2014, January 3). "Badging from Within." *Inside Higher Ed.* http://www.insidehighered.com/news/2014/01/03/uc-davis-groundbreaking-digital-badge-system-new-sustainable-agriculture-program

Falluca, A., and Lewis, E. (2013). "Promoting Student Affairs Buy-In for Assessment: Lessons Learned." *Assessment Update, 25*(3), 4–5, 13–14.

Feldmann, M. L., and Jackson, K. (2011). "Took Survey. Got Shirt: Using Effective Educational Practices to Maximize NSSE Response Rates." *Assessment Update, 23*(6), 1–2, 15.

Ferren, A., and Paris, D. (2013). "How Students and Faculty Can Fulfill the Promise of Capstones." *Peer Review, 15*(4). http://www.aacu.org/peerreview/pr-fa13/Ferren.cfm

Fifolt, M. M. (2013). "Applying Qualitative Techniques to Assessment in Student Affairs." *Assessment Update, 25*(4), 5–6, 12–13.

Fitch, P., and Steinke, P. (2013). "Tools for Assessing Cognitive Outcomes of Experiential Learning." Paper prepared for the NCA HLC Annual Conference on Quality in Higher Education. http://departments.central.edu/psychology/files/2011/07/HLC-2013-Paper-Fitch-Steinke.pdf

Flateby, T. A (2010). "System for Fostering and Assessing Writing and Critical Thinking Skills." *Assessment Update, 22*(3), 1–2, 14–15.

Flick, A. (2009). "The Humanities and Interrater Reliability: A Response to R. Stephen RiCharde." *Assessment Update, 21*(1), 1–2, 15–16.

Florida State University. (2011). "Career Portfolio User's Guide." http://www.career.fsu.edu/IMAGES/PDFS/Guides/CareerPortfolioGuide.pdf

Florida State University. (2014). "Overview of Chalk and Wire for Students." http://www.coe.fsu.edu/Current-Students/Student-Academic-Services-OASIS/For-Undergraduates/Overview-of-Chalk-and-Wire-for-Students

Ford, T. (2010). "Growth in Disciplinary Resources for Assessment in the Liberal Arts." *Assessment Update, 22*(6), 1–2, 13–15.

Fulcher, K. H., and Bashkov, B. M. (2012). "Do We Practice What We Preach? The Accountability of an Assessment Office." *Assessment Update, 24*(6), 5–7, 14.

Fulcher, K. H., and Good, M. R. (2013). *The Surprisingly Useful Practice of Meta-Assessment.* Urbana: University of Illinois and Indiana University, National Institute for Learning Outcomes Assessment.

Fulcher, K. H., Swain, M., and Orem, C. D. (2012). "Expectations for Assessment Reports: A Descriptive Analysis." *Assessment Update, 24*(1), 1–2, 14–16.

Gaff, J. G. (2004, Fall) "What Is a Generally Educated Person?" *Peer Review.* http:// www.aacu.org/peerreview/pr-fa04/pr-fa04feature1.cfm

Gansemer-Topf, A. M., and Wohlgemuth, D. R. (2009). "Selecting, Sampling, and Soliciting Subjects." In J. H. Schuh and Associates, *Assessment Methods for Student Affairs.* San Francisco: Jossey-Bass.

Gardner, P. D. (1998). "Are College Students Prepared to Work?" In J. N. Gardner, G. Van der Veer, and Associates, *The Senior Year Experience: Facilitating Integration, Reflection, Closure and Transition.* San Francisco: Jossey-Bass.

Gaston, P. L. (2010). *General Education and Liberal Learning: Principles of Effective Practice.* Washington, DC: Author.

George Mason University. (2014). "Office of Institutional Assessment." (2014). https://assessment.gmu.edu/

Georgia Institute of Technology. (2014). "FAQs." https://www.assessment.gatech .edu/faq/Office of Assessment

Gettysburg College. (2014). "College Life." http://www.gettysburg.edu/about/ offices/college_life/co-curricular-goals.dot

Gilchrist, D., and Oakleaf, M. (2012, April). *An Essential Partner: The Librarian's Role in Student Learning Assessment* (NILOA Occasional Paper No. 14). Urbana: University of Illinois and Indiana University, National Institute for Learning Outcomes Assessment.

Goldman, G. K., and Zakel, L. E. (2009). "Clarification of Assessment and Evaluation." *Assessment Update, 21*(3), 8–9.

Grand Valley State University. (n.d.). "University Assessment Committee." http:// www.gvsu.edu/uac/

Greville, E. C. (2009). "A Rose by Any Other Name: Grading and Assessment." *Assessment Update, 21*(5), 1–2, 13.

Griffin, M. (2009). "What Is a Rubric?" *Assessment Update, 21*(6), 4,13.

Griffin, M. (2010). "Collaborative Online Assessments for Validity and Reliability." *Assessment Update, 22*(4), 1–2, 15–16.

Griffin, C. B., and Burns-Ardolino, W. (2013). "Designing and Implementing an Integrative, Collaborative, Problem-Solving-Based General Education Capstone." *Peer Review, 15*(4). http://www.aacu.org/peerreview/pr-fa13/Griffin.cfm

Grinnell College. (n.d.). "Sure III." http://www.grinnell.edu/node/25713

Gustafson, M., and Bochner, J.(2009). "Assessing Critical Thinking Skills in Students with Limited English Proficiency." *Assessment Update, 21*(4), 8–10.

Hall, A., and Palmieri, M. (2012). "Tracking, Documenting, and Assessing Experiential Learning." http://www.uc.edu/content/dam/uc/provost/docs/ undergraduate_affairs/Palmieri_Hall%20OAIRP%20Fall%202012.pdf

Hanson, J. M., and Mohn, L. (2011). "Assessment Trends: A Ten-Year Perspective on the Uses of a General Education Assessment." *Assessment Update, 23*(5), 1–2, 14–15.

Hardin, B. E. (2012). "Assessing Institutional Assessment: One Institution's Progress in Developing Quality Assessment Practices." *Assessment Update, 24*(4), 8–9, 12.

Harper V. B., Jr. (2010). "Developing Cost-Reporting Guidelines for Learning Assessment and Accountability in Virginia." *Assessment Update, 22*(1), 7–10.

Harrell, Mara. (n.d.). "Pre and Post Tests for Assessing the Effectiveness of an Argument Mapping Tool for Teaching." http://www.cmu.edu/teaching/assessment/examples/courselevel-bytype/preposttests/course_preposttest-techglobaldev.html

Hart Research Associates. (2009). *Learning and Assessment: Trends in Undergraduate Education A Survey among Members of the Association of American Colleges and Universities.* http://www.aacu.org/membership/documents/2009MemberSurvey_Part1.pdf

Hart Research Associates. (2013, April). *It Takes More Than a Major: Employer Priorities for College Learning and Student Success.* http://www.aacu.org/leap/documents/2013_EmployerSurvey.pdf

Harvey, L., and Williams, J. (2010). "Fifteen Years of Quality in Higher Education." *Quality in Higher Education, 16*(1), 3–36.

Harvey, V., and Avramenko, A. (2012). "Video Killed the Radio Star—Video Created the Student Star!" *Assessment Update, 24*(2), 5–6, 9.

Hartwick College. (2014a). "Committee on Assessment of General Education." http://www.hartwick.edu/academics/academic-support-services/office-of-academic-affairs/dean-of-assessment-and-retention/assessment-at-hartwick/cage—general-ed-assessment

Hartwick College. (2014b). "Organizing Principles and Strategic Framework." http://www.hartwick.edu/about-us/office-of-the-president/organizing-principle-and-strategic-framework

Hatfield, S. (n.d.). "Assessing Your Program Level Assessment Plan" (IDEA Paper 5). http://www.theideacenter.org/sites/default/files/IDEA_Paper_45.pdf

Hawthorne, J., and Kelsch, A. (2012). "Closing the Loop: How an Assessment Project Paved the Way for GE Reform." *Assessment Update, 24*(4), 1–2, 15–16.

Hazelkorn, E. (2013, May 23). "Has Higher Education Lost Control over Quality?" *Chronicle of Higher Education.* http://chronicle.com/blogs/worldwise/has-higher-education-lost-control-over-quality/32321

Heer, R. (2012). "A Model of Learning Objectives–Based on *A Taxonomy for Learning, Teaching, and Assessing: A Revision of Bloom's Taxonomy of Educational Objectives.*" http://www.celt.iastate.edu/teaching/RevisedBlooms1.html

Hersh, R. H., and Keeling, R. P. (2013, February). "Changing Institutional Culture to Promote Assessment of Higher Learning" (Occasional Paper No. 17). Urbana: University of Illinois and Indiana University, National Institute for Learning Outcomes Assessment.

Hinton, M. D., and MacDowell, M. A. (2012). "Assessment as a Communication and Management Tool for Presidents and Trustees." *Assessment Update, 24*(4), 7, 13–14.

Houlette, F. (2012). "Borrowing Techniques from Computational Linguistics to Process Qualitative Data." *Assessment Update, 24*(1), 7–8.

Hoyt, J. E. (2009). "Integrating Assessment and Budget Planning: A Good or a Bad Idea?" *Assessment Update, 21*(5), 9–10, 16.

Hubert, D., and Lewis, K. (2013). "e-Portfolio Assessment of General Education. Quantitative and Information Literacy." http://facultyeportfolioresource.weebly .com/uploads/2/1/5/3/2153229/assessreport2013.pdf

Hughes, R. L., and Jones, S. K. (2011). "Developing and Assessing College Teamwork Skills." In J. D. Penn (Ed.), *Assessing Complex General Education Student Learning Outcomes* (New Directions for Institutional Research No. 149). San Francisco: Jossey-Bass.

Hutchings, P. (2009). "The New Guys in Assessment Town." *Change: The Magazine of Higher Learning, 41*(3), 26–33.

Hutchings, P. (2010, April). *Opening Doors to Faculty Involvement in Assessment.* Urbana: University of Illinois and Indiana University, National Institute for Learning Outcomes Assessment.

Ickes, J. L., and Flowers, D. R. (2013). "Student Interpretation of Selected Degree Qualifications Profile Outcomes." *Assessment Update, 25*(4), 1–2, 14–16.

Illinois College. (n.d.). "Assessment in the Divisions of the Colleges." http://www.ic.edu/ RelId/606788/ISvars/default/Assessment_in_the_Divisions_of_the_College.htm

Illinois State University. (2013). "Progressive Measures." http://assessment. illinoisstate.edu/downloads/Spring2013Volume8Issue2.pdf

Indiana State University. (2014). "Community Engagement." http://www.indstate .edu/publicservice/

Indiana University. (2013). "SnaapShot 2012." http://snaap.indiana.edu/snaapshot/

Indiana University. (2014). "IU Undergraduate Program Entrepreneurship and Corporate Innovation." http://kelley.iu.edu/Management/Undergraduate/ requirements/page14581.html#entrepreneurship

Indiana University-Purdue University Indianapolis. (n.d.a). "Information Management and Institutional Research." www.imir.iupui.edu/

Indiana University-Purdue University Indianapolis. (n.d.b). "Planning and Institutional Improvement." www.planning.iupui.edu/apbrv2

Iowa State University. (n.d.) "Classroom Assessment Techniques." http://www.celt .iastate.edu/teaching/cat.html

Jacobson, W. (2012). "Crowd-Sourcing the Analysis of Institution Level Survey Responses." Paper presented at the Higher Learning Commission Annual Conference, Chicago. http://www.uiowa.edu/~outcomes/HLC2012/agenda.pdf

James Madison University. (2013a). "Information Seeking Skills Test." http://www.lib .jmu.edu/gold/isst.htm

James Madison University. (2013b). "Undergraduate Catalogue 2013–2014. Student Assessment." http://www.jmu.edu/catalog/13/policies.html#studentassessment

James Madison University. (n.d.). "Center for Assessment and Research Studies. (n.d.). JMU Assessment." https://www.jmu.edu/assessment/JMUAssess/Overview.htm

Jankowski, N. (2011a, July). *Juniata College: Faculty Led Assessment.* Urbana: University of Illinois and Indiana University, National Institute for Learning Outcomes Assessment

Jankowski, N. (2011b, August). *Capella University: An Outcomes-Based Institution.* Urbana: University of Illinois and Indiana University, National Institute for Learning Outcomes Assessment

Jankowski, N. (2012, April). *St. Olaf College: Utilization-Focused Assessment.* Urbana IL: University of Illinois and Indiana University, National Institute for Learning Outcomes Assessment

Jankowski, J., Hutchings, P., Ewell, P., Kinzie, J., and Kuh, G. (2013). "The Degree Qualifications Profile: What It Is and Why We Need It Now." *Change: The Magazine of Higher Learning, 45*(6), 6–15. http://www.changemag.org/Archives/Back%20 Issues/2013/November-December%202013/Degree_full.html

Jankowski, N., Ikenberry S. O., Kuh, G. D., Shenoy, G. F., and Baker, G. R. (2012). *Transparency and Accountability: An Evaluation of the VSA College Portrait Pilot.* Urbana: University of Illinois and Indiana University, National Institute for Learning Outcomes Assessment

Jankowski, N., and Makela, J. P. (2010). *Exploring the Landscape: What Institutional Websites Reveal about Student Learning Outcomes Activities.* Urbana IL: University of Illinois and Indiana University, National Institute for Learning Outcomes Assessment

John Carroll University. (n.d.). "Assessment." http://sites.jcu.edu/vpsa-assessment/

Johns Hopkins University. School of Medicine. (n.d.). "Standardized Patient Program." http://www.hopkinsmedicine.org/simulation_center/training/ standardized_patient_program/

Joint Committee on Standards for Educational Evaluation. (2011). "Program Evaluation Standards Statement." http://www.jcsee.org/program-evaluation-standards-statements

Jones, E. A. 2009. "Expanding Professional Development Opportunities to Enhance the Assessment Process." *Assessment Update, 21*(3), 3–4.

Jones, E. A., Hoffman, L. M., Ratcliff, J., Tibbets, S., and Click B. A., III. (1994). "Essential Skills in Writing, Speech, and Listening, and Critical Thinking for College Graduates: Perspectives of Faculty, Employers, and Policy Makers." NCTLA Project Summary. University Park: Pennsylvania State University.

Joyes, G., Gray, L., and Hartnell-Young, E. (2010). "Effective Practice with E-Portfolios: How Can the UK Experience Inform Implementation?" *Australian Journal of Educational Technology, 26*(1), 15–27. http://blogs.ubc.ca/hoglund/ files/2011/05/e-port3-EJ877550.pdf

Juniata College. (n.d.a). "Institutional Research." http://www.juniata.edu/services/ research/

Juniata College. (n.d.b). "Just the Facts." http://www.juniata.edu/justthefacts/ outcomes.html

Kabik, M. (2013, January 9). "The Difference between Reporting and Communication." http://www.acceleratingitsuccess.com/uk/Articles/tabid/1661/ ArticleId/5596/The-Difference-Between-Reporting-and-Communication.aspx

Kahn, S. (2014). "E-Portfolios: A Look at Where We've Been, Where We Are Now, and Where We're (Possibly) Going." *Peer Review, 16*(1). http://www.aacu.org/ peerreview/pr-wi14/Kahn.cfm

Keeling, R. P. (Ed.). (2004). *Learning Reconsidered: A Campus-Wide Focus on the Student Experience.* Washington, DC: Student Affairs Administrators in Higher Education.

Keeling, R. P. (Ed.). (2006). *Learning Reconsidered 2: Implementing a Campus-Wide Focus on the Student Experience.* Washington, DC: American College Personnel Association, Association of College and University Housing Officers-International, Association of College Unions-International, National Academic Advising Association, National Association for Campus Activities, National Association of Student Personnel Administrators, National Intramural-Recreational Sports Association.

Keeling, R. P., Wall, A. F., Underhile, R., and Dungy, G. J. (2008). *Assessment Reconsidered: Institutional Effectiveness for Student Success.* Washington, DC: Student Affairs Administrators in Higher Education.

Kelderman, E. (2014, January 30). "Conference Gives Hints of How Accreditation May Change." *Chronicle of Higher Education.* https://chronicle.com/article/ Conference-Gives-Hints-of-How/144313/

Kerrigan, S., and Carpenter, R. (2013). "Culminating a College Education While Fostering Civic Agency." *Peer Review, 15*(4). http://www.aacu.org/peerreview/ pr-fa13/Kerrigan.cfm

King, J. (2011). "Beyond the Grade: Developing Opportunities for Course-Embedded Assessment." *Assessment Update, 23*(5), 9–10.

King, P. M., and Kitchener, K. S. (1994). *Developing Reflective Judgment.* San Francisco: Jossey-Bass.

Kington, R. (2012, February 4). "Can You Apply 'Pay for Performance' to Higher Education?" *Huffington Post.* http://www.huffingtonpost.com/raynard-kington/ can-you-apply-pay-for-performance_b_4717504.htm

Kinzie, J. (2010). "Perspectives from Campus Leaders on the Current State of Student Learning Outcomes Assessment." *Assessment Update, 22*(5), 1–2, 14–15.

Kinzie, J. (2011, August). *Colorado State University: A Comprehensive Continuous Improvement System. NILOA Examples of Good Practice.* Urbana: University of Illinois and Indiana University, National Institute for Learning Outcomes Assessment.

Kinzie, J. (2012, June). *Carnegie Mellon University: Fostering Assessment for Improvement and Teaching Excellence. NILOA Examples of Good Practice.* Urbana: University of Illinois and Indiana University, National Institute for Learning Outcomes Assessment.

Kinzie, J. (2013). "Taking Stock of Capstones and Integrative Learning." *Peer Review, 15*(4). http://www.aacu.org/peerreview/pr-fa13/Kinzie.cfm

Klein, S., Liu, O. L., and Sconing, J. (2009). "Test Validity Report." Washington, DC: US Department of Education, Fund for the Improvement of Postsecondary Education.

Klein-Collins, R. (2013). *Sharpening Our Focus on Learning: The Rise of Competency-Based Approaches to Degree Completion.* Urbana: University of Illinois and Indiana University, National Institute for Learning Outcomes Assessment.

Klemic, G. G., and Lovero, E. (2011). "Closing the Loop: Assessing SLOs for Quantitative and Qualitative Models in Business Courses. *Assessment Update, 23*(1), 9–10.

Knerr, A. R. (2013) "Data Collection." In D. M. Timm, J. D. Barham, K. McKinney, and A. R. Knerr (Eds.), *Assessment in Practice: A Companion Guide to the ASK Standards.* Washington, DC: American College Personnel Association.

Knerr, A. R., and Gold, S. P. (2013)."Using and Sharing Assessment Data." In D. M. Timm, J. D. Barham, K. McKinney, and A. R. Knerr (Eds.), *Assessment in Practice: A Companion Guide to the ASK Standards.* Washington, DC: American College Personnel Association.

Kohlberg, L. (1981). *The Philosophy of Moral Development.* San Francisco: Harper & Row.

Konwerski, P. A., Sonn, A. C., and Hamluk, B. F. (2010). "Assessment on the Road: Benchmarking Student Services Through Site Visits." *Assessment Update, 22*(2), 3–5.

Kramer, P. I. (2009). "The Art of Making Assessment Anti-Venom: Injecting Assessment in Small Doses to Create a Faculty Culture of Assessment." *Assessment Update, 21*(6), 8–10.

Kramer, P. I., Knuesel, R., and Jones, K. (2012). "Creating a Cadre of Assessment Gurus (at Your Institution)." *Assessment Update, 24*(4), 5–6, 11–12.

Krathwohl, D. R., Bloom, B. S., and Masia, B. B. (1956). *Taxonomy of Educational Objectives Handbook II: Affective Domain.* New York: McKay.

Krueger, D. W. (1993). "Total Quality Management." In T. W. Banta (Ed.), *Making a Difference.* San Francisco: Jossey-Bass.

Kuh, G. D. (2008). *High-Impact Educational Practices: What They Are, Who Has Access to Them, and Why They Matter.* Washington, DC: Association of American Colleges and Universities.

Kuh, G. D. (2010). Foreword. In J. H. Schuh and A. M. Gansemer-Topf. *The Role of Student Affairs in Student Learning Assessment.* (NILOA Occasional Paper No. 7). Urbana: University of Illinois and Indiana University, National Institute for Learning Outcomes Assessment.

Kuh, G. D. (2013). *What If the VSA Morphed into the VST? Viewpoints.* Urbana: University of Illinois and Indiana University, National Institute for Learning Outcomes Assessment.

Kuh, G. D., and Ikenberry, S. (2009). *More Than You Think, Less Than We Need: Learning Outcomes Assessment in American Higher Education.* Urbana: University of Illinois and Indiana University, National Institute for Learning Outcomes Assessment.

Kuh, G. D., Jankowski, N., Ikenberry, S. O. and Kinzie, J. (2014). *Knowing What Students Know and Can Do: The Current State of Learning Outcomes Assessment in U.S. Colleges and Universities.* Urbana: University of Illinois and Indiana University, National Institute for Learning Outcomes Assessment.

Kuh, G. D., Schuh, J. H., Whitt, E. J., and Associates. (1991). *Involving Colleges: Successful Approaches to Fostering Student Learning and Development Outside the Classroom.* San Francisco: Jossey-Bass.

Kuratko, D. F. (n.d.). "Entrepreneurship and Corporate Innovation Major." http://kelley.iu.edu/Management/Undergraduate/requirements/page14581.html#entrepreneurship

Kyllonen, P. C. (2013, November–December). "Soft Skills for the Workplace." *Change: The Magazine of Higher Learning, 45*(6), 16–25.

LaGuardia Community College. (2014). "The Role of Students and Recent Graduates in Peer Mentorship Positions as Student Technology Mentors: Project Portfolio." https://c2l.digication.com/laguardia_community_colleges_cuny_c2l_project_portfolio/profile//

LaGuardia Community College. (n.d.). "About Outcomes Assessment." http://www.lagcc.cuny.edu/Assessment/About/

Lederman, D. (2009, October 22). "Dashboard Fever." *Inside Higher Ed.* http://www.insidehighered.com/news/2009/10/22/cupa

Lehman College. (2013). "Dean's Office Assessment Workshop." http://www.lehman.edu/research/assessment/documents/AHWorkshop_10072013–1.pdf

Lehman College (n.d.). "Office of Assessment and Planning." http://www.lehman
.edu/research/assessment/

Lewis, K. L., and Swerdzewski, P. J. (2009). "The Internal Consultant Model for
Assessment." *Assessment Update, 21*(6), 5–7.

Lindemann, D. J., and Tipper, S. J. (n.d.). "Painting With Broader Strokes.
Reassessing the Value of an Arts Degree." http://snaap.indiana.edu/pdf/SNAAP_
Special%20Report_1.pdf

Liu, M. (2011). "Junior Faculty Members' Involvement in University Assessment."
Assessment Update, 23(5), 6–8.

Loacker, G., and Mentkowski, M. (1993). "Creating a Culture Where Assessment
Improves Learning." In T. W. Banta and Associates (Eds.), *Making a Difference.* San
Francisco: Jossey-Bass.

Long Beach City College. (2012). "Adjunct Faculty Participation." http://outcomes.
lbcc.edu/pdf/Adjunct-WhitePaper-rev_4-12.pdf

Long Beach City College. (n.d.). "Student Guide to Learning Outcomes." http://
outcomes.lbcc.edu/StudentGuide.cfm

Long Island University. (2013). "Annual Assessment Report Forms. Post OA
2013 Memo. Assessment Exemplars." http://www.liu.edu/Academic-Affairs/
Outcomes-Assessment/CWPost-Campus

Louisiana State University. (n.d.). "Student Success Outcomes." http://studentlife
.lsu.edu/student-success-outcomes

Love, A. G. (2012). *Discussing the Data, Making Meaning of the Results.* Urbana IL:
University of Illinois and Indiana University, National Institute for Learning
Outcomes Assessment.

Loyola Marymount University. (2014). "Celebrating Assessment at LMU." http://
academics.lmu.edu/spee/officeofassessment/celebratingassessmentatlmu

Lumina Foundation. (2011). "The Degree Qualifications Profile." Indianapolis, IN:
Author.

Lynn University. (2014). "Core Curriculum." http://www.lynn.edu/academics/
core-curriculum/core-curriculum

Macalester College. (2012). "Assessment Office." http://www.macalester.edu/
assessment/

Magoulias, C. H. (2011). "Repairing a Broken Assessment System." *Assessment Update,
23*(6), 5–6, 14.

Malone University. (n.d.). "Resources for Assessment. Program Assessment Template."
http://www.malone.edu/academics/assessment/background-resources/

Marquette University. (2014). "Assessment at Marquette." http://www.marquette
.edu/assessment/

Martin, K. S., and Martinez, E. E. (2010). "Using Student Focus Groups to Facilitate
Communication and Improve the Learning Environment." *Assessment Update,
22*(6), 6–7, 15–16.

Martins, D. S. (2010). "Changing the Climate for Assessment." *Assessment Update,
22*(6), 3–5.

Marx, J. I., Crew Solomon, J., and Tripp, B. G. (2011). "The Presentation of the
Student Role in Everyday Classroom Life: An Assessment." *Assessment Update,
23*(1), 1–2, 14–15.

Marymount University. (2012). "Student Learning Assessment Template." http://www.marymount.edu/offices/ie/assessment.aspx

Massachusetts College of Liberal Arts. (2013). "What Is Assessment? Assessment FAQs." http://www.mcla.edu/Academics/institutionalresearch/assessment/

Massey, J., and Gouthro, K. (2011). "Community Outreach: Assessment and Program Planning for Off-Campus Students." *Assessment Update, 23*(1), 6–8.

Massey, J., Griffiths, B., and Corrigan, N. (2011). "Assessment in Times of Turbulence: Using Assessment Tools to Understand and Change Processes in Student Services." *Assessment Update, 23*(6), 7–9, 14.

Maternoski, K. (2009, August 4). "Inside Higher Ed. The Unheard Voices." http://www.insidehighered.com/news/2009/08/04/serviceqa#ixzz2ih6zDoBL

Matthews-DeNatale, G. (2014). "Are We Who We Think We Are? ePortfolios as a Tool for Curriculum Redesign." *Journal of Asynchronous Learning Networks, 17*(4). http://jaln.sloanconsortium.org/index.php/jaln/article/view/395

McCollum, D. L. (2011). "The Deficits of Standardized Tests: Countering the Culture of Easy Numbers." *Assessment Update, 23*(2), 3–5.

McCullough, C. A., and Robinson, R. (2014). "The Role of an Institution-Level Assessment Committee in Faculty Professional Development Initiatives." *Assessment Update, 26*(2), 9–10, 12–13.

McKendree University. (2013). "Current Assessment Activities." http://www.mckendree.edu/offices/provost/assessment/current-assessment-activities.php

Mentkowski, M., and Associates. (2000). *Learning That Lasts: Integrating Learning, Development, and Performance in College and Beyond.* San Francisco: Jossey-Bass.

Miami Dade College (n.d.a). "General Education Assessment Process." http://www.mDCedu/learningoutcomes/documents/LearningOutcomes_AssessmentProcess.pdf

Miami Dade College. (n.d.b). "The Process." http://www.mDCedu/learningoutcomes/theProcess.aspx

Miami University of Ohio. (2013). "Crunchtime." http://www.fsb.miamioh.edu/programs/crunchtime

Miami University of Ohio. (n.d.). "Corporate Partners." http://www.fsb.miamioh.edu/corporate-partners

Miller, M. A. (2013). "Editorial: Benefit/Cost=Value." *Change: The Magazine of Higher Learning, 45*(2): 4–5.

Millett, C. M., Payne, D. G., Dwyer, C. A., Stickler, L. M., and Alexiou, J. J. (2008). *A Culture of Evidence: An Evidence-Centered Approach to Accountability for Student Learning Outcomes.* Princeton, NJ: Educational Testing Service. https://www.ets.org/Media/Resources_For/Higher_Education/pdf/4418_COEII.pdf

Mills, S., Bennett, B., Crawford, C. B., and Gould, L. (2009). "A Model for Integrating Assessment across an Undergraduate Political Science Major." *Assessment Update,* 21(6), 1–2, 14–16.

Mince, R., Mason, L. A., and Bogage, N. (2011). "Community College Strategies: Improving Faculty Ownership of General Education and Its Assessment." *Assessment Update, 23*(6), 11–13.

Missouri State University. (2013). "University Surveys and Tests." http://www.missouristate.edu/assessment/90579.htm

Montgomery College. (2011). "Student Learning Outcomes Assessment Handbook: QA Handbook. Fall 2011." https://cms.montgomerycollege.edu/EDU/Department.aspx?id=13752

Montgomery College. (2013). "Outcomes Assessment Plan Fall." https://cms.montgomerycollege.edu/EDU/Department.aspx?id=12479

Montgomery College. (n.d.). "Learning Outcomes Assessment." http://cms.montgomerycollege.edu/EDU/Department.aspx?id=13649

Moon, J. (2010). "Learning Journals and Logs." http://ar.cetl.hku.hk/pdf/ucdtla0035.pdf

Mort, D. L. (2012). "The Third Rail of Assessment—Dangerous But Powerful." *Assessment Update, 24*(2), 3–4, 14.

Mourtos, Nikos J. (2003). "Defining, Teaching, and Assessing Lifelong Learning Skills." http://www-engr.sjsu.edu/nikos/pdf/FIE%2003%20-%20Boulder.pdf

Mueller, John. (2012). "Authentic Assessment Toolbox. What Is Authentic Assessment?" http://jfmueller.faculty.noctrl.edu/toolbox/whatisit.htm

Munzenmaier, C., and Rubin, N. (2013). "Perspectives. Bloom's Taxonomy: What's Old Is New Again." Learning Guild Research. http://educationalelearningresources.yolasite.com/resources/guildresearch_blooms2013%20(1).pdf

National Association of Colleges and Employers. (2011). "Position Statement US Internships." http://www.naceweb.org/advocacy/position-statements/united-states-internships.aspx#sthash.pvOHmdGL.dpuf

National Association of Colleges and Employers. (2013a). "Candidate Skills/Qualities Employers Want. http://www.naceweb.org/about-us/press/skills-qualities-employers-want.aspx

National Association of Colleges and Employers. (2013b). "Class of 2013 Majority of seniors participated in Internships and Coops." https://www.naceweb.org/about-us/press/class-of-2013-internships-co-ops.aspx.

National Communication Association. (2012). "Speaking and Listening Competencies for College Students." https://www.natcom.org/uploadedFiles/Teaching_and_Learning/Assessment_Resources/PDF-Speaking_and_Listening_Competencies_for_College_Students.pdf

National Council of Teachers of English/Council of Writing Program Administrators. (n.d.). "NCTE-WPA White Paper on Writing Assessment in Colleges and Universities." www.wpacouncil.org/whitepaper

National Institute for Learning Outcomes Assessment. (n.d.). "Transparency." http://www.learningoutcomeassessment.org/TFComponentUSLE.htm

National Survey of Student Engagement. (2012). *Moving from Data to Action.* Washington, DC: Author.

National Survey of Student Engagement. (2013). *A Fresh Look at Student Engagement.* Washington, DC: Author.

New Media Consortium. (2014). "The NMC Horizon Report: 2014 Higher Education Edition." http://www.nmc.org/pdf/2014-nmc-horizon-report-he-EN.pdf

New York City College of Technology. (2008). "Assessment and Institutional Research. Test Blueprint Guidelines." http://air.citytech.cuny.edu/air/TestBlueprintGuidelines.aspx

Niemi, E., and Douglass, C. (2013). "Including Students in Student Assessment. *Assessment Update, 25*(2), 7–8, 14.

North Carolina Campus Compact (n.d.). "Journals/Publications Related to Civic Engagement in Higher Education." http://www.elon.edu/e-web/org/nccc/CivicRelatedJournals.xhtml

North Carolina State University. (2006). "Guiding Principles for Assessment at NC State." http://upa.ncsu.edu/asmt/foundations/principles

Northeastern Illinois University. (2012). "Assessment." http://www.neiu.edu/oapr/assessment/

Northeastern Illinois University. (n.d.a). Academic Development Program Template for Review." http://www.neiu.edu/oapr/program-review/resources.html

Northeastern Illinois University. (n.d.b). "Legislative Mandate." http://www.neiu.edu/oapr/program-review/legislative-mandate.html

Northern Arizona University. (2014a). "Annual Assessment Reporting." http://nau.edu/OCLDAA/Assessment-Process/Annual-Assessment-Reporting/

Northern Arizona University. (2014b). "Assessment Awards." http://nau.edu/Provost/OCLDAA/Assessment-Awards/

Northern Illinois University. (2014). "Office of Assessment Services." http://www.niu.edu/assessment/

Northern New Mexico College. (2011). "Improvements Report Form." http://site.nnmc.edu/page/assessment

Nulty, D. (2008). The "Adequacy of Response Rates to Online and Paper Surveys. What Can Be Done?" *Assessment and Evaluation in Higher Education, 33*(3), 301–314. http://www.uaf.edu/files/uafgov/fsadmin-nulty5–19–10.pdf

Nunley, C., Bers, T., and Manning, T. (2011, July). *Learning Outcomes Assessment in Community Colleges.* Urbana: University of Illinois and Indiana University, National Institute for Learning Outcomes Assessment.

Nyack University. (2014). "Frequently Asked Questions." http://www.nyack.edu/content/AssessmentFAQ

Oakland Community College. (2009). "Classroom Assessment Techniques." https://oaklandcc.edu/Assessment/Classroom/how-does-this-apply.aspx

Oakleaf, M., Belanger, J., and Graham, C. (2013). "Choosing and Using Assessment Management Systems: What Librarians Need to Know." www.ala.org/acrl/sites/ala.org.acrl/files/content/conferences/confsandpreconfs/2013/paper/oakleafbelangergraham_choosing.pdf

Ohia, U. O., and Diallo, Y. (2012). "Lessons from Multiple Institutional Assessment Measures of Specific Student Learning Outcomes and Satisfaction." *Assessment Update, 24*(5), 7, 13–14.

Ohio State University. (2014). "Center for the Study of Student Life." http://cssl.osu.edu/

Oklahoma State University. (n.d.). "Assessment and Testing." https://uat.okstate.edu/

Old Dominion University. (2014). "Office of Assessment." http://www.odu.edu/assessment

O'Neill, N. (2010). "Internships as a High-Impact Practice: Some Reflections on Quality." *Peer Review, 12*(4). https://www.aacu.org/peerreview/pr-fa10/pr-fa10_oneill.cfm

Oregon State University. (2012). "OSU Perspective May 2012: Improving Response Rates; iPod Touches "R" Us; What Should I Know BEFORE I Create and Launch a Survey." *Perspective, 9*(3), 1–4. http://oregonstate.edu/studentaffairs/sites/default/files/docs/volume_9_3_2012.pdf

Oregon State University. (2014). "Assessment-OSU Perspective." http://oregonstate
.edu/studentaffairs/assessment-osu-perspective

Oregon State University. (n.d.). "Departmental Assessment." http://oregonstate.edu/
studentaffairs/assessment-departmental-assessment

Ory, J. C. (1992). "Meta-Assessment. Evaluating Assessment Activities." *Research in
Higher Education, 33*(4), 467–481.

Palo Alto Community College. (2013). "Assessment Calendar." http://pacweb.alamo
.edu/assessment/development/assessment-calendar.aspx

Palomba, C. A., and Banta, T. W. (1999). *Assessment Essentials: Planning, Implementing,
and Improving Assessment in Higher Education.* San Francisco: Jossey-Bass.

Papadimitriou, A. (2009). "Motivating Freshman Students in a Business Management
Course via Portfolios: Practice from a Greek Public University." *Assessment Update,
21*(1), 10–12.

Papadimitriou, A., and Mardas, D. (2012). "Assessing an Internship Program by
Listening to Students and Employers." *Assessment Update, 24*(3), 6–8, 14.

Paradis, T. W., and Hopewell, T. M. (2010). "Recognizing Progress in Degree-Program
Assessment: The Seals of Assessment Achievement and Excellence." *Assessment
Update,* 2010, *22*(4), 8–9, 11.

Paris, D. C. (2011). *Catalyst for Change: The CIC/CLA Consortium.* Washington, DC:
Council of Independent Colleges.

Pascarella, E. T., and Terenzini, P. T. (1991). *How College Affects Students: Findings and
Insights from Twenty Years of Research.* San Francisco: Jossey-Bass.

Pascarella, E. T., and Terenzini, P. T. (2005). *How College Affects Students: A Third Decade
of Research.* San Francisco: Jossey-Bass.

Patton, M. Q. (2008). *Utilization-Focused Evaluation.* Thousand Oaks, CA: Sage.

Penn, J. D. (2011). "My Own Worst Enemy: Five Ways My Best Intentions Impair
Assessment." *Assessment Update, 23*(6), 3–4.

Penn, J. D. (2012). "Assessing Assessment: Strategies for Providing Feedback on
Assessment Practices." *Assessment Update,* 2012, *24*(6), 8–9, 13.

Penn, J. D., Ray, C. M., and Kominsky, T. K. (2010). "Using Inter-Rater Reliability to
Understand the Assessment of General Education Outcomes." Presentation at the
Assessment Institute, Indianapolis, IN.

Pennsylvania State University. (2012). "Assessment Report Template." http://www
.assess.psu.edu/

Pennsylvania State University. (n.d.a). "Penn State Learning Design Community
Hub." http://ets.tlt.psu.edu/learningdesign/

Pennsylvania State University. (n.d.b). "Welcome to Student Affairs Research and
Assessment." http://studentaffairs.psu.edu/assessment/

Pennsylvania State University. (n.d.c). "Working with Student Teams Assessing
Teamwork." http://sites.psu.edu/schreyer/assessing-teamwork/

Penny Light, T., Chen, H., & Ittelson, J. C. (2012). "Using ePortfolios to Support
Assessment." In T. Penny Light, H. Chen, and J. C. Ittelson (Eds.), *Documenting
Learning with ePortfolios* (pp. 95–104). San Francisco: Jossey-Bass.

Perkins, J. A., and Fifolt, M. M. (2013). Analyzing Data. In D. M. Timm, J. D. Barham,
K. McKinney, and A. R. Knerr (Eds.), *Assessment in Practice: A Companion Guide to the
ASK Standards.* Washington, DC: American College Personnel Association.

Peterson, M. H., and Gustafson, A. (2013). "Using Curriculum-Embedded Assessments of Student Learning: Establishing a Model for Internal Benchmarking." *Assessment Update, 25*(2), 9–11.

Phillips, K. R., and Thompson, S. S. (2011). "Developing an Assessment Plan for a Professional Program: A Collaborative Success." *Assessment Update, 23*(2), 8–9, 15.

Pike, G. R. (2009). "Assessing Program Outcomes in the Absence of Random Selection for Participation." Assessment Measures. *Assessment Update, 21*(6), 11–13.

Pike, G. R. (2012a). "Criteria for Evaluating Campus Surveys." Assessment Measures. *Assessment Update, 24*(1), 10–12.

Pike, G. R. (2012b). "The ACT Engage Survey." Assessment Measures. *Assessment Update, 24*(5), 8–9.

Pike, G. R. (2013a). "ExamSoft Examination Management." Assessment Measures. *Assessment Update, 25*(2), 12–13.

Pike, G. R. (2013b). "The Updated National Survey of Student Engagement." Assessment Measures. *Assessment Update, 25*(4), 10–11.

Pike, G. R., and Ouimet, J. A. (2009). "Using Theory and Expert Opinion, Focus Groups, and Student Interviews to Improve Campus Surveys." Assessment Measures. *Assessment Update, 21*(1), 7–9.

Pike, G. R., and Thomas, J. C. (2010). "The Defining Issues Test:" Assessment Measures. *Assessment Update, 22*(6), 11–12.

Pikes Peak Community College. (2011). "Information Literacy Results." http://www.ppcc.edu/files/3513/3856/8231/Information_Literacy_Assessment_Results_Fall_2011.pdf

Pikes Peak Community College. (n.d.). "Assessment." https://www.ppcc.edu/academics/assessment/

Porter, S. R. (2011). "Do College Student Surveys Have Any Validity?" *Review of Higher Education, 35*, 45–76.

Portland Community College. (2013). "Report Template." www.pcc.edu/resources/academic/degree-outcome/documents/2012_2013_LAC_report_template.doc

Portland Community College. (2014). "Overview of Assessment Reporting." http://www.pcc.edu/resources/academic/learning-assessment/sac-resources.html#assessmentwin

Portland State University. (2011). "Assessment Handbook." http://www.pdx.edu/studentaffairs/sites/www.pdx.edu.studentaffairs/files/PSU_EMSA_Assessment Handbook_0.pdf

Portland State University. (2014a). "Assessment Vision." http://www.pdx.edu/studentaffairs/assessment

Portland State University. (2014b). "CWLO Development Process." http://www.pdx.edu/intitutional-assessment-council/cwlo-development-process

Possin, K. A. (2013). "Fatal Flaw in the Collegiate Learning Assessment Test." *Assessment Update, 25*(1), 8–9, 12.

Prince George's Community College. (2013). "Student Learning Outcomes Assessment Handbook." https://www.pgcc.edu/uploadedFiles/Pages/About_PGCC/opair/Student%20Learning%20Outcomes%20Assessment%20Handbook(2).pdf

Princeton University. (2014). "The Senior Thesis." http://www.princeton.edu/admission/whatsdistinctive/experience/the_senior_thesis/

Prineas, M., and Cini, M. (2011, October). *Assessing Learning in Online Education: The Role of Technology in Improving Student Outcomes* (NILOA Occasional Paper No. 12). Urbana: University of Illinois and Indiana University, National Institute for Learning Outcomes Assessment.

Provezis, S. (2010, October). *Regional Accreditation and Student Learning Outcomes: Mapping the Territory* (NILOA Occasional Paper No. 6). Urbana: University of Illinois and Indiana University, National Institute for Learning Outcomes Assessment.

Provezis, S. (2011, July). *Augustana College: An Assessment Review Committee's Role in Engaging Faculty. NILOA Examples of Good Practice.* Urbana: University of Illinois and Indiana University, National Institute for Learning Outcomes Assessment.

Provezis, S. (2012, June). *LaGuardia Community College: Weaving Assessment Into the Institutional Fabric. NILOA Examples of Good Practice.* Urbana: University of Illinois and Indiana University, National Institute for Learning Outcomes Assessment.

Purdue University. (2013). "Signals." http://www.itap.purdue.edu/studio/signals/

Purdue University. Purdue Assessment. (2012). "Welcome to Assessment. Office of the Provost." http://www.purdue.edu/provost/assessment/

Redman, P. (2013). "Going beyond the Requirement: The Capstone Experience." *Peer Review, 15*(4). http://www.aacu.org/peerreview/pr-fa13/Redman.cfm

Reed, S. (2011a). "Duke University: Creating a Culture of Evidence." In R. J. Sternberg, J. Penn, and C. Hawkins (Eds.), *Assessing College Student Learning: Evaluating Alternative Models Using Multiple Methods.* Washington, DC: Association of American Colleges and Universities.

Reed, S. (2011b). "Miami Dade College: Assessment Supports the American Dream." In R. J. Sternberg, J. Penn, and C. Hawkins (Eds.), *Assessing College Student Learning: Evaluating Alternative Models Using Multiple Methods.* Washington, DC: Association of American Colleges and Universities.

Reedley College. (2012). "SLO Assessment Summary 2011–2012." http://www.reedley college.edu/index.aspx?page=1149

Reedley College. (2013). "Course SLO Assessment Report Format." http://www .reedleycollege.edu/index.aspx?page=1148

Reid, A., and Paster, D. (2013, October 11). "Digital Badges in the Classroom." *Inside Higher Ed.* http://www.insidehighered.com/advice/2013/10/11/how-use-digital-badges-help-your-classroom-teaching-essay

Research and Planning Group for California Community Colleges. (n.d.). "CTE Employment Outcomes Survey." http://rpgroup.org/projects/CTE-Employment-Outcomes-Survey

Rest, J. (1993). *Guide to Using the DIT, Revised.* Minneapolis: University of Minnesota Center for the Study of Ethical Development.

Reynolds, D. (n.d.). "Assessment: Survey for Assessing Students' Motivation, Confidence, and Goals for Writing." http://www.cmu.edu/teaching/assessment/examples/courselevel-bycollege/hss/course_writingsurvey-arthistory.html

Reynolds-Sundet, R., and Adam, A. J. (2014). "Community College Strategies. Creating Change and Buy-In for Assessment through Faculty Learning Communities." *Assessment Update, 26*(1) 12–14.

Rhodes, T. L. (2011). "Making Learning Visible and Meaningful Through Electronic Portfolios." *Change: The Magazine of Higher Learning, 43*(1), 6–13.

Rice University. (n.d.). "Office of Institutional Effectiveness." http://oie.rice.edu/

RiCharde, R. S. (2008). "The Humanities vs. Interrater Reliability." *Assessment Update,* *20*(4) 1–2, 11.

RiCharde, R. S. (2009). "Response to Arendt Flick." *Assessment Update, 21*(1), 3.

Rochester Institute of Technology. (2011). "Assessment." http://www.rit.edu/studentaffairs/arts/assessment.php

Rochester Institute of Technology. (n.d.). "Assessment Office Student Learning Outcomes." http://www.rit.edu/academicaffairs/outcomes/

Rodgers, M. (2011). "A Call for Student Involvement in the Push for Assessment." *Assessment Update,* 23(1), 4–5.

Rogers, R. F., Cravalho, P. F., and Boyajian, J. G. (2010). "Implementing the Class-Level Survey of Student Engagement: First Impressions and Findings." *Assessment Update, 22*(4), 5–7.

Rollins College (2013). "Academic Internship Program Course Syllabus (Fall 2013)." http://www.rollins.edu/academic-internships/documents/Fall%202013%20Syllabus#Fall%202013%20Syllabus

Ross, A. (2013). "Reflective Pedagogy Practice: About Artifacts." http://lc.mcnrc.org/ref-practice-2/

Rubin, R. B. (1995, November). "The Undergraduate Student Canon: Standards and Assessment." Paper presented at the annual meeting of the National Communication Association, San Antonio, TX.

St. Ambrose University. (2013). "Assessment and Evaluation Plan." http://www.sau.edu/Documents/Offices/Assessment/2013plan(1).pdf

St. Ambrose University. (2014). "Assessment." http://www.sau.edu/Assessment.html

St. John's University. (2014). "Unpacking Assessment." http://www.stjohns.edu/about/administrative-offices/provost/assessment-materials/unpacking-assessment

St. Olaf College. (2012). "General Education Student Learning Report." http://wp.stolaf.edu/ir-e/files/2013/07/report.pdf

St. Olaf College. (2013). "Student Learning in the Fine Arts." http://wp.stolaf.edu/ir-e/files/2013/07/FineArts.pdf

St. Olaf College. (2014). "Institutional Research and Evaluation." http://wp.stolaf.edu/ir-e/

St. Olaf College. (n.d.). "St. Olaf College Data Collection Schedule." http://wp.stolaf.edu/ir-e/files/2013/07/DataCollectionSchedule2012–18.pdf

Salisbury, M. (2013, April 22). "Delicious Ambiguity: 'Treat Us like Freshmen or Treat Us like Juniors; I Don't Care. Just Pick One.'" http://www.augustana.edu/blogs/ir/?p=787

Salt Lake Community College (2014). "Faculty e-Portfolio Resource Site." http://facultyeportfolioresource.weebly.com/

Salt Lake Community College. (n.d.a). "Reflection Handout for Students." http://facultyeportfolioresource.weebly.com/uploads/2/1/5/3/2153229/reflectionhandoutstudent.pdf

Salt Lake Community College. (n.d.b). "Reflective Writing: A Common Sense Rubric." http://facultyeportfolioresource.weebly.com/uploads/2/1/5/3/2153229/commonsensereflectivewritingrubric.pdf

Samford University. (2013). "Assessment Homepage." http://www.samford.edu/assessment/

Saunders, K., and Cooper, R. M. (2009). "Instrumentation." In J. H. Schuh and Associates, *Assessment Methods for Student Affairs.* San Francisco: Jossey-Bass.

Saunders, K., and Wohlgemuth, D. R. (2009). "Using Existing Databases." In J. H. Schuh and Associates, *Assessment Methods for Student Affairs.* San Francisco: Jossey-Bass, 2009.

Schermer, T., and Gray, S. (2012). "The Senior Capstone: Transformative Experiences in the Liberal Arts. Final Report to the Teagle Foundation." http://www.teagle foundation.org/teagle/media/library/documents/resources/Augustana-Final-Report.pdf

Schneider, C. G. (2013). "Afterword. The DQP and the Assessment Challenges Ahead." In P. T. Ewell, *The Lumina Degree Qualifications Profile (DQP): Implications for Assessment* (Occasional Paper No. 16). Urbana: University of Illinois and Indiana University, National Institute for Learning Outcomes Assessment.

Schneider, C. G., and Rhodes, T. L. (2011). "Foreword." In R. J. Sternberg, J. Penn, and C. Hawkins (Eds.), *Assessing College Student Learning: Evaluating Alternative Models Using Multiple Methods.* Washington, DC: Association of American Colleges and Universities.

Schoepp, K. (2012). "Lessons Learned: Building a Sustainable Assessment Program in the United Arab Emirates." *Assessment Update, 24*(6), 10–11, 14.

Schuh, J. H., and Associates. (2009). "Assessment as an Essential Dimension of Student Affairs Practice." In J. H. Schuh and Associates, *Assessment Methods for Student Affairs.* San Francisco: Jossey-Bass, 2009.

Schuh, J. H., and Gansemer-Topf, A. M. (2010, December). *The Role of Student Affairs in Student Learning Assessment* (NILOA Occasional Paper No. 7). Urbana: University of Illinois and Indiana University, National Institute for Learning Outcomes Assessment.

Schuh J. H., Upcraft, M. L., and Associates. (2001). *Assessment Practice in Student Affairs: An Applications Manual.* San Francisco: Jossey-Bass.

Schuurman, S., Berlin, S., Langlois, J., and Guevara, J. (2012). "Mission Accomplished! The Development of a Competence-based E-portfolio Assessment Model." *Assessment Update, 24*(2), 1–2, 14–16.

Seattle University. (2014). "UAC Guidelines for Assessment Project Report." www .seattleu.edu/WorkArea/DownloadAsset.aspx?id=121882

Secolsky, C., and Wentland, E. (2010). "Differential Effect of Topic: Implications for Portfolio Analysis." *Assessment Update, 22*(1), 1–2, 15–16.

Seifer, S. D., and Conners, K. (2007). "Faculty Toolkit for Service-Learning in Higher Education." http://www.servicelearning.org/filemanager/download/HE_toolkit_ with_worksheets.pdf

Seton Hall University. (2014). "Stillman School of Business. Undergraduate Assessment." http://www.shu.edu/academics/business/undergraduate-assessment

Seton Hall University. (n.d.). "Departmental Assessment Worksheet." http:// www.shu.edu/offices/provost/assessment/upload/Departmental-Assessement-Reporting-Worksheet-20110125.pdf

Sexton, S. M. (2012). "Assessment Plans: A Tool for Sanity." *Assessment Update, 24*(5), 5–6, 12.

Seybert, J. (n.d.). "An Introduction to Dashboards in Higher Education: Graphic Representation of Key Performance Indicators." http://www.zogotech.com/ demoFiles/presentations/intro_to_dashboards_in_higher_ed.pdf

Seyferth, T. (2012). "E-Portfolios in Higher Education: Investigating Validity in Web-Based Competency Assessment." Chalk and Wire Learning, Inc. http://chalkandwire.com/images/uploads/support/Validity_White_Paper_Jan2012.pdf. 2012.

Sharpe, N. R., Reiser, R. I., and Chase, D. C. (2010). "Developing a Collaborative Assessment Framework." *Assessment Update, 22*(1), 4–6.

Shepherd University. (2014). "Minigrants for Faculty and Staff." http://www.shepherd.edu/ctl/minigrants_faculty_staff.html

Siefert, L. (2013). "Use of AAC&U Value Rubrics." http://www.aacu.org/value/casestudies/

Slater, J. B., Burson, T. E., and McArthur, J. A. (2011). "Connecting Assessment to Resource Allocation: A Demonstration Project at Queens University of Charlotte." *Assessment Update, 23*(4), 9–11.

Smith, D. N. (2009). "Challenges to the Credible Assessment of Learning. *Assessment Update, 21*(5), 6–8.

South Mountain Community College. (2011). "Academic Assessment Week." http://about.southmountaincc.edu/About/AcademicAssessment/AssessmentWeek.htm

Southeastern Oklahoma State University. (2010). "Assessment Plan for General Education. Appendix I." http://homepages.se.edu/gus/files/2010/01/assessment-plan-for-general-education.pdf. 2010

Southeastern Oklahoma State University. (n.d.). "Assessment." http://homepages.se.edu/gus/general-education-degree-program/assessment/

Southern Illinois University Edwardsville. (n.d.). "Assessment." http://www.siue.edu/innovation/assessment/assessmentplans.shtml

Souza, J. M. (2013). *Embedded Assessment and Evidence-Based Curriculum Mapping: The Promise of Learning Analytics.* Urbana: University of Illinois and Indiana University, National Institute for Learning Outcomes Assessment

Spangehl, S. D. (2007). "Assessment Reconsidered: What Higher Education Should Have Learned from the Past Twenty Years." http://assessment.tamu.edu/resources/conf_2007_presentations/Spangehl.pdf

Stanford University. (2014). "Assessment: FAQ." http://www.stanford.edu/dept/pres-provost/irds/assessment/faq.html

State University of New York at New Paltz. (2013). "Co-Curricular Transcript Program." http://www.newpaltz.edu/saus/co-curricular.html

Steinke, P., and Fitch, P. (2003). "Using Written Protocols to Measure Service-Learning Outcomes." In S. H. Billing and J. Eyler (Eds.), *Advances in Service-Learning Research: Vol. 3. Research Exploring Context, Participation, and Impacts* (pp. 171–194). Greenwich, CT: Information Age Publishing.

Steinke, P., and Fitch, P. (2007). "Assessing Service-Learning." *Research and Practice in Assessment, 1*(2), 1–8. http://www.rpajournal.com/dev/wp-content/uploads/2012/05/A32.pdf

Steinke, P., and Fitch, P. (2011). "Outcomes Assessment from the Perspective of Psychological Science: The TAIM Approach." In J. D. Penn (Ed.), *Assessing Complex General Education Student Learning Outcomes* (New Directions for Institutional Research No. 149). San Francisco: Jossey-Bass.

Sternberg, R. J., Penn, J., and Hawkins, C. (2011). *Assessing College Student Learning: Evaluating Alternative Models Using Multiple Methods.* Washington, DC: Association of American Colleges and Universities.

Stoecker, R., and Tryon, E. (2009). *The Unheard Voices: Community Organizations and Service Learning.* Philadelphia: Temple University Press.

Sum, P. E., and Light, A. (2010, July)." Assessing Student Learning Outcomes and Documenting Student Success through a Capstone Course." *Teacher.* http://www .units.miamioh.edu/celt/events/docs/CFLING/assessing%20SLO%20and%20 docuiming%20student%20success%20through%20a%20CAPSTONE%20course .pdf

Suskie, L. (2009). *Assessing Student Learning: A Common Sense Guide* (2nd ed.). San Francisco: Jossey-Bass.

Swain, M. S., Finney, S. J., and Gerstner, J. J. (2013). "A Practical Approach to Assessing Implementation Fidelity." *Assessment Update, 25*(1), 5–7, 13.

Swing, R. L., and Coogan, C. S. (2010, May). *Valuing Assessment: Cost-Benefit Considerations* (NILOA Occasional Paper No. 5). Urbana: University of Illinois and Indiana University, National Institute for Learning Outcomes Assessment.

Talisman, N., and Westcott, K. (2012). "Cultural Event Attendance: A Qualitative Analysis." Poster. https://ncurdb.cur.org/ncur/archive/Display_NCUR.aspx?id= 61183

Tennessee Tech University. (2014). "Critical Thinking Assessment Test." http://www .tntech.edu/cat/home/

Texas A&M University. (2014). "Student Life Studies. Division of Student Affairs." http://studentlifestudies.tamu.edu/

Texas A&M University. (n.d.). "Student Leaders Learning Outcomes Project." http:// sllo.tamu.edu/

Thelk, A. D. (2014). "Building a Better Course Evaluation System." *Assessment Update, 26*(2), 6–7.

Tilghman, S. (2012). "The Uses and Misuses of Accreditation." http://www.princeton .edu/president/tilghman/speeches/20121109/

Timm, D. M., Barham, J. D., McKinney, K., and Knerr, A. R. (Eds.). (2013). *Assessment in Practice: A Companion Guide to the ASK Standards.* Washington, DC: American College Personnel Association.

Timm, D. M., and Lloyd, J. (2013). "Ethical Assessment." In D. M. Timm, J. D. Barham, K. McKinney, and A. R. Knerr (Eds.), *Assessment in Practice: A Companion Guide to the ASK Standards.* Washington, DC: American College Personnel Association.

Towson University. (2014). "Civic Engagement and Leadership." http://www.towson .edu/studentaffairs/civicengagement/serviceLearning/index.asp

Triton College. (2014). "Assessment Process." http://www.triton.edu/assessment/

Triton College. (n.d.). "Part VI. Using Assessment Results." http://www.triton.edu/ uploadedFiles/Content/About/Academic_Senate/Academic_Senate_Sub committees/Assestment_Committee/Part_VI.pdf

Troy University. (2012). "Institutional Research Planning and Effectiveness." http:// trojan.troy.edu/employees/irpe/effectiveness.html

Truman State University. (2011). "Portfolio Assessment." http://assessment.truman .edu/almanac/2011/Chapter%208%20%20Truman%20Portfolio.pdf

Truman State University (2014). "Portfolio." http://portfolio.truman.edu/

Truman State University. (n.d.). "Portfolio Permission Form." http://assessment .truman.edu/components/portfolio/Permission_Form07.pdf

Tweedell, C. (2011). "Assessment on a Budget: Overcoming Challenges of Time and Money." *Assessment Update, 23*(5), 4–5.

University of Alaska. (n.d.). "The Assessment Cycle." https://www.uaa.alaska.edu/
studentaffairs/assessment/assessment-cycle.cfm

University at Albany. (n.d.). "Student Success Assessment." http://www.albany.edu/
studentsuccess/assessment/

University of Arizona. (2013). "Assessment Exemplary Website-Journalism." http://
assessment.arizona.edu/exemplary/ug/journalism

University of California Irvine. (n.d.). "Guidelines for Reviewing Assessment Plans."
http://www.assessment.uci.edu/assess/documents/GuidelinesforReviewingProgram
AssessmentPlans.pdf

University of Central Florida. (n.d.). "Success Stories." http://www.assessment.ucf.edu/

University of Cincinnati. (2014). "Frequently Asked Questions." http://www.uc.edu/
propractice/intern/frequently-asked-questions.html

University of Cincinnati. (n.d.). "College Portrait." http://www.collegeportraits.org/
OH/UC/learning_outcomes

University of Connecticut. (n.d.). "How to Write Program Objectives/Outcomes."
http://assessment.uconn.edu/docs/HowToWriteObjectivesOutcomes.pdf

University of Delaware. (n.d.). "Center for Teaching and Assessment of Learning."
http://ctal.udel.edu/

University of Florida. (2014). "Institutional Assessment." http://assessment.aa.ufl
.edu/news

University of Florida. (n.d.). "Assessment Team." http://www.ufsa.ufl.edu/faculty_
staff/committees/assessment/

University of Georgia. (n.d.). "About the DSAA." http://studentaffairs.uga.edu/
assess/about/index.htm

University of Hawaii at Manoa. (2012). "What's Good Enough." http://www.manoa
.hawaii.edu/assessment/workshops/pdf/whats_good_enough_standard_setting_
2012–11.pdf

University of Hawaii at Manoa. (2013). "Definitions/Glossary." http://manoa.hawaii
.edu/assessment/resources/definitions.htm

University of Iowa. (2011). "Painless Assessment Meetings." http://www.uiowa.edu/~
outcomes/papers/Painless.pdf

University of Iowa. (2013a). "Annual Outcomes Assessment Update-2013." .http://
www.uiowa.edu/~outcomes/documents/2013AssessmentSummary.pdf

University of Iowa. (2013b). "Learning from Assessment." http://www.uiowa.edu/~
outcomes/learning.htm

University of Iowa. (2014). "About the Survey." http://uc.uiowa.edu/about-survey

University of Maryland Baltimore County. (2014). "Your Voice Speaks Volumes."
http://www.umbc.edu/reslife/survey/

University of Minnesota. (2012). "Center for Teaching and Learning. Selected
Journals about Assessment and Evaluation." http://www1.umn.edu/ohr/teach
learn/journals/assessment/index.html

University of North Carolina Asheville. (2014). Assessment Process. http://student
affairs.unca.edu/assessment-process

University of North Carolina Chapel Hill. (n.d.). "Assessment Framework. Division of
Student Affairs." http://studentaffairs.unc.edu/sites/studentaffairs.unc.edu/files/
DSA%20Assessment%20Framework%2012-2010.pdf

University of North Carolina Wilmington. (n.d.). "Student Affairs Assessment
Research and Planning." http://uncw.edu/studentaffairs/assessment/

University of North Dakota. (2011). "2011 Faculty Survey of Student Engagement." https://und.edu/research/institutional-research/surveys/2011-fsse.cfm

University of North Dakota. (2012). "Annual Report Guidelines." https://und.edu/research/institutional-research/_files/docs/annual-reports/guidelines-2012.pdf

University of North Dakota. (2014a). "Getting Assessment Completed and Reported." http://und.edu/university-senate/assessment/getting-done.cfm

University of North Dakota. (2014b). "University Assessment." http://und.edu/university-senate/assessment/

University of North Dakota. (n.d.). "Understanding Your Review." https://und.edu/university-senate/assessment/_files/docs/understand-your-review.pdf

University of North Texas. (n.d.). "Student Portraits Symposium." http://studentaffairs.unt.edu/student-portrait-symposium

University of Oregon. (n.d.). "Student Affairs Assessment and Research." http://sa-assessment.uoregon.edu/Home.aspx

University of South Carolina. Columbia. (2013). "Carolina Core." http://www.sc.edu/carolinacore/

University of Southern California. (n.d.). "Assessment Center." https://sait.usc.edu/assessment/Certificate.html

University of Southern Maine. (2013). "USM Core Learning Outcomes." http://usm.maine.edu/core/usm-core-learning-outcomes

University of Texas at Austin. (2013a). "Assessment and Program Effectiveness." https://www.utexas.edu/provost/planning/assessment/

University of Texas at Austin. (2013b). "Handbook for Institutional Effectiveness." http://www.utexas.edu/provost/planning/assessment/iapa/resources/pdfs/Handbook%20for%20Institutional%20Effectiveness.pdf).

University of Utah. (2012a). "Office of Assessment Evaluation and Research. About Our Services." http://studentaffairs.utah.edu/assessment/services.php

University of Utah. (2012b). "Survey Administration Methods." http://studentaffairs.utah.edu/assessment/documents/planning/Survey%20Administration%20Methods.pdf

University of Utah. (n.d.). "Student Affairs Assessment Matrix." http://studentaffairs.utah.edu/assessment/documents/sa-assessment-matrix.pdf

Upcraft M. L., and Schuh, J. H. (1996). *Assessment in Student Affairs: A Guide for Practitioners*. San Francisco: Jossey-Bass.

Upcraft, M. L., and Schuh, J. H. (2002, March–April). "Assessment vs. Research: Why We Should Care about the Difference." *About Campus*, 16–20.

US Congress. (1991). *Higher Education Amendments of 1992*. 102nd Congress. www.GovTrack.us. http://www.govtrack.us/congress/bills/102/s1150

US Department of Education. (1988). "Secretary's Procedures and Criteria for Recognition of Accrediting Agencies." *Federal Register, 53*(127), 25088–25099.

US Department of Education. (2006). *A Test of Leadership: Charting the Future of U.S. Higher Education*. Washington, DC: Author, 2006.

Vanderbilt University. (n.d.). "Designing an Assessment Plan." http://virg.vanderbilt.edu/AssessmentPlans/plan/Home.aspx

Vernon, R., Lynch, D., and Tandy, C. (n.d.). "Assessing Student Learning Competencies Through Second Life." 2009–10 IUPUI PRAC Assessment Grant Summary of Progress. http://www.planning.iupui.edu/376.html#1112

Virginia Polytechnic and State University. (2014a). "ePortfolios for Assessment." https://eportfolio.vt.edu/gallery/Gallery_Presentation/assessmentgallery.html

Virginia Polytechnic and State University. (2014b). "Office of Assessment and Evaluation." http://www.assessment.vt.edu/

Voluntary System of Accountability. (2014). "College Portrait Participants by State." http://www.voluntarysystem.org/participants

Vroeijenstijn, A. I. (1994). "Preparing for the Second Cycle: External Quality Assessment in Dutch Universities." In D. F. Westerheijden, J. Brennan, and P.A.M. Maassen (Eds.), *Changing Contexts of Quality Assessment: Recent Trends in West European Higher Education.* Utrecht, Netherlands: Lemma.

Walvoord, B. E., and Anderson, V. J. (1995). "An Assessment Riddle." *Assessment Update,* 7(6), 8–11.

Walvoord, B. E., and Anderson, V. J. (1998). *Effective Grading: A Tool for Learning and Assessment.* San Francisco: Jossey-Bass.

Washington State University. (2014). "Course Evaluations and Surveys." http://oai.wsu.edu/online_course_evals_surveys/

Weber State University. (2014a). "Affective Skills." http://www.weber.edu/mls/degrees/campus/affectiveskills.html

Weber State University. (2014b). "Student Affairs Assessment." http://www.weber.edu/SAAssessment

Wehlburg, C. M. (2013). "'Just Right' Outcomes Assessment: A Fable for Higher Education." *Assessment Update,* 25(2), 1–2, 15–16.

Weinstein, D. A., and Schneller, B. (2009). "The Degree Specification Project: A Case Study in Departmental Outcomes Assessment." *Assessment Update,* 21(2), 8–9.

Weinstein, S., Ching, Y., Shapiro, D., and Martin, R. L. (2010). "Embedded Assessment: Using Data We Already Have to Assess Courses and Programs." *Assessment Update,* 22(2), 6–7.

Welsh, J. (2013). *Student Involvement in Assessment: A Three-Way Win.* Urbana: University of Illinois and Indiana University, National Institute for Learning Outcomes Assessment.

Wenk, L., and Rueschmann, E. (2013). "Hampshire College's Division III: To Know Is Not Enough." *Peer Review,* 15(4). http://www.aacu.org/peerreview/pr-fa13/Wenk.cfm

West Virginia University. (2014). "Student Affairs Assessment." http://studentaffairs.wvu.edu/sa_resources/assessment

White House. (2013). "College Scorecard." http://www.whitehouse.gov/issues/education/higher-education/college-score-card

Wiggins, G. (1998). *Educative Assessment: Designing Assessments to Inform and Improve Student Performance.* San Francisco: Jossey-Bass.

Wiggins, G., and McTighe, J. (2005). *Understanding by Design, Expanded Second Edition.* Upper Saddle River, NJ: Pearson.

Wisconsin Technical College. (2013, September 13). "Fox Valley Tech Agriculture, Health Simulation Centers Nearly Ready for Students." *Wisconsin Technical College News.* http://wistechcolleges.wordpress.com/tag/health-simulation-and-technology-center/).

Woosley, S. (2009). "Focus Groups." http://cms.bsu.edu/about/administrative offices/studentaffairs/studentaffairsassessmentplan/assessmentresources/guidesandtoolsforassessment

Woosley, S., and Miller, C. (n.d.). "Surveys." http://cms.bsu.edu/about/administrative offices/studentaffairs/studentaffairsassessmentplan/assessmentresources/guidesandtoolsforassessment

Wright, B. (2013). "Origins of the WASC Assessment Leaderhip Academy." *Assessment Update, 25*(6), 1–2, 16.

Wright, C. W. (2011). "A Kind of Heresy: Assessing Student Learning in Philosophy." *Assessment Update, 23*(3), 4–6.

Yancey, K. B. (2009). "Electronic Portfolios a Decade into the Twenty-First Century: What We Know, What We Need to Know." *Peer Review, 11*(1), 28–32.

Yavapai College. (2008). "Guiding Principles and Good Practice." http://www.yc.edu/v5content/student-learning-outcomes/docs/docs/The%20Guiding%20Principles%20and%20Good%20Practice%20of%20Assessment.pdf; http://www.yc.edu/v5content/student-learning-outcomes/

Zis, S., Boeke, M., and Ewell, P. T. (2010). *State Policies on the Assessment of Student Learning Outcomes: Results of a Fifty-State Inventory.* Boulder, CO: National Center for Higher Education Management Systems.

Zubizarreta, J. (2004). *The Learning Portfolio.* San Francisco: Jossey-Bass.

NAME INDEX

SUBJECT INDEX

Page references followed by *e* indicate an exhibit.

A

AACSB International, 266

ABET 2000 standards (1997), 5

ABET accreditation, 187

About Campus journal, 213

Academic Program Assessment Template (Malone University), 30

ACAT (Area Concentration Achievement Tests), 106

Accountability: general education assessment and voluntary system of, 175–178; international perspective on quality assurance and, 7–9; outcomes assessment purposes of improvement and, 265–266; tension between improvement and, 265, 274; U-CAN initiative on, 229; The Voluntary Framework of Accountability for community colleges, 6; Voluntary System of Accountability (VSA), 175–178, 229

Accreditation: assessment activity levels linked to visits for, 265–266; Calvin College's redesigned assessment program after receiving, 10; caution against using as enforcement, 51; debate over next reauthorization of, 264–265; Higher Learning Commission of the North Central Association of Colleges and Schools, 242; IUPUI's assessment used to support institutional and disciplinary, 244, 250–251. *See also* Disciplinary accreditation; Institutions; Regional accreditation

Accrediting agencies: ABET engineering, 187; HEA Amendments of 1992 codifying assessment by, 5; impact on outcomes assessment by, 5; intended outcomes specifically addressed by, 191; international development of, 7; outcome statements guidelines by, 70; pioneering assessment efforts by, 4; pressures for evidence of assessment accountability from, 196. *See also* Disciplinary accrediting agencies; Regional accrediting agencies

ACT Engage survey, 60, 130–131

ACT exam, 103

If you enjoyed this book, you may also like these:

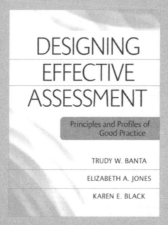

Designing Effective Assessment:
Principles and Profiles of
Good Practice
by Trudy W. Banta, Elizabeth A.
Jones, Karen E. Black
ISBN: 9780470393345

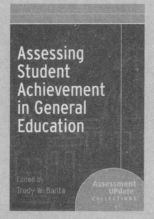

Assessing Student Achievement
in General Education:
Assessment Update Collections
by Trudy W. Banta
ISBN: 9780787995737

Assessing the Online
Learner: Resources and
Strategies for Faculty
by Rena M. Palloff,
Keith Pratt
ISBN: 9780470283868

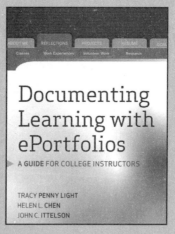

Documenting Learning with
ePortfolios: A Guide for
College Instructors
by Tracy Penny Light
Helen L. Chen
John C. Ittelson
ISBN: 9780470636206

Want to connect?

Like us on Facebook
http://www.facebook.com/JBHigherEd

Subscribe to our newsletter
www.josseybass.com/go/higheredemail

Follow us on Twitter
http://twitter.com/JBHigherEd

Go to our Website
www.josseybass.com/highereducation